W9-CUW-329

INTRODUCTIONS TO ENGLISH LITERATURE
GENERAL EDITOR: BONAMY DOBRÉE

VOLUME I

THE BEGINNINGS OF ENGLISH
LITERATURE TO SKELTON 1509

THE BEGINNINGS
OF
ENGLISH LITERATURE
TO SKELTON

1509

By
W. L. RENWICK
Professor of Rhetoric and English Literature, University of Edinburgh
And
HAROLD ORTON
Professor of English Language, University of Leeds

DOVER PUBLICATIONS, INC.
NEW YORK 19, N.Y.

CONTENTS

CONTENTS

EDITOR'S PREFACE

IF there is a danger of literature becoming separated from life, and at times the danger becomes actuality, there is a still greater one of the same thing happening in the study of literature. For one thing, it is apt to become that most arid of studies, literary history, in which history is largely, and literature, in any real meaning of the word, entirely ignored. The literature of the past is only of value in so far as it has significance to-day, just as history is only of use if it can throw a light upon the contemporary scene. But in the same way as history becomes illuminating by study, by finding out not only what people did, but why they did it, what circumstances, thoughts and emotions brought them to act, so we enlarge the boundaries within which the literature of the past has value if we gain an insight into the circumstances, thoughts and feelings which produced not only the writers, but also the readers of any particular period.

People of different ages speak different languages; not that the words are necessarily different, but the implications are. We of the twentieth century mean very little when we speak of the "social virtues", whereas to an eighteenth-century writer the phrase implied a whole philosophy of civilisation. For us to understand what Donne meant when he wrote:

> On man heavens influence works not so,
> But that it first imprints the ayre,
> Soe soule into the soule may flow. . . .

we have to be at least aware of a whole body of philosophic thought, we might say of philosophic apprehension, to which most of us are likely to be strangers, but which was common at the beginning of the seventeenth century. Thus one of the objects of literary study should be to enable us to translate the language of another day into that of our own, which we can only do if we realise that these divergencies of expression are not merely a question of literary allusion, but of what entered the minds of educated people every day, coloured the spectacles through which they looked at life, and moulded the form in which they uttered their feelings. Thus it is not altogether idle to ponder why Ben Jonson should have written:

> What beckoning ghost besprent with April dew
> Hails me so solemnly to yonder yew
> (Elegy on Lady Jane Pawlett)

while Pope should have preferred:

> What beckoning ghost athwart the moonlit glade
> Invites my steps, and points to yonder shade
> (In Memory of an Unfortunate Lady)

for there is a reason which lies deeper than personal idiosyncrasy.

It has become a platitude to say that an age is reflected in its literature, and like all platitudes the saying has ceased to have any force. Moreover, an age is often much better represented by what is no longer read, than by the works which we still take from our shelves. If, for instance, we try to reconstruct the Restoration period from the plays of the time, we shall get a view which is, to say the least of it, misleading: the age is far better represented by the turgid flood of pamphlets which issued from the inkpots of Penn and Muggleton, Thomas Hicks, John Faldo, and a dozen other forgotten and vituperative sectarians. We tend to read Dryden's plays, or certain of the satires, in preference to his other work, but he is far nearer his age in *Religio Laici* and *The Hind and the Panther* than in his now more popular writings. And if each age brings forth its own recognisable progeny, how is it that Milton and Etherege appeared together? or Thomas Hardy and Max Beerbohm? Each age has so many facets, that it is difficult to pitch on any as being its outstanding mirror though each age will have certain peculiarities not shared by the others. But these peculiarities are often merely the surface of fashion, accidental rather than essential, and until we know something of the age, we cannot tell which peculiarity, when explained, can have any significance for us.

Yet, if it is dangerous to regard literature as the looking-glass of its time, every age has certain problems which seem to it to be of major urgency. In the Shakespearian age it was to incorporate the "new learning" into life; later in the seventeenth century, the politico-religious issue was the important one; the eighteenth century, again, was lured by a vision of civilised man. That is to say that each age has its philosophy, its scale of values. But philosophy, which to some extent conditions literature, is itself conditioned, partly by the way people live, and partly by the influx of thought from foreign countries, though it is as well to remember that such thought will only penetrate or take root in a country already prepared for it. Therefore, the way people live, their social and political grouping, their economic formation, to some extent determine the way they write. Much has lately been made of the influence of economics: too much, for Marx cannot account for Milton, and it is as easy to argue that the economic development of the eighteenth century was due to the idea of the universe as defined by Newton as that "Dutch finance", commercialism, and the expansion of trade, gives a clue to the philosophy of history which runs through Gibbon's *Decline and Fall*. Yet economics have an effect on literature; we can see it to some extent in *Piers Plowman*, and without the rise of the middle classes at the end of the seventeenth century we could not have had Defoe, Steele, or Addison; the polite essayist could not have come into being, quite apart from whether or not he preached the bourgeois virtues.

The influence of foreign thought is a subject that has loomed too large, perhaps, in most histories of literature, mainly because literature has on the whole been treated as separate from life. The influence of something on somebody has been a favourite subject for theses, and the answers have

been as dubious as the theme has been ill-defined. Because
Chaucer, having read Dante's

> *Quali i fioretti di notturno gelo*
> *chinati e chiusi, poi che il sol gl'imbianca,*
> *si drizzen tutti aperti in loro stelo;*

> *tal mi fec' io. . . .*
>
> (*Inferno* II, 127. . . .)

or, more probably, the corresponding lines in the *Filostrato*
of Boccaccio, proceeded to sing

> But right as floures, thorugh the colde of night
> Y-closed, stoupen on hir stalkes lowe,
> Redressen hem a-yein the sonne bright,
> And spreden on hir kinde cours by rowe:
> Right so gan. . . .
> . . . .Troilus. . . .
>
> (*Troilus and Criseyde*, II St. 139)

that is not to say that Chaucer was influenced by Dante or by
Boccaccio; indeed no prettier contrast to the *Divina Commedia*
could be found than *The Canterbury Tales*, though it is clear
that there is some connection between them and the *Decameron*. No one really familiar with the comedy of France and
England in the seventeenth century, with an understanding
of what they were up to, can believe that the English were
influenced by the French to more than a superficial degree.
Nevertheless, the thought of one country, or of one individual,
can very profoundly affect a period, and the scepticism of
Montaigne is apparent throughout the seventeenth century
from Shakespeare to Halifax. In the same way, German
thought obscured the clarity of Coleridge, and puffed the
thought and style of Carlyle to an almost intolerable smoki-
ness.

The writer, therefore, is, besides being a unique individual,
the product of the forces of his time. However much we
may regret it, we have to abandon Shelley's contention that

"poets are the unacknowledged legislators of the world", though we need not altogether throw over the position; for though, no doubt, thought does sometimes influence action, it is more usually the successor of deeds, and it will not be denied that Locke is a child of the Revolution just as Hobbes was of the Great Rebellion. It is truer to say with Arnold that poetry is a criticism of life, though not quite true, for literature is, rather, a growth from life itself, a part of life, not its harvest only. We can go further and say that it is so ravelled with life that it can be described also as the soil and the seed. But that a metaphor should lead to such confusion is enough to indicate how closely tangled with life literature is, how complex the relation between them, and how impossible it is to separate one from the other.

.   .   .   .

The object of the Introductions in this series is to give the student some idea of the soil out of which the works of literature grew, so as to be able to grasp with fuller understanding the books mentioned in the Bibliographies. This, then, is not yet another History of English Literature, but rather, to exaggerate a little, a History of England in which not kings, battles, diplomatic or constitutional struggles, nor even economic development, are given pride of place, but literature. As is suitable to our age in which economics have come to be given a high place as determinants not only of our lives, but of our manner of thinking and feeling, and even of our religion, economics will be given more stress than they have hitherto been allowed in books on literature, but not, as some would no doubt wish, to the exclusion of everything else. For instance, though the question of the control of money no doubt played a larger part in the Great Rebellion than we were most of us brought up to believe, it would be absurd to neglect the religious elements in the struggle: indeed, as Professor R. H. Tawney has shown, it was religion itself that largely determined the economic trend of the eighteenth century. The effect of religion on literature is more easily traceable; it begins with Beowulf and runs through the whole, most markedly in the periods where the Church to a large extent stamped the nature of society, or when controversy raged high, as it did from the Reformation—or at least from the time of the *Marprelate Tracts*—to the foundation of the Bank of England. Philosophy also plays an important part, not only as being the matter of much admirable writing, but also in the general attitude towards life exhibited by writers who unconsciously, rather than in full awareness, absorbed the ideas of their time. But philosophy again is affected by economics, for no one can doubt that the individualism of the nineteenth century was largely the result of the Industrial Revolution, and that Carlyle's Cromwell must own as forebears Adam Smith and James Watt. Science also can affect literature, and without Huxley there would probably have been a different Hardy.

Another addition to the view of literature is made in these volumes by giving due place to the sister arts where they rose to any height, or seem to have importance with respect to writing. Thus music had an effect on poetry in the seventeenth century, while painting and architecture affected the poetry, and perhaps the prose, of the eighteenth. Wherever, in short, the literary "movement" of a time seems congruous with that of the other arts, they are included in the survey. Most important of all, however, is the social background, the changes of milieu indicated, say, by the decay of the guilds or the rise of nationalism; for these are the things which most affect the way people live, and therefore what they will most wish to write and to read.

The Bibliographies which form the major part of each volume are designed to give the reader a detailed view of the literature of each period, and being classified and commented will enable him to study or to enjoy either any special branch, or the whole literature of the period. Only the specialist can read everything; but the aim of this series is to enable anyone who so wishes, to get a clear idea of any one period by reading with a certain degree of fervour for a year, a clear notion not only of what was written, but, so to speak, of why and how, from what impulses, with what objects, and in what conditions morally speaking. It is hoped by this method to integrate literature with life, and so give the writings of the past that meaning without which to read is to be baffled, and to miss that greatest of all pleasures, a sense of unity of feeling with the writer of any work. Lacking this, literature is too far separated from living, and can have but little value.

The manner in which English literature has been split up in this series no doubt demands an explanation. There are many ways in which it can be split up. This has been done variously, sometimes rather arbitrarily by centuries or other irrelevant measuring rods, more often by grouping it around great figures: The Age of Wordsworth and so on: or by literary movements: The Romantic Revival, for instance. These divisions have their uses, but for our purpose here they tend to subordinate life to literature. It is admitted that there is an element of arbitrariness in the present divisions also, but the object is to relate literature to life, disregarding movements, which may only be different aspects of the same thing. The divisions here correspond in the main with social sense; roughly indeed, with what reservations you will, and with contradictions of a rule which cannot be rigid, since human nature refuses to fit into compartments.

In the first period, after the Conquest, you can say with some plausibility (though it is in this period that our structure is weakest) that literature was much more diffused among different classes; it was written for no particular brand of person. Everyone would read *Piers Plowman*, or applaud the miracle plays. There is, it is true, much that is courtly about Chaucer, but there is much that is not. When we get to Spenser, say, we feel that literature is being written for an aristocracy: the drama still maintained its general appeal (though even as early as the moralities and interludes there is a shift away from the people), but it became more and more aristocratic, till under Charles II it was entirely courtly. This period, then, we can describe as the aristocratic period: Donne, Jeremy Taylor, Sir Thomas Browne, Milton, are writers for an aristocracy, and this social sense we may say was established by the Tudors, and exploited by the Stuarts, till it came to an end at the Revolution of 1688. Then, with great suddenness, there appeared a literature written by the middle class, of the middle class, and for the middle class:

17   B

the pamphleteers, the essayists, and soon Defoe and the novelists. Even the drama changed with startling rapidity, with the anti-aristocratic satire of Farquhar, and the sentimental comedy of Steele.

The ideas of the middle class, with its strong sense, as it then had, of an organised society, gave place in the last century to the idea of individualism, due partly to the French, and partly to the Industrial Revolution. It had been begun by the romantic poets, with their break-away from the idea of "society" so dear to the eighteenth century. It might grieve Shelley to think that he was the forerunner of the excellent Dr. Smiles, but so it is. At all events, individualism dominated literature until the War. But even before that it was breaking down (having somewhat oddly consorted with a blatant imperialism), as can be seen from the plays of Mr. Bernard Shaw, and still more, perhaps, from the novels of Mr. E. M. Forster. The post-War period has its own characteristics; a new twist has been given to our view by the recent investigations into psychology, ethnology, physics, and by the Russian Revolution.

There are, of course, several objections to this sort of division: odd elements appear everywhere: you cannot, for instance, rank Bunyan among aristocratic writers. But some division has to be made along chronological lines. It may be objected that the first period needs at least two volumes: it is so long and so varied. That is true, but the number of works which remain which can be of interest to the general reader are comparatively few, and it was thought better to devote more space to our more recent heritages, as being both fuller of works we are likely to read, and as having a closer influence upon our present day approach to living.

BONAMY DOBRÉE

PREFACE TO THE FIRST EDITION

THE method of this volume differs perforce from that of the rest of this series, for any reader will require more and more varied help here than in later periods. It does not follow that every reader will need everything. We have tried to point out to the general reader the most helpful studies of each work listed, to give a little more guidance to any reader who has special interest in any one, and to show where more may be found. No one need be afraid of long lists, but must pick what he himself needs out of them. The method varies within the volume, according to a rough judgment of the difficulty and the importance of the subject. Thus the pre-Conquest literature is treated more systematically than the later mediaeval because of its greater technical difficulty. We have tried to bear in mind both the average reader with a general interest in life and literature and the serious student of what is called "Old and Middle English". It will be obvious that the volume is a mixed effort by one of each; and that the former is solely responsible for the opinions expressed in the introduction.

W. L. R.
H. O.

1939

PREFACE TO THE SECOND EDITION

IN the decade that has elapsed since the publication of this book, few works of the first importance have appeared, for the War and its complications have inevitably absorbed much of the time and energy of many of those whose contributions would have rightfully secured mention in this Second Edition. In consequence we have not found it necessary to add much in our endeavour to bring the book up to date. We have, however, tried to correct errors in the First Edition, and in doing so, we have been much helped by information received from Professor F. W. Baxter, Professor Bruce Dickins and Mr. W. A. G. Doyle-Davidson, to each of whom we now express our grateful thanks. The introduction is untouched.

W. L. R.
H. O.

1952

THE BEGINNINGS OF ENGLISH
LITERATURE TO SKELTON 1509

INTRODUCTION

I

THE terms *Ancient*, *Mediaeval*, *Modern*, are useful as chronological references or compendious mnemonic labels. They have no critical value, for there is no Time-Factor in art. What matters is experience, which is the whole content of knowledge, however acquired and however retained, present in consciousness or latent in the mysterious reserves of the mind. It may be argued that knowledge is cumulative and so the later ages have more experience than the earlier, but, though individual ability varies indefinitely, even the greatest can use only part of a limited experience; and for all its complexity, art depends upon the emotions, and they are few and common. The scale of experience matters not at all. Emotions are not to be measured statistically, and our judgments—which are our registration of emotional contacts—are qualitative, not quantitative. A clachan in Glencoe went up in flame one snowy night in 1692, and the pibroch *Muinntir a Glinne so* is a greater work of art than the Great War produced in ten nations. And man has a pitiful and merciful capacity for forgetting. We can be carried to Australia in five days, but how many of us (I write on the Border) could ride forty miles across difficult country in misty weather and bring back a dozen cows in the face of an armed population?

Yet I am not sure but that we might speedily recover that craft, if the immediate value of solid edible cows became more pressing than the clipping of the Australian record. So—returning to the arts with which we are here concerned—I conjure the reader to abolish from his mind the notion that "old" means "dead". The dead is the superseded. Old text-books are dead, but not old poems, old sermons, old philosophies (for philosophy also is a creative art), so long as they are what we call "good"—that is, so long as we find or divine in them some emotional power or intellectual interest—which is also an emotion—so long as they attach themselves to our experience, in prospect as addition to experience or in retrospect of memory recalled. Some things may have been done better since they were done first. It is interesting to watch men improving on their predecessors. But we must keep our chronology innocent of the flattering concept of "progress". And above all we must eschew the metaphor "evolution", for poem does not beget poem nor play give birth to play. Such things are made by wilful men wilfully, as well as they know how, for their present ends, and the discussion of epic and drama as if they were strains of moths or primulas is on a level with the treatment of political history as the Acts of an anthropomorphic Providence or a demonic Financier. On the other hand, there is no great point in nostalgia. Those who look back with longing to a Golden Age unconsciously identify themselves with a Golden Class; but Mr. Yeats in ninth-century Ireland may not have been a bard, William Morris may have been a thrall in Iceland, and it might be our cattle that were lifted.

In this essay—or, rather, this series of hints and glimpses—we wish to be there or thereabouts, not here and now patronising our rude forefathers or dramatising ourselves in hauberks and chasubles; still less should we treat the visions and designs of our forebears as if we had dug them out of a quarry. In so far as we succeed in remembering that these books were written by *people*, about *people* and for *people*, we shall find ourselves among people, men and women, artists and thinkers. It is difficult. The content of daily life, from which we draw the imagery that is the medium of expression, has changed—not only the clothes and the buildings, but the familiar avocations. How many of us have seen the potter's thumb, the beggar's dish, "the dyer's hand subdued to what it works in"? To most of us these are intellectual concepts; not so long ago they were daily things in every village, and directly visual. We can still say "swift as an arrow", but only members of certain clubs know just how swift that is. So also the content of education—that is, of deliberately acquired experience—has changed. Our history shows Venus and Hercules and Cæsar usurping the place in men's thoughts and dreams once held by Isoude and Lancelot and Gawaine, who ousted Brynhild and Offa and Hrothgar—not only as stories, but as images, subjects for comparison and standards of social and moral judgment, and spells to call up specific memories and emotions in the mind. For the most part they have lost their powers, yet each was relevant, proper, modern, in its time, and may be recovered.

Bede is simple, because he represents, and very purely, two things that have lasted to this day, the Latin language and the Latin Church; but for our generation, now that the dangerous times are back, even his lay contemporary is not so very difficult. In the year 1912, after several peaceful generations, Professor W. Macneile Dixon prefaced his *English Epic and Heroic Poetry* with a good sonnet which closed thus:

> Wiglaf is dead, and Hrothgar long ago
> At the last rampart met the stroke of fate.
> No journeys now the byrnie by his side
> Makes with the earl or atheling lying low;
> Nor thee a second time can time create,
> Viking and kinsman, in thy mournful pride.

Three years, and a young London scholar engraved on the wall of his earth-house the refrain of Deor,

> þæs ofereode: þisses swa mæg——

and a year after—though the Ordnance Corps did not persevere with their adaptation of the byrnie—a helm-bearer,

Robert Graves, was going behind his Cavalier reminiscence to discover a pure Anglian sentiment:

> It is no courage, love or hate
> That lets us do the things we do;
> It's pride that makes the heart so great;
> It is not anger, no, nor fear—
> Lucasta, he's a Fusilier,
> And his pride keeps him here.

Another year, and the war-leader of the Angle-kin said to his warriors: "Our backs are to the wall, let us stand and fight it out"—which is very much what one Byrhtnoth, according to the poet, said at Maldon in 991. Such things are neither ancient nor modern, and may be dismissed only when staunchness and self-respect and sacrifice cease to be virtues. And vices are as eternal as virtues. Things are being done in our Europe which Froissart would understand much better than most of our publicists; Robin Hood with an automatic pistol is the same Robin Hood who made himself a public nuisance with the long-bow, and the Black Prince was not the last hero to perpetrate a massacre.

Yet the stubborn fact of change confronts us still. The change of speech matters little: the oldest English is easier than any foreign language. The change of tradition matters a great deal, for value in any art depends on the interaction of an individual creative will and a valid tradition of thought, imagery, and technique. Technique can be learned, but three-quarters of our study must always be the attempt to reacquire the traditional content of the imagination. This is true at all times, in the study of Dryden and Wordsworth as in that of Cynewulf. The translucent medium of expression must become transparent to us, at least in patches, before we can see the individual whose emotions, thanks to some miracle of art, we share; and though the medium of the older artists can never come quite clear, if we will take a little pains it need not be quite opaque. Or if in another phase of criticism we regard the artist as maker and his work as an *objet d'art* for inspection, then we are equally bound to examine the material and the process before we can enjoy aught but a vague pleasure and a gaping wonder. In *Widsith*, for instance, the oldest of our poems, we meet at once this primary difficulty of imaginative content, for *Widsith* is a sort of catalogue of Germanic tribes and chieftains, some of whom we cannot even identify or locate, but all of whom carried, for the poet and the audience he wrote for, an image, a story, and an appropriate emotion. We have lost touch, because the tradition is that of the Germanic confederacy and the great migrations, yet before we dismiss it as dead we should realise that these names are but the strings of a harp whose fingering is forgotten—and whose tones, though roused only by wandering winds of romanticism, have revived their power in Germany.

Widsith, then, presents, in a sort of catalogue and therefore with tantalising aridity, some of the inherited experience, charged with imaginative and emotional power, that the English brought to England. As we have it—for what we have is probably a late and revised edition—it shows also contact with a force which was eventually hostile to the tradition it represents, the Roman Church, for among the tribes of his world the poet numbers the Israelites, the Assyrians, the Hebrews, the Jews and the Egyptians, names manifestly gathered from biblical instruction. The advent of Christianity need not have harmed the native literature, as the examples of Ireland and Scandinavia prove. A monotheistic religion, of course, entails a notion alien to polytheism, the notion of heresy, but the extent to which the missionary feels bound to change the imaginative content of his people depends on the range and intensity of his desire for orthodoxy as well as upon their affection for their own legendary. The Irish contrived to be Christians without giving up their heroes or even forgetting their gods. The Scandinavians had learned how to preserve their stories before the missionaries made them disreputable as relics of heathendom. In England, Augustine confined himself to a Kentish tribe whose whole importance was its strategic position, but if Paulinus had stayed away from York for another century, or, better still, had left the North to Lindisfarne, early English literature would be much more interesting.

The question is, when a new body of imaginative experience arrives, whether it is to be assimilated or whether it is to supersede the old. So much of our early literature is lost that it is difficult to make out a history, but *Beowulf* at least remains to us. The Christian infiltration into this piece of Germanic legendary has long been recognised, but it is another matter to say that the Christian notions were the poet's main object and the legendary was but the vehicle. There is a tendency to suggest that a reference to Cain and a hint of gentle righteousness prove that the author was a priest,[1] but that does poor justice to the missionaries on one hand and to the poet's nose for a good story on the other; nor need we assume that the righteous heathen is an impossibility. *Beowulf* reads to me like a secular poem, written by a cultivated layman, who though a Christian, had a pious and proper respect for the tradition of his own people—not only the traditional stories, but the moral and social tradition; for *Beowulf* belongs to a settled and civilised society with clear notions of ethics and behaviour, and possessed of culture, different indeed from the composite civilisation and composite culture that have supplanted those of the seventh century, but none the less authentic and influential, and contributory to the ordinary ideas of life and conduct by which we are still governed. Certainly it is far removed from monkishness.[2]

We cannot tell whether *Beowulf* represents its age exactly: but if Gibbon had been luckier at Oxford he might have met those who could have taught him that it is not quite true that "All beyond Cæsar and Tacitus is darkness or fable in the antiquities of Germany". First, however—though Gibbon would have found it difficult—we must rid our minds of the

[1] Mr. Kemp Malone even argues that the references in *Widsith* are only possible to a priest, but I think my point holds there even more firmly.
[2] For a brief example of what monkishness means, see the *Narratio de Uxore Aernulfi* appended (from a thirteenth-century MS.) to Gaimar's History: Rolls Series, Vol. I. The same mentality may be studied in some Communist criticism.

notion that Latin culture is the only culture, and a knowledge of Latin synonymous with education. The Roman missionaries did not arrive among a mindless people. They brought a new culture with different racial and geographical connections, and the two existed for a time side by side. Bede, whose orthodoxy imbued even mathematics with emotion, was "skilled in the native minstrelsy", and, as he closed his lifetime of service to the Roman Church, sang on his deathbed in his native strains. The fact that his *Historia Ecclesiastica* was translated into English proves that his Latin was a hindrance to some, but it proves also that there were men who could read English, and who cared to know. The native ability was there, or Lindisfarne, Monkwearmouth, and the schools of York that bred the teachers of Charlemagne's clerks, would never have come into being; nor is it possible to assume that the ability was lying fallow until it yielded such marvellous crops under the Roman plough.

It may be asked, then, if cultivation existed apart from the churches, what became of it? The answer can never be complete, but some reasons may be found for the loss of so many of its monuments.[1] First, the Viking invasions of the ninth century destroyed the books along with the society that made them. Northumbrian poetry survives only in transcripts adapted to the dialects of happier and safer districts, and there was no more chance of a literature to correspond to the art of the manuscripts and crosses, bred between the Anglian tradition, the Irish instruction, and the Roman importation. Of the culture of the Scandinavian settlers themselves little is known. It would seem as if the best-bred of these tough-minded·races had gone to Iceland to work out their own freedom far from settled lands, and with it their own inimitable literature; but those who settled in England cannot have lacked their share of the tradition and the brains. They correspond indeed to the English of some three centuries earlier, only with a greater knowledge of the world, and they had their influence on law. There was barely time, however,

---

[1] The loss has been so admirably expressed by Professor R. W. Chambers that I need only refer to his paper *The Lost Literature of Mediaeval England* in *The Library*, 4th ser., 5 (1925).

for anything to come of those new-settled regions before the
Norman Conquest changed the whole situation, and the
Conqueror's devastations threw them back once more. The
story of Havelok, and a few late ballads, alone testify to
possibilities, for by the time the Scandinavian districts had
consolidated themselves, the Germanic tradition had lost its
prestige and was reduced to a folk-lore.

The mechanical factor of destruction certainly operated,
but another, also mechanical, was operating continuously.
We must not confuse Latin and culture; we must not confuse
culture and literacy. Reading and writing are useful accom-
plishments, but as the cinema and radio are showing us, they
are not identical with, nor even essential to, intellectual and
emotional cultivation. The illiterate chieftain or baron who
listened to *scop* or *jongleur* instead of reading in a book might
be more cultivated in person, behaviour, and imagination
than most products of our public and secondary schools. As
Professor Chadwick has pointed out,[1] the first things men
need to write down are laws and the boundaries of lands,
because these must be fixed and precise, and must be
preserved intact. Literacy is useful up to that point, but so
long as each party to a dispute can produce a reader, literacy
need be spread no wider. Men write down what is useful to
themselves. The clerics in their turn wrote down, not all they
knew, but what they required—their own history, and the
dogma which also must be preserved intact and precise as a
safeguard against heresy. The writing of what early English
poetry remains was probably done by ecclesiastics who were
interested in poetry but whose memories were spoiled by
books, who had changed from oral learning to book learning
and needed their literature in that form.

Quite apart from any question of literacy, again, men
regard things differently out of habit. There are the things
that are in books and the other things that are not. Bede did
not write down the native minstrelsy he knew; he sang it.
The monks of Lindisfarne could certainly write, and that
magnificently; they knew poems about Ingeld, for in an
often-quoted letter Alcuin rebuked them for their taste for

[1] *The Growth of Literature*, Vol. I, Chap. XVI.

such heathen things; but so far as we know they kept their skill for the place to which it was appropriate, the service-books of the church. King Alfred is witness that St. Aldhelm was versed in English song, but—though we would gladly exchange all we have of the abominable Latin that Aldhelm learned in the Celtic schools for one leaf of what he sang in the streets—Alfred, himself a lover of English poetry, did not think fit to record one line. It probably never occurred to him. So likewise, at the end of the Middle Ages, Caxton printed what suited his serious courtly clientèle, but not the lyric and dramatic masterpieces of his own time. He did not necessarily despise them; he left them where they belonged, in the taverns, at the cross-roads, in ladies' bowers and in the church-yards. This habit of mind persists into the nineteenth century, and we have only hints of what it has lost us. To take one example: from the twelfth century to the late fourteenth we have allusions to a hero called Wade,[1] but what must have been a familiar and persistent image has dropped clean out of the imaginative experience of the English. One can hardly even complain.

An unwritten literature, again, is not necessarily uncritical. "Folk" song and "art" song differ only in obeying different rules, and our illiterate chieftain—or the illiterate rustic—though he might not check at textual niceties, knew how a poem or a story ought to go, and paid for a good one when he heard it: both of which are more important. The cleric also, who wrote down those fragments which seemed not unedi-fying or appealed to some personal sentiment, knew the rules and encouraged their application to his own purposes. *Beowulf* is anonymous, but we are told about Cædmon, because he marks a stage at which the tradition was made serviceable to the Church. People were singing songs, and Cædmon was inspired by a new subject. The old subjects were superseded by the new, the Old Testament stories and the Lives of the Saints, matter of instruction and edification expressed in the imagery and rhetoric of the secular tradition and deriving—for us at least—what interest they possess

[1] Walter Map, *de Nugis Curialium*, II. xvii, to Chaucer, *Merchant's Tale* 179. See Skeat's note on the latter.

largely from the reminiscences of that tradition which they contain. The use of the local tradition to make men listen to scriptural instruction instead of heathen legends is good missionary technique. The content of the imaginative experience is most easily changed in such a fashion, so that the hymning of Christ in terms proper to a Germanic hero would induce hearers of *The Dream of the Rood* to accept Him into their imaginations as something familiar and admirable. It is also true to say that the poet of *Genesis B* who sees Abraham as another Hrothgar or Offa, and the poet of *Andreas*, who sees the apostle as another Beowulf, are at exactly the same stage imaginatively and culturally as the fifteenth-century writers who told the stories of the good knight Sir Jason and his friend Sir Hercules.

In the work of King Alfred we can recognise another attempt at assimilation, this time at a more advanced position than that of the missionaries. Alfred deplored the low estate of learning,[1] but he must have had some faith both in the literacy and in the intelligence of his people, or the mere translation of useful books would have been pointless. But however sound his plans and methods, this second *Beowulf* stage, this second chance for a native culture strengthened and refined by foreign contacts, did not last long. The Danish wars and dynastic troubles gave the English little time or peace for study, and it was a makeshift at best. Nor could the Church at large or at headquarters take very seriously this concession to local weakness. Once, and in the North, there had been men like the Northumbrian king of Bede's youth, Aldfrith, "well skilled in holy Scripture", who gave eight hides of land for a book of Geography,[2] pupils of the Irish heretics whom Bede fought with all his theological and mathematical resources, but that chance was lost, while the power of Rome pressed steadily towards uniformity. The content of the mind had to be controlled. Any modification or eccentricity in this remote and barbarous province would be suspect; if it proved harmless it would meet indifference

[1] Preface to translation of the *Cura Pastoralis*.
[2] Bede, *Life of Abbot Ceolfrid*.

30

at best. Successive clerical reformers, already associated in English minds with the export of bullion but accepted in simple docility, checked any prospect of a true assimilation, and with it any prospect of an original English contribution to European thought.

Whether the English aspired greatly to any such contribution is doubtful. Then as ever an odd mixture of conservatism and docility, ready to be impressed by any foreigner who arrived with a sufficient display of authority, the simple Oswys were no match for the Wilfrids. A stiffer-backed race might have upheld their traditions in spite of the priests, but the power of institutions must be reckoned with, and also their attraction. Wilfrid broke with his Celtic teachers for the sake of the wider Roman opportunities and the stronger Roman power. Alcuin, whose school at York might have been such a centre of intellect in England as the school of Chartres became in France, was tempted away to the Carolingian empire. And, when all external influences are allowed for, the fact remains that the Anglian tradition was not advancing. It was already a fully-developed tradition when the English brought it to England, and no later poet achieved the stylistic security, any more than the grave dignity, of *Beowulf*, or its clear pictures of sea and shore and moorland. So much is lost that we cannot dogmatise, but the sailorman who loves and curses the sea, the *Seafarer*, appears as unique in Old English as in early European poetry. Cynewulf is indubitably a great religious poet; seventy years before the Conquest, someone could write a good poem on the battle of Maldon; but slackening of the verse and stiffening of the style betray a tradition on the down grade, and it may be that little of value was being done when the Normans landed. That does not mean that the poetic tradition was destroyed—as we shall see in another connexion, its shadow stretches right down into the sixteenth century—but it could not compete with the new tradition that was growing up, the third great European tradition in which we still work, the tradition of France.

II

We must not imagine, however, that the Norman Conquest meant the introduction into England of the French tradition, for the simple reason that that tradition was not yet made. If Taillefer the jongleur did indeed sing the *Chanson de Roland* before Senlac, he sang something—glorious as it is—more primitive than the English had sung round their watch-fires the night before—more primitive, in all likelihood, than the scops sang to Hengist and Horsa while Rowena, after the old English custom, carried round the wine-cup. In any case, the Normans were not missionaries of culture. They were keen business men like their Viking ancestors, from whom they inherited a gift of discipline and a power of organisation which the needs of settled life and the revelation of Continental régimes fostered into political genius. It is assumed by some historians that the Normans brought a new gaiety and liveliness to the melancholy English, but the English melancholy is a generalisation from the scanty relics of the selection made by clerics who were continually upbraiding their countrymen for their love of women and feasting and general frivolity, and who were themselves taken to task by reformers for their own love of gaudy clothes and bright ornaments. The Normans brought better architecture—or, what is perhaps even more important, better building—but beyond that their direct effect on art in England was negligible, and even depressing.

On the other hand, the indirect effects are almost incalculable. The Normans brought discipline and organisation into a land that was in some need of both, and since they appreciated the discipline and organisation of the Roman Church, they drew upon it at once for reinforcement of their secular rule. The stiffening of Roman uniformity accompanied the new system. Though they had little or nothing to put in place of the English literary tradition which they reduced along with the language to political and social inferiority, they reoriented the English outlook, for they abolished the Channel as a political frontier, and closed the northern seas. It was not that the Channel had ever been an impassable barrier to the English. English mercenaries mounted guard in Constantinople. English scholars attended the schools of France, and English missionaries converted Germany and Sweden from heathenism. Alfred recorded the voyages of his merchants, and encouraged the old habit of the Roman pilgrimage. We hear much of the travels of the Irish monks: a people whom one of their countrymen, the apostle of Germany, reproached because "There are few cities in Lombardy or Francia or Gaul in which there is not a harlot of English race"[1] might not feel such pride in its exports—and its religious enthusiasms, since this was one outcome of the Roman pilgrimage—but it could not be described as cloistered in its island. The new political situation, however, ended the old cultural situation. The English had looked east, west, and south: east to their ancestral tradition, west to Ireland, and south to Rome. Now they looked only south, to Rome and to France, and there began, for one thing, the drain of intellect to the south-east which made impossible an intellectual centre in the north to succeed Alcuin's school, and for another, more direct contact with the French thought and art that were rising so rapidly and to such brilliance during those first two or three generations after the Conquest. And this contact was possible not only to those who sought the schools of Chartres and Paris: thanks to the southern queens and to the family relations of the third and later generations with central and southern France, French poets as well as French theologians and administrators came into England. It took time, but in Henry I's reign the contact was clearly established, and by Henry II's it was strong.

Henceforth there were three traditions, three bodies of thought and imagination articulate and inarticulate, each possessing its own appropriate matter, language, and technique: the Latin, the French, and the English. The relations between them are not easy to disentangle. To set down Latin as the language of the clerks, French as that of the governing classes, and English as that of the labourers,

[1] Quoted by Hodgkin, *History of the Anglo-Saxons*, II, 419.

would look neat and systematic; it might even be roughly true. The implied negative, however, would be quite untrue. Of the three tongues, two were maternal and one merely professional. Any man who knew Latin must know at least one of the others. If English was his mother tongue he would almost certainly know French as well, and many French speakers must have found English necessary to their business. It is essential that the student should appreciate the fact that mediaeval England had two vernaculars *plus* one habitual language; that though French was shared with a preponderant body overseas and Latin with all Europe, each passèd current in England by full right of citizenship; and that all three must be taken into account.[1] Thereafter he must realise that the three tongues were not insulated one from another. Even in the early generations the two races were intermarrying, and the three languages were intermarrying. The presence of both French and English songs in the manuscript from which Wright printed his *Specimens of Lyric Poetry*,[2] the presence there and elsewhere[3] of bilingual and macaronic poems, prove that there were people round about the year 1300 who could appreciate both tongues, for the game of playing with two languages at once—and occasionally with three—is a sophisticated pastime. The audience which was amused by such things as

> Cest est ma volunte
> That I mighte be with thee
> Ludendo.
> Vostre amour en moun qoer
> Brenneth hote as the fyr
> Cressendo . . .[4]

was composed neither of Saxon yokels nor of race-arrogant Normàns. It was perhaps a specialised audience, but it was the kind of specialised audience by which literature is made and fostered.

[1] Lest some be discouraged let me add that the crucial documents have all been translated either then or since. See the bibliography.

[2] MS. Harleian 2253; Percy Society, Vol. IV, 1842.

[3] As in Wright's *Political Songs*, in the Rolls Series.

[4] Chambers and Sidgwick, *Early English Lyrics*, p. 16.

An elementary difficulty indeed confronts the literary historian—that is, anyone who attempts to assess the intellectual and imaginative experience of those who walked the English soil: how to construe the term "English Literature". If we confine ourselves to things written in the English tongue we do not only obtain a distorted view of the Middle Ages, but make incomprehensible the later history of things written in the English tongue. If we include all subjects of the Kings of England, we not only include half France, but make a false unity between groups whose only relationship was that they owed political allegiance to the same person. If we define English literature as anything written in England, we saddle ourselves not only with various latinists who were here on purely professional business, but with one or two learned Hebrews, and we might disturb the shades of some others, like Garnier of Pont-Sainte-Maxence, who wrote of his *Vie de S. Thomas* in the late twelfth century:

> Ainc mes mieldre romanz ne fu fez ne trovez:
> A Cantobire fut et fet et amendez . . .
> Mes languages est buens, car en France fui nez . . .[1]

for when Garnier says "France", he means the royal kingdom, not Normandy, and he means us to notice the difference.

Not all the latinists can be disregarded, by any means. At certain times, official, ecclesiastical, and learned works in Latin, and even frivolities and psalmodies, might be set aside as extremely important indeed, but not central to our present purpose. But when we turn to the twelfth and early thirteenth centuries, where there is something in English but nothing vital—Anglo-Norman never did produce anything very exciting—we find a notable body of Latin writings: Walter Map and Giraldus Cambrensis, as lively a pair of characters as any age brought forth; John of Salisbury, a remarkable intellect; a whole group of historians who on occasion are as living writers as any historian need be: and Geoffrey of Monmouth, author of one of the main source-

---

[1] Quoted by Vising, *Anglo-Norman Literature*, p. 80.

books of European literature. They were all churchmen, but that means little. They vary indefinitely between courtier, civil servant, don, philosopher, humorist; nor is "monk" a sufficient pigeon-hole for Matthew Paris, historian, calligrapher, traveller, artist, and man of business. These men were not divorced from the life of their country and of Europe, from the common speech or the tales and songs of the people.

There is no complete solution, yet by following his own interests and trusting to his own intelligence the student may pick his way. If Gerald de Barri, half Norman, half Welsh, and writing in Latin, does not belong to us, to whom do the descriptions of his tours belong? John of Salisbury, on the other hand, is ours by the local and personal reminiscences which help us to understand what twelfth-century men were like; but when we attempt to trace his intellectual affiliations, to define his contribution to intellectual life, or to assess his intellectual quality, we become involved in international (or supra-national) institutions, the Church and the University, since much of his working life was spent in Chartres where he was Bishop, and Paris where he taught. If we were to try to deal exhaustively with the history of the mind in England, we should have to follow the philosophical and scientific adventures of Western Europe; which would lead us from ancient Athens to Syria, Bagdad, along North Africa with the Moslem cavalry into Spain, and north again to Paris, meeting Arab physicians and Jewish rabbis and French logicians, and one Athelheard of Bath, a remarkable person. It is too long a journey, and we must leave it to the historians of philosophy and science—always remembering that it is there, and that it matters.

Even cutting free from that busy and fascinating society, we are left with a sufficient tangle of peoples and tongues. One, though far from irrelevant, we may dismiss: the consolidation of Scandinavian tradition that coincided in time—though in little else apart from a tincture of Latin—with the flourishing of the new French school, and thanks to which the allusions of our early poets are less of a puzzle than they might be. In its place there appears another tradition, the

Celtic. After all, the Norman Conquest was crucial, and to other literatures as well as to English. It is amusing, if impractical, to speculate on what might have been, had that strong man Harold Godwinsson broken William the Bastard at Senlac—English, a *sermo regius*, its tradition refreshed from Scandinavia, enriched in content by continuing connections with the Latin world and in technique by relations (already opened under the Confessor) with the new arts of France, hospitable to the Irish arts and scholarship, and controlling all with its own sober good taste, might have reached earlier and more naturally a fuller synthesis than that which appears only in Chaucer's time: or it might not. What did happen is still more curious. After the English settlement, such Britons as retained some political cohesion shut themselves up in the west, refusing even to share the true religion with their supplanters. Christianity, and along with it some mixed intellectual and artistic cultivation—certain in fact though disputable in amount[1]—came to northern England through the Gaelic branch, and apart from incidents like the recruiting of Asser to assist Alfred's latinity, the relations between Briton and Saxon remained, at best, distant. The Normans, however, overran the English bounds into South Wales, where de Clares, de Barris and the like, formed a narrow line of connection.

In time, the adaptable stock from northern France threw roots in the island, and the natural and normal first leafage appears in their growing interest in the past of their new land, which was not merely annexed to the Duchy of Normandy but held—and most importantly reflected on them—the higher status of a kingdom. There was wherewith to feed that interest. The Anglo-Saxon Chronicle was continued for some eighty years after the Conquest in the strength of Alfred's organisation of it; and as it failed, William of Malmesbury, a scion of mixed Norman and English stock who died about 1143, was writing *de Gestis Regum Anglorum*, out of a desire to preserve for posterity what could be sought

---

[1] The distribution through north-west Europe of techniques and decorative motives—*quaere*, from Scythia?—awaits investigation and co-ordination by impartial archaeologists.

out *de nostra gente*, and supplementing the Chronicle from other histories, monastic files, lives of saints and kings, the reminiscences of Norman officials, and the tales and ballads of the countryside. At the same time or little later, Geoffrey Gaimar, a Norman poet domiciled in Lincolnshire, wrote *Lestorie des Engles*, of which the extant second Book is solidly based on the Chronicle, filled out from local memory and including the deeds of Hereward and the Danish tale of Haveloc. But here enters the new factor. For the British part of the story, if anyone cared to include it, there had been available the eighth-century *Historia Britonum* of Nennius and the sixth-century *de Excidio Britanniæ* of Gildas; but Gaimar's lost First Book contained British history, and he lists among his sources a Welsh book translated by order of Robert Earl of Gloucester, the son of Henry I, and borrowed for his use from Walter Espec, the Norman lord of Helmsley. He also mentions

> Le bon liuere de Oxford
> Ki fust Walter larcediaen.[1]

Now it was on "a very ancient book in the British tongue" lent him by Walter, Archdeacon of Oxford, that Geoffrey of Monmouth, according to his dedication to the same Earl of Gloucester, based his *History of the Britons*. Whether there ever was such a book—for Gaimer was probably referring to Geoffrey's work—to what extent Geoffrey reproduced it, whether his is an inflated version of misunderstood history or (as his younger contemporary and fellow Cambro-Norman Gerald insisted) a pack of lies of his own invention, no man can tell. But the thing was launched. The Britons had their revenge. The British tradition became the tradition of England.

Thus when a good poet of King John's time, Layamon[2] of Worcester, an Englishman and son of an Englishman, was moved, about the year 1200, to write a history of the English—

[1] Ed. Hardy and Martin, Rolls Series, Lines 6465–6.
[2] I use the form that has become familiar. The historical forms are *Laʒamon* and *Laweman*. *Lawman* is the correct modernising.

Hit com him on mode and on his mern þonke
þet he wolde of Engle þa æðelæn tellen,
Wat heo ihoten weoren and wonene heo comen
þa Englene londe ærest ahten——

he paid lip-service to the historical reputation of Bede, but
himself produced a version, in form and style derived from
the Anglo-Saxon poetic tradition, of the version in eight-
syllable Norman verse which Wace the Jerseyman had made
of Geoffrey's *Historia Britonum*. So it goes on, through Robert
of Gloucester and Mannying of Bourne a hundred years
after Layamon, until it is almost accepted into serious
history. Almost, not quite. Henceforth historians might be
divided into those—headed by William of Malmesbury—who
held that all beyond Bede and the Anglo-Saxon Chronicle
was darkness or fable in the antiquities of England, and those
who, like Gray in later years, were attracted by darkness and
fable. Verse is the badge of this latter tribe; and history in
verse denotes a transference of artistic (that is imaginative)
allegiance from the grave English tradition to the less
mature but more exciting fashions of the French.

Geoffrey's success, however, does not explain the concentration upon Arthur. There were other stories in the
Historia Britonum, but Lear and Cymbeline had to await
their poet. Research into the origins of the Arthurian legend
is of little avail. There are the meagre annals of a Romano-
British chieftain who fought against the English; primitive
folk-tales of uncertain antiquity about which Celtic scholars
are not agreed—and when Celts fall out other races do well to
stand by; triads little more revealing than *Widsith*; solar,
oceanic, and vegetation myths once fashionable among the
learned. There is Geoffrey's setting-out of the main lines.
And there are the Anglo-Norman and French poems in
which we first meet the tales cherished ever since in the
imagination of Europe. It is not so much a matter of historical
veracity as one of literary psychology. How did it happen?
It has long been accepted that generations of Welsh bards
and Breton harpers carried the perfect tales of their tribes-
men to Norman and Angevin courts, but no one has traced

the process much beyond the assertions of Gaston Paris, whose parallel theories about the origins of the Charlemagne cycle have been shown by M. Bédier to be illusory. We can be sure of this, that Celticism had a success among the Normans of the twelfth century and—still more, perhaps—among their wives. The legend is removed from Armorican mists to the daylight of a shrewd and mundane generation. As part of the island tradition, Arthur possessed the negative advantage as against Anglo-Saxon heroes such as Offa, Athelstan, and Alfred, and against British heroes like Cadwalla, of arousing no inconvenient emotional implications. The Normans, again, coveted Brittany. Henry II thrust his son Geoffrey into the dukedom, and counter-attacked the Bretons' belief in the return of Arthur by the "discovery" of his tomb at Glastonbury and the naming of Geoffrey's unlucky son who fell a victim to King John. The Arthurian legend had political value. An appeal was made to the imagination for specific temporary ends; and an effective addition was made to the content of the imagination which endured for centuries.

Once launched, the thing succeeded by its own merits. It suited the new mixed Angevin civilisation that was growing out of the Norman grimness. And it was a good story, a unity from the mysterious birth to the tragic close, a nebula whose perfect form attracted innumerable wandering tales and became the nucleus and shell of an imaginative cosmos. When all the suppositions and presumptions are laid out on the board—Celtic legends, Celtic bards, mythologies, archidiaconal libraries—there is another to put beside them: the presumption that professional men of letters know their trade. At the Angevin courts of the twelfth century Wales and Brittany were "news". Also, an initial success, whatever its reasons and motives, is sure to be exploited. Again, a story has to have its appropriate setting, as every gossip-writer knows, so that *this* kind of story, wherever it be collected or invented, had to be told of Brittany or Cornwall, *that* of Moslem Spain, the other of Trebizond or Babylon; and a setting may be valued according to the readiness with which it will receive new accretions. Wace wrote a *Roman de Rou*

which was a history of the Normans from Rollo down. He
enlivened it with speeches and picturesque details of his own
invention—the trick has been rediscovered of late years—just
as Layamon added to his *Brut*, and every mediaeval quasi-
historian after him, but there were limits: he could not
engraft irrelevant fairy-tales into the annals of Duke Richard
or Duke William without question or explanation, and his
scene was Normandy and its borders. The figure of Charles
the Great, again, however fantasticated by successive
romancers, had behind it a material historical personage; and
however it may wander into the marvellous lands of the
paynim, is sited centrally on the map of Europe. But Arthur
was always the shadow of a shade, hovering in a topography
which, despite efforts to identify and familiarise it, remained
as vague as the strange creatures that inhabited it—a shadow
that stimulated the imagination by offering certain decorative
motives and throwing the mind into a certain attitude, and
then left it free to create what it created or what the owner's
will required.

Personality and topography cease to have any significance.
Anything could go into the story of Arthur—fairy-tale,
mystical symbolism, straight poetry, courtly sentiment,
social instruction—with only the barest reference to legitimise
it. It was in other ways than as history that it became a useful
part of the imaginative inheritance of Europe. As the cycle
widened, and as it became a common possession of all
Europe from Dante to the Wife of Bath, the principal figures
took on an heraldic precision and expressiveness. Their names
recalled the stories, the appropriate emotions, and the social
ideals over which they came to preside, while the historical
significance disappeared with the temporary political use
that had called it up, except in so far as Englishmen took
pride in their ownership of one of the Nine Worthies. The
common position.was probably that of the worthy Caxton[1],
who doubted whether Arthur had ever lived, but was very
ready to be convinced, for the honour of England and
because the stories were such good stories and so full of
lessons of conduct. But even Caxton—even Manning of

[1] Preface to Malory's *Morte Darthur*.

Bourne—understood well enough that an historical Arthur was one thing and the poets' tales another. It was only in the nineteenth century that another kind of historical inquiry began, and it was understood that the Celts invented love and song, beauty and adventure—the French, gaiety, story-telling, and manners—and the English nothing. We must read our Renan and Matthew Arnold, however, with the clarity of mind they recommend. If we had *The Wife's Complaint*[1] only in an Anglo-Norman version, the critical experts would doubtless acclaim its Celtic strangeness and Celtic force of emotion. And some of the most delicate of the Arthurian versions are German. The gulf between Arthurian origins and the *matière de Bretagne* is a passage perilous. As the mathematicians say, there are too many variables; for we are confronted not only with an historical problem and the migration of folk-tales, but with the social experience of a dozen generations and the wilfulness of a hundred artists.

Meanwhile, events had filled the imagination with new images and called it into the service of new desires, and the French genius responded as brilliantly. When Christendom began to counter-attack the Moslem, men looked back to the great leaders of the defence, and the cause received its imaginative embodiment in the *matière de France*. In England, the Charlemagne cycle has not had the continuous success of the Arthurian cycle. With the disappearance of the European unity, the European cause lost its emotional value along with its activity. From the 1090's till the 1490's—from the First Crusade to the reconquèst of southern Spain, from the aftermath of Pope Gregory's triumph to the childhood of Luther—Christian Europe had a common enemy, the Saracen, in whose likeness all the foes of religion could be portrayed, as were the Norsemen in the French romance of *Gurmand et Isembard*. But when the national cause was more important in men's eyes than the European, when irreligion was identified with other Christians—heretic or papist—

[1] I use the customary title. Given the moral code of early Germanic poetry, which escaped mediaeval and modern conventions, it may be correct: but some difficulties of interpretation would disappear if marriage were not assumed. Either way, this Anglian fragment could be made the nucleus of a romance.

Roland and Oliver became mere subjects of amusement to Ariosto, and, even in those parts which had best reason to retain some emotion against the Saracen, dwindled into Sicilian marionettes. Political and religious nationalism made them of little force in the new England of Spenser and Shakespeare, and the new criticism, which grew out of national feeling as much as out of classical precedent, prescribed the national legend as the proper subject of great poetry. One greater power existed to carry the Arthurian legend over the transition and to fix it in the English imagination: while chivalry was yet a living emotion and a social code, but the language had changed enough to be intelligible to later readers without philological preparation, there had appeared one Thomas Malory, endowed (by some accident inscrutable to all our sciences from Mendelian genetics to Marxian economics) with a prose style incomparably suited to the subject, in whose strength all our later romancers have carried on.

The Charlemagne cycle, however, was by no means neglected in England. There was room for both Arthur and Charles, because they did not cover the same emotional field: Arthur stands for fighting and society, Charlemagne for fighting and religion. Religion, of course, comes into the Arthurian cycle with the Grail, but it is just in these symbols that the difference of tone is clearly felt. In the Arthurian tales the relics of the Passion are mysterious and magical treasures, laid up in strange castles in sunset lands, revealed in vision or ritual to the elect initiate. Their appearance in the Charlemagne cycle commemorates the historical fact that Charles, who had a cult of relics, brought many into France: the relics are brought from Rome, lost and regained in the ordinary course of warfare; they are the sort of relics one might see in any great church, and if they work miracles, they work honest miracles such as a man might hear in any saint's-day sermon. So it is also with the people. When Sidney Lee claimed for the Arthurian tales, among other virtues, a "greater abundance of human interest"[1] he was thinking no doubt of such things as the tragedy of Balin and Balan and the immortal tale of Tristram, and

[1] Introduction to *Huon of Bordeaux*, E.E.T.S., 1882, p. xviii.

indeed there is nothing in all the Charlemagne stories so penetrating as the picture of Lancelot in what should have been a moment of triumph: "Thenne kyng Arthur and alle the kynges and knyghtes kneled doune and gaf thankynges and louynges vnto god and to his blessid moder. And euer syre Launcelot wepte as he had ben a child that had ben beten."[1] But when on Loch Lomond side King Robert the Bruce

> merely
> Red to thaim that war him by
> Romanys off worthi Ferumbras . . .
> And made them gamyn and solas,[2]

he read them something livelier and heartier than any Arthurian tale. If the anecdote is of Barbour's invention it is well invented, and it shows also where Barbour learned something of his own splendid way. Only once in all Malory's book do we hear the authentic voice of the fighting man-at-arms: "And so syre launcelot passed on a paas and smyled and said god gyue him ioye that this spere made, for there came neuer a better in my hand."[3] But I dare undertake (in the words of Sir Philip Sidney) honest Sir Oliver will never displease a soldier—who, when the hungry douzepers were beaten off a convoy they had captured,

> him be-thouȝth as man that hadde nede.
> Sone he rauȝt to hym a pece ful of wyn,
> And to swannes that were y-bake wel and fyn,
> ffyue white louves; and turned hys destrer.[4]

The one woman in all Malory who has any individuality—for even Isoude is only fair and faithful—is Enid, and she (as Tennyson felt) is dropped for the sake of a negative female

---

[1] Malory, *Morte Darthur*, XIX, xii.
[2] Barbour,'*The Bruce*, III, 435-7, 465.
[3] *Morte Darthur*, Book VI, Chap. XIII.
[4] *Firumbras*, ed. O'Sullivan, E.E.T.S., 1935, 459–62. I quote the Fillingham version because it seems to me livelier here.

of higher financial standing. But one would like to see Tennyson confronted with that forth-coming damsel Floripas the
Emir's daughter, who rescued the knights for love of Sir
Guy whom she had seen perform in a tournament long
before, and encouraged them when (like human beings but
not like the Round Table) they were disheartened:

> "Lordynges", sayde floryp, "ne haue ȝe no doute:
> The tour hys strong y-now, with-Inne and with-oute.
> There whyle þat ȝe hit hald, schal no man it wynne.
> Take we it alle in myrþe þat we haue here-Inne!
> ffyftene maydenes we beȝt now here.
> Eche man chese hym a mayde þat hym lyketh to fere!
> y haue y-chose þere me lykeþ, my lemman Gy."[1]

> þan gan Florippe þat ientail maide Gyon hure lef a-scrye;
> "Kys me, gode lef," þanne sche sayde, "ones for al þys
>   nuye."
> Al y-armed as þay wer þan, a kuste hure as a myȝte:
> "Grant mercy," said sche, "swete lemman; now am y
>   prest to fiȝte."[2]

I have tried to translate the princess into Malorian prose,
but it cannot be done. Sir Oliver, however, runs easily into
Elizabethan: " 'There is none of us all,' said Roland, 'so
valiant but he will lose his strength if meat fail.' 'Lordings,'
said Oliver, 'let be your complaining. For a dinner I am
the first man in the world.' With that he plucks forth his
prey and lets them all see. . . ."[3]

The douzepers are more like people, just as the issues are
more real, the wandering and fighting more intelligible
than the motiveless jousting and knight-errantry of the
Round Table. The sentiments are not delicate, but they
are not entangled with a social code, and grow naturally
out of permanent humanity. Anyone can sympathise with
Sir Richard as he casts loose his wounded horse:

[1] Ib., 853–9.
[2] Bodleian version, ed. Herrtage, E.E.T.S., 1879, 3237–40.
[3] Fillingham version, 502–6.

45

Well sore he syked and sayde, "stede, thou were myn.
By god," he sayd, "thou art a noble stede,
And ofte thou haste me holpe at my nede.
Nowe thou schalt brydeles away fro me reche.
[To] Ihesu crist of hewn y the by-teche!"
he blessyd hys stede, and aftyr let hym go:
the terys of hys ey3en ronne to his to.[1]

I have quoted *Ferumbras* because it was popular, because
King Robert the Bruce—or John Barbour—is good enough
authority for anyone, because it is enjoyable, but also because it succeeded and succeeds by its natural human
quality, for it draws comparatively little of its force from
the memory of European crisis, depends less on an historical
background than even the *Chanson de Roland*. It has none
of the vague attraction that the aura of Celtic prestige
lends, for many readers, to the Arthurian stories, for it is a
straightforward piece of book-making, manufactured, as M.
Bédier has shown,[2] to advertise the relics kept at S. Denis
and to exploit the crowds that attended a religious fair.
The seriousness of the old *chansons de geste* may have disappeared, but its place is taken by the keenness with which
the poet identifies himself with the persons of his poem,
their dangers and their feelings. Well read or recited, with
those lines to throw straight at the audience:

Now prey we for Gy that god be hys waraunt,
That ys blyue fecched before the amaraunt!

Now speke we of balam, that wicked thef,
That was in gret yre,—god 3eue hym euyl pref!—

it must have been exciting: it is still better than Zane Grey
and even Stanley Weyman. This normality of sentiment in
the Charlemagne cycle makes it able to receive even comedy.
There is no drastier jester in English literature than Sir

[1] Ib., 923–9. I have added the word *To* in the fifth line, and removed the
editor's exclamation mark after *hewn*.
[2] *Les Legendes Epiques*, IV.

Dinadan, but *Rauf Coilȝear* is comedy well handled and zestfully enjoyed by its author.[1] Incidentally it is the one addition to the cycle for which there is no French original: it is claimed for Scotland, and whatever the philologists decide about the dialect, the story of Charlemagne and the charcoal-burner is the sort of story men told about the Stewart kings. It is not parody, of which there is no lack elsewhere. Roland, as he appears on the road to meet the collier, is a figure to take the eye, and neither Charlemagne nor Rauf is diminished in stature by their encounter. It is as if a *fabliau* of the less scurvy type had crossed the border-line between simple and gentle, or a poet of *chansons de geste* had suddenly developed that peculiar kind of wisdom we call a sense of humour.

Perhaps that could have happened only in this illogical island; but it is a mistake to think in diagrams. In the Middle Ages there was free trade in stories, and in the Norman world, which touched the Celtic lands in the west, shared a language with the French kingdom and a country with the English, and reached out to Sicily, southern Italy, Greece, and Jerusalem, stories and ideas could travel far and easily. A Persian story of two lovers might drift through by Bagdad and Constantinople; it does not follow that every mediaeval story about an Emir's son or a Sultan's daughter is of oriental origin, or that we solve a problem at every turn by invoking ethnology or history. In our own time Mr. James Bridie, having served in the North Persia Expeditionary Force, put a bit of that experience into a play; the critics damned *Marriage is No Joke* for its impossibly fantastic William le Queux second act; and the fantastic touch in Mr. Bridie might be traced quite seriously to his Scottish descent. It does not follow that the next playwright who introduces us to an exotic lady in a trans-Caspian setting is a Scot, or has read William le Queux, or has served in a North Persia Expeditionary force, or is writing history. But we can be sure that a mediaeval audience would recognise in Mr.

---

[1] The original poem, that is, before some heavy-handed rhymester pinned on a conventional sequel to it. We are dependent on a late text, printed in Edinburgh in 1572.

Bridie's play something of the *fabliau* setting, of romance of the Charlemagne or Alexander type, and of the difficult *jeunesse* of a hero. Some might criticise his restraint, and others, with minds trained on Aristotelian logic though unclouded with the *Poetics*, might criticise the mixing of social *genres*, but they would know what had happened to Mr. Bridie, and receive his images willingly into an imaginative experience that contained many more of the same kind.

III

The separation of social classes, and still more the separation of class literatures—*fabliau* for *bourgeois*, romance for knightly circles—was not so rigid in practice as in theory. Schematic political diagrams constructed on the artificial or sentimental "class" basis, whether mediaeval or modern, are bound to break down before natural ability—especially if it be perpetuated in a natural group such as the family—and before the need of a political society for certain kinds of ability. The history of families like the Pastons, the de la Poles, the Chaucers, shows it clearly, and if Professor Manly is right in insisting that Chaucer wrote for "a handful of courtiers, gentlemen, churchmen, professional men, officials, and city merchants",[1] then we must believe that they shared the same tastes, that the knight appreciated a lively *fabliau* and the merchant a chivalric romance, or Chaucer would not have mixed them. That indeed might be expected, for a good story contains something for everybody. Human nature overrides class, and no class is self-contained either economically, emotionally, or intellectually.

Yet there is one separation that is vitally important to our understanding of the Middle Ages: the separation of the clerk from the layman. That separation allowed mediaeval learning to develop its peculiar character, its special triumphs and its special vices. The Church took learning to be her province, but unfortunately attempted to preserve it as her exclusive province. It was necessary that clerics should be

[1] *Some New Light on Chaucer*, p. 76. I fancy Dr. Manly exaggerates a little the natural circumstances of authorship, but his point is good.

educated, and the converse was accepted, that laymen need not be educated. This set a dangerous distance between ecclesiastical and lay thought. Learning was professionalised, and so was the Church. Little attention was paid to aught but what immediately concerned clerics, so that the Universities lacked the useful pressure of lay opinion and lay requirements. The intellectual professionals exercised their minds within the closed circle of their own speculations; and the Church saw to it that those speculations should be kept within the bounds of orthodoxy. Orthodoxy depends on authority, and, though new authority was cautiously admitted at intervals—once the Church had accepted what was known of Aristotle, other parts of his work, filtering through Arab scientists, were covered more or less by the same acceptance—the content of knowledge on the whole was little increased, and too much deference was paid to what had once been accepted. Inquiry was discouraged, partly because departure from authority is heresy, and partly because the Church, whose only concern was with the human soul, forbade undue interest in the things of this miserable and transitory world.

Nor was the balance redressed by the one province of learning which escaped the rigid control of Rome. The Common Law also required, and trained, well-educated practitioners, but here also, though a certain literary training was given and became a tradition in the Inns of Court, the primary purpose of study was professional, and it too rested upon authority. Young men, certainly, attended the Inns merely for the sake of a general training in administration, without binding themselves to the lifelong obedience required of the cleric, and the conflict of lay and ecclesiastical authority is conspicuous in the history of England; but the habits of mind induced by the methods of study were not so very different. Even the empirical Common Law confuses precedent with authority, and is entangled in the same processes of distinction, definition, and interpretation which were the staple activity of the civilians and the philosophers. Beyond this one restricted—and jealously watched—province, thought was exercised only within the forms of

49   D

deductive logic, a machine of extraordinary power and accuracy which was so highly regarded as the one producer of intellectual conclusions that it was kept turning after conclusions had been reached, and was either applied to problems for which it was unsuited or prevented any discussion of them, until the inductive methods which should have been its complement became its enemy perforce, and, triumphing, shackled thought in its turn to the laboratory practice which is to-day producing even worse results.

We must not make the mistake, however, of regarding mediaeval thought as existing within watertight compartments; the organic metaphor of differentiation of functions is nearer the truth. The very fact that the Church did interfere shows that the Church recognised the close relations that exist between all forms of knowledge. In all the wars down to those of Huxley, science lost little, and the Church gained by being forced to review the premises upon which her deductive dogmas rested; and it is uncertain whether the equanimity with which modern churchmen have viewed the theories of Dr. Einstein and other physicists is due to caution, indifference, or inability to recognise the theological implications. In any case, absolute stability and complete separation, however desirable from the Roman point of view and convenient for the political diagram called "Respublica Christiana", were impossible to human nature. The clerk was employed in secular business, and small wonder if he developed social usefulness and social ambitions, especially as his quality exempted him from the long absences of the fighting man and left him available for the amusement of the ladies.

Story-telling is the basis of literature, but there are always those to whom dynamic imagery is a distraction, who prefer to dwell upon states of mind and discriminations of emotion, to treat of such things, like Henry James, by direct analysis, and, though they may find some story necessary, accept the necessity as Mr. E. M. Forster does, with regret.[1] Inherited legend, physical experience, and far fetched tale are not the only sources of the imaginative medium. Intellectual habits as well as intuitive observation come into play when the

[1] *Aspects of the Novel*, Chap. II.

clerk occupies himself with the pastimes as well as the office-work of the world. For long he had had his own pastimes in his own professional Latin, and they have their place in literary history, though too little vernacular poetry of the lesser forms has survived for us to dogmatise about their relationships. When in the fourteenth century or so he brought his training into society, he united the two important extremes, the University and the ladies' bower; and there were clever people in both.

Since the intellectual habits of the clerk were induced by the methods of philosophy, and since that philosophy was strictly metaphysical, the clerkly poet was put to considerable strain. It is not that the philosopher cannot be an artist: the theological metaphysician may have as much regard for the elegance of his demonstration as the metaphysician of number; but the elegance of theologian and mathematician is a specialised elegance, an extreme example of functional beauty. The poet, who, like the painter, works through his senses as well as through his intellect, has to embody the universal entities of the metaphysician before he can make anything of them. Hence grew the habit of allegory, which is the treatment of intellectual universals as if they had physical individuality, the appearances and actions of which are to be understood as purely intellectual or emotional activities. The thing is ancient, and the example of Boethius—the junction-point of classical and Christian worlds, acceptable to both—may have suggested or assisted the vogue. That poets should be infected by the habit of the thinkers is nothing surprising: the allegorical school is the contribution of the clerks to secular poetry. From the fourteenth century, and especially through the enormously successful *Roman de la Rose*, the poetic imagination had another set of figures to work or play with.

These allegorical figures appear in painting as well as in poetry, and though the poets were free as the painters were not, it is possible that their use of them was suggested by pictures and tapestries. There is a continuous cross-influence between literature and painting—despite all theories, it is inescapable. The decorators of churches and cloisters worked to the dictation of ecclesiastics trained in metaphysical thinking, who would demand figures of the Theological Virtues and so on, just as the baron might order a Tristram or a Lancelot, for men surround themselves with the images of their preoccupations. The poets would see the pictures as well as hear the arguments, were perhaps more interested in them, and would receive from them images which they could use immediately. The opening of the *Roman de la Rose* certainly suggests it, and since that opening became a common convention, it must have been an easily assimilated and therefore a usual experience. In a dream, which removes the mind from mundane physical fact, the poet sees certain figures painted on the walls of a garden—an enclosed place, not a plain or greenwood—then meets others, and even some that were at first only painted, in human form walking and talking. It is as if the figures stepped down off the wall; and that is in effect what happened.

There are, of course, many modes of allegory: parable and *exemplum*, collected for the use of preachers in the *Gesta Romanorum*; symbolism that attempts to express the inexpressible, a very ancient resource for a religion that includes its share of mysticism and one that became a vice in the fifteenth century; the heraldic allegory which is taken straight out of social custom, and of which Chaucer's *Parlement of Foules* is a prime example. The method of the *Rose* is partly symbolic, but largely it is an elaborate series of personifications, an affair of the intellect. The conception of love taught in this Lovers' Manual corresponds with its method: the poem is quite unmoral, unphilosophical, unspiritual, entirely mundane and social in its judgments, concerned with the conduct of leisurely flirtation rather than with the communion of souls. The method suits only certain subjects and moods. It is sophisticated and deliberately decorative, meditative rather than active. Its value is, that it can discourse of states of mind and emotion directly, without much need of narrative relation between the delicate movements of sentiment which are its true subject. It may be put to the credit of Guillaume de Lorris that he invented a way of such discourse, and it may be observed that his success proves the existence of a settled, sophisticated, and imaginative society. Thanks to him, the poets of the fourteenth and fifteenth centuries had another imaginative tradition to draw upon. There were the two ways: one could tell a story about Gawaine to illustrate or teach courtesy, or one could picture forth a decorative Courtesy which might or might not remind the audience of Gawaine, but could teach directly. The imagination now held the figures of Fair-Welcome and Evil-Speech, Friendship and Danger, along with Gawaine and Kay, Bedwar and King Mark, and gave them up—and even then not entirely, as Spenser proves—only when their place was taken by the greater figures of the reborn Gods.

Somewhat the same process may be observed in drama. The Mystery is a story, first and last, more serious than the Romance but concerned like it with life and conduct. The Morality grows out of the methods of the Schools. In essence it is a disputation between the personified metaphysical entities themselves instead of one between a group of scholars about those entities. The story is trivial; the real business lies in the speeches. Thus young Thomas More, according to a well-known anecdote, was able to break into the acting in hall. He did not need to know the plot, for the plot was the speeches, and the speeches ran on the well-understood logical principles. Here also there was a connection between poet and painter. The painter was employed in scenic design, costume and property-making. He and the poet worked together: the dramatic scene taught the painter some of the tricks of composition, as the arrangement of figures in many early pictures proves,[1] and the poet's eye was filled with clear and precise images. The necessary team-work between poet, painter and musician must have helped all three. In drama, above all, the connection between notions and images is most easily made. Anyone who has seen—or, better still, acted in—a Mystery knows that it is not a mere anti-quarian curiosity or primitive precursor of Shakespeare, but something in itself, having value and interest of its own without reference to anything else. The Morality, on the other

[1] See two suggestive if over-emphatic articles by Oskar Fischel, *Art and the Theatre*, in *The Burlington Magazine*, Vol. LXVI, Jan. and Feb. 1935.

hand, succeeds only when the thesis concerns permanent human emotions as in *Everyman*, or when it is enlivened with humorous realism. Like other allegories, it depended on accidentals or on intellectual lucidity, for the original interest lay in the proper conduct of the disputation, and when that academic habit was superseded—let some of us take heed!—the real point of the affair disappeared.

The *Roman de la Rose*, however, is really two poems. The first, that of Guillaume de Lorris, is a chivalric allegory of mid-thirteenth-century sentiment: into the second, Jean de Meung fifty years later poured the whole bucket of social satire and miscellaneous information. Satire is endemic, and can be discussed at a more appropriate point; the geography, natural history, ethnology which were current in the later Middle Age came from these same clerks. For though the Church might deprecate inquiry, people like miscellaneous information. Fortunately, few people are equally anxious about the strict accuracy of that general knowledge whose value is its intrinsic interest and not its technical utility, and fewer still make the awkward correlations that lead to heresy. Nor did the Church ban what was already current. Consequently, as literacy grew more common to answer the needs of international trade and the complications of politics, more and more laymen demanded miscellaneous information. The most delicate gift of the clerk to the lay mind had been the sentimental, decorative poetry of Ovid; the heaviest was the congeries of facts and fancies gathered from Pliny and Isidore and who-knows-where that swelled the encyclopædia of Bartholomew the Englishman.

It has often been remarked, and with reason, that the same fund of information satisfied the Middle Ages from first to last. Bartholomew compiled his *de Proprietatibus Rerum* about 1250 from collections already six to twelve centuries old. It was translated by Trevisa about 1398, printed about 1470 in Latin, about 1495 in English, and was still worth printing in 1535, and even, in selection, in 1582. Dullness of mind is no explanation of such complacency, for men were no duller then than now; but under the intellectual régime we have indicated, the facts that were raised to the level of knowledge existed as professional knowledge restricted to the professionals who required them, and much remained at the level of information, which exists as imagery. Accuracy was irrelevant, and the imagination was the judge of value: the state of mind is common still, as every shrewd journalist knows. It seems to be intensified, even, as the generations passed. King Alfred noted down the narratives of Ohthere and Wulfstan, which Hakluyt quite properly included among *The Principall Navigations, Voiages, and Discoveries of the English Nation* for the same reason as Alfred wrote them: they were intelligent *comptes rendus* of practical work by honest merchant sailors. The travels attributed to the mythical Mandeville are quite another matter. They stimulate the imagination, which is all that any modern travel-book does to the stay-at-home. We demand a show of accuracy nowadays, but that is merely because our palate is tickled with different spices.

The ecclesiastical authorities were wise in their generation, for by maintaining general knowledge at the level of imagery they kept it from usurping in men's lives the preponderance enjoyed by religion. Whereas in the nineteenth century the intellectual position of the clerics was challenged by the scientists in the name of truth, in the Middle Ages the intellectual position of the scientists—for they did exist— was denied by the Church in the name of salvation. It was one of the experiments Europe has made. The Greeks measured all things by the scale of man, but their system broke down under a wave of otherworldliness. The mediaeval Church measured all things by what it conceived to be the purposes of God, but broke down under a new wave of interest in what Bacon called "the book of God's works". The eighteenth century measured by the needs and nature of civilised society. Nowadays both God and man are abandoned, and all studies hanker after the blessed irresponsibility of science. Everywhere there is a lack of balance, and no century may justly blame the others. So the visitor to the Zoo who fails to observe the pelican in her piety need not despise his mediaeval ancestor who was less concerned with the physiology of *Pelecanus onocrotalus* than with the love of

55

God for His creatures. Once that is clear, understanding will follow. For *Urbs Syon aurea, patria, cive decora* and the streamlined shape of Things to Come are dreams alike, however variable the imagery: human dreams that rest on faith —and the prospect of whose reality promises only boredom to the Aucassins of every age.

IV

The protest of Aucassin might almost be held to symbolise the radical separation of mundane and clerical thought in the Middle Ages: "For to Hell go the fine clerks and the fine knights who have died in tourneys and in rich wars, and the brave soldiers and the free-born men. With those will I go. And there too go the gracious ladies who have two friends or three beside their lords; and there go the gold and silver, and the vair and the gris; and there too go harpers and minstrels and the kings of the world. . . ." Let it remind us at least that the secular mind existed. The domination of religion in the "Age of Faith" is exaggerated by writers who fail to balance the breviaries with the romances, the love-allegories, the witchcraft that may be the survival of the older cults, the curiosity of alchemists, and the common recalcitrance of human nature. They see how the church-spire dominates the village, and forget in the first place the castle, which has disappeared not merely through the hates of the Roses, the prudence of Henry VII and the strategy of Cromwell, but through the changes of society and the changes of fashion; and in the second place they forget the tavern, which has not disappeared at all.

We must remember also that the organised Church supplied moral, intellectual and social needs which other agencies, from the Rural District Council to the Registrar-General, have gradually taken over. The student of literature must try to discriminate between spiritual enlightenment and the organisation of life under religious sanctions. Joshua's Camp Standing Orders are sanitary regulations though they appear in the Bible, and much that is discussed in chapters on The Religious Life of the Middle Ages has the same practical motive as led a modern Highland minister to fiddle at village dances—it gave an outlet for the natural desire for amusement and enabled him to keep an eye on the morals of his young parishioners at the same time. We have little trace in England of the complementary process, so obvious in southern Europe and even in Ireland, by which the Church sanctified the places and festivals of pagan cults and superstitions. The British Church may have done so, but the English had not been long enough in England, perhaps, for true local observances to have grown up so strongly as to require careful handling, and the ease with which the English accepted Christianity suggests that their own religion was already decadent and discredited. Foreign reformers found things to reform, of course, but since religious observance was of the official kind, it was on the whole reasonably correct, and easily brought to uniformity without much need for compromise or syncretism. On the other hand the magical element in ritual objects and in the sub-religious notions and customs that gather round the Church or are carried over from the elder religions seems to flourish but little in England. The three horse-skulls built into the church-tower of Elsdon in Northumberland may be relics of a pagan survival, but if so they are its only relics: there exists neither legend, proverb, nor custom to explain their mysterious presence there. Nor do we advance the claims of a liqueur or a tooth-paste, as in France, by appealing to the notion of a body of secret knowledge held by old Curés.

Yet Aucassin is not everybody. The Church did bulk large in mediaeval life, and, though variably in time and place, religion occupied much of the mediaeval mind. Indeed the only periods at which true religious literature has appeared in English in any quantity were the central Middle Age and the seventeenth century. On the whole, the seventeenth-century poetry is the better. Ineffable experience requires for its expression some intellectual material—sand-grains round which the surcharged emotion may crystallise. Thus Dante could go far beyond St. Catherine of Siena not only because he was a great literary artist, but because he had the intellectual system of St. Thomas Aquinas for a medium of expression, and so also Donne and Vaughan and Herbert—to vary the metaphor—were able to reflect from their philosophical, scientific, and social knowledge some broken rays of the great Light which otherwise would have dispersed invisible in daylight or spread blindingly upon the mist. Otherwise, beyond the description of equivocal physical symptoms and inarticulate impulses such as made Margery Kempe such a nuisance to her neighbours and travelling companions,[1] the divine visitation can be recorded only in symbols which only the initiate can really interpret, or by analogies of *light, sweetness, fire, love*, the reiteration of which may help such as recognise in those terms a known experience but does not elucidate it to the profane, and though it may produce a kind of hypnosis in minds willing to surrender, may only weary—and, from the lesser erotic symbolists, disgust—the serious inquirer.

Of the splendour and importance of these mystics, and especially those who wrote in prose, others have treated in a magistral fashion, with a knowledge and an insight to which I can lay no claim.[2] It is to be observed, however, that the mystical writers are as rare as they are precious. They were English eccentrics whom the Roman Church was chary of encouraging, perhaps because their English language and style were unofficial, perhaps from a sound general notion that eccentricity and heresy are near neighbours, perhaps from a not ill-founded suspicion of those uncouth and un-disciplined islanders. The Latin mind seems uncomfortable unless it can rest upon a complete and closed intellectual system: it was an Italian that produced the *Summa Theologiæ* accepted by the Church, and an Italian that was inspired by its intellectual grandeur to the mystical ecstasy of the *Paradiso*. Such a system, however, is apt to cause only discomfort to the English mind, so much less logical and so much surer and more sensitive in intuition. In religion as in society, the English temper is at once more sedate and less conformist. England has always produced—and, within

[1] See *The Book of Margery Kempe*.
[2] e.g., R. W. Chambers, *The Continuity of English Prose*, Miss Emily Hope Allen, etc.

limits, permitted—her eccentrics, and it is not without reason that we can trace a resemblance between Margery Kempe and George Fox: they are products of the same social and intellectual complex. For though religion may be the same in any clime, its outward manifestations are moulded in different regions by social habit and by the imaginative inheritance, and that so deeply that one does not always find theologians capable of making the distinction.

The Church is a Mediterranean institution, which inherited, for instance, along with Greek mystery and Roman organisation, the Greek and Roman notions of the position of women. Asceticism may have strengthened the disapproval with which orthodox Mediterranean ecclesiastics regarded the married secular clergy of England as an heretical abuse to be reformed at once; but their predecessors must merely have been astonished at the existence of double monasteries, celibate indeed but linked, such as the Abbess Hilda ruled with notable success at Whitby. Such a thing was possible to those who inherited the social habit, the morals, of the northern barbarians. It seems to have worked as well as any other monastic plan. But to the Mediterranean theologians it was impossible. The steadiness of temper which made such institutions possible in England has ensured also her freedom from the excesses of asceticism. The one English rule of religious life, laid down about 1130 by St. Gilbert of Sempringham, is notable in its sobriety. The English *Rule of Anchoresses* is inspired with common sense and kindliness as well as with holiness. Even a mystical eccentric like Richard Rolle is very far from the extreme practices of the Irish anchorites—anything like the enthusiastic asceticism of the Thebaid is as inconceivable in England as the enthusiastic discipline of the Spanish Inquisition—and the devoted solitaries seem to have had their place and even their function in the community around their hermitages.

In England, indeed, religious literature has usually been marked by reflective piety rather than enthusiasm. The best mediaeval poems of religious sentiment are those which sublimate normal human emotion, like those colloquies of the Saviour on the Cross and his Mother.[1] In these poems of the cloister, theology adds the tremendous weight of its universality to emotions isolated and concentrated in the silent meditations on set themes at set hours prescribed by monastic rule. These formal meditations on the Seven Sorrows or the Five Joys of Our Lady, or on the incidents of the Passion, can be monotonous enough, and their conformity to direction emphasises their obvious inequality in value— they may have been of equal spiritual value to their makers at the time, but are not to us now. Let us remember once more how subject our study is to accidents of survival. If we had more of this poetry, we might find more to associate with that grand fragment—if fragment it be, and not an inspired ejaculation—written about 1240:

> Nou goþ sonne vnder wod,—
> me reweþ, marie, þi faire Rode.
> Nou goþ sonne vnder tre,—
> me reweþ, marie, þi sone and þe.[2]

From what cloister-garth in what green valley that sunset was seen in the evening hour of meditation, we do not know. Part of its strength lies in its power to conjure up a situation, as the writer has been tempted to hint in the last sentence. It has all the emotional intensity of the set theme, and, with that, something else—a thing seen at that moment of concentration, which suddenly and completely fuses with it and extends its power. Perhaps it was a breach of discipline. The eyes should not have strayed beyond the cloister cross. Would it be presumptuous to claim as peculiarly English this complete fusion of the natural observation and the brooding thought? The sun dipping behind the wooded hill, the meanest flower that blows, become so naturally for our poets the origin and vehicle of universal sorrow and universal joy. The unknown monk and the Wordsworth of *Tintern Abbey* had

[1] e.g., in Carleton Brown's *English Lyrics of the XIII Century*, No. 49. I quote lyrics where possible from Dr. Carleton Brown's excellent collections, for economy's sake.

[2] Carleton Brown, *XIII Century Lyrics*, No. 1.

something of the same experience, however different their terms and images, and it is a humane sorrow, a humane pity that is made universal—divine—in their meditation.

Critical reading among such works resolves itself into the selection of the best of each kind—the most convincing of the confessions of sin, the grimmest of the admonitions of death and doom,[1] the neatest of the poor translations of well-known Latin hymns, the least offensive of the erotic-mystical imitations of Thomas of Hales' *Love Ron*. Many of these religious hymns are eternally valid—prayers for forgiveness or intercession, for help in trouble and in the hour of death, and preachings of holy living or, on the borderland of religion and ethics, injunctions for the regulation of conduct like the well-known and admirable *Moral Ode*. Yet a layman may confess to a certain sense of relief on coming across a religious poem done *ad hoc* and not in the way of custom and duty, as when a cynical satire on the times provokes a religious rejoinder.[2] Here we are freed from the routine of institutions and touch the world's life directly. We gain touch again, less directly, when we find the professional man of religion setting himself to adapt the themes, phrases, or forms of secular lyric. Religious parody of popular song is a common technical device of evangelists at all times, but desperately precarious. With all respect for motives, good poets are rarer than good Christians, and to have a first-rate human love-song to sing might, we feel, do us more good than a clumsy perversion of it into the conventional terms of religiosity.[3] The pious intentions of *The Gude and Godlie Ballads* are frustrated as we read

> Quho is at my windo? quho, quho?
> Go from my windo, go, go!
> Quho callis thair, sa lyke a strangair?
> Go from my windo, go![4]

[1] *XIV Century Religious Lyrics*, 28–30, 48.
[2] Carleton Brown, *XIV Century Religious Lyrics*, No. 120, answering No. 103, which does not read to me like a specifically religious poem.
[3] Ib., e.g., Nos. 73, 132: probably 9, 10, 69.
[4] Ed. Laing, 1867, p. 116. This is late (1542), but mediaeval things stayed long in Scotland: *vide infra*.

Burns wrote a good set of verses for it, but despite the Wedderburns' sincerity and their real gifts, we wonder what people were singing in sixteenth-century Aberdeen to that lovely tune. Such things depend too on our knowing the original: without that, much of the force is lost. Whatever our religious opinions, we are less apt to regret the original when the adaptation has such authentic, self-generated force as the joyous, ribald triumphing of

> The Paip, that pagane full of pryde,
>   He hes vs blindit lang;
> For quhair the blind the blind dois gyde,
>   Na wonder thay ga wrang:
> Lyke prince and king he led the ring
>   Of all iniquitie:
> Hay trix, tryme go trix,
>   Vnder the grene wod tree . . .
>
> The blind Bischop he culd nocht preiche,
>   For playing with the lassis;
> The syllie Freir behuffit to fleiche,
>   For almous that he assis;
> The Curat his creid he culd nocht reid,
>   Schame fall the cumpanie:
> Hay trix, tryme go trix,
>   Vnder the grene wod tree.[1]

So when we are jerked back from the springtime meadows to hearken to the conventional drone of the preacher, we are not so grateful as perhaps we ought to be.[2] We are very ready to be "thankful were it but for this fair day and the fine weather for the lambs", and feel thankfulness easier out of doors. Nor is it in a gracious mood that, having paused to hear the minstrel singing his goodnight verse, we wonder whether the comedian is putting on a pietistic snuffle or whether it is only a parson trying to jockey us into his

[1] Ib., p. 178.
[2] Carleton Brown, *XIII Century Lyrics*, No. 63; Lydgate, ed. MacCracken, Part I, No. 12.

church.[1] Religious sentiment, like any other, must spring direct from the fountain. Only rarely—much less frequently than in the mysteries where form and inspiration are fresh and local—are our emotions touched as when Bach lets us hear, between the pious phrases of the chorale, the echo of the shepherds' piping.

We take pleasure indeed in those secular refrains, however mishandled by well-meaning evangelists, but the pleasure is not always what the evangelists intended. Yet they too may have enjoyed their excursions in unregenerate *motifs*. They were doing in verse somewhat as their musical colleagues were doing when they used secular tunes as *canti fermi* in their Church services[2]—a custom condemned by the Council of Trent but not so easily broken. This dubious usage of the musicians was an instinctive (or—who knows?—deliberate) escape from their own elaborate conventions as well as from the restrictions imposed upon them by ecclesiastical authority. The musicians were restricted to the fixed words of the Canon—that is, to fixed forms, rhythms, and emotions. They could progress only in pure musical form, and any elaboration or constructional alteration had to be a logical development, not too violent an innovation to be impossible of performance by choirs who sang by theory as much as by notation, or to be alarming to the temperamental and theological conservatism of the authorities. Musical skill and enthusiasm, canalised by their function, wrought marvels in their fight for their art, so that they had to be called to order at intervals. Meanwhile, secular music renewed itself by its constant alliance with free poetic change, with dance and labour and fashion. A whole world of varied movement was denied to the Church musician who elaborated his art in the isolation of the sanctuary, until he contrived to inlay those fragments of it into his professional practice. So also the religious poet may have tried to refresh himself and his tradition; but his problem was more complex.

There was—and is—more possibility of refreshment in

[1] Ib., No. 97. Compare also the Latin hymn written to *Somer is i-cumen in*; though that is perhaps nearer the device noted in the next paragraph.
[2] The *Westerne Wind* Mass is the most famous English example.

hymn and sequence, where more variation of form, though still within limits, was permissible. In these, original inspiration is needed rather than recapitulation or contrapuntal elaboration, and their popularity among folk proves that they were singable as well as spiritual.[1] Full freedom comes with the expression of religious sentiment in the secular tradition. The makers of carols were free of emotion, phrase, metre, rhythm, form, alike and together. It is not that secular music was unprincipled or accidental: it was the work, once more, of the cultivated layman, who is not necessarily irreligious. He might indeed be in holy orders but learned, like Bede before him, in the native minstrelsy; or he might be a layman not unacquainted with the hymnal tradition of the Church: the point is that he worked outside the ceremonial tradition, produced religious poetry and music as they existed outside the cloister, in the freedom of daily life.

This refreshing inflow of secular forms is the more welcome that the cloister-poets, unlike the church musicians, have obvious artistic limitations. A rapid survey would suffice to show that, so far from developing poetic form or style, or forming new schools of religious art, the fourteenth and fifteenth century men were, if anything, duller and less competent than their elders: which is not surprising, considering their circumstances. Interest revives, however, when among the anonymous crowd we meet a recognisable personality like John Lydgate. Not that Lydgate's is a particularly fascinating personality, but at least we have it at full length. Lydgate was a professional poet with a large practice, and from his religious poems we can gather what forms of religious poetry commended themselves or prescribed themselves to a Monk of Bury. And since we have enough and to spare of Lydgate's output—the term is used advisedly—we can attempt to gauge and assess the quality of a sober discreet man of professed religion in the early fifteenth century. Routine work preponderates: versions of psalms, hymns, and portions of services with glosses on the same, legends of the Saints and invocations to them, poems to Our Lady, original

---

[1] The sequence *Angelus ad Virginem*, which Chaucer's Nicholas sang, is No. 52 in *The Oxford Carol Book*.

and translated; three edifying tales, a couple of spiritualised courtly motives, and so on. None of this is very original. There is more fresh interest in the half-dozen occasional pieces; a Corpus Christi procession which is the religious counterpart of his secular Mummings and "Soteltyes"—a commission from the Prior instead of from the King—a prayer for King, Queen and People that links him with political events, and four poems which commemorate happenings within the Abbey.[1]

These last may remind us of another artistic relationship, already touched upon: that of poetry with the plastic arts; for the events commemorated are the setting up of pictures and sculptures. The evidence for mediaeval painting in England is as fragmentary as that for poetry and music. Secular examples have practically disappeared; of church painting, damaged examples remain, long neglected, lately recovered, surprising in their quantity and sometimes too in their quality, enough to prove the ubiquity and the occasional power `of church decorators in both town and village. Although Lydgate is no art critic—it might be as injudicious for the disciplined cleric to criticise the *res dedicata* (not to mention the *res consecrata*) as for the courteous beneficiary to criticise the gift made to his Abbey—there is a social interest in these occasional poems from the community at Bury.[2] And there is something more. Lydgate never reveals the power of the handmaid of religion with the intensity of Villon in the Ballade *feist à la requeste de sa mère pour prier Nostre Dame*. He was not a great poet, nor was he a poor old woman in whom the pictures of the parish church struck fear and hope, but a sedate churchman to whom such things were a daily environment. But he was by no means insensitive, and in his poems on the Passion, for instance, he does feel, and make us feel, the force of the visual impression.[3] In the most

---

[1] Ed. MacCracken (E.E.T.S. CVII), Nos. 11, 41, 47, 48, 56, 62.

[2] Ed. MacCracken, No. 56, on a picture of Our Lady set up by Ralph Gelebronde.

[3] Ib., No. 47, on a Pietà; 62, on the same. I take No. 48 to be inspired by a picture or crucifix. Cf. Wright, *Political Poems* (Rolls Ser.) I, p. 268, where the writer remembers (to very different purpose) pictures of the miracles of St. Francis.

personal of his religious poems, indeed—one hesitates to say the *truest*, for sincerity is a different question and a difficult one—the force of that art is felt as it rarely is in English poetry. The poem, or, rather, series of poems, called *The Testament of Dan John Lydgate*[1] might be taken as the sampler of his religious verse. His special devotion (as a monk of Bury) to Our Lady does not appear clearly in it, but the prayers to Jesus are religious of the heart, the allegory after the fashionable manner of the *Rose* and the recurrence of the spring-song relate it to his secular poetry, and among the personal reminiscences in the fourth section he tells how his careless and boisterous childhood was rebuked:

> Wythinne .XV. holdying my passage
> Myd of a cloyster, depicte vpon a wall,
> I saugh a crucifix, whos woundes were not smalle,
> With this (word) "Vide" wrete there besyde,
> "Behold my mekenesse, O child, and leve thy pryde."

But in the last resort Lydgate, however practised in his profession, was always a churchman, subject to a churchman's restraints; and, however genuine in feeling, he is never more than an estimable poet. There is a world of difference between him and his anonymous fourteenth-century predecessor who wrote *Cleanness*, *Patience*, *Pearl*, and *Gawain and the Green Knight*.

Lydgate can be discerned in isolation as the producer of a received *corpus* of works, but he stands out only in low relief from the common background of cloister poets. The *Gawain* poet is a distinct personality: a layman, a poet of original power, and one of the most accomplished technicians that ever wrote verse in English. This last point is of more importance than some clerical writers seem to suspect. In the desperate battle for expression, technique is as valuable as knowledge. It is by his carillon of rhymes that Dunbar, a magnificent craftsman, informs the liturgical *Hail, sterne superne* with mystical feeling, which distils from the hypnotic repetition of sounds while the sense flows forward; it is by the

[1] Ed. MacCracken, No. 68.

skilful shaping and disposition of the phrases that he creates the reverent joy of Christmas in *Rorate Coeli desuper*. So Milton in the Nativity ode. So too the nameless poet in *The Pearl*. To convey personal sorrow and theological consolation he devised an allegory wherein emotion and intellect could interfuse, and he enshrined it cunningly in recurrent alliteration and the interplay of interlacing rhymes. It is not a question of personal emotion, which some critics are unable to feel, *plus* theological argument, over whose orthodoxy learned heads have shaken, *plus* a clever layman's trick of juggling with words. The elaborate craftsmanship may have been itself a beguilement of sorrow; but the artificer may well be praised who spends his most accomplished handiwork for the thing he loves. Any tin pot will hold the consecrated wine at need, and be consecrated by its service; but if we are to have a golden chalice, it is all the better if it be a goldsmith's masterpiece.

Craftsmanship, however, is not this poet's only gift. *Cleanness* and *Patience* contain Bible stories, and here the literary tradition of the Lives of the Saints may have helped. The Saints are intermediaries between earth and heaven, and in their stories human pity and terror and admiration may rightly mingle with spiritual awe and jubilation and devotion: *Juliana* and *St. Margaret* and *St. Erconwald* may serve as English examples. Here the poet's distance from his subject is much the same: these are biblical tales and therefore charged with divine spirit, but the protagonists are human beings. What is more, the Saints' Lives preserved, while French example dwindled into prettiness and triviality, an inherited portion—little enough sometimes, but genuine —of the grand style of the Old English heroic poets. In the hands of a poet who possessed the sense of magnificence and the sentiment of grandeur, the tradition revived. Here was a poet whom wind and rain elated, who knew the strength of the seas and the pride of kings, and who believed in God. He was not the professional preacher who tells an impressive tale and appends a lucid moral: he was a poet like Spenser and Milton and Wordsworth, a poet of wide powers and wide knowledge, guiding his fellow-men in the way of good, seeking purity of heart and submission to the divine will.

This poet is an individual—that is, one whose habits of feeling and observation, intellectual interests, and artistic tastes can be distinguished from the common run of his kind. For the religion of the ordinary man in town and village we may turn to *The Lay Folk's Mass Book*, *The Prymer*, the legends of the saints and the more familiar homilies; to the instructional writings of John Myrc, from which we may gather some notion of the daily work of the village priest and the religious duties the ordinary man was expected to observe; and, best of all in some ways, to the fifteenth-century Miracles. Here we have best exemplified the interpenetration of secular life and religion, and the intimate mingling of familiarity and awe which is possible only to implicit faith. The scenes in which a scriptural episode is doubled with a realistic episode of contemporary life may be regarded in various ways. No doubt Noah and his wife, the shepherd complaining of the oppressiveness of barons' retainers, the tricks of Mak the sheepstealer, had "entertainment value", and worked the audience's imagination into the action, and, in the better moments—and with the best performers—lifted its emotion from earth to heaven. But such scenes are more than naïve accidents. The miracle-writers knew the value of contrast, and of what we can only call parody—the tricks Shakespeare used throughout *Henry IV*. Falstaff's diatribe against honour does not cancel Prince Henry's aspiration or Hotspur's high-mindedness, because both author and audience believe in honour. So the scenes of realistic comedy act as a foil to the serious and undisturbed religion of the rest. Further, both writers and audience were well drilled in symbolism. The linked Old and New Testament "types" appear together in church paintings, block-books, and drama; the symbolic use of realistic scenes is carrying the method only a little further. Noah's recalcitrant wife is a comic figure from the street where the audience are standing. She heightens the terror of the flood that God sent upon a generation busy with its own affairs, like this one, and she is a foil to the saving faith of Noah. And she is the recalcitrant human soul that will not believe in the wrath to come and the means of salvation. How it was gradually built up, and to what extent each individual in the crowd appreciated its full significance, is another matter. Serious-minded priests must sometimes have watched anxiously to see that the balance was preserved. But the significance was there, and would no doubt be expounded when necessary for the instruction of the simple.

Somewhat the same justification might be found for the innumerable anachronisms. We feel it incongruous that Old Testament characters should swear by St. Peter or Our Lady of Walsingham. But again, when Old and New are painted on the same panel, they exist together. The concepts of time and space had not the hold over mediaeval minds that they have over ours. The learned dealt in abstract universals, and the unlearned dealt only in the particulars of their own surroundings. To most people, after all, 55 B.C. and A.D. 1066, Madagascar and Timbuctoo, are not far apart. They exist together in the modes of "long-ago" and "far-away". If that is so, after many generations of scientific method—that is, of history and measurement—how much more for our ancestors? They did not begin a mental process from given points of time and space, but from concepts presented to them by metaphysical theologians. In their dogmatic theology there is no *then* and *now*, *here* and *there*. God the Spirit exists from eternity and to eternity, and in Him all things are comprised and co-exist. Thanks to the psychologists and the physicists, we are arriving again at some comprehension of such a condition, though neither state their conclusions in religious terms and though the corresponding art ends in romantic individualism rather than in any universal understanding such as embraced those whose thought was based on God and the Church *quod semper, quod ubique, quod ab omnibus*. The condition was not, of course, consciously present to the audience, though it was the justification of the learned writer. To the crowd it was a necessary and unremarked premise. The ordinary layman would have found our explanation hard to understand—as hard to understand as our difficulty.

This much would be clearly present in his mind: this was a religious affair, and it was his affair. A priest no doubt wrote it down in the beginning, and perhaps rehearsed it— that is one of the things priests are for, writing things down— but now it was his, the Butcher's, the Shipwright's, or whatever his trade was. It was part of the activity of the guild, like admitting apprentices or fixing the minimum scantlings for deck-beams, and it was part of his duty as a guildsman to pay, to help, to act if need be, and at least to see that it was done well, for the honour of the guild, the town, and Holy Church. The order in which these three came in his mind altered as time went on, and this is worth notice, for the end of a phenomenon may be as significant as its origins, and is usually less conjectural. From our memory of the text-books we are apt to assume a chronological diagram: Miracle begat Morality which begat Elizabethan Drama. They were not of course disassociated, but their ends betray the essential difference between them. The Miracle dwindled into local observance or festival custom, into procession or disguising. The Morality died when the new learning drove the meaning out of the time-honoured disputation in the schools and the new humanism displaced the old metaphysical entities with human values. The point is reinforced, that the Miracle was a local observance, a regulated custom of the lay organisations; and it was a religious observance. So we find in it the common mind, inconsequent, vague, tender and pitiful and comic and ready to give worship where it is due. It is not perhaps an uncontaminated spiritual exercise—we cannot tell, for instance, from what ancient store of superstition is derived that northern eccentricity, the comic Devil, who may be Loki himself, exiled from Asgard—but it is a very human mixture, and perhaps all the truer religion in consequence.

V

At this point—since we have drifted towards the subject— we may break off to remind ourselves of the importance of technique: that is, first, of verse and rhetoric. Every real

artist has his own technique, by which his work is recognisable. That technique is his selection, variation, and invention
within a body of knowledge and skill which is traditional
and common, concerned with the overcoming of difficulties
and the exploitation of qualities inherent in his material.
Thus the poet has at his disposal a language held in common
with his fellow-countrymen, and certain ways of arranging
that language which have been found valuable by his
elders—ways which, to begin with at all events, he is apt
to accept as natural. He may argue interminably over
details—all controversies between artists are either technical
or irrelevant—but it is only rarely, when some violent
contrast or contradiction strikes him, that he will question
the fundamentals.

There have been in our Europe three great traditions of
verse-making: the Graeco-Roman, the Germanic, and the
French; and it is no small proof of the capabilities of our
language that English verse can be written according to
all three. The first, though it has always been influential
because it was clearly formulated, and though it has been
usefully practised as a scholarly exercise, we may leave
aside as an affair of the intellect. The other two are in our
blood and nerves—and on our tongues, for, as M. Emile
Legouis says, in the wisest words ever written on this thorny
subject: "Les sonorités d'une langue sont sa plus intime et
plus essentielle poésie. La prosodie et la versification s'organi-
sent spontanément autour des vertus élémentaires contenues
dans les vocables."[1] That is to say, the song-smiths in their
working generations hammer out the shapes that will best
exploit and display the qualities of their metal. But crafts-
men like to examine each other's work, and when the
English iron-workers met the bronze-workers of France,
they learned something of their methods; and with good
reason, for beyond all questions of fashion and prestige
there lay the sheer hard fact that their iron was changing
its crystals. To set metaphor aside: throughout the Middle
Ages the accidence of the English language was changing
and simplifying itself, so that about Chaucer's time it had

[1] *Défence de la Poésie Française* (Constable, 1922), p. 39.

reached, roughly speaking, the stage at which French had arrived about the time of the Norman Conquest. French versification, the youngest of the three traditions, would have been of little use to Cynewulf; it helped to solve difficulties for later generations who worked out the shapes, finally polished by the Elizabethans, which still hold good. For even those moderns who most loudly protest their independence and proclaim the downfall of traditions have invented no new principle: they are but searching for new effects, and more than half their success, when they do succeed, is that we find the new tunes make a pleasant counterpoint with the old tunes we have in our ears.

In dealing with language, and with the organisation of language, we are concerned not merely with sounds, but with meanings; and meanings are made clear not only by words, but by the connexions between them. As English first modified its inflexions and then shed most of them— the great change that differentiates Old from Middle and Middle from Modern English—word-order largely took their place as a method of expressing the connexion between words, and thus word-order became less variable. The Latin poet is free to display his words in the best rhythmical and rhetorical relationship to one another, while the inflexions continue to declare their grammatical relationships: only his prepositions are invariable in position, and they are fewer than ours. The Old English poets—that is, those late ones whose works we have—never exploited this freedom as, say, Horace did, but the possibility was there and was used, and as inflexions were lost it disappeared. The modern English poet has to work with longer, more complex and less tractable rhythm-units than the Latin: his unit is not the word, but the phrase. Thus the shedding of inflexions changed the shapes and sizes of the rhythm-units which the poets had to fit together to make their verses. The variable syllables at the ends of nouns and adjectives were removed, interstices filled up with prepositions, the articles became essential, the usage of auxiliary verbs extended, and so on; the cadence and the incidence of accentuation altering perforce.

This second change must have troubled the English poets, for of all phenomena of language accent is the most conspicuous. It is precisely the difference between English and French that the accentuation of English words is so much more marked, that there is such a difference between the heaviest and the lightest accents, and such an infinite range of intermediates between them, compared with the comparatively level accentuation of French. The main result, for our present purpose, is that English verse has always been controlled by the incidence of heavy accents, while French poets have to reckon their syllables. The Old English poets organised *les sonorités* by organising the heavily-accented syllables, emphasising and connecting them, since they were normally the first syllables of important words, by alliteration; the French counted off their syllables in groups, and emphasised and connected the groups with rhyme, which they could do the more easily because they had comparatively few inflexions left. There are of course other phenomena, but this is not a treatise on comparative versification: suffice it that quantity in English and accent in French are of roughly equivalent importance; and that the student of Old English poetry must not be dismayed by the lists of verse-types, A. B. C. and so on, compiled by German scholars. These are quite correct, but they are only statistical formulas and have nothing to do with the principle of beauty, which is, then as now, the principle of controlled variation. Let the student mark the alliterated syllables upon which the line depends, and trust his native ear. If he is in difficulties with any particular line, then he may consult the type-formulas.

The change of versification is clearly marked in Layamon's *Brut*. Just as Layamon accepted the new imaginative tradition, so he experimented in the new French verse. It may be that as he worked over the lines of Wace his ear became attuned to the new cadence. It may be that like a good craftsman he tried to reproduce the form as well as the meaning of his original; or perhaps he realised as he went on that this French system really suited his English speech. All these may have been in his mind, but we need not attempt to make out what at best would be a disjointed history. English verse as practised by Gower and Chaucer, and by all English poets since, has been a compromise or reconciliation between the two systems. Gower, indeed, a highly respectable poet in each of the three tongues, is almost symbolic of English culture in the fourteenth century. There is a regrettable sedateness about Gower. He has a gift of quiet expressiveness to which justice has scarcely been done, but he never attempts a broad effect. To him, it would seem, verse was just an efficient way of telling stories, rather than the best way of infecting his reader with varied emotion or achieving the *mimesis* of vision and passion. So he remains the respectable Gower, whom no one can neglect, who is full of felicities but excites us little about either his own world or ours. His very success in the three tongues damns him as "accomplished". Yet he proved one point very clearly and finally: that French verse could be written in English. The proof exists only in the eight-syllable couplet, but it is complete.

Chaucer on the other hand attempted more, had his greater successes and those in many verse-forms, but was never so completely secure as Gower. Ten Brink and others have worked out his type-formulas. Here again let the student use his ear, speak the verse aloud as if it were French rather than English, and consult the formulas only when he sticks completely. The verse goes to a lighter run of accent than most English verse, but the tune is familiar, and where a reasonably sensitive and experienced modern Englishman sticks in the reading, it is highly probable that Chaucer stuck in the writing. He was not a miraculous earth-born virtuoso. On the contrary, he was one of those poets like Drayton and Keats, who have to work for their mastery, whom we can watch improving and who keep on improving. He knew it himself, for he knew what he was trying to do, which was to write, in English, verse after the manner of the fashionable court school of French poets, of Eustache Deschamps, Otes de Granson, Jean Froissart, his contemporaries and acquaintances with whom French poetry was decaying, as French movements decay, in elegant doctrinaire rigidity. This formalism was no great harm: English and French vices tend to counteract one another, the fresh language made excessive formalism unlikely, and Chaucer was all the better for bracing himself to a high standard of formal precision, even if it was too high for him. The versifier who could spin the catherine-wheel at the end of *The Clerk's Tale*—is it a sign of graceless relief at seeing the last of Griselda?—was the better able to write *Troilus and Criseyde*.

It is doubtful whether Chaucer learned anything of verse from those other pupils of the French, Dante and Boccaccio. He knew the sonnet, but translated Petrarch without trying to reproduce his form as he reproduced the French rondel. Indeed there were—and are—few technical lessons to be learned from Italian versification compared with those to be learned from French. To carry over the latter into English was task enough for one man, and was perhaps the most useful thing Chaucer could have done. Yet his restriction to a highly-specialised school, however natural to a man who belonged to another branch of the same society that produced it, was a restriction; and however praiseworthy the determination that made him force English to purposes which would doubtless have been easier to accomplish in French and Latin, however admirable his modernism, those very virtues entailed some neglect of the possibilities of English. There were things to be learned on this side of the Channel that Chaucer did not learn.

The alliterative verse of *Piers Plowman* is indeed symbolic of opposition to the society and politics of which Chaucer was an apparently contented part. It may have been chosen for that symbolic purpose by a poet who wrote to recall Englishmen to pristine virtue, but in fact the old English way of writing did not die when Layamon discovered the new. More or less ably adapted to the new accidence, more and more thrust into the background by French fashion, it lingered in the uplands of the west and north, and that as late as 1513, when an unknown bard in Cheshire or Lancashire celebrated Flodden and the Stanleys in *Scotish Field*. Langland's great poem was not a solitary phenomenon, nor a

75

piece of artificial archaism, but grew out of a habit of verse, well understood, and admirably suited to its purpose. If we compare Langland's verse with Gower's—which might be within the competence of more men than the court verse of Chaucer—we appreciate more fully its gravity, its strength, its capacity for adaptation to a language more purely English than Chaucer's, its capacity for variation to suit the theme and especially for the emphatic lyrical declamation for which the English poets have such a peculiar genius. It is perhaps well that Chaucer kept to his own task, for the virtues and devices he neglected are endemic in the English language, and were instinctively engrafted into his forms by later poets. It is well also that another great poet should have arisen with him to reinforce those virtues and devices by his example.

The synthesis made by Gower and Chaucer was the synthesis of French verse and style with English words and grammar, but before the Elizabethans made the final synthesis, there was another intermediate—a combination rather than a true synthesis of French and English versification. The alliterative poets of the fourteenth and fifteenth centuries were not ignorant of the other schools. They took the *laisse*, the long stanza of the French romancers, and wrote it with alliteration, sometimes with and sometimes without rhyme. The greatest artist in this school was the unknown fourteenth-century Midlander who wrote *Cleanness*, *Patience*, *Gawain and the Green Knight*, and *The Pearl*. The skill displayed is astonishing, whether in plain alliteration or in the rhymed and alliterated stanzas, intricately connected by repetition, of *The Pearl*. But it was achieved at a cost, for it demanded a rich vocabulary, and this poet's, especially in *Gawain and the Green Knight*, is so extensive and peculiar as to make his poem extraordinarily difficult—a grave pity, since *The Green Knight* is the best romance there is. If Gower represents the trilingualism of fourteenth-century England, *Gawain and the Green Knight* is an exaggeration of the fusion of English, French, Danish, Norse, Latin, that was producing modern English. It has been conjectured that it was written for a feast of St. George at Windsor, but no poet in his senses would offer a poem of such difficulty on an official occasion and to such an audience.

Since alliteration requires a rich vocabulary, the exploitation of vocabulary was a great part of Old English rhetoric. The inflected language made possible a rhetoric of parallelism which is difficult to translate into our uninflected English. The effect seems monotonous, but the monotony is due largely to our ignorance of the imaginative heraldry as well as of the imaginative processes of our forefathers. The so-called synonyms of Old English poetry are concise descriptions or allusions, and their choice and their placing in relation to one another can be made to yield expressive variety of tone and that counterpoint of meanings by which figures of rhetoric enrich the sense with cross-lights and superimposed images. We may take it that there are extremes: that for the sake of his alliteration the most careful poet was sometimes forced to use a synonym whose variation (the thing that first brought it into being or made it into a synonym) did not add to his image, and that the least careful would at least avoid incongruities of allusion. Even the least careful, again, must arrange his synonyms in some order. To say "The sun rose, God's candle" is good; to say "God's candle rose, the sun" is weak. To say "The man spoke, poured forth the treasures of his speech, the warrior wise in council" is good rhetorical development;[1] to say "The warrior wise in council poured forth the treasures of his speech, the man spoke" is merely futile explanation.

The system makes at least for conciseness, economy, and precision. It demands a certain quickness of apprehension in the hearer, and creates a compressed and masculine style. A Tennyson might spend a page on describing the sea, but in a few phrases the old poets could call up sharply the one or two images required to effect their purposes. "The whale's road", "the gannet's bath"—there are the shapes and movements of the sea-creatures, and the open space of the sea surrounds them. Such observation is at first individual. It is ever renewed, but ever tending to fixity under the impulsion of powerful individuals. The great artists teach us

[1] Though spoiled by modern grammar: the original would be in six words.

to see and to express our seeing, so that to see things afresh, and to record them afresh, requires a violent breach of habit; and vision and technique, acquired together from their example, interact to the reinforcement of habit when our seeing has to be set down in words or paint. Thus like all technical systems the Old English rhetoric became fixed, the images became stock properties, the legendary allusions (so far as we can judge) were introduced out of custom or to meet the exigencies of the verse. Such degeneration may have set in before the English language and its poetic art came to the western island. It is perhaps well that the new subjects and the new schools intervened before that art could stiffen into the mere learned ingenuity that mars the later Norse poetry.

The cultivated Old English prose was a greater loss than the rhetoric of Old English poetry, yet it must be observed that centuries had to pass before the English poets contrived to combine the gravity of the native school with the speed and lightness of the French, and invent another medium of continuous verse suited to the qualities of the language and to the native temperament. Drama seems to have grown out of music as well as out of story-telling, but no such history is required to account for the semi-lyrical stanzas in which the writers of Miracles framed the speeches of their characters. They accepted the French formulas, and, however well adapted the stanzas are to certain emotional passages and metaphysical entities, they do not make a true dramatic speech-verse in English, and the formulas cramp the expression in the realistic scenes. Association with music no doubt helped to carry forward the long romances, but the time had to come for that association to be broken, for speech to become speech and song, song. The French learned that naturally; the lesson, for some reason, seems harder for the English, who sing by nature and, until eighteenth-century snobbery nearly destroyed it, had the oldest tradition of part-song in all Europe.

In musical matters there is little help available to the amateur. The historians of music in England confine themselves to church music, where a continuous history is traceable in purely musical idiom, and rarely risk a remark

upon the scattered relics of the flourishing but less calculable
music of the world at large. In our present state of knowledge,
the formation of the lyrical measures is a mystery. The
origins will be traced to whatever source is fashionable at the
moment—the Palermo of Frederick Barbarossa, the Milan
of St. Ambrose, Provence, or Ireland. If, as Saintsbury
insisted, the origins are to be found in Latin hymnology,
what made a change like this?

> Solvitur acris hiems grata vice veris et Favoni
> Trahuntque siccas machinae carinas;
> Ac neque iam stabulis gaudet pecus aut arator igni,
> Nec prata canis albicant pruinis . . .

> Levis exsurgit Zephyrus
> et sol procedit repidus;
> iam terra sinus aperit,
> dulcore sus diffluit . . .[1]

The influence of the Church is too simple an explanation.
The hymn of Lucretius

> Æneadum genetrix, hominum divumque voluptas,
> Alma Venus . . .

may well be superseded in doctrine by

> Veni, Sancte Spiritus,
> Et emitte coelitus
> Lucis tuæ radium.

> Veni, pater pauperum,
> Veni dator munerum
> Veni lumen cordium . . .

but where in Gospel or in Fathers is the change of form
dictated? The Church may have provided an energetic,
though not the unique, vehicle of transmission: to explain
the formation would require the analysis and re-synthesis of
a linguistic complex and of a world of social habit and of

---

[1] Horace, Od. I, iv, and *The Cambridge Songs*, ed. K. Breul, p. 60.

instinctive biological response to stimulus. There are life-times of fascinating work in it for well-equipped students, for there is no single answer. Calling a truce to speculation, let me hazard one suggestion: where the tune is discoverable, it is the clue to reality—that is, to how the thing sounded to the people who made it—and when the tune is lost—or, by the indifference of our musicians, not available—the verse may be tested by trying to fit it to known tunes, especially to the tunes of nursery rhymes and to traditional hymn and carol tunes which descend from the metrical habits of the Middle Ages. It will be noticed that the best secular lyrics demand each a tune for itself, and that is evidence of long and high cultivation.

If we knew how Old English poetry was recited it would help our understanding of it more than all the metrical tables in Germany. The technical term was *singan ond secgan*, to sing and say, and we know that the harp was used to accompany the voice—"the clear sound of the harp" is in *Beowulf* and elsewhere a symbol of cheerful human companionship that mocked the outcast and the exile—but whether in recitation of the heroic poem we do not know, though one can imagine it used most effectively. By what dramatic arts the professional reciters enforced the excitement of the romances we cannot tell, nor how gesture and music seconded the modulation of the voice. The Latin writers use the term *cantare*, to sing, when speaking of the recitation of tales,[1] but mediaeval Latin is too fluid a language to allow of precise deduction from a single word, and those who recite ballads learned by heart, and have not suffered from the good intentions of elocution-teachers, fall naturally into a strong and very effective cadence which approaches plainsong. Many ballads, of course, have their own tunes. W. P. Ker showed clearly the place of the French *carole* in the formation of the ballad,[2] and one can understand it in things like *Binnorie*, but did the historical ballad begin in the same way? Or did it merely take over a habit

[1] See, e.g., the remarks of Thomas of Cobham in Chambers, *Mediaeval Stage*, II, App. G.
[2] *Collected Essays*, XXII, XXV–XXVI; *Form and Style in Poetry*.

which at first sight seems a hindrance? Or is it a different inheritance that makes *Sir Patrick Spens* so impressive when it is carried on that thin air like the wind in the rigging, and makes *Hobbie Noble* ride to its tune at a livelier canter? My mother used to tell us how in her girlhood an aunt, born at the opening of the nineteenth century when tradition was still active, had store of ballads. One[1] ended somewhat thus:

> "Ye're welcome to me", said Captain Ogilvy,
> "Ye're welcome, thrice welcome to me.
> Ye're welcome, thrice welcome", said Captain Ogilvy,
> "The Duchess of Northumberland to be".

And as Auntie Jean pronounced the last emphatic line, she rose from her stool, took her skirts in her hands, and swept a full curtsy to the floor. It might be a personal idiosyncrasy, or a reminiscence of the sole Scottish dramatic custom, the custom of competitive performance of *The Gentle Shepherd* which she knew well; or it might, in that odd corner of the Lowlands, be a lingering relic of the proper way to "produce" a ballad. However such speculations may one day be resolved, we should at least remember that when we read *Beowulf* or *Ferumbras* or *Clerk Saunders* in our scholarly edition with the textual footnotes we are doing something eccentric, like examining cinema "stills" with a magnifying glass, that we are adding to our imaginative experience something in-complete and exanimate, and that it behoves us the more to keep awake what imagination we have. Here again, as in other technical difficulties, reading aloud is the best specific.

Beyond the insuperable difficulty of recovering the poems as they were recited—there is still hope of hearing a few sung —there is another, more easily removed: that of seeing them as they were seen. Not that we can see them with the same eyes. In five hundred years we have acquired the habit of reading type, learning meanwhile to appreciate the austere beauty of black and white. We have lost the elasticity of spelling and word-form, and the tricks of abbreviation.

---

[1] A version of *The Duke of Gordon's Daughter*, No. 237 in Childs Collection.

Reading is made too easy for us, so that we approach the deciphering of a mediaeval manuscript as a task, and one not lightened by scholarly demands for precision.

Here also we must allow for losses, and for presuppositions. When it is assumed that literacy was confined to Churchmen, then our notion of book-production and circulation imposes the cloister on our historical imagination. Legend and the museum-cases, again, impose the notion that monastic books were invariably noble masterpieces of illumination. Such masterpieces, however, were not the staple product—much less the only product—of the scriptoria. Many manuscripts of artistic value disappeared when the monasteries were dissolved, but, as we may judge from catalogues and from survivals, the monastic libraries contained, for the most part, text-books and treatises—theological, philosophical, medical, and even scientific—written in economically crabbed hands. To imagine otherwise is to do less than justice to those monasteries which were centres of learning, and could not afford to provide *editions de luxe* for study any more than the mediaeval or modern colleges which have taken over their task. We must allow also for the professional "stationers" like Chaucer's Adam Scrivener, who produced books for students and for amateurs of literature, not all of whom could indulge in such splendid volumes as are the pride of the British Museum and the Bibliothèque Nationale. We must remember the *jongleur* who occasionally wrote out his repertory to save his memory, and also the amateurs themselves like Robert Thornton and a dozen anonymous compilers.

There is yet another, though minor, artificial obstacle. Early and mediaeval literature are presented to us as "texts", isolated or classified. That is not how they appeared in the book-chests of mediaeval readers. We have of late been given the opportunity of seeing the great Old English poetic collections complete, and, at the other end of our period, the Scottish Text Society have done good service by publishing Bannatyne's and Maitland's manuscripts as they stand. But to gather some idea of the tastes and habits of the intermediate years we must turn to such catalogues as that of the Harleian collection and study the contents of such collections as No. 2253. So doing—thanks to the excellent Humphrey Wanley and his successors it can be done very well—we find a variety and comprehensiveness for which our common notions of the Middle Ages prepare us as little as our formal studies. Or if we take, say, the Auchinleck Manuscript in the Scottish National Library, we find its owner had a similarly wide taste both in English and French. He collected together forty-three pieces: seventeen romantic, ten religious and moral, seven saints' lives and the like, five miscellaneous and two historical works, and did not classify them. The manuscript is a little library of mixed reading, testimony to the mixed interests of a moderately serious general reader, and also, like the Thornton Manuscript in Lincoln Cathedral, to the free circulation of copies throughout the island. If the good student will remember a little of the many kinds of mediaeval book he will have a better notion of the Middle Ages than the best-recognised authority on one, and if he will compare catalogues he will gather the relative popularity and importance of different books and authors. Confining himself for the time being to English poetry he will realise, by that most practical test, the paramount importance of Chaucer.

VI

Among the individual poets of the European Middle Ages, two stand out: Dante and Chaucer. Strictly speaking, they are incomparable. Intellectually, Chaucer is tentative, inquisitive, where Dante, resting on the closed system of St. Thomas Aquinas, is magnificently certain. On the other hand, though Dante inhabits heights and abysses to which Chaucer never even aspired, his range on earth is the more restricted of the two, and however incapable Chaucer might be of the rapture and glory and scorn, the desperate intensity of Dante, his feelings were not circumscribed by a political party. Incomparable or not, we can think of them together: we are rarely tempted to group Chaucer with the French masters from whom he learned his trade of poetry. They are final: when they had done their work, that kind of work was done for good. So also, for very different reasons and to very different purpose, Dante is final. Chaucer is a link in a chain. He leads us back to the old world whose unmoved ghosts haunt manuscripts and tapestries, and he leads forward to Shakespeare and Smollett and Dickens, and can never be final while men walk and talk.

Chaucer, the first poet since Horace who was a man of the world and made poetry out of it, touched life at more points than the average man in any age, and at more than a mediaeval man could normally expect. Not that mediaeval society was quite such a system of insulated compartments as the mediaeval mind makes it appear, but Chaucer had unusual opportunities. A London merchant's son enjoyed more freedom than anyone, for, unlike both squire and serf, he was not bound to one piece of land, and he had his choice of occupations. As a layman, he was not subject to a cleric's restrictions either intellectual or physical. The fact that he acquired somehow and somewhere a useful acquaintance with Latin literature, with philosophy, and with astronomy, suggests that lay education was not so backward as we are sometimes told, and that it was available to him. Trained in a princely household, in the conventions of chivalry and among the arts to which feudal society gave both form and meaning, he knew the veterans of Edward III's wars as Sterne knew those of Marlborough's, and better than Scott knew those of the '45; he himself had experience, though it was short and unlucky, of real warfare; employment on three embassies showed him foreign lands and foreign potentates, and something of government and diplomacy, without hedging him in, as a great place would, with dignity. Then he settled down to a busy official life, and that in the Customs, a service that meant dealings with merchants, shipmasters, warehousemen, between the variegated life of a busy seaport on one hand and the machinery—and the accidents—of government on the other. And in all these various activities he was more than a looker-on. He was part and parcel of them, considered, so far as we can see, useful and efficient. With all his attitude (in later life at any rate) of the detached and amused observer, with all his consuming love for books, he was never a mere bookman or *promeneur solitaire*, but one who, like Fielding and William de Morgan, learned the world in the course of his business and so learned it naturally and truly.

Of Chaucer's view of the world, what can one do but quote Dryden and say "Here is God's plenty?" Yet the pleasure of writing about Chaucer is too great to be forgone, and—since this essay is already desultory enough—we may be allowed some desultory remarks. Desultory, because any real study of Chaucer would have to cover his own range. That range is important. The difference between Chaucer and Chrestien de Troyes is that Chaucer wrote *fabliaux* as well as romances; between Chaucer and Otes de Granson, that Chaucer wrote an astronomical text-book as well as courtly poems; between Chaucer and John Holywood, that Chaucer wrote courtly poems as well as an astronomical text-book; and so on. The neat phrase that "Chaucer was the half-disillusioned child of the Middle Ages" is quite beside the mark: Chaucer was the child of the XIV century, and enjoyed it so much that he was in touch with everything that men were doing in his time, and tried his hand at most of them. He was not, of course, a miraculous intellect embracing the human universe with equal sympathy and equal understanding: he was Geoffrey Chaucer, not Buddha. But he looked out very frankly on so much of the world as chanced to present itself before his friendly eyes.

Friendly, but not uncritical: when Matthew Arnold found fault with Chaucer for lack of seriousness, he was forgetting—perhaps he never realised—what a various and insidious thing "humour" is. The humorist enjoys things as they are, gets most of his fun out of life by watching the differences between people and watching each behave so like himself. But what of the effect on his reader? Is he entirely unconscious of it, entirely without motive or intention? Browning, another humorist, has stated the case for art:

For, don't you mark, we're made so that we love
First when we see them painted, things we've seen
Perhaps a thousand times nor cared to see.

The artist, as Wordsworth maintained, makes us see things afresh. Then we can love them—or not. The Wife of Bath is accepted for her sheer Rabelaisian vitality. The Doctor and the Lawyer pass, with a touch of traditional satire. The townsmen are perceived to be rather self-important and rather dull. It is a different matter when we look with Chaucer's eyes at the ecclesiastics.

There is nothing fortuitous about the tradition of Chaucer's anticlericalism. Professor Manly has shown that the old story that Chaucer got into trouble for beating a friar in Fleet Street, though now impossible to verify, rests upon good authority.[1] In any case it should be kept for its symbolic value, for however freely Chaucer may have accepted the generality of mankind, he is frankly critical of the Church; and his criticism, however humorously conveyed, is serious. The one ecclesiastic who is anything but a comic figure is the Parson, and he is set up in contrast to the rest. It may be that Chaucer was merely taking the popular English side in the long quarrel between the seculars and the regulars. It may be that he merely shared the old endemic English dislike of the proud prelate, a dislike that may go back to the Norman Conquest if not further, and was connected with the steady opposition to the foreign beneficiaries who drew such a handsome revenue out of England. Both of these motives count for much; yet surely it was something more than a party quarrel or a common prejudice that made Chaucer so comprehensive in his criticism, and made his criticism so much the more dangerous that it was so varied and so deadly good-humoured. The Pardoner and the Somnour are plain rascals; that was nothing new, and Chaucer handles them as roughly as they deserve. The Prioress on the other hand, he treats with all courtesy, and what are we left with when he has finished? A slip of provincial over-refinement, a gentlewoman from Cranford; and there is one elevated ecclesiastical figure reduced to charming insignificance. There are more ways of killing a cat than drowning it in cream, but a cat drowned in cream is a dead cat all the same. His treatment of the Monk is even more devastating.

[1] *New Light on Chaucer.*

Quite clearly, he must have approved of an institution that produced types he admired, and the only people (except the Parson and his obscure brother) whom Chaucer treats with serious respect are the Knight, the Squire, and the Yeoman. The Yeoman is conclusive, for here no "class feeling" can enter, and if Chaucer had wanted to include an Ancient Pistol or an Old Bill, there was nothing to stop him: he cannot have lacked the knowledge, and he certainly had the skill. To describe the Knight as a "chivalric" figure might be misleading to some people, but we must guard against our own preconceptions, and avoid confusing "chivalry" with "knight-errantry". That we are apt to do so is natural enough, for there did exist a highflown theoretical "chivalry" which is demonstrated in some of the best and some of the worst romances, which was a power for good in men's minds, brought disaster to Scotland at Flodden, and died of a cold fever in the works of Cervantes, of arthritis in those of La Calprenede, and of the vapours with Margaret Duchess of Newcastle. That it survives (to our confusion of mind) is a tribute to Malory, to literature which remains intact when political issues, social needs, and the notions bred of them, have disappeared from the common memory of every day. Chaucer's Knight is chivalric, but not theoretical. He comes out of Froissart, not out of Malory, and it is an unlucky battalion that has not had him in its Mess.

The Knight's Tale must be read candidly. It is not a love-story, but the story of two friends who behave like gentlemen. So far as character is concerned, the one character in it—and it is a brilliant one—is that of Theseus. Theseus is a Duke, not a Knight; a chivalric figure, but not an irresponsible Lancelot. Rather he is a Chandos or a Talbot, a General Officer Commanding who is confronted with a serious breach of military law and discipline, takes prompt action, and, when things are explained to him, is sympathetic enough to reprieve the culprits on condition that their affair is settled decently and in order, to ensure which he takes charge of it himself. Given the articles of war and the duelling code, the whole business is entirely correct, and Theseus is neither shadowy nor diagrammatic.

He does not "represent" a social order, but belongs to a type moulded by circumstance. His best battalion was doubtless commanded by the Knight of the Prologue, and his Army Corps was happy and efficient. Chaucer knew them both, and so did I. And by a further stroke of genius, he has endowed his Duke with a sense of humour. To this experienced soldier, the high romantic vein of Palamon and Arcite is funny. Yet he is experienced enough to know that it is real and natural—youthful and foolish, but right and fitting in foolish youth, like the Squire's taste in clothes, to be regarded with all sympathy by men of the world like Theseus and Chaucer, who have been through it in their time:

> Al moot been assayed, hoot or cold;
> A man moot ben a fool or yong or old;
> I woot it by my-self ful yore agoon.[1]

After all, Palamon and Arcite were actuated by love and honour, and neither Theseus nor Chaucer were men to laugh at those motives. The tale goes on, neither made ridiculous by the jest of Theseus nor refuting it: but it has been set in perspective.

This art of perspective is one of the things Chaucer had learned while writing *Troilus and Criseyde*. Any story exists in three planes: that of the writer, that of the characters, and that of the reader. The writer may lean across, as Thackeray does and Chaucer himself sometimes, to comment for the reader's benefit upon what is happening on the plane of the characters, but he is apt to get in the way or to distract attention. In the character of Pandarus Chaucer invented a fourth plane, and was able to keep out of his reader's way in confidence that the stereoscopic effect was there. He repeated it in Theseus, and Shakespeare picked up—or re-invented—the device in Enobarbus and Menenius and (tilting the plane a little) in Falstaff. Beside the heroes of romance is set a man of the world. The heroes are not belittled by his presence. He serves like a portrait-painter's mirror, to cast a reflected light that shows them in the round

[1] *Knight's Tale*, 953-5.

—the light of all the facts and all the values to which they are blinded. Chaucer did not learn this from Boccaccio or any other Italian. It is just the thing we miss in the Clerk's Tale, which he took over complete, and reverently, from Petrarch; it makes just the difference between the setting and conversations of the *Decameron*, which are on the same plane with the stories, and those of *The Canterbury Tales*, which are on the fourth plane. The Pandarus-figure might be likened to the Greek chorus, intermediate between the audience and the tragedy, but it is not the same, for it is part of the tragedy; not *on* the picture-frame but well within it. And it is a humorous figure.

It makes Chaucer's attitude to romantic chivalry seem rather equivocal. Romantic chivalry seems an affair for the young. The Squire is given a marvellous romantic Tale—and Chaucer did not finish it. He did finish the story of Beauty and the Beast as it was caught up in the Gawain cycle and made to illustrate Gawain's traditional virtue of courtesy; but whether the Wife of Bath's Tale is a comment on her Prologue, or her Prologue a comment on the tale, or whether Chaucer kept them quite separate in his mind, are questions no man can answer. He left unreported the remarks of the Host on the Franklin's Tale; nor is it easy to pronounce dogmatically, when one has allowed that *The Rime of Sir Thopas* is a satire on a debased form of literature, whether Chaucer wrote it because he despised those who had debased the form, or despised the form because it was debased. A reasonable conclusion might be, that he enjoyed the knightly romance, but admired the knightly reality whose fundamentals he defined in one noble line:

> he loved chivalrye,
> Trouthe and honour, fredom and curteisye.

This divorce from romance need not be regarded as entirely congenital idiosyncrasy in Chaucer. His earlier work shows how completely he accepted the sophisticated society in which he was brought up, and though in later work he overstepped its restrictions, he could not rid himself of its sophistication. He could make delightful things out of classical legend as it appeared to the mediaeval imagination and out of philosophy as it interested a clever amateur whose humour would keep breaking in; he could rhyme his wise, dry conversation with his friends; above all, he could turn *Troilus and Criseyde* into something infinitely greater than the sentimental labyrinth in which it began. But neither in earlier days when he inhabited the courtly world of Deschamps and Granson, nor later, when he had moved towards a wider reality, could he go back to the generous simplicities of romance. Old stories like the Wife of Bath's Tale and the Franklin's Tale, which carried a plain moral of universal application, had some value for him, but he was too civilised for irrational adventures. *Gawain and the Green Knight*, if he knew it, probably seemed to him as rough and provincial in subject as in form. The advance is obvious, the gain is great, but something too is lost. The vocational chivalry which gave contemporary—and for us antiquarian—interest to the Gawain-poet's precise descriptions of knightly equipment was not in the inheritance of the emancipated bourgeois Chaucer, and that was a small loss, compensated and more in *The Hous of Fame* and *The Knight's Tale*. The loss of the "romantic" landscape and the "romantic" atmosphere is more serious, for these exercise powerful and permanent influences on the English mind.

Chaucer was a Londoner, who walked for pleasure in the daisied meadows, or in formal gardens enclosed after the French mode. What would he be doing in a Cumberland glen among the snow-wreaths, or on the misty shores of the Tarn Wathelin?[1] Yet to so many Englishmen, even before Cynewulf and even after Meredith, the enclosed garden would be an exile indeed, were they never to feel that cold wind on their faces. What, again, would our plump official, who had so keen an eye for the human spectacle—Troilus riding through the streets with the dust of fighting on him, the face of the criminal led to the gallows, the Man in Black bearing his sorrow about with him—what would he do at

[1] *Gawain and the Green Knight; The Awntyrs of Arthur.*

a three days' hunting of hart and boar and fox?[1] Watch hounds at work, with Shakespeare? Ride the hill with Scott and screech with Surtees? That was not his game, though the four of them would agree admirably over the evening tankard afterwards; and though he might rise politely with the rest to toast the Unknown as the master huntsman among poets, he might be a little bored if they discussed the day's run too long. So there is little landscape in Chaucer, and no weather except the winter that keeps him indoors and the spring that lets him out for his walk. It was not from him that his disciple Gavin Douglas learned to see the light in the northern sky, or his later disciple Spenser to love running water. He was a townsman, and—though he had an eye for a horse—his business was with men and books. And he comes in an imaginative interregnum between belief and the willing suspension of unbelief. Before Gawain could "come ageyn out of Faerye",[2] the garden where Chaucer read to Richard II had to be broken down. A wilder, ruder life had to bring fresh adventure into England, and men arrive to whom the free play of fancy was as dear as the exercise of the observant humour.

The ballade on *Lak of Steadfastness* shows that he was not unobservant of the political faults that brought about the tragic change, but of all great poets he was the least of a politician. When Sir Walter A. Raleigh wrote of Shakespeare that "he is worlds removed from Chaucer, who understands social differences as Shakespeare never did, and to whom, therefore, social differences count less",[3] he was remarking upon social history as much as on individual character. Though the rigidity of mediaeval society must not be exaggerated, it was a more definite organisation than any that followed until the invention of Soviet Russia. To Chaucer, as to Langland, social differences were differences of function. He could not foresee the confusion of function to be caused by pestilence and civil war, still less the social

---

[1] *Gawain and the Green Knight*. The hunt in *The Boke of the Duchesse* is seen as by a visitor at the meet, not by a hunter.
[2] *The Squire's Tale*, 96.
[3] *Shakespeare* (English Men of Letters), p. 193.

revolution of the new Tudor monarchy or the new alignments of sentiment that were to arise out of the Reformation.
The bourgeois Chaucer about 1390 could take for granted
social differences which by 1590 had become precarious
and were therefore more to be insisted on by the bourgeois
Shakespeare. It is not entirely a question of date, however.
Chaucer took less heed of the social order than Langland,
whose subject indeed is just that. As a result, he misses what
Langland expresses so strongly, the sense of the dignity of the
poor man—not a personal dignity maintained in spite of
his poverty, but a dignity held by right of his function. A
northern peasant like Burns could proclaim his independence
—independence, not revolt—but again that is something
different. The southern Chaucer could view his Plowman
sympathetically enough, but he does not suggest that the
Plowman had any status at all. The Miller is a comic figure,
and the comic description removes him from consideration.
Chaucer could not imagine that the strength that could
break a barn door might one day help to break a Cavalier
charge. What is more to the point, he did not perceive, as
Langland would, that a miller was an important person
in a village community and therefore weighted with responsibility. With all his force, the Miller does not matter,
for by that dangerous English trick of humour which works
not indeed to destroy but, by its very tolerance, to weaken,
the drunken bully is rendered harmless.

Chaucer, in short, takes little heed of function or status.
In the same way, he takes little interest in passion as a
force in the soul: that is how *Troilus and Criseyde* differs
from *Il Filostrato* on which it is based. What is best, and is
new, in Chaucer's judgment is that it is aesthetic, concentrated on the value of the appearance as appearance, not
on its cause or its end. For a parallel we must go back to
Homer—beyond Virgil, who was thinking always of im-
perial Rome—or to *Beowulf*. Chaucer sees values like Scott,
who wrote of the ruffian he sentenced: "This is a turbulent
fierce fellow. Some of his attitudes were good during the
trial."[1] Chaucer may not have thought the matter out as

[1] *Journal*, Aug. 20, 1827.

Keats was trying to do when he wrote: "Though a quarrel in the Streets is a thing to be hated, the energies displayed in it are fine; the commonest Man shows a grace in his quarrel"[1]—but he would doubtless have agreed with the notion.

It is this mode of judgment that incapacitates him, as has so often been observed, for tragedy. The silent films showed this fundamental difference between comedy and tragedy, that appearance can be funny in itself, but not tragic. Chaucer, like Charlie Chaplin, can achieve pathos, but not tragedy: for tragedy, appearance is not enough. Nor is it enough for politics. Chaucer never had a vision of the face of England as the Gawain-poet saw it, but his knowledge of men and his emancipation from theoretical judgment saved him from the weakness of *Gawain and the Green Knight*, wherein the motive is too special and too artificial to balance the grandeur of the imagery. He never had a vision of the people of England as Langland saw them, and that might have been more serious. Chaucer saw people one at a time, not in groups and kinds like Langland. Langland was saved from mere schematism by the peculiar nature of his vision. For allegory is not a single or a simple thing: there are varieties. A metaphysical allegory like *The Romance of the Rose* depends upon the reader's intellectual appreciation of the abstractions of which it is made; an allegory like *Piers Plowman* is made of human life, and its success depends on the reader's knowledge of life and the writer's ability to create types which, though stripped of the accidents of individuality, are yet alive. *Piers Plowman* gives an accurate picture (so far as we can judge) of the ordinary human scene in the fourteenth century, just as *The Pilgrim's Progress* gives one of England in the seventeenth. Chaucer indeed selected his pilgrims with care and economy to cover the larger part of society. If he had gone higher than the Knight, or lower than the Plowman, he would have been forced into political problems. As it is, he restricted himself entirely to the social and casual relations of people. Time takes queer revenges. The real purpose and aim of Langland, the attempt

[1] Letter to George Keats, March, 1819.

95

to cure the woes of England by recalling each class to the conscientious discharge of its function, is dead, for it was only temporary. Politics is "the endless adventure", and any fixed system will serve only for a little. People are eternal. Historians read *Piers Plowman* for its exposition of feudal theory; others besides historians may read it for its pictures of the street, the London tavern, the cleric dodging parish duty for the sake of a salaried post, the judges on circuit—and for the sake of one most valuable thing, the acquaintance of an honest man of God, William Langland. But the reader will not judge the people he finds there. He cannot help judging Chaucer's, for the aesthetic judgment, the innate gift which the artist cannot but use, to whatever end he use it, is the lasting judgment, for it demands the reader's confirmation. So Chaucer is justified in his work; and so we may say "Here is God's plenty" and read him again.

VII

One thing is certain: after such a master used it, English could no longer be regarded as a subordinate language. At what date it can be said to have prevailed over French is difficult to determine, for the two quotable events, John Cornwall's substitution of English for French as the official medium of instruction in schools[1] and the statute of 1362 permitting the use of English in law courts, must be understood as terminal rather than crucial points in the process, for it is highly improbable that such conservatives as schoolmasters and lawyers were anticipating a future situation. Cornwall was merely recognising the fact that French was a foreign language to be studied as such—unless this was a fact, why did men translate so many romances from French into English? The lawyers were merely recognising the fact that witnesses were appearing in court who could give lucid evidence only in English and yet were too reputable and responsible to be spoken for like Saxon

[1] Recorded by Trevisa, 1385, as the beginning of a custom universal in his day.

serfs to whom Norman courts were foreign. How exactly the *fait accompli* was established cannot be traced in detail: political feeling, the needs of daily business on the land, habits caught from nurses and servants, intermarriages—all these might be invoked, or deduced from the fuller evidence as to the prevalence of Gaelic among the Anglo-Irish. Behind them all lies the dominant condition, that the low estate of English was a purely political circumstance which, however important and influential, could not destroy the innate strength of the language nor efface the cultural tradition embodied in it, whereas Anglo-Norman was a dialect separated from its parent stock, not in itself strong enough to develop a separate culture and always over-shadowed by the French of France. The wars must have made it plain to many a simple knight that Anglo-Norman "after the scole of Stratford-atte-Bowe" had become an out-lying patois, and the discovery would be enough to throw the weight of *amour propre* to the side of the language which could assert itself a *sermo regius* and therefore at least the political equal of the French of Paris. At worst it stamped the speaker as a foreigner, which is better than being treated as an uneducated and boorish provincial. In the immediate entourage of kings of England who were also sovereigns of parts of France, French was obviously necessary, and no one could escape the dominance of French culture. Elsewhere in England, the English language seems to have been accepted during the fourteenth century as the natural tongue. It is part of Chaucer's greatness, and of the service he rendered to England, that he recognised the new status of English, and, realising also its artistic possibilities, wrote in English on subjects that might be considered to belong rather to Latin and French, and so gave to the English language a cultural status (in England at least, where it mattered most) to correspond with social habit and political development.

That political development must be traced within England as well as in the international relations of which it becomes possible to speak. National consciousness grew as local antagonisms and dynastic quarrels hardened the frontiers of the new nations, but within the boundaries of the narrow seas it is possible also to observe some signs of social consciousness, and even, with that development known to historians as "the rise of the middle classes", of something like a body of public opinion. Social consciousness, indeed—the appreciation of the varied social scene and the sense of being part of it—is the new inspiration of *The Canterbury Tales*. Chaucer set the example of its expression, and if, as Dr. Manly says, he wrote first for a small audience, the number of existing manuscripts shows that it was soon a large one. And the example was followed. The anonymous continuator of *The Canterbury Tales* cannot be dismissed as a mere imitator, for an observer so shrewd and so appreciative was certainly inspired by his model's humane interest as well as by his success. Those others who wrote *London Lickpenny*—now denied to Lydgate, to the no small impoverishment of his reputation—and *The Voyage to Compostella* had also found out that the contemporary scene is lively and amusing in itself. These men differ from Langland and resemble Chaucer in that their satire has its end in enjoyment, not in change or reformation. They tell much, and advocate nothing. They can see themselves along with their neighbours in one picture, with no other criticism than a comic ruefulness that reflects enjoyment of the picture rather than any moral notions about it. Of these poets of the social scene the one identifiable personality is Hoccleve, who tells us too much about himself to be lost in the crowd.

Hoccleve was a poor creature at best, and, despite his clinging to the skirts of Chaucer, no great poet; but he is a recognisable individual, and he provides firsthand evidence that some sort of society had formed in London before 1450, and even before 1400. In the first place, he was that well-known figure, the civil servant of literary tastes. An enlarged royal service, less personal to the monarch and seated in permanent offices, might be expected to breed, or attract, intelligent and articulate men of education with no special professional or clerical bent, and to stimulate gregarious habits in them. The later history of the civil service warrants the supposition, and Hoccleve allows us glimpses of a society for which at least we have no earlier evidence but whose character is familiar to later generations. For, in the second place, Hoccleve was a clubman, and so ranks as a social phenomenon with Pope and Dr. Johnson and Thackeray. To write versified epistles to friends is one thing, to write to fellow-members is in a different range of relationship and of feeling, and to include the epistles among one's works involves the assumption that there are others, outside the immediate circle in which they were written, who will understand and appreciate that relationship and the tone and feeling appropriate to it. Hoccleve's "Board of Green Cloth" did not centre round a tribal chieftain or a church or a king. The members were not of equal rank, and their bond of relationship was just their membership of an organisation that existed for its own sake, for no other purpose than the association of its members. Thus the London of Prince Hal's riotous youth knew the meaning, if it had not the word, of "clubbability". Now the great ages of the clubs are the reigns of Queen Anne, of George III, and Victoria, and it is fair to reason that the appearance of the social club is an indication of social stability. It did not last long, but it did exist.

Hoccleve's habit of personal revelation is of the same nature and growth. Chaucer had it, and for the same reason, though Chaucer did not exaggerate it. A man who has no adventures to relate, either of soul or body or mind, and who has no definite doctrine to promulgate, does not make his own ordinary self the subject of his art unless he is aware of a society of men like himself, and thinks it is large enough, and will last long enough, to make the revelation even of weaknesses and defects likely to meet with sympathetic fellow-creatures. There must be an audience, and one interested in character for its own sake without regard to its moral or intellectual value or its effect on others. And there must be time for it, since self-revelation, whether naïve or romantic, is the fruit of leisure. This society of the years round 1400 was not yet fully formed, and was soon to break up. Hoccleve is only a rudimentary Boswell without a Johnson—if only he had Boswellised Chaucer instead of merely eulogising him!—but he, like Boswell, introduces us into a social circle which was the happiest thing in his life, and expects us to take pleasure in it. And, like Boswell, he was interested in himself and his own frailties. Behind both there lies a general interest in human behaviour which is the growth of a settled society conscious of itself and its varieties.

It might be argued that this pleasure in mere existence legitimises also the nonsense poem, of which a much earlier period produced an admirable example in *The Land of Cockaigne*. This has been read as a satire on the monasteries, but no such explanation is required. It is just comic nonsense, a thing with many variants in many languages, but of a kind perhaps best preserved in the old-established society of England. How old the nonsense poem is, as a *genre*, we cannot tell, but one admirable example, *The Man in the Moon*,[1] dates from before 1300. Here is a daft little poem which is neither satire nor sentiment nor religion nor morals nor philosophy nor incantation: it is plain nonsense and the most English thing in all mediaeval literature. But nonsense is possible only when a common understanding can be assumed, and that is as much social as intellectual. You cannot play games with reason or religion unless you believe in them. Without the ground of faith to play on, the games are meaningless—and, which is worse, dangerous. The ground of common understanding may be small, but it must be there, and the significance of *The Man in the Moon* and *The Land of Cockaigne*, for our present argument, is that they rest on the widest ground. The Reformation killed ecclesiastical nonsense like the Boy Bishop and the Litany of the Ass, because it was safe only when faith was unshaken. Only the clerks of the universities could appreciate the excellent academic nonsense of some of the student songs. But *The Land of Cockaigne* is a matter of food and drink and laziness, and the kindly, muddled, half-intelligence of *The Man in the Moon* is equally within the competence of anyone with a sense of humour. These are social poems, written for an unspecialised society. But they are not written

[1] Carleton Brown, *XIIIth Century Lyrics*, No. 89.

in such specifically social terms as the fifteenth-century poets used.

The appearance of stability, however, which is suggested by the very grouping of named and recognised poets round the year 1400, was temporary and insecure. The fifteenth century was soon occupied with changes in every department of life—changes whose early stages Chaucer saw and whose discords were resolved for English poetry only by Spenser. Chaucer's linguistic and cultural synthesis provided the basis upon which later poets rested, but linguistic change destroyed his versification, religious and political difficulties unsettled men's minds and drove them into hostile parties, and finally the great shift of thought and desire which we call the Renaissance re-oriented the whole content of mind and imagination. The literary results of these movements lie for the most part beyond our scope. The general turbulence settles down into a rhythm only in the latter part of Henry VIII's reign, and no clear history of the interim can be made out. The court tradition was carried on with varying success. It seems to grow less and less valid as the century proceeds, until in Stephen Hawes it is swamped in erudition and morality, redeemed only by occasional neatness of phrase and one famous couplet.[1] The critic finds himself reduced to the reviewing of single, and usually anonymous poems, many of them, like that graceful piece *The Flower and the Leaf*, far from devoid of merit. But for the philologists he could quite well include a review, say, of *The Owl and the Nightingale*, which belongs to the early thirteenth century, for its prettiness and its touch of humour were not beyond the scope of the fifteenth, and its methods and ideals are not recognisably alien. There is a slightly faded charm in these things, but they are only continuations with little variation; and the current was running into other channels. Only John Lydgate stands up, were it but by sheer bulk.

The great reputation enjoyed by this very mediocre poet seems extraordinary to a later age, and explicable only by

[1] See *The Oxford Book of Verse*, No. 33, for the only living fragment of Hawes.

the hypothesis that the others were worse, which is not quite true. Lydgate wrote a great deal, wrote it in competent verse, and wrote for a notable clientèle, something of whose prestige reflected, as is usual, on himself. But that is not enough to create quite such a reputation. When a writer seems to have been heavily over-praised, it is safe to conclude that the reasons lie outside the aesthetic values in his work, and that he represents in a high degree the interests of his time. We have a useful check on fifteenth-century interests in the catalogue of Caxton's publications, and if we analyse the work of Lydgate, it presents much the same mixture—so many religious poems, so many moral, so many recreative. If we add the works of Hoccleve (omitting his most personal poems) the general effect is unaltered. Apparently this was the taste of the upper and upper-middle classes: respectable, sedate, rather old-fashioned and solid— the taste of that thriving family the Pastons, of Caxton's noble and ecclesiastical patrons, of the royal circle itself. Which is perhaps what one might expect. Lydgate's later reputation has not benefited by the citation in every primer of the titles only of his two unconscionable masterpieces *The Troy Book* and *The Falls of Princes*, which between them account for 66,433 lines out of the 145,500 with which he is credited.[1] The short poems contain all the quality which a facile versifier untrammelled by an artistic conscience could muster, and the long ones are only skilled labour.

Verse was too easy, and prose too difficult. It was difficult even for Chaucer, who could write such distinguished verse and such undistinguished prose. In the Middle Ages nobody needed prose very much. The learned wrote their treatises in Latin, the lawyers drafted their documents according to their Latin or French formularies, and the men of letters followed the French fashion, which concentrated mainly on verse, except for memoirs such as those of Joinville and Villehardouin, written in that style of gentlemanly discourse which is a peculiar national possession of the French and had never an English counterpart, except perhaps in Halifax

[1] Dr. MacCracken's calculation: I have not counted them myself.

and Sir William Temple. This state of affairs is a sad degeneration from the days of Alfred, but in the fifteenth century prose began to revive. How Sir Thomas Malory, who seems to have been an ordinary unscrupulous man-at-arms fighting in a most unchivalrously-conducted war, was inspired to produce the first monument of artistic prose since the days of Ælfric is (as we have said) a mystery. It was one of those happy accidents that occur to men of genius like Sidney and Fielding and Walpole. This we can say, however, that the new qualities that come into Malory's prose come from his working over poetic originals. These new qualities are harmony of rhythm and emotional power, qualities neglected by men whose only use for prose was exposition, but so vital to the poets that they infected the translator and informed his prose with their power and grace, just as the great, grave tradition of liturgical Latin was to infuse its qualities into the Bible of Tyndale and the Prayerbook of Cranmer. But that assumes that Malory could feel and appreciate the qualities of his originals, and it merely defines, without explaining, his achievement of a new art, "the other harmony of prose".

Of such an art Lydgate had no conception. That is why *The Troy Book* and *The Falls of Princes* are dead. For the same reason, Hoccleve's less enormous *Regiment of Princes* is dead. Yet they were successful in their time, because they contained the kind of material the age desired. To us, who have forgotten the conception that verse is the finest vehicle for the general purposes of vernacular writing, it seems stupid to translate Boccaccio's quite adequate Latin prose into slack English verse; it was more important at the time that Boccaccio's compilation should be made available to Englishmen somehow, and verse came natural to Lydgate and to his readers. In that they were really behind the times. Laurent de Premierfait, who translated Boccaccio's *de Casibus Virorum Illustrium* into French, did not make that mistake, and if Laurent's style was no great model, Froissart, the stiffest of versifiers, had adapted the memoir style to history, so that there were French examples if they had been heeded. It was the incentive that was lacking. I fancy that the secret of Malory was just this, that in the weariness of prison he desired to write, but thought he could not write verse (which was probably true) and set himself to write as he could, with poetry in his mind and no preconceptions about prose.

Others, however, had other incentives. Dr. R. W. Chambers has pointed out very admirably and forcibly that a continuous tradition of English prose exists among the writers of religious meditation.[1] His case is complete, but two remarks fall to be made. Behind the prose of Dame Juliana and the other fifteenth-century mystics there lie not only the prose of Richard Rolle and other predecessors, but for one thing the echo of liturgy and plainsong, and for another, the natural rhythms into which the musing mind naturally falls. These arise eventually from physical facts— the necessity of making the voice of the celebrant or preacher heard, the cadences inevitable in the frequent repetition of identical phrases, and the nervous reactions of solitude. Again, it must be allowed that this continuity is along a narrow and specialised line. "How shall the world be served?" Even in the religious sphere something more was done. With the Reformation we have little to do, for Lollardry was apparently suppressed. It did not produce, on either side, any great literary monument. Wyclif's own works are readable only by theological historians, and would be easier as well as comelier in the academic Latin in which they were begotten. But however difficult it be to assess its effects, a movement cannot be ignored which created so much stir, which numbered adherents from Kent to Ayrshire and which tried to enlist non-professional interest in theological disputation by spreading abroad theological treatises in English and (what might have been more important if it had been better done) an English Bible. Lollardry created at least a public opinion. It was its whole basis that the public should have an opinion.

For the time being, however, the political movement was both more urgent and more productive. Signs of anxiety

[1] *The Continuity of English Prose*, introductory to Harpsfield's *Life of Sir Thomas More*, E.E.T.S., and separately.

appear along with the signs of social consolidation, and the two are not unconnected. Chaucer's Merchant who

> Wolde the see were kept for any thing
> Bitwixe Middelburgh and Orewelle.[1]

had many brethren, and more than one expressed the same wish in prose and in verse.[2] Good police at sea was a test of good government, and the merchant, who was strong enough to make himself heard, was not inclined to waste his time and goods in fighting. Casual verses on contemporary affairs—the cry of the oppressed commons, and the song of exultation over fallen enemies—may be expected at any time. There are few better than those of that fourteenth-century journalist Laurence Minot, and his best is no better than the song of Lewes made in 1264, years before he was born, and both are better than Skelton's song on Flodden. The significant thing in the fifteenth century is the number of treatises on government, ranging from the commercial disquisition—a very interesting one—called *A Libel of English Policy*[3] to Fortescue's legal and constitutional *Monarchia*. The troubles of Richard II's reign, the usurpation of Henry IV, the foreign wars, the minority of Henry VI, the Wars of the Roses, coincide not only with notable poems like *Piers Plowman* and *Mum and the Sothsegger*, but also with treatises on political morality which occupy the place held in our own troubled times by treatises on political science. Whether the change from moral responsibility to scientific irresponsibility is a sign of human progress, and whether either does more than provide phrases for practical politicians, are not questions to be debated here. The point is, that men were thinking about the technique and the ethics of government, and trying to influence others, creating the rudiments of a public opinion.

Hoccleve's own *Regiment of Princes* is (in every sense) a weighty example. Except for the personal reminiscences in the long prologue, which is now the interesting part of the

---

[1] Prologue to *Canterbury Tales*, 276–7.
[2] e.g., Wright, *Political Songs*, Vol. II, *Of Keeping the Seas*.
[3] Wright. *Political Songs*, Vol. II.

book, it is by no means original, but there is surely some significance in its appearance so soon after a lineal succession of seven kings had been violently broken by the father of the Prince Henry to whom it is dedicated, when merchants and people alike were calling for better government. Originality or translation does not matter. When three men in three parts of the realm[1] set themselves to translate the treatise *Secreta Secretorum*, it means that men were worrying about government. Other works besides those bearing directly on government might be taken as issuing from the same habit of mind. The *Faits and Gestes of Chivalry* and still more *The Order of Chivalry* printed by Caxton deal with the law as well as the conduct of war, and with international law as well as personal conduct. Again these authors draw on ancient authority, but they give their contemporaries the precedents and the principles by which opinion is formed. Nor are they unenlightened. According to *The Order of Chivalry*, for instance, "enemy alien" undergraduates are not only to continue their studies unmolested, but are to receive supplies from home and even, in emergency, visits from specified relatives. Whether such excellent rules were observed in practice may be doubtful, but what chance would even the proposal stand with any modern government? Such cases were thought out, and Caxton laid them before Englishmen in their native language. Even the *Morte Darthur* itself might well have been intended as Caxton read it, like *Piers Plowman*, to remind men of the pristine virtues that were conspicuously absent from the Wars of the Roses.

The popularity of history is a more direct symptom of the same state of mind. The writing of chronicles was indeed the oldest literary tradition in England, and in the monastery of St. Albans particularly, a strong tradition and, in the hands of such men as Matthew Paris and Thomas Walsingham, productive of admirable work. The monastic tradition, however, ever since the days of William of Malmesbury, was a Latin tradition. In the late fourteenth century, and still more in the fifteenth, it was not confined to the monasteries

[1] Including Ireland, which otherwise scarcely comes into our story. See the edition by Robert Steele, E.E.T.S.

nor to Latin. Here again originality is of less account than the desire to know. Capgrave of Norfolk, a monk and a man of some note, provides a more useful source-book for historians, but the men for whom Trevisa translated Higden's *Polychronicon* into a lively colloquial prose that makes Lydgate's instructional verse seem more old-fashioned than ever, the men who compiled or adapted a *Brut*, were feeling a need which betrays the effort—perhaps only half-conscious —to understand vaguely-felt difficulties and to look for help in the past. It is in time of trouble that history becomes useful.

All these things have their interest, though few of them could be claimed as literature of the highest class. Again we must make the sorrowful comment that the things that last are not always those that are most conspicuous and most urgent at the time, and the judgments that remain are not necessarily those of the most honest mind or of the most serious import. Human sympathies and intrinsic beauty are the only preservatives. The letters of the Paston family and the merchant house of Cely remain when even the treatises of Pecock, who really could write English prose—why do heretics so often write better than the orthodox?—are relegated to the specialists. The two literary products which (along with the *Morte Darthur*) are the glory of the fifteenth century are those that were not printed till the nineteenth[1] —the Miracles, and the century's brilliant share in the most continuous of English literary traditions, the song.

If it could be proved that Lydgate, who devised entertainments for the court and for the city of London, had a hand also in any of the Miracles, he would look less like a stranded log. But an annual output of over 20,000 lines during his working life was probably occupation enough, and so conspicuous a name could scarcely fail to remain attached to any work of the magnitude of a play. The suggestion emphasises the contrast between the official poetry of the schools and the forms which grew in close contact with ordinary life, the drama which drew its vitality from the everyday scene of town and countryside no less than from

[1] Except for a few songs printed in the Catalogue of the Harleian MSS,

religious feeling, and the song which, however elaborate its artistic cultivation, arises always from the simpler emotions.

To these may be added the ballad, the intermediate form which is supposed to have taken its shape in the fifteenth century. Much theorising and more contention have been spent on its nature and history. W. P. Ker derived it from the *carole*, the dance-song which spread as a social fashion from France, and so partly solved the mystery of the appearance of the same ballad in different countries. Professor Gummere argued the theory of "communal authorship", which, if it means anything, means simply that textual accuracy was not considered a virtue, and that any reciter could adapt or improve, or patch where his memory failed: which is not astonishing to anyone who thinks in terms of people rather than of theories. It has been lauded as "folk-art" and slighted as "the débris of romance". All these notions are probably correct. There are ballads that are *caroles* and ballads that are simplified popular recensions of romantic tales, and ballads that relate stories and superstitions preserved among the most conservative and least distracted portions of the community, and there is constant interchange between the professional and the amateur, the product of the schools and the product of the fields and workshops. The soldier songs of the last war are good evidence of how some things of the kind arise, bred between the events, feelings and humour of the community, the professional—in this case the music-hall in which capitalist enterprise has exploited the eternal *jongleur*—and the floating memory of evangelistic hymns and schoolroom lessons. Again, it is a tradition well understood in all sections of the community that notable events ought to be celebrated in rhymes. The rhymer does it in the way he knows best, as well as he can. Once a form is established, and familiarity gives some ease in the handling, the result may be good. Ballads are still produced and sold to the crowd. They may not be very good, but they are not always bad; and we do not know how many bad ballads have been luckily forgotten. The ballad is best regarded as a thing of diverse, natural, social, and cultural origins, which grew into a recognised form which was then exploited with varying success.

Nothing is gained by attempting close definition of a variable form. The best are the best-remembered, possibly also those that were made in circles where the art was well and critically appreciated either through high cultivation or through the absence of competing artistic ideals. The best examples arrive when the form was disentangled from its origins and established as a thing having its own ideal; and that was probably later than the fifteenth century.

After we have noted these genuine glories of the century, we are faced with the fact of decline, not only in literature, but in other arts. The first part of the century, in which the best of its literature was written, saw the church-building which was financed by the wool trade and the new weaving industry, but when all has been allowed for—civil and foreign war, religious unrest, linguistic change, agrarian and commercial difficulties—there was an artistic and intellectual collapse, an emptiness which goes far to explain the eager welcome given a little later to the revived classics, and the intellectual refreshment and the renewal of artistic enterprise that followed the revival. Music may have enjoyed continuous development from John Dunstable's school in the first half of the century, and, as we have said, the history and criticism of lyric poetry would be easier if we knew more of secular music; but music, like embroidery (the other art for which England was famous and whose activity is continuous) is comparatively independent. The arts that depend more upon society and upon intellectual collaboration, and notably painting, seem to have all but died. It is not through mere carelessness that we are only now coming to understand that England had valuable schools of wall-painting, nor is the Reformation a sufficient explanation of the loss of tradition and technique; for before the old liturgical and theological customs were abandoned there was a lively outburst of secular building to employ decorative artists if they still existed in any activity or had vitality enough to adapt themselves to the demand. Fashion changes; and the most important oversea connexions of England both in trade and in politics were with the Low Countries— which might explain some deficiencies, for, as has been suggested, contact with France is most valuable to England if only because of their differences—but if the French "primitives" were to have little influence, why did not the English painters learn from the school of the van Eycks? The skill of the alabaster-carvers survived to build fine monuments for sixteenth-century worthies, but was it only the prestige of Italian art that led Henry VII to put Torrigiano in charge of his works at Westminster? The decline in heraldic design alone would prompt the question.

The whole condition can be observed at once in the history of English printing. Caxton's venture has all the casual amateurism that, if we like, we can call typically English. The new art was introduced not by Stationers, whose business was the making of books, but by a middle-aged Mercer who came to it by accident. Nor do we find English calligraphers exchanging into print as a later generation of sailors "changed into steam", for Caxton's immediate successors, Wynkyn de Worde and Pynson, were foreigners.[1] They did not realise, apparently, the importance of the new craft, nor—what is more to the point—the relation of the new technique to the old, or how little they had to learn. Thus England, with a manuscript tradition unsurpassed anywhere and equalled only in those parts of France which shared the same civilisation, produced books artistically worthless beside the contemporary masterpieces of Venice and Paris. Caxton knew how to set type and make-up formes, but the inherited craft of lettering died without translation into type, so that England depended on foreign supplies based on foreign penmanship; and what was perhaps worse, the inherited craft of layout, spacing, all that makes for beauty in a book, died without passing on its secrets to the amateur Caxton and his followers. The same helplessness is even more obvious when we study the decoration of books. England, which had bred the great schools of Lindisfarne, Jarrow, Winchester, St. Albans, Canterbury, East Anglia, and had bred woodworkers of incomparable skill, was apparently unable to grasp the notion of the wood-block.

[1] An attempt was made in that home of good writing, St. Alban's, but it was so evanescent that it merely emphasises the point.

What cuts were produced in England were wretched imitations of foreign work. Except for a few antiquarian experiments by John Day, late in the sixteenth century, the English presses for three hundred years produced nothing better than the commonplace and second-rate. Conservatism does not explain the failure, for no good manuscripts were produced either. Such inertia proves that the great tradition of bookmaking was dead, for—though the English have an extraordinary trick of abandoning their own achievements—sheer necessity might have driven intelligent stationers into the new branch of their trade.

The necessity, however, does not seem to have existed. Caxton's patrons were an intelligent aristocracy, lay and ecclesiastical, and their demands were simple. There was no scholarly demand for his services. In the first half of the fourteenth century William of Ockham had called a halt to the extravagances of metaphysics, and no comparable thinker arose to continue his work. Philosophy was waiting for the new content which it was one special function of the Renaissance to recover from Cicero and Plato and Lucretius, and for the new method which Roger Bacon had been unable to force on the orthodox schools. In the great revival which was the vital thing in fifteenth-century Europe, England had no part. Thus no English printing-house ever became a centre of intellectual activity and a source of intellectual sustenance like those of Aldus and Froben and Plantin, or bred a family like the Estiennes. The custom of the English printers remained what Caxton's amateur initiative could compass, serving the desires of the casual reader as well as might be—valuable, no doubt, but serving neither scholarship and philosophy nor their own art. One can only conclude that art and scholarship and philosophy were not there, and meanwhile the continental printers went so far ahead that the next generation were content to import what they needed. There are many reasons why Italy, the former home of the oldest and greatest of the three European traditions and the latest to develop a vernacular literature, should be first to recover that tradition and to fuse it into her still malleable arts, but the history of the Parisian book-trade

shows that the same city could contain the strongest intrench-
ment of mediaeval dogmatism and a lively centre of the new
art and the new learning at the same time.

Returning to literature, we can see how difficulties sur-
rounded such an energetic mind as that of John Skelton, who
was training in Oxford in the 1480's. Classical scholarship
was in the air. The embroidery of poetry now had to be
classical. Yet the classical material is only applied, not of the
stuff. Except that as a professional scholar Skelton used it
more heavily than the amateur Chaucer, he used it in exactly
the same way, though he lived to see the new humanism
firmly established. As we have seen, Chaucer's imagination
was comparatively little excited by romance. In Skelton,
romance disappears, or, to be more precise and even more
conclusive, romantic allusion is used only as invective
against Garnesche. On the other hand he retained, as
Chaucer did not, the academic invention of metaphysical
personification—of all mediaeval traditions the least forceful,
the least generative, and the one which gave least control and
direction to the user. Classical learning weighted his mind
without revitalising his imagination or forcing him to revalue
his artistic ideals, for Skelton came at the dead centre of the
movement, after the wheel had spent its momentum and
before it turned over, with ever-increasing speed, toward the
new learning and the new poetry. Boccaccio had abandoned
his Tuscan verse and prose to supply the age with less attractive but very useful Latin books of reference. We regret it, but
it was the result of a complete conversion from mediaeval to
classical, and an honest man's conscientious attempt to
advance the studies he believed in. Caxton translated from
Raoul le Fevre the stories of the Æneid and of Jason, in
which the classical tales were adapted for pastime to
chivalric convention without any attempt to change mediaeval ideas or ideals, producing a bastard form of romance
which to us seems merely incongruous. Skelton could do
neither. His times gave him a wide but uncritical reading in
Latin authors, a text-book training in deductive logic that
was more formal than practical, in rhetoric as it was understood before the rediscovery of Cicero, and in philosophy

that was mere dogmatic metaphysics; gave him Gower and Chaucer and Lydgate as masters of English poetry[1] and at the same time a speech that differed from theirs; and gave him the habit of personified abstraction as a means of imaginative expression.

Nature, however, gave him a great deal more, and I cannot but feel that he was himself dissatisfied with his equipment. Not that he did not believe in it; on the contrary, he belonged, by chance or temperament, to the conservative group at Oxford as against his contemporaries Grocyn, Linacre, Colet. He mocked the new fashion of learning Greek, and complained, like any member of any old school, that the young were no longer being thoroughly grounded before they proceeded to the higher studies. But the informal rush of his verse betrays the impatience of a temper too energetic for the slow procedure imposed by the allegory of abstraction to which he was thirled, and desiring also a more forcible means of expression, some medium less sober than Gower's, less equable than Chaucer's, lighter and swifter than Lydgate's. So he hammered at alliteration, used rhyme like a clapper, loaded his diction with aureate terms and Latin tags. There is nothing in Skelton that is new, whether it be among his religious poems which only continue the custom of earlier ecclesiastical poets, or among his invectives. In poetry as in scholarship he looks back rather than forward. There is nothing in Skelton which we cannot find better done elsewhere. Except for the venom of its personal attack on Wolsey, *Colin Clout* is not so good as *The Plowman's Tale* before him or the comparable sections of *The Shepheardes Calender* after him; *The Garlande of Laurell* is not so good as *The House of Fame;* even *Phyllyp Sparowe* is not so good as Joachim du Bellay's epitaphs on his dog and his cat, or *Elinour Rummyng* so good as *Gammer Gurton;* in "flyting" and in grotesque description Dunbar is his superior. Yet we feel that Skelton is an original, and that he is indispensable.

Skelton is a *person*. He exists in three, even four dimensions. We can see him and know him as we can see and know few men before him—perhaps only one, Chaucer himself. He

---

[1] See *The Garlande of Laurell.*

was himself intensely self-conscious, even self-centred. It is small wonder that this exuberant, violent, frustrated character that sweetens at times into tenderness, this powerful wit untempered by self-embracing humour but plumed with a flying fancy, should fascinate some modern minds. It is small wonder that in his own day this insubordinate cleric and uncelibate priest, this reckless satirist and fearless inveigher against prelatic abuses, should live and die in trouble. The difficulty for most of us is the obstinate doubt whether the immense research required for the understanding of Skelton's allusions, and even his phrases, will be repaid. His mind, too rapid for the heavy material of expression—much of which was intellectual accretion rather than a true imaginative content—ejected lumps of crabbed allusion, enigmas whose complete solution would require a fifteenth-century educational curriculum as well as a knowledge of history and gossip. We feel they are rather like the pellets under an owl's perch. Yet we are always tempted back. We want to know more, if only to identify the mice and beetles that have been crushed in that powerful beak and claws. So too his mind was too agile for the verse and language he inherited, and too impatient—even if the time had come, which was not yet—to labour over the rehandling of them. His charming pictures of young women—Jane Scrope, the group of ladies in the Countess of Surrey's household—begin with the precision of Holbein drawings and then are tagged with trails of embroidered allusion. Yet the phrases have a poise or a perfume which cannot fail of effect, the manner of approach is perfect and the distances are kept exactly. In these we feel what we miss in *The Tunnyng of Elinour Rummyng*, which is purely objective, without either Chaucer's humorous reality or Langland's moral strength or Hoccleve's comic attitudes. Yet the vigour with which the crude colours are handled is enough to justify it. There is authentic value in the strong strokes of the brush—or, rather, the palette-knife—over the rough texture of the canvas. We are best to read Skelton as we can: to take what we want from Dyce's notes and supplement them if we care to go further; to let the colours blur and come clear as they will. There is

114

refreshment and enjoyment enough, in this academic priest, the last of the mediaeval English poets.

VIII

It is of course quite wrong to separate Scottish from English literature. They use the same language, and they belong to the same European tradition. Yet there are differences to be observed. One of these differences we cannot estimate—the extent to which the character of Scottish literature is affected by Gaelic. At present the tendency is to emphasise Scottish Celticism, but nothing can be proved, and the question must be left as it is, subject to the waves and currents of general feeling, influenced more by sentiment, politics and economics than by ethnology or solid cultural history. Existing Gaelic literature itself lies outside my competence, and identifiable Gaelic influences, which are not (as yet) very important at best, come into the story much later than this volume can reach. Our subject is that northern branch of English literature whose differences from the southern largely originated in the castle hall of Norham, on a day in 1292 when Edward I gave a palmary example of the English politician at his worst. All we have from Scotland before that is the scrap of verse—by no means devoid of rhythmical art —which laments the unhappy change that befell *When Alisandre our King wes deid* and Edward rent this friendly island in twain and created, in his own despite, the first self-conscious nation in Europe. The next generation saw its proud isolation embodied in and stimulated by the first great Scottish poem, John Barbour's *The Bruce*. Henceforth, every motive and every condition of literature was set in a new way, local differences of language were accentuated, and the relations of the two island groups with the continental part of the European tradition differed along with their different political alignments. However ethnographers may speculate, the political situation, and it alone, need be invoked to explain the literary differences that can be summed up in the primary facts that the Tweed is a frontier and that the average Scot is more at home in Bordeaux or Auxerre than in Dorset or Sussex.

Except, however, for local linguistic habits—much less different from those of northern England than those of northern England from southern—and for local peculiarities of spelling—which have nothing to do with language at all—Barbour's poem falls entirely within the bounds of the secular literature we have been discussing. One new value has arisen: national feeling accompanies such general European traditions as the religious feeling of the Charlemagne romances; the Southron as well as the Saracen is an object of execration. Otherwise the moral values are those of the rest of Europe, and so are the aesthetic values. *The Brus* can be placed with Wace's *Roman de Rou*, as history written in the technique of romance. In the next century, Sir David Lyndsay did the same thing with biography in *Squire Meldrum*, the life of one of his friends which the Early English Text Society classifies, by some inexplicable failure of intelligence, as "Burlesque Romance", but which is just a stylised biography, lacking the olympian acidity of Lytton Strachey and more competent than Herr Ludwig's. Blind Harry's[1] *Wallace* is in the lower grade of the same kind, more given to marvels and vituperation—a typical good schoolwork. Both have in full measure the essential virtue of gusto. They believe in their subject, and drive on with it. Each achieves the effect he aims at, and if Barbour is the greater it is because he aims at the greater effect. His is a book to read, for its variety of scene, adventure, and feeling, and for its clear presentation of the many details by which Barbour builds up his picture of the king who found himself. But no one can listen to Henry the Minstrel without catching some excitement and exhilaration from his violent tale.

It is just this strength of pervading sentiment, this fierce

[1] "Blind Harry", as who should say "Homer". Whether he was blind, whether he had any other name, whether the name is generic and not particular, are questions whose importance has not been demonstrated. No one as yet has resolved him into a syndicate, and for me "Blind Harry" means "the man who wrote *The Life and Acts of the Most Famous and Valiant Champion Sir William Wallace, Knight of Ellerslie; Maintainer of the Liberty of Scotland*".

faith, that we miss in the romances which have—perhaps by a not unprecedented national possessiveness—been claimed for Scotland: *Sir Eger, Sir Grime, and Sir Graysteele, The Awntyrs of Arthur*, and so on. They certainly were known in Scotland, but whether they were written there is another story: they provide indeed a prime example of that island unity at which we have already glanced. *Rauf Colzear* is the only beast out of the herd—home-bred or raided—that Scotland need be anxious to earmark. They are very readable, however, and without them we should lack not only a clue to the Scotland of the Stewarts, but some understanding of the course of literature, since these are of the same school as *Gawain and the Green Knight*—which without them would appear an isolated phenomenon—and since they gave to the Scottish poets certain habits of verse and style that continued in vogue for generations. It is thanks to these northern poets that we can trace a continuous history of verse-forms from the Old English poets on one hand and the troubadours on the other, down to Burns himself, for in the north the two great innovators Chaucer and Spenser, however influential, were not so completely victorious as in the south.

The influence of Chaucer is, of course, more than obvious; it was acclaimed, with pride and with humility, by the Scottish poets themselves. And they are not unworthy of their master. For one thing, they were less troubled by basic technical problems than their southern contemporaries. James I could write better Chaucerian verse than Hoccleve, because he learned the language along with the style and the verse, and could keep it, an artificial accomplishment, uncontaminated by later developments. Henryson, Dunbar and the rest, who did not write Chaucerian English, had a dialect to write in that was reasonably fixed and settled in its forms, and whose variations were trifling compared with those that worried Caxton.[1] Fifteenth-century Scots is nearer modern Scots than fifteenth-century English is to modern English; there have been changes indeed, but apart from vocabulary its main difficulty arises from the fact that

[1] The problem of language arose a hundred years later and became acute after 1603; and even then it was a different problem.

our modern spelling is the creation of London printers. To this fundamental linguistic security we may attribute, to some extent at least, the greater skill of the Scottish poets, and even their greater show of personality. They could concentrate on the style and spirit of Chaucer without being tempted to reproduce a versification which was impossible in their dialect. For them, the great lesson of Chaucer was freedom. He was not their only teacher, but he freed them from slavery to alliteration or to the eight-syllable verse, and he, and still more his English disciples, taught them—a more perilous lesson—the trick of allegory.

His broad humanity he could not teach them, for that grows from experience as well as temper, and each man must gain his own experience; but he gave the salutory example of personality in poetry, so that Henryson could allow his own very different humour and sentiment to have free play in his *Fables*, and even to differ from the master himself in *The Testament of Cresseid*, the one poem—since *The King's Quair* is so imitative—worthy to be bound up with *The Canterbury Tales*. So strong, and so self-possessed, is Henryson's personality, that the title of "Scottish Chaucerian" seems unnecessary. He exists in his own right, sober, devout, quietly observant of beasts and people. Both his meditative sadness, as in *The Abbey Walk*, and his humour, as in that admirable "pastourelle"[1] *Robyn and Makyn* and in the *Fables*, seem restful in comparison with the black melancholy and the noisy rough-and-tumble of his compatriots. These quiet traits are indeed Scottish, but they stand outside the common literary habit that was handed down to Burns; and they are more difficult of expression. Whether Dunbar needed any encouragement to express his individuality may be doubted, but his expressed admiration proves that it was from Chaucer that he too learned to reproduce in his Scots the graces of the French school. It is not, however, *The Thrissill and the Rois* or any other allegory, however graceful and well-wrought, that gives Dunbar his high place among his country's poets, but the revelation of a mortal man.

[1] The French term is used of set purpose; the poem is not a "pastoral" in the classical or Renaissance sense.

It is pleasant to trace the things Dunbar and Chaucer had in common, and how, even in these, they differed. The difference is almost climatic—between the Thames-side garden and the bleak ridges of Edinburgh and Stirling. Both men disliked the regular orders of clergy: compare *The Somnour's Tale* and *How Dunbar was desierit to be a Frier*. Both were much about courts: compare any of Chaucer's polite, composed court-poems with *The Dance in the Queen's Chalmer*. Both had fits of melancholy: compare the *Envoy to Scogan* with *Timor Mortis Conturbat Me*. Comparison comes to a speedy end. *Troilus and Criseyde* stands clear of all comparisons, then or afterwards. *The Parliament of Foules* should be compared with Holland's *Buke of the Howlet*—both poems come out of it honourably, by virtue of very different qualities— rather than with anything in Dunbar. Dunbar took warning, if he needed it, not to begin anything like *The Legend of Good Women* or *The Monk's Tale;* he was incapable of anything like the Prologue to the *Legend*, or, for that matter, the Prologue to the *Tales*. On the other hand he could manage a fabliau with anybody; and he was possessed of a riotous and fantastic devil that never haunted Chaucer or the banks of Thames. It is a familiar spirit of the north, lewd, foul, comic both in joy and in despair, infinitely vigorous. Skelton knew it, but Skelton's is a ragged double-shuffle compared with the accurately-executed enormities of Dunbar when he set himself capering. It is not satire, nor burlesque, but something on the far and windy side of both. Turn the page, and in *Suete Rois of Virtew*, or *Rorate Coeli Desuper*, the torch-flare changes to cool summer morning or the light of altar-candles. Dunbar's moods are as incalculable as his attitudes: aristocrat, sinner, worshipper at the feet of Our Lady, painter by turns in the school of Hieronymus Bosch and Holbein, he postures, kneels—and disappears. If there are two men to study in all our history from *Beowulf* to Skelton, they are Chaucer and Dunbar.

Dunbar, so intimately related to that typical Renaissance monarch James IV, might be thought to lead us beyond the Middle Ages. Yet we must continue even further forward, since mediaeval habits of feeling and of technique remained active in Scotland so much longer than in England—if indeed they have quite died. The debate-form, for instance, a clerkly trick from France which produced in England two admirable poems in *The Owl and the Nightingale* and *The Flower and the Leaf*, is found more freely in Scotland, down to Burns's *Twa Dogs* and *Twa Brigs*. To explain this would mean writing a history of Scotland; but here we may note this difference, that the old Church in Scotland bred no group of humanists like the More-Colet group in England, to establish the New Learning, with all it implied of a breach with the past as well as a hope for the future, before the entangled domestic and religious troubles began. The Scottish humanists came later, and coincided with the time of civil strife, whereas the English had coincided with a period of political settlement. They were of the reforming party, and both ecclesiastical and civil politics made such claims upon them that the scholarship even of a Melville or a Buchanan, valuable as it was to the universities, had little chance to ripen and spread, still less to influence the vernacular literature. Thus while Scotland under James IV and James V was in advance of contemporary England in some respects, the artistic and scientific culture of the sixteenth century was but sporadic, lacking a philosophic nexus and a critical discipline, such as England, with a richer society, more leisured scholarship, and political stability, was in process of developing. The breach of continuity came later, after the Stewart poets, and was indeed a violent attenuation rather than a complete breach. As there was no hiatus, so there was no New Poetry. Even Hume, Drummond, and their generation, which learned the new art from England and Italy and France, retain some memory of the older Scotland and the Middle Ages.

A successful translation of Virgil might well entitle Gavin Douglas to inclusion among the poets of the new Renaissance, and indeed it is a world away from the chivalric travesty Caxton had printed in Douglas's childhood. But Douglas wrote also *King Hart* and *The Palice of Honour*, as typical fifteenth-century allegories as need be, though fuller of noise and movement than their southern congeners. This touch of rough vitality which he contrives to impart into a somewhat lifeless form is the sign of his nationality, and also of the originality of feeling and vision that gives value to—and has earned recognition for—the prologues to his *Æneados*, and it saves the translation itself from the over-smoothness that comes of too much academic respect for Virgil. In Sir David Lyndsay the same quality and the same originality are not only displayed, but cultivated. If not the greatest poet to be mentioned in this survey, he is certainly the most original; and his abiding popularity among his own people testifies to his integral Scotticism. With Lyndsay we have reached the Reformation—and *The Satyre of the Three Estaitis* goes far to explain the course it took in Scotland—but he remains within the mediaeval tradition, "aureate" in diction, romantic in feeling, and undisciplined in construction.

Lyndsay, however, is rarely dull. The headstrong verse does not degenerate through loss of control, for he has all the native delight in ingenious rhyming. And in speaking his mind plainly to his master, the good servant of James V spoke for all conditions of the Scottish people. Had he been listened to, the history of Scotland would have been happier. Perhaps it was too much to expect men to listen to the whole of *A Dialogue betwix Experience and ane Courteour*. The whole history of the early world, continuously moralised and applied to contemporary conditions, is a heavy lesson despite its shrewdness. But at least Lyndsay, unlike Hawes, saw the danger, and saved his poem from some of the deadlier kinds of dullness by variations of metre which admit—or perhaps intentionally invite—its absorption in small doses. Even here, where it is more difficult than in his shorter works, he continues to combine an earnest character and a lively mind.

Small doses of this salt meat might be recommended, and most of this Scottish poetry is highly flavoured. Yet though it smell rank at times, it is with the honest effluvia of the stable and the farmyard. Aristocrat as he was, Lyndsay understood and thought for the plain folk. None of these court poets, indeed, are confined to a court circle or a courtly convention. James I is credited with *The Kingis*

Quair, but shares also with James V the credit of *Christis Kirk on the Grene:* if both attributions are false, the legends do not lose significance. The noisy rough-and-tumble was not a class-character, but the expression of something national. Our weaker-headed generation may weary of it in the unrelieved length of *Christis Kirk* and *Peblis to the Play* and *Cokilby's Sow*, and may even regret the convention they created for later Scottish poets who imitated the rowdiness without learning either the high skill of verse or the finer temper that accompanied it; yet it may be argued that it was just that coarse fibre that gave life and strength to the whole, and kept it alive, under the worst conditions, when the southern branch died of inanition and good manners. At least it testifies to some force and liveliness, and its comic inconsequence is part of the Scottish birthright—a spirit that invades even the serious historians and makes Pitscottie, for instance, the best reading of any historian since Giraldus Cambrensis. And some day Scotland may remember the art and the music that those same generations made, and may set this part of her tradition in its place when she rebuilds.

IX

The stage is now set for the new generation and the new literature. Many of the new stories have arrived, sometimes in strange guises. The new learning has come with Linacre and a new type in that scholarly butcher Tiptoft, Earl of Worcester. Feudalism has expired in a flurry of unchivalric throat-slitting, the Church is under a cloud, scholastic logic is spinning more and more mechanically, a mill without grist. Men's speech has changed, the content of the imagination has changed. The economics of the manor have changed. Europe is organising itself in nations under despotic kings, and the pious voyages to Jerusalem will soon be forgotten in the material excitements of the Indies. The world is new.

One vital thing has still to come: the new criticism. How that is to affect politics, religion, and society is not our affair, but a glance forward helps to define the literary weakness that inevitably reflects the decline of the Middle Ages.

After a generation of humanist discipline men will learn to use prose for every purpose. What is more easily remarked, English poets were to become conscious of form, the great lesson of classicist criticism. Chaucer learned it for himself, by hard experience. We can see him learning as *Troilus and Criseyde* changes from the leisurely manner of the first three Books, full of divagations and pauses, to the swifter economy of the last two. We can see it better as we compare the elaborate entry into *The Boke of the Duchesse* with the Canterbury prologues. Other men never learned. It takes Hoccleve 1200 lines of introduction, duplicating his effects and hovering about, before he gets down to the business of *The Regiment of Princes*. Hawes is as bad. Skelton, having abandoned the discipline of narrative, finds no other guide to the conduct of his matter. Spenser, when the time comes, "thrusteth into the middest" as no mediaeval poet dared, because he knows—only too well—the rules of the epic game. The dramatists, though less subservient to the new legislation, learn how to lay out and carry through a complex structure.

But it is not our duty in the close to draw conclusions or present a balance-sheet of profit and loss. In the following pages we try to help our fellow-student to find the most useful material from which to make up his own mind. If in the foregoing we have started some hares for him to keep or kill—provoked an idea or two for him to clarify, complete, or disprove—then we have done what we intended.

If he is bound to some curriculum of study, we hope to be useful to him. If he is in the more fortunate position of being able to follow his fancy, we say follow it, without caring where it leads, but follow a line. If one piece of advice to the free student be permitted, it would be this. In order to gain some acquaintance with the general average content of mediaeval life, he could make an intensive study of a small area he knows. There is enough to form a nucleus in innumerable villages in England, and in more Scottish ones than appears at first sight. The church can be taken as an instrument of ritual worship. If one will study the uses of the various parts, then such accidents as chantries and tombs, the exact meaning of decorative carving, glass and painting, then, with such elders to help him as John Myrc and such moderns as Professor Hamilton Thompson, and with (above all) the service-book, he will learn about mediaeval notions of religion and legendary naturally, as his ancestors learned them. He will soon discover the significance of its status as parish, collegiate, or monastic church, may take up the aesthetics of architecture and decoration, the economics and organisation of its building, its founders and benefactors, and so on. Lay monuments—castle, manor-house, almshouse —will serve in the same way, the student always remembering that secular life leaves few traces compared with religious observance—that the best-preserved castle preserves less than the most pillaged and restored church. The publications of the local archaeological society are usually full of fragments, and also of useful references.

Along with these studies, the student will read the poetry and prose which were arts contemporary with the buildings, which thrilled and amused the people who lived in them. Thus a fourteenth-century chantry will remind him that Langland denounced the abuse of chantries—*Piers Plowman* will remind him of chantry-chapels he has seen in his churches. The vogue of chantries, thoughtfully ruminated in the study or in the church, will reveal one prevalent emotion in the fourteenth-century mind, which will lead him perhaps to The Monk's Tale and Lydgate, and to salutary meditation on death and the soul. In those ruins, again, he may trace hall and bower. In this soler they read Chaucer and *Emare*— wearing what clothes? In this cloister they transcribed Roger of Wendover, thinking what thoughts, and poring over what technique? Refurnish Tattersall, that stands bare, with songs and arguments as well as with tapestries and armours. Read the legend and the truth of Warwick. Or begin with a poem or a story, and follow it back. Anything will do for a starting-point, but follow your fancy; and follow up the references, for there is no knowing where they may lead. We can promise you some labour and much delight.

LIST OF ABBREVIATIONS

Angl.—*Anglia, Zeitschrift für Englische Philologie*, Halle, 1877–.

Angl. B-bl.—*Beiblatt zur Anglia*, Halle, 1890–.

Archiv.—*Archiv für das Studium der Neueren Sprache und Literaturen*, ed. Herrig *et al*, Brunswick, 1846–.

Billings.—*A Guide to the M.E. Metrical Romances* by A. H. Billings, New York, 1901.

Bonner Beitr.—*Bonner Beiträge zur Anglistik*, Bonn, 1898–1908.

Brandl.—*Geschichte der altenglischen Literatur*, by A. Brandl, Strassburg, 1908.

Brandl-Zippel.—*Mittelenglische Sprach und Literaturproben*, by A. Brandl and O. Zippel, Berlin, 1917, etc.

B.M.—*British Museum*.

C.B.E.L.—*The Cambridge Bibliography of English Literature*, 4 vols., London, 1941.

C.H.E.L.—*The Cambridge Hist. of Engl. Lit.*, C.U.P., 1907–26.

Chambers, Beow.—*Beowulf and the Finnsburg Fragment*, ed. A. J. Wyatt, rev. with Introduction and Notes by R. W. Chambers, C.U.P., 1914, etc.

Chambers, Beow. Introd.—*Beowulf, an Introduction to the Study of the Poem*, by R. W. Chambers, 2nd ed., C.U.P., 1932.

Chambers, Eng. Norm. Con.—*England before the Norman Conquest*, by R. W. Chambers, London, 1926.

Clarke, Sidelights.—*Sidelights on Teutonic History during the Migration Period*, by M. G. Clarke, C.U.P., 1911.

Classen-Harmer. — *An Anglo-Saxon Chronicle*, ed. E. Classen and F. E. Harmer, Manchester, 1926.

Cockayne, Leechdoms.—*Leechdoms, Wortcunning and Starcraft of Early England*, 3 vols., by O. Cockayne, London, 1864–6.

Cook, Elene.—*The Old English Elene, Phoenix and Physiologus*, by A. S. Cook, New Haven, 1919.

Craigie, Specimens.—*Specimens of A.S. Poetry*, 3 vols., ed. W. A. Craigie, Edinburgh, 1923–31.

Dickins, Run. Poems.—*Runic and Heroic Poems*, by B. Dickins, C.U.P., 1915.

D.N.B.—*Dictionary of National Biography*, London, 1885–.

Earle-Plummer, Sax. Chron.—*Two of the Saxon Chronicles Parallel*, 2 vols., ed. C. Plummer, Oxford, 1892–9.

E.E.T.S. (O.S./E.S.).—*Publications of the Early English Text Society* (Original Series/Extra Series).

Encycl. Brit.—*Encyclopaedia Britannica*, 14th ed.

Engl. Hist. Rev.—*English Historical Review*, London, 1886–.

E.L.H.—*A Journal of English Literary History*, Baltimore, 1933–.

English Studies.—*A Journal of English Letters and Philology*, Amsterdam, 1936–.

Essays and Studies.—*Essays and Studies by Members of the English Association*, Oxford, 1910–.

E.St.—*Englische Studien, Organ für englische Philologie*, Leipzig, 1877–.

Ev. Lib.—*Everyman's Library*.

French and Hale.—*Middle English Metrical Romances*, ed. by W. H. French and C. B. Hale, New York, 1930.

Gordon, A.S. Poetry.—*Anglo-Saxon Poetry*, tr. by R. K. Gordon, Ev. Lib., 794.

Grein-Wül(c)ker, Poesie.—*Bibliothek der angelsächsischen Poesie*, 3 vols., ed. C. W. M. Grein and R. P. Wül(c)ker, Cassel, 1883–98.

Grein-Wül(c)ker, Prosa.—*Bibliothek der angelsächsischen Prosa*, ed. C. W. M. Grein, R. Wül(c)ker, H. Hecht, Cassel, 1872–.

Hall. Beow.—*Beowulf and the Finnesburg Fragment*, tr. J. R. C. Hall. New ed. rev. C. L. Wrenn and J. R. R. Tolkien, London, 1950.

Hall, Sels.—*Selections from Early Middle English*, 2 vols., ed. J. Hall, Oxford, 1920.

Hall, Jud. Phoen.—*Judith, Phoenix and other Anglo-Saxon Poems translated*, by J. L. Hall, London, 1902.

H. and B.—*A Bibliographical Guide to Old English*, by A. H. Heusinkveld and E. J. Bashe, Iowa, 1931.

Hibbard, Med. Rom.—*Medieval Romance in England*, by L. A. Hibbard, Oxford, 1924.

Hoops, Reallexikon.—*Reallexikon der germanischen Altertumskunde*, 4 vols., ed. J. Hoops, Strassburg, 1911–19.

Horstmann, A.E.Leg.—*Altenglische Legenden*, ed. C. Horstmann Paderborn, 1875.

Horstmann, A.E.Leg. 1878.—*Sammlung Altenglischer Legenden*, ed. C. Horstmann, Heilbronn, 1878.

Horstmann, A.E.Leg. 1881.—*Altenglische Legenden, neue Folge*, ed. C. Horstmann, Heilbronn, 1881.

Huchon, Hist. Lang. Angl.—*Histoire de la Langue Anglaise*, 2 vols., by R. Huchon, Paris, 1923–30.

Jansen.—*Die Cynewulf-forschung*, by K. Jansen, Bonn, 1908.

J.(E.)G.Ph.—*Journal of English and Germanic Philology*, Evanston, later Urbana, 1897–.

Kennedy, Cynewulf.—*The Poems of Cynewulf*, by C. W. Kennedy, London, 1910.

Kershaw.—*Anglo-Saxon and Norse Poems*, by N. Kershaw, C.U.P., 1922.

Klaeber, Beow.—*Beowulf and the Fight at Finnsburg*, ed. F. Klaeber, 3rd ed., London, 1941.

Kölbing, A. E. B.—*Altenglische Bibliothek*, ed. E. Kolbing, Heilbronn, 1883–.

Liebermann, Gesetze.—*Die Gesetze der Angelsachen*, 3 vols., ed. F Liebermann, Halle, 1903–16.

Medium Ævum.—*Medium Ævum* Oxford, 1932–.

M.L.N.—*Modern Language Notes*, Baltimore, 1886–.

M.L.R.—*Modern Language Review*, C.U.P., 1905–.

M.Ph.—*Modern Philology*, Chicago, 1903–.

Morris (and Skeat), Specimens.—*Specimens of Early English*, Pt. I, ed. R. Morris, rev. Mayhew and Skeat, 2nd ed., Oxford, 1898. Pt. II, ed. Morris and Skeat, 4th ed., Oxford, 1898.

Neilson and Webster, Ch.—*Chief British Poets of the 14th and 15th Centuries*, ed. W. A. Neilson and K. G. T. Webster, Boston, 1916.

Oakden, Allit. Poetry.—*Alliterative Poetry in Middle English; The Dialect and Metrical Survey*, by J. P. Oakden, Manchester University Press, 1930.

Owst, Lit. Pul.—*Literature and Pulpit in Medieval England*, by G. R. Owst, C.U.P., 1933.

Palaestra.—*Palaestra, Untersuchungen und Texte*, Leipzig, Berlin, 1898.

Phil. Quart.—*Philological Quarterly*, Iowa, 1922–.

P.M.L.A.—*Publications of the Modern Language Association of America*, Baltimore, 1884–.

R.E.S.—*The Review of English Studies*, London, 1925–.

Rickert, Rom. Friendship.—*Romances of Friendship*, vol. I of *Early English Romances in Verse*, by E. Rickert, London, 1908.

Rickert, Rom. Love.—*Romances of Love*, vol. 2 of *Early English Romances in Verse*, London, 1908.

Ritson, A.E.M.R.—*Ancient English Metrical Romances*, ed. J. Ritson, London, 1802.

S.A.T.F.—*Publications de la Société des anciens Textes Français*, Paris, 1875–.

Sedgefield, Bk. A.S. V.P.—*An A.S. Book of Verse and Prose* by W. J. Sedgefield, Manchester, 1928.

Sedgefield, Maldon.—*The Battle of Maldon and Short Poems from the Saxon Chronicle*, ed. W. J. Sedgefield, London, 1904.

Shackford, Leg. Sats.—*Legends and Satires from Medieval Literature*, by M. H. Shackford, Boston, 1913.

Sisam.—*Fourteenth Century Verse and Prose*, ed. K. Sisam, Oxford, 1921.

Smithson, Christian Epic.—*The O.E. Christian Epic*, by G. A. Smithson, Berkeley, 1910.

S.P.E.—Society for Pure English.

Speculum.—*The Speculum, a Journa of Medieval Studies*, Boston, 1926-.

S.T.S.—*Publications of the Scottish Text Society*, Edinburgh, 1884-.

Thomas, Engl. Lit.—*English Literature before Chaucer*, by P. G. Thomas, London, 1924.

Thorpe, A.S.C.—*The A.S. Chronicle*, ed. B. Thorpe, London, 1861.

Trounce, Engl. Tail Rhyme.—"The English Tail-Rhyme Romances" by A. McI. Trounce in *Medium Ævum*, Oxford, 1932-3.

Wardale.—*Chapters on O.E. Literature*, by E. E. Wardale, London, 1935.

Weber, Metr. Rom.—*Metrical Romances of the XIII, XIV and XV Centuries*, ed. H. Weber, Edinburgh, 1810.

Wells, (Manual).—*A Manual of the Writings in Middle English*, by J. E. Wells. With Eight Supplements. New Haven, 1916-.

Weston, Ch.M.E.P.—*The Chief M.E. Poets*, by J. L. Weston, Boston, 1914.

Weston, Rom. Vis. Sat.—*Romance, Vision and Satire*, by J. L. Weston, Boston, 1912.

Williams, Gnomic Poetry.—*Gnomic Poetry in A.S.*, by B. C. Williams, New York, 1914.

Z.f.d.A.—*Zeitschrift für Deutsche Alterthum und Deutsche Litteratur*, Leipzig, Berlin, 1841-.

CONTENTS

CHAPTER II

GENERAL BIBLIOGRAPHIES OF
OLD AND MEDIAEVAL ENGLISH LANGUAGE
AND LITERATURE

The following bibliographical items will be found useful. For others, especially German bibliographies, see Heusinkveld and Bashe below.

Annual Bibliography of English Language and Literature. Ed. for the Modern Humanities Research Association. Cambridge, 1921–.

American Bibliography for 1921–, in *Publications of the Modern Language Association of America*, Baltimore, 1884–. [See the March number.]

Brandl, A. *Geschichte der altenglischen Literatur*. Strassburg. 1908. [Offprint from Paul's *Grundriss der germanischen Philologie. Passim.*]

Cambridge Bibliography of English Literature, ed. F. W. Bateson, 4 vols. London, 1941. [This supersedes the bibliographies contained in *C.H.E.L.*]

The Cambridge History of English Literature, edited by A. W. Ward and A. R. Waller, C.U.P., 1907–1926. See 1.446 ff., and 2.432 ff. [A cheap reprint, omitting the bibliographies, was published in 1932.]

Cross, T. P. *Bibliographical Guide to English Studies*. 9th ed. Chicago, 1947.

Edwardes, M. *A Summary of the Literatures of Modern Europe (England, France, Germany, Italy, Spain) from the Origins to 1400.* London, 1907. [A useful guide, with summary lives of authors, synopses of writings, and select bibliographies.]

Gayley, C. M., and Kurtz, B. P. *Methods and Materials of Literary Criticism—Lyric, Epic, and Allied Forms of Poetry*. Boston and New York, 1920.

Gross, C. *The Sources and Literature of English History from the Earliest Times to about 1485.* 2nd ed. London, 1915.

133

Heusinkveld, A. H., and E. J. Bashe. *A Bibliographical Guide to Old English. A Selective Bibliography of the Language, Literature, and History of the Anglo-Saxons.* Iowa, 1931. [Excellent.]

Kennedy, A. G. *A Bibliography of Writings on the English Language from the Beginning of Printing to the End of 1922.* Cambridge (Mass.), 1927. [Indispensable for advanced study.]

Kennedy, A. G. *A Concise Bibliography for Students of English.* 2nd ed. O.U.P., 1946.

Lawrence, W. W. *Selected Bibliography of Mediaeval Literature in England.* New York, 1930. [Useful for beginners.]

Modern Language Notes. Baltimore, 1886–. [Each number lists recently published books.]

The Modern Language Review. Cambridge, 1905–. [Lists new books quarterly.]

Northup, C. S. *A Register of Bibliographies of the English Language and Literature.* New Haven, 1926. [New ed. in preparation.]

P.M.L.A. [Includes annual lists of new American publications.]

R.E.S. [Contains quarterly summaries of periodical literature.]

Schofield, W. H. *English Literature from the Norman Conquest to Chaucer.* London, 1914. [See pp. 466–86.]

Van Patten, N. *An Index of Bibliographies and Bibliographical Contributions Relating to the Work of British and American Authors, 1923–32.* London, 1934.

Wells, J. E. *A Manual of the Writings in Middle English, 1050—1400.* With eight supplements. New Haven, 1916–. [A handbook to all the extant writings in print composed in England. It "groups each piece with the others of its kind; indicates its probable date, or the limitations as to its date, its MS. or MSS., the probable date of its MS. or MSS., its form and extent, commonly the dialect in which it was first composed and its source or sources when known; presents comments on each longer production, with an abstract of its contents; and supplies a bibliography for each composition." Invaluable and indispensable.]

The Year's Work in English Studies. Published by The English Association, Oxford, 1921–. [A valuable critical review of current publications.]

CHAPTER III

OLD ENGLISH PERIOD—PEOPLE, INSTITUTIONS, LANGUAGE

1. PEOPLE AND INSTITUTIONS

For excellent résumés of current knowledge about persons, peoples, places, institutions, customs, etc., see the *Encyclopaedia Britannica* (14th ed.). For articles on individuals see the *Dictionary of National Biography*. The *Cambridge Medieval History* (Cambridge, 1911–1936) should also be regularly consulted.

A. GENERAL BIBLIOGRAPHY

A Guide to Historical Literature. Compiled by G. M. Dutcher, H. R. Shipman, S. B. Fay, A. H. Shearer, W. H. Allison. New York, 1931.

Gross, C. *The Sources and Literature of English History, from the Earliest Times to about 1485.* 2nd ed. London, 1915. [An invaluable annotated bibliography of English historical writings. Indispensable.]

Paetow, L. *Guide to the Study of Medieval History.* 2nd, rev. ed. London, 1931. [Not confined to English History.]

Annual Bibliography of English Language and Literature, ed. for the Modern Humanities Research Association. Cambridge, 1921– . [Contains sections devoted to historical topics.]

The English Historical Review. London, 1886– . [A quarterly journal, the July number of which includes a bibliography of books published during the year.]

B. ETHNOLOGY

Beddoe, J. *The Races of Britain.* Bristol, 1885. [See Chaps. V (Anglo-Saxon Period and Conquest), VII (Danish Period), VIII–XI (Normans)].

Chadwick, H. M. *The Origin of the English Nation.* 2nd ed. C.U.P., 1924. [Based upon "all branches of ethnological study—history, tradition, language, custom, religion and antiquities". Does not accept Bede's distinction of Angles and Saxons.]

Chadwick, H. M. and N. K. *The Growth of Literature.* 3 vols. C.U.P., 1932–9. See in particular, Vol. I.

Chambers, R. W., ed. *Widsith.* C.U.P., 1912.

Fleure, H. J. *The Peoples of Europe.* London, 1922. [Useful introd.]

Fleure, H. J. "Distribution of Races and Languages" in Vol. I of the *Oxford Survey of the British Empire.* Oxford, 1914.

Fleure, H. J. *The Races of England and Wales: a Survey of Recent Research.* London, 1923.

Hoops, J. *Reallexikon der germanischen Altertumskunde.* 4 vols. Strassbourg, 1911–19.

Jolliffe, J. E. A. *Pre-Feudal England. The Jutes.* London, 1933.

Peake, H. J. "The English Village" in Vol. I of the *Oxford Survey of the British Empire.* Oxford, 1914.

Ripley, W. Z. *The Races of Europe: A Sociological Study.* London, 1913. [First pub. New York, 1899. Standard work. See especially Chap. XII on the peoples of the British Isles.]

Schütte, G. *Our Forefathers: The Gothonic Nations. A Manual of the Ethnography of the Gothic, German, Dutch, Anglo-Saxon, Frisian and Scandinavian Peoples.* 2 vols. Trans. from the Danish by J. Young. Cambridge, 1929–33. [A standard work. Indispensable.]

Wadstein, E. *On the Origin of the English.* Upsala, 1927.

Weldon, B. de W. *The Origin of the English.* London, 1928.

C. SOCIAL HISTORY

Allison, T. *Pioneers of English Learning.* Oxford, 1932.

Andrews, C. McL. *The Old English Manor.* Baltimore, 1892.

Benham, A. R. *English Literature from Widsith to the Death of Chaucer. A Source Book.* London, 1916. [A comprehensive collection of extracts in translation illustrating the political, industrial and cultural backgrounds of the period.]

Browne, G. F. *The Importance of Women in Anglo-Saxon Times; and other Addresses.* London, 1919.

Collingwood, R. G. *Roman Britain.* O.U.P., 1924. [An excellent introd.]

Chadwick, H. M. *Studies on Anglo-Saxon Institutions.* Cambridge, 1905. [Brilliant survey. Indispensable.]

Chadwick, H. M. *The Heroic Age*. Cambridge, 1912, 1926. [See especially Chaps. XVI–XVIII.]

Files, G. T. *The Anglo-Saxon House*. Leipsic, 1893.

Gramm, W. *Die Körperpflege der Angelsachsen. Eine Kulturgeschichtlich-etymologische Untersuchung*. Heidelberg. 1938.

Gummere, F. B. *Founders of England, With Supplementary Notes*, by F. P. Magoun. New York, 1930. [A new and improved ed. of *Germanic Origins: a Study in Primitive Culture*.]

Haverfield, F. J. *The Roman Occupation of Britain*. Revised by G. Macdonald. Oxford, 1924. [See pp. 261–8 on "Roman Britain and Saxon England".]

Hodgkin, R. H. *A History of the Anglo-Saxons*. 2 vols. Oxford, 1935. [Contents:—Vol. I: The Angles and Saxons in Germany, The End of the Roman Period, The Conquest of Kent, The First Stage of the Saxon and Anglian Conquest, General Character of the Saxon Conquest, The Second Stage of the Conquest, Heathen Society, The Conversion, The Golden Age. Vol. II: The Struggle for Supremacy, The Church in the Century after Bede, The Results of Christianity, The Vikings, The Coming of the Great Army, The Danish Wars [871–8], War and Peace [878–92], The Restriction of Order of Learning, Alfred's Foreign Policy, Alfred's Last War, and Alfred, the Man and his Message. An excellent "attempt to adjust the new views and the old". Non-partizan and well-illustrated. Indispensable.]

Leach, A. F. *The Schools of Medieval England*. London, 1915. [See especially Chaps. III–VI.]

Leeds, E. T. *The Archaeology of the Anglo-Saxon Settlements*. Oxford, 1913. [Standard.]

Maitland, F. W. *Domesday Book, and Beyond*. Cambridge, 1907. [See Essay 2 on "England before the Norman Conquest".]

Parry, A. W. *Education in England in the Middle Ages*. London, 1920. [Bk. I (pp. 3–30)deals with the A.S. period. Excellent.]

Pfändler, W. "Die Vernügungen der Angelsachsen" in *Angl.*, 29.417–526. 1906.

Philippson, E. *Germanisches Heidentum bei den Angelsachsen*. Leipzig, 1929.

Quennell, M. and C. H. B. *Everyday Life in Anglo-Saxon, Viking and Norman Times*. London, 1926. [A concise, popular account, well illustrated.]

Rösler, M. "Erziehung in England vor der normannischen Eroberung" in *E. St.*, 48.1–114. 1915. [A well-documented and comprehensive account.]

Stenton, F. M. *Anglo-Saxon England*. Oxford, 1943. [Vol. 2 of the *Oxford History of England*. Indispensable.]

Strutt, J. *Glig-gamena Angel-ðeod. The Sports and Pastimes of the People of England*. New ed., enlarged by J. C. Cox. London, 1903. [Detailed description, with excellent illustrations, of pastimes of the people and an account of their origin. Very good reading-matter.]

Traill, H. D. *Social England. A Record of the Progress of the People in Religion, Laws, Learning, Arts, Industry, Commerce, Science, Literature and Manners by various writers*. Illustrated ed. [revised] by H. D. Traill and J. S. Mann. 6 vols. London, 1901–4.

Vinogradoff, P. *The Growth of the Manor*. 2nd ed. London, 1911. [Contents: Chaps. on Celtic Tribal arrangements, Roman influence, the English Conquest, the grouping of the folk, the shares in the township, the open field system, the history of the holding, Manorial origins, the principles of the Domesday Survey, ownership and husbandry, and social classes. See especially Bk. II (pp. 117–287) on the O.E. Period.]

Vinogradoff, P. *English Society in the Eleventh Century*. Oxford, 1908. [Account of military organisation, jurisdiction, taxation, government and society, land tenure, rural organisation, social classes, land and people. Standard.]

Wingfield-Stratford, E. C. *The History of British Civilisation*. 2nd ed. London, 1930. [See Chaps. I–III.]

Wright, T. *The Homes of Other Days. A History of Domestic Manners and Sentiments in England*. London, 1871.

D. POLITICAL HISTORY

Bense, J. F. *Anglo-Dutch Relations*. O.U.P., 1925. [Surveys from the earliest times to the death of William III. Forms an introd. to the author's *Dictionary of the Low Dutch Element in the English Vocabulary* (see p. 146)].

Chambers, R. W. *England before the Norman Conquest*. London, 1926. [Source book of English History from Teutonic times to 1066. Excellent reading-matter.]

Collingwood, W. G. *Scandinavian Britain*. London, 1908. [A comprehensive survey.]

Collingwood, R. G., and Myers, J. N. L. *Roman Britain and the English Settlements*. 2nd ed. Oxford, 1937. [Bks. I–IV, by Collingwood, on Roman Britain. Chaps. XIII (Romano-British Agriculture), XV (Romano-British Art), XIX

(Britain in the fifth century) may be noted. Interesting suggestions as to Arthur on pp. 320–4. Bk. V, by Myers, on the English Settlements. Not such smooth reading as Bks. I–IV, but the better for its lesser degree of conjecture, frank acknowledgment of paucity of evidence and avoidance of dogmatic conclusions. Valuable use of archaeology.]

Ekwall, E. *Scandinavians and Celts in the North-West of England.* Lund, 1918. [Study of Goidelic influence on local and personal nomenclature of North-West England.]

Freeman, E. A. *History of the Norman Conquest: its Causes and Results.* 6 vols. Oxford, 1867–79; 2nd ed. of Vols. I–IV, 1870–6; 3rd ed. of Vols. I and II, 1877. [Standard.]

Hodgkin, T. *The History of England from the Earliest Times to the Norman Conquest.* London, 1906. [Standard.]

Hoops, J. *Reallexikon der germanischen Altertumskunde.* 4 vols. Strassburg, 1911–19. [An indispensable reference book for more advanced studies. See I, 593–613 on A.S. Settlements, and IV, 529–53 on the Vikings.]

Kemble, J. M. *The Saxons in England.* 2nd ed. by W. de G. Birch. London, 1876. [Still useful.]

Kendrick, T. D. *A History of the Vikings.* London, 1930. [For advanced students particularly.]

Levison, W. *England and the Continent in the Eighth Century.* Oxford, 1946. [Erudite and authoritative.]

Lappenberg, J. M. *History of England under the Anglo-Saxon Kings.* Translated by B. Thorpe. Rev. ed. 2 vols. London, 1881. [Still useful.]

Mawer, A. *The Vikings.* Cambridge, 1913. [An excellent introductory survey.]

Oman, C. *England before the Norman Conquest. Being a History of the Celtic, Roman and Anglo-Saxon Periods down to the Year A.D. 1066.* London, 1910. [Authoritative.]

Ramsay, J. H. *The Foundations of England, or Twelve Centuries of British History, 55 B.C.–A.D. 1154.* 2 vols. London, 1898. [See especially Vol. I, Chaps. X, XXV, XXXI.]

Sayles, G. O. *The Medieval Foundations of England.* London, 1948. [A history of ideas in action.]

Shetelig, H. and Falk, H. *Scandinavian Archaeology.* Translated by E. V. Gordon. Oxford, 1937. [A summary of the whole of the pre-history and early history of the Scandinavian countries from the Stone Age to the end of the Viking period. Excellently illustrated. The best book in English on this subject.]

THE BEGINNINGS OF ENGLISH LITERATURE

Stenton, F. M. *Documents Illustrative of the Social and Economic History of the Danelaw.* Oxford, 1920.

Stenton, F. M. "The Danes in England" in *Proc. of the B.A.,* XIII, 203–46. 1927. [Surveys relations between Danes and English in the tenth century.]

Stephenson, C. *Borough and Town.* Camb. (Mass.), 1933. [Study of beginnings of town life in England.]

Tait, J. *The Medieval English Borough. Studies on its Origin and Constitutional History.* Manchester U.P., 1936.

Williams, M. W. *Social Scandinavia in the Viking Age.* New York, 1920.

Young, G. M. *The Origin of the West Saxon Kingdom.* O.U.P., 1934.

E. LAW, CONSTITUTION

Darlington, R. R. *A Constitutional History of England: From Anglo-Saxon England to 1066.* [In preparation. Methuen.]

Holdsworth, W. S. *A History of English Law.* 12 vols. London, 1922–38. [See Vol. II, Bk. II, on Anglo-Saxon Antiquities.]

Jenks, E. *A Short History of English Law.* 4th ed. London, 1938. [See Chap. I.]

Liebermann, F. *Die Gesetze der Angelsachsen.* 3 vols. Halle, 1903–16. [1. Text and German Translation. 2. Glossaries. 3. Introductions and Notes to each. A monumental edition. "For those who desire to make a study of the texts and their history, or to enter into a full discussion either of the Laws themselves or of the terms which are employed therein (this edition) is indispensable", Attenborough, *Laws of the Earliest English Kings,* Preface, C.U.P., 1922.]

Morris, W. A. *The Constitutional History of England to 1216.* New York, 1930.

Pollock, F. "English Law before the Norman Conquest," in A. Bowker's *Alfred the Great.* London, 1899, pp. 209–39. [Useful introd.]

Pollock, F. and Maitland, F. W. *The History of English Law before the Time of Edward I.* 2 vols. 2nd ed. Cambridge, 1911. [See especially Vol. I, Chap. I (The Dark Age in Legal History) and Chap. II (Anglo-Saxon Law).]

Stubbs, W. *The Constitutional History of England.* 3 vols. Oxford 1874–8. [Often reprinted. Standard work.]

Taswell-Langmead, T. P. *English Constitutional History.* [9th ed. by A. L. Poole.] London, 1929. [See Chap. I, "From the Teutonic Conquest of Britain to the Norman Conquest of England."]

F. THE CHURCH

Allison, T. *English Religious Life in the Eighth Century.* London, 1929.

Bede. *Ecclesiastical History of the English Nation.* Translated by A. M. Sellars. Also translated by J. E. King. 2 vols. London, 1930. [The latter gives Latin text.]

Bright, W. *Early English Church History.* Oxford, 1897. [Standard.]

Deanesly, M. *A History of the Medieval Church, 590–1500.* London, 1925. [Deals with Church as a whole.]

Duckett, E. S. *Anglo-Saxon Saints and Scholars.* London, 1947. [A safe guide for students of 7th and 8th century England.]

Duke, J. A. *The Columban Church.* O.U.P., 1932.

Encycl. Brit. sub. *England, The Church of.*

Howorth, H. H. *The Golden Days of the Early English Church from the Arrival of Theodore to the Death of Bede.* 3 vols. London, 1917.

Hunt, W. *The English Church (597–1066).* London, 1901. [Standard.]

Knowles, D. *The Monastic Order in England: a History of its Development from the Times of St. Dunstan to the Fourth Lateran Council, 943–1216.* C.U.P., 1940.

Mills, J. S. *The Great Days of Northumbria.* London, 1911.

Plummer, A. *The Churches in Britain before A.D. 1000.* Vols. I and II. London, 1911–12. [Standard.]

Robinson, J. A. *The Times of St. Dunstan.* Oxford, 1923. [Studies of Athelstan, Dunstan, Ethelwold and Oswald. Standard.]

Ryan, A. M. *A Map of Old English Monasteries and Related Ecclesiastical Foundations. A.D. 400–1066.* London, 1939.

Tidball, T. A. *The Making of the Church of England A.D. 597–1087.* Boston, 1919.

Wall, J. C. *The First Christians of Britain.* London, 1907.

Williams, H. *Christianity in Early Britain.* Oxford, 1912. [Standard.]

2. GENERAL HISTORY OF LANGUAGE

Bloomfield, L. *Language.* London, 1935. [A revised version of the author's *Introduction to the Study of Language,* 1914. Intended for the general reader, and for those who are beginning their linguistic studies. Excellent.]

De Laguna, G. A. *Speech: Its Function and Development.* London,

1927. [Inquiry into the origin and function of speech and its relation to thought and other human activities.]

Gardiner, A. H. *Speech and Language.* Oxford, 1932. [Outlines a "general theory of speech and language, and deals with the sentence, both form and substance, in some detail. The author is chiefly concerned with the function of speech as an instrument for conveying meaning", Preface, 13.]

Graff, W. L. *Language and Languages.* New York, 1932. [A general introd. to linguistic science, and a survey of modern knowledge.]

Gray, L. H. *Foundations of Language.* New York, 1939.

Jespersen, O. *Language, Its Nature, Development, and Origin* London, 1922, etc. [Bk. I deals with the history of linguistic science; Bk. II, with the speech of the child; Bk. III, with the individual and the world; Bk. IV, with the development of language. Excellent.]

Jespersen, O. *The Philosophy of Grammar.* London, 1924.

Meillet, A. and Cohen, M. *Les Langues du Monde.* Paris, 1924. [Its linguistic maps are excellent. New edition in preparation.]

Palmer, L. R. *An Introduction to Modern Linguistics.* London, 1936.

Paget, R. *Human Speech. Some Observations, Experiments, and Conclusions as to the Nature, Origin, Purpose and Possible Improvement of Human Speech.* London, 1930. [An extremely interesting book which others besides the general reader, for whom it is intended, will appreciate.]

Pederson, H. *Linguistic Science in the Nineteenth Century.* Translated by J. W. Spargo. O.U.P., 1931. [A most stimulating book, as well as a useful guide.]

Pillsbury, W. B. and Meader, C. L. *The Psychology of Language.* London, 1928. [Designed to "give a general survey of the facts of language and a psychological interpretation of those facts" for students of both language and psychology.]

Sapir, E. *Language: An Introduction to the Study of Speech.* London, 1921. [Attempts to show the variability of language in point of place and time and its relationship to other fundamental human interests.]

Schlauch, M. *The Gift of Tongues.* London, 1942. [Illustrated from English.]

Schmidt, P. W. *Die Sprachfamilien und Sprachenkreise der Erde.* Heidelberg, 1926.

Scott, H. F., Carr, W. L. and Wilkinson, G. T. *Language and its Growth. An Introduction to the History of Language.* Chicago, 1935.

Sturtevant, E. H. *Linguistic Change. An Introduction to the Historical Study of Language.* Chicago, 1917.

Sturtevant, E. H. *An Introduction to Linguistic Science.* Oxford, 1947.

Sweet, H. *The History of Language.* London, 1900.

Vendryes, J. *Language: A Linguistic Introduction to History.* Translated by P. Radin. London, 1925. [Deals with the origin of language, sounds, grammar, vocabulary, structure of languages, writing and the progress of language.]

Wyld, H. C. *The Historical Study of the Mother Tongue. An Introduction to Philological Method.* London, 1906, etc. [Includes chapters on the aims of historical linguistic study, the sounds of speech, how language is acquired and handed on, sound change, the development of dialects, linguistic contact, analogy, methods of comparison and reconstruction, the Aryan mother-tongue and the derived families of languages, the Germanic languages, the history of English during the O.E., M.E. and Modern Periods. An excellent introductory book.]

3. A. GENERAL HISTORY OF THE ENGLISH LANGUAGE

Alexander, H. *The Story of Our Language.* Toronto, 1940. [A thoroughly sound and comprehensive introduction.]

Armour, J. S. *The Genesis and Growth of English: an Outline of Philology for Students.* O.U.P., 1935.

Baugh, A. C. *A History of the English Language.* London, 1935 [Includes a good account of the relationship between the French and English languages in England during the M.E. period. Useful reading-lists end each chapter. A very readable book.]

Bradley, H. *The Making of English.* London, 1904, etc. [Primarily intended to "give educated readers, unversed in philology some notion of the causes that have produced the excellences and defects of modern English as an instrument of expression". Includes chapters on the making of English Grammar, foreign elements, word-making, changes of meaning, and some makers of English. A classic, introductory survey.]

Brunner, K. *Die Englische Sprache, ihre Geschichtliche Entwicklung. Erster Band, Algemeines, Lautgeschichte.* Halle, 1950. [A handbook dealing with origins, records and distribution, the development of vowels in both stressed and unstressed syllables, and the consonants. A second volume on the

143

inflexions and on English outside Europe is ready for the press.]

Classen, E. *Outlines of the History of the English Language*. London 1919, etc. [Contains chapters on the ancestry of English, syntax, vocabulary, development of meaning, word-formation, accidence, development of sounds, standard English, and the history of English spelling. A useful, but somewhat unconventional book.]

Emerson, O.F. *The History of the English Language*. London, 1894. Reprinted, 1924. [Contains five main sections. 1: The Relativity of English to other Languages. 2: The Standard Language and the Dialects. 3: The English Vocabulary. 4: The Principles of English Etymology. 5: The History of English Inflections. Valuable.]

Huchon, R. *Histoire de la Langue Anglaise*. Tome I: Des Origines à la Conquête Normande. Tome II: De la Conquête Normande à l'Introduction de l'Imprimerie. Paris, 1923–30. [Vol. I deals with the Indo-Germanic and Germanic periods, primitive O.E., O.E. morphology, the vocabulary, dialects, and the characteristics of both prose and poetry. Vol. II: the Transition Period, the dialectal literature of the thirteenth century, the origin of the Standard Language, and includes a chapter on the origin of Scots.]

Jespersen, O. *Growth and Structure of the English Language*. 8th ed. London, 1935. [Particularly useful for the foreign elements in the English vocabulary.]

Jespersen, O. *A Modern English Grammar on Historical Principles*. Parts I–VII, 1922–49. [Pts. I—IV, publ. Heidelberg. Pts. V–VII, publ. London, 1946–9. Pt. I: Sounds and Spellings. Pts. II–V: Syntax. Pt. VI: Morphology. Pt. VII: Syntax.]

Krapp, G. P. *Modern English, Its Growth, and Present Use*. New York, 1909.

Lindelöf, U. *Elements of the History of the English Language*. Translated by R. M. Garrett. Seattle, 1911. [Good introd.]

Lounsbury, T. R. *English Spelling and Spelling Reform*. London, 1909.

Lounsbury, T. R. *History of the English Language*. New York. 1894.

Luick, K. *Historische Grammatik der englischen Sprache*. Leipzig, 1914–29. [The most detailed study of the phonological development of English, including the dialects. Includes valuable bibliographical information about texts and monographs. Indispensable for the philologist.]

Marckwardt, A. H. *An Introduction to the English Language*. O.U.P., 1942. [Starts from a study of the living language and works backwards to O.E.]

Mathews, M. M. *A Summary of English Dictionaries*. Oxford, 1933. [A brief but stimulating account of English lexicography, with an indication of the characteristic features of English and American dictionaries now in use.]

McKnight, G. H. and Emsley, B. *Modern English, in the Making*. New York, 1928. [Designed to "show the principal changes that have taken place in the English language since the adoption, in the fourteenth century, of the East Midland dialect as the standard form of English". Much attention is given to the influence of classicism.]

Moore, S. *Historical Outlines of English Phonology and Middle English Grammar*. Ann Arbor, Michigan, 1919, etc.

Mossé, F. *Esquisse d'une Histoire de la Langue Anglaise*. Lyons, 1947. [A first-rate survey of the external history of the language from prehistoric times to the present day. Specially interesting on French influence on English. Gives useful reading-lists.]

Onions, C. T. *An Advanced English Syntax*. London, 4th ed., rev. and enlarged, 1927, etc. [Includes an "account of some notable archaic and obsolete constructions" intended for students of early Modern English.]

Robertson, S. *The Development of Modern English*. London, 1936, etc. [The emphasis has throughout been placed on present-day English, especially American English. Contains chapters on the nature and origin of Language, the ancestry of English, Old and Middle English, Modern (British and American) English, English Inflexions, English sounds and their history, contemporary pronunciation, spelling and spelling reform, sources of the vocabulary, the making of words, the changing meanings and values of words, and syntax and usage. At the end of each chapter is a selection of books recommended for further study A useful and readable book.]

Smith, L. P. *The English Language*. London, 1912, etc. Home Univ. Lib. [Includes chaps. on origins, foreign elements, modern English, word-making, historical development. Good introd.]

Sweet, H. *A Short Historical English Grammar*. (Corrected Impression), Oxford, 1924. [Abridged from the historical parts of the author's *New English Grammar*.]

Thomas, P. G. *An Introduction to the History of the English Language.* London, 1920.

Toller, T. N. *Outlines of the History of the English Language.* Cambridge, 1900. [A useful, elementary account of the changes in vocabulary, grammar and prose style, chiefly of the earliest periods.]

Weekley, E. *The English Language.* London, 1928, etc. 80 pp. [*Benn's Sixpenny Library*, 35.] [An excellent introductory sketch.]

Wrenn, C. L. *The English Language.* London, 1949. [Discusses relationships, origin of vocabulary, spelling and pronunciation, making and ordering of words, development of meaning, influence of important individual writers and works, the language today. A lively introduction for the serious student.]

Wyld, H. C. *A Short History of English, with a Bibliography of Recent Books on the Subject, and Lists of Texts and Editions.* 3rd ed. London, 1927. [Includes chapters on the sounds of speech, the general principles of the history of language, the history of English sounds in the O.E. period, etc. It also contains useful bibliographical information, and its phonetic explanations, a feature of the book, are particularly helpful. Indispensable.]

*Wyld, H. C. *A History of Modern Colloquial English.* 3rd ed. Oxford, 1936. [While its chief aim is to give an account of the history of English pronunciation from the early fifteenth century to beginning of the nineteenth century, it describes the salient features of M.E. phonology. Based on the "occasional-spelling" method. Most stimulating.]

Wyld, H. C. *Studies in English Rhymes from Surrey to Pope.* London, 1923, etc. [Intended primarily for those interested in the study of literature. Phonetic symbols purposely omitted.]

3. B. SEPARATE STUDIES OF THE VOCABULARY

Behrens, D. *Französiche Elemente im Englischen.* In Paul's *Grundriss*, I.2. Strassbourg, 1901.

Bense, J. F. *A Dictionary of the Low-Dutch Element in the English Vocabulary.* The Hague, 1926–39. [Standard.]

Bentley, H. W. *A Dictionary of Spanish Terms in English, with Special Reference to the American Southwest.* Oxford, 1932.

Björkman, E. *Scandinavian Loanwords in Middle English.* Halle 1900–2. [Standard.]

Carr, C. T. *The German Influence on English Vocabulary.* S.P.E., Tract 42. Oxford, 1934. [Valuable.]

Clark, G. N. *The Dutch Influence on the English Vocabulary*. S.P.E., Tract 44. Oxford, 1935.

Dellit, O. *Über lateinische Elemente im Mittelenglischen*. Marburg, 1905.

Förster, M. *Keltisches Wortgut im Englischen*. Halle, 1921. [Standard.]

Funke, O. *Die gelehrten lateinischen Lehn- und Fremdwörter in der altenglischen Literatur*. Halle, 1914.

Greenough, J. B. and Kittredge, G. L. *Words and their Ways in English Speech*. London, 1902. [Includes accounts of origin of language, learned and popular words, class dialects, historical development, the vocabulary, development of words, change in meaning, etc.]

Holthausen, F. *Altenglisches etymologisches Wörterbuch*. Heidelberg, 1934. [Unique and invaluable.]

Johnson, E. L. *Latin Words of Common English*. New York, 1931.

Jordan, R. *Eigentümlichkeit des anglischen Wortschatzes*. Heidelberg, 1906. [Important for the study of word-distribution in O.E.]

Keiser, A. *The Influence of Christianity on the Vocabulary of Old English Poetry*. Urbana, 1919.

Llewellyn, E. C. *The Influence of Low Dutch on the English Vocabulary*. O.U.P., 1936. [Excludes words used only in dialectal English, but includes words that have been borrowed in South Africa, North America, the East and West Indies, Guiana, and the West Coast of Africa. The words are classified according to the probable "channels of entry" (e.g. warfare, trade, fishing, land-drainage, industry, and the arts), and each group is prefaced by an account of the historical and economic relations between England and the Low Dutch countries concerned.]

Luick, K. "*Zu den lateinischen Lehnwörtern im Altenglischen*" in *Archiv*, 126, 1911.

MacGillivray, H. S. *The Influence of Christianity on the Vocabulary of Old English*. Halle, 1902.

Mettig, R. "*Das französische Element im Alt- und Mittel-englischen*" in *E. St.*, 41.177–252. 1910.

Pogatscher, A. *Zur Lautlehre der griechischen, lateinischen und romanischen Lehnwörter im Altenglischen*. Strassburg, 1888.

Praz, M. "*The Italian Element in English*" in *Essays and Studies*, 15. Oxford, 1929.

Rasner, F. *Die französiche Lehnwörter im Frühneuenglischen*. Marburg, 1907.

Serjeantson, M. S.   *A History of Foreign Words in English*. London, 1935. [Indispensable.]

Skeat, W. W.   *Principles of English Etymology*. 2nd series. *The Foreign Element*. Oxford, 1891.

Smock, J. C.   *The Greek Element in English Words*. Edited by P. W. Long. London, 1931.

Taylor, W.   *Arabic Words in English*. S.P.E., Tract 38. Oxford, 1933.

Toll. J. M.   *Niederländisches Lehngut im Mittelenglischen*. Halle, 1926.

4. OLD ENGLISH GRAMMAR, PHONOLOGY, SYNTAX

(Since English provides unrivalled documentation throughout twelve centuries of change, it is the predestined prey of philologists; and since change is continuous and drastic, linguistic study must be historical, so the innocent student who asks the librarian for a grammar of early English may be confronted with something more scientific, complete, and alarming than the tabulated dogma presented as standard Latin or French grammar. If his bent is that way, he will find no better philological pabulum than the works of Sievers, Luick, Morsbach, and so on. If he merely wishes to be able to read intelligently, he must not allow them to frighten him off. Old English is about as difficult to a modern Englishman as Italian is to one who knows Latin and French—that is, after a preliminary acquaintance with the principal forms, he will soon learn to allow for the differences. Early acquaintance with any local dialect is no disadvantage. The West Saxon of King Alfred is a useful fixed medium for the learning of the forms, and a comparatively slight knowledge of the principles will enable the student to recognise them in other periods and dialects. W.L.R.)

Andrew, S. O. "Some Principles of O.E. Word Order" in *Medium Ævum*, 3. 167–88, 1934.

Andrew, S. O. *Syntax and Style in Old English*. C.U.P., 1940. [A sketch.]

Bright, J. W.   *An Outline of Anglo-Saxon Grammar*. New and rev. ed. by J. R. Hulbert. London, 1936.

Brunner, K.   *Altenglische Grammatik nach der Angelsächsischen Grammatik von Eduard Sievers*. Halle, 1942. [Authoritative.]

Bülbring, K.   *Altenglisches Elementarbuch. I Teil: Lautlehre*. Heidelberg, 1902. [Standard book on O.E. phonology.]

Cook, A. S.   *A First Book in Old English: Grammar, Reader, Notes and Vocabulary*. 3rd ed. London, 1903. [Useful introd. especially for the private student.]

Girvan, R. *Angelsaksisch Handboek*. Haarlem, 1931.

Huchon. *Hist. Lang. Angl.*, I, 193–270. [Syntax.]

Luick. *Hist. Gram.* [Indispensable for philologists.]

Moore, S., and Knott, T. A. *The Elements of Old English*. 5th ed. Ann Arbor, 1927.

Ross, A. S. C. *The Essentials of Anglo-Saxon Grammar*. Cambridge, 1948.

Sedgefield, W. J. *A Skeleton Outline of Old English Accidence*. Manchester, 1917, etc. [Easily memorised.]

Sievers, E. *An Old English Grammar* (translated and edited by A. S. Cook). 3rd ed. Boston, 1903. [Scarcely for beginners. Use, if possible, the new, thoroughly revised German edition by Brunner, mentioned above.]

Wardale, E. E. *An Old English Grammar*. 4th ed. London, 1938. [Intended as an introd. to the "standard works of Sievers and Wright".]

Wright, J. and E. M. *An Elementary Old English Grammar*. Oxford, 1923.

Wright, J. and E. M. *Old English Grammar*. 3rd ed. Oxford, 1925. [Standard.]

Wülfing, J. E. *Die Syntax in den Werken Alfreds des grossen*. Bonn, 1894–1901. [The only extensive work on O.E. syntax.]

Wyatt, A. J. *An Elementary Old English Grammar*. (Early West-Saxon.) Cambridge, 1897.

Wyld. *Short Hist.* [Chap. V, on O.E. phonology.]

N.B. Useful outlines of O.E. grammar will be found in the *Readers* of Anderson and Williams, Bright, Flom, Krapp and Kennedy, Sweet, and Turk (see pp. 152–3).

5. OLD ENGLISH DICTIONARIES

Bosworth-Toller. *An Anglo-Saxon Dictionary based on the Manuscript Collections of the late Joseph Bosworth* . . . edited and enlarged by T. N. Toller. Oxford, 1882–98. *Supplements*, by T. N. Toller. Oxford, 1908–20. [The best.]

Grein, C. W. M. *Sprachschatz der angelsächsischen Dichter*. New edition by J. Köhler and F. Holthausen. Heidelberg, 1912–14. [Complete for poetic monuments.]

Hall, J. R. C. *A Concise Anglo-Saxon Dictionary for the Use of Students*. 3rd ed. Cambridge, 1931. [Reliable working dictionary.]

Sweet, H. *The Student's Dictionary of Anglo-Saxon*. London, 1911.

CHAPTER IV

OLD ENGLISH LITERATURE—GENERAL

A. HISTORY AND CRITICISM

Anderson, G. K. *The Literature of the Anglo-Saxons*. O.U.P., 1949. [A descriptive history. The bibliographical notes should be treated cautiously.]

Baldwin, C. S. *Three Mediaeval Centuries of Literature in England*. 1100–1400. Boston [U.S.A.], 1932. [See Chaps. I–II. Designed as a "compact guide-book", and intended specially for those who wish to study privately.]

Baugh, A. C., and others. *A Literary History of England*. London, 1948. [Comprehensive and authoritative.]

Brandl, A. *Geschichte der altenglischen Literatur*. Strassburg, 1908. [Offprint from Paul's *Grundriss der germanischen Philologie*. Excellent.]

Brooke, S. A. *The History of Early English Literature*. 2 vols. London and New York, 1892 [reprinted 1914]. [Literary criticism is specially valuable.]

Brooke, S. A. *English Literature from the Beginning to The Norman Conquest*. London, 1898, etc. [Noteworthy literary criticisms. Fine verse translations of O.E. poetry.]

C.H.E.L., Vol. I, 1907. [Indispensable.]

Chadwick, H. M. and N. K. *The Growth of Literature*. Vol. I. Cambridge, 1932.

Chambers, R. W. *"The Lost Literature of Mediaeval England"* in *The Library*, 4th Ser. 5.293–321. London, 1925. [Summarises the sources of our knowledge of O.E. literature.]

Courthope, W. J. *A History of English Poetry*. 6 vols. London, 1895–1910. See Vol. I, 1895. [Chap. III deals with A.S. poetry.]

Earle, J. *Anglo-Saxon Literature*. London, 1884. [Useful guide.]

Harvey, P. *The Oxford Companion to English Literature*. 3rd ed. Oxford, 1946. [*Passim.*]

Encyclopaedia Britannica, 14th ed.

Jusserand, J. J. *A Literary History of the English People*.

London, 1905. [See particularly, Chaps. III and IV on A.S. literature.]

Ker, W. P. *English Literature, Medieval.* London, 1912. Home Univ. Lib. 43. [See Chap. I.]

Ker, W. P. *The Dark Ages.* Edinburgh, 1904. [A classic. See especially Chap. IV on the literature of the Teutonic languages.]

Legouis, E., and Cazamian, L. *A History of English Literature, 650-1914.* Translated by H. D. Irvine and W. D. MacInnes. 2 vols. London, 1926-7. [A translation with revised select bibliographies of the authors' *Histoire de la Littérature Anglaise.* Paris, 1924. Chap. I. (pp. 3-54) deals with O.E. literature, but rather unsympathetically.]

Legouis, E. *A Short History of English Literature.* Translated by V. F. Boyson and J. Coulson. Oxford, 1934. [Chap. I (pp. 1-15) devoted to A.S. literature.]

Martin-Clarke, D. E. *Culture in Early Anglo-Saxon England.* London, 1947.

Sampson, G. *The Concise Cambridge History of English Literature.* C.U.P., 1941. [A free summary of the 14 vols. of *C.H.E.L.*, but brought up to date.]

Schirmer, W. F. *Geschichte der englischen Literatur von den Anfängen bis zur Gegenwart.* Halle, 1937.

Snell, F. J. *The Age of Alfred, 664-1154.* London, 1912. [A useful elementary study.]

Stephen, L. and Lee, S. *Dictionary of National Biography.* London, 1885-. [Indispensable.]

Ten Brink, B. *Early English Literature.* Translated by H. M. Kennedy. London, 1883. [This is translated from the first edition of the author's *Geschichte der englischen Litteratur,* Vol. I. Berlin, 1877. A second ed. of the latter, revised by A. Brandl, was published in Strassburg, 1899. Indispensable.]

Thomas, P. G. *English Literature before Chaucer.* London, 1924. [A summary sketch, but reliable.]

Wardale, E. E. *Chapters on Old English Literature.* London, 1935. [Sound, though conservative. Contains many excellent translations, chiefly of poetical passages.]

Wilson, F. P., and Dobrée, B. (eds.). *The Oxford History of English Literature.* 3 of the 12 vols. already published. O.U.P., 1944-. [See Vol. II, Part I: *Chaucer and the Fifteenth Century,* by H. S. Bennett; and Part II: *The Close of the Middle Ages,* by E. Chambers.]

Wright, C. E. *The Cultivation of Saga in Anglo-Saxon England.*

Edinburgh, 1939. [Demonstrates the existence of a fairly well developed oral literature.]

B. BOOKS OF OLD ENGLISH SELECTIONS

Anderson, M. and Williams, B. C. *Old English Handbook. A Grammar with a Reader Prepared from Actual Manuscripts.* London, 1938.

Bright, J. W. *An Anglo-Saxon Reader, with Notes, a complete Glossary, a Chapter on Versification and an Outline of Anglo-Saxon Grammar.* Revised and enlarged by J. R. Hulbert. New York, 1935, etc. [Chapter on versification is brief but excellent.]

Cook, A. S. *A First Book in Old English, Grammar, Reader, Notes and Vocabulary.* 3rd ed. London, 1903. [The prose, but not the poetical extracts, are normalised to an early W.S. basis. Includes a brief but useful bibliography and appendices containing short specimens of non-W.S. and Old Germanic dialect.]

Craigie, W. A. *Easy Readings in Anglo-Saxon.* Edinburgh, 1927. [An excellent introduction to early English.]

Craigie, W. A. *Specimens of Anglo-Saxon Prose.* 3 vols. Edinburgh, 1923-9. [Useful and cheap collections of extracts, with vocabularies.]

Craigie, W. A. *Specimens of Anglo-Saxon Poetry.* 3 vols. Edinburgh, 1923-31. [Handy collections.]

Flom, G. T. *Introductory O.E. Grammar and Reader.* Boston, 1930. [Designed for beginners. Includes a good variety of selections both W.S. and non-W.S. The brief account of versification is very helpful.]

Krapp, G. P. and Kennedy, A. G. *An Anglo-Saxon Reader.* New York, 1929.

Mossé, F. *Manuel de l'anglais du moyen age des origines au XIVe siècle. I. Vieil-anglais. Tome premier: Grammaire et textes. Tome second: Notes et glossaire.* Paris, 1945. [An excellent text-book. Has a useful account of syntax.]

Sedgefield, W. J. *An Anglo-Saxon Book of Verse and Prose.* Manchester, 1928. ["In the present volume are bound up the [author's] *Anglo-Saxon Verse-Book* and the *Anglo-Saxon Prose-Book*, each of which is published separately." Excellent.]

Sweet, H. *A Second Anglo-Saxon Reader. Archaic and Dialectal.* Oxford, 1887. [Provides linguistic material from the non-West Saxon dialects for advanced students. A "cheap and handy abridgement of Sweet's *Oldest English Texts*". Consists largely of glosses.]

Sweet, H. *An Anglo-Saxon Primer, with Grammar, Notes and Glossary*. 8th ed., rev. Oxford, 1905. [Spelling of texts is normalised on an Early W.S. basis.]

Sweet, H. *An Anglo-Saxon Reader in Prose and Verse, with Grammatical Introduction, Notes and Glossary*. 10th ed., revised by C. T. Onions. Oxford, 1946. [A classic.]

Turk, M. H. *An Anglo-Saxon Reader*. Rev. ed. New York, 1930.

Williams, O. T. *Short Extracts from Old English Poetry, chiefly for Unseen Translations*. Bangor, 1909.

Wyatt, A. J. *An Elementary Old English Reader*. [*Early West Saxon.*] Cambridge, 1901.

Wyatt, A. J. *An Anglo-Saxon Reader, edited with Notes and Glossary*. Cambridge, 1919, etc. [Contains good collection of extracts, but is deficient in illustrative non-W.S. material. The notes are excellent.]

Wyatt, A. J. *The Threshold of Anglo-Saxon*. Cambridge, 1926. [Normalised texts.]

CHAPTER V

OLD ENGLISH LITERATURE—POETRY

1. Modern Collections
2. Books of Translations
3. History and Criticism
4. Versification
5. Authors, Texts and Manuscript Collections

1. MODERN COLLECTIONS

Craigie, W. A. *Specimens of Anglo-Saxon Poetry.* I: *Biblical and Classical Themes.* II: *Christian Lore and Legend.* III: *Germanic Legend and Anglo-Saxon History and Life.* Edinburgh, 1923–31. [Intended for students of O.E. literature. Short bibliographies, but no apparatus. Cited as Craigie, *Specimens I, II and III.*]

Dickins, B. *Runic and Heroic Poems of the Old Teutonic Peoples.* Cambridge, 1915. [With full critical apparatus and translations. Contains *Runic Poem, Waldere, Fight at Finnsburh* and *Deor.*]

Grein, C. W. M. *Bibliothek der angelsächsischen Poesie. Neu bearbeitet, vermehrt und nach neuen Lesungen der Handschriften.* Ed. R. P. Wül(c)ker. 3 vols. Cassel, 1883–98. [Almost complete collection of poetical texts. Indispensable. Cited as Grein-Wülker, *Poesie I, II and III.* Vol. III is in two parts (IIIa and IIIb) paginated separately.]

Holthausen, F. *"Kleinere altenglische Dichtungen"* in *Angl.,* 41.400–4. 1917. [Contains texts not printed by Grein-Wülker, above.]

Kershaw, N. *Anglo-Saxon and Norse Poems.* Cambridge, 1922. [Contains *Wanderer, Seafarer, Wife's Lament, Husband's Message, Ruin* and *Battle of Brunanburh.* With full critical apparatus and translations.]

Krapp, G. P. (and Dobbie, E. v. K.). *The Anglo-Saxon Poetic Records.* I: *The Junius Manuscript,* ed. Krapp. II: *The Vercelli*

Book, ed. Krapp. III: *The Exeter Book*, ed. Krapp and Dobbie '
IV: *The Beowulf Manuscript*, in preparation. V: *The Paris
Psalter and the Meters of Boethius*, ed. Krapp. VI: *The Anglo-
Saxon Minor Poems*, ed. Dobbie. London, 1931– . [Excel-
lent critical apparatus. Indispensable. Cited under name of
editor(s).]

Schücking, L. L. *Kleines angelsächsisches Dichterbuch. Lyrik und
Heldenepos.* Cöthen, 1919. [With full apparatus.]

Sedgefield, W. J. *An Anglo-Saxon Book of Verse and Prose.* Manchester, 1928. [A complete volume comprising the author's
Anglo-Saxon Verse Book and *Anglo-Saxon Prose Book*, each
published separately. Good apparatus.]

Note. See also the *Readers* and anthologies mentioned above
(pp. 152–3).

2. BOOKS OF TRANSLATIONS

Cook, A. S., and Tinker, C. B. *Select Translations from Old
English Poetry.* Rev. ed. London, 1926. [Compiled from
various authors. Prose and verse.]

Faust, C., and Thompson, S. *Old English Poems.* Chicago, 1918.

Gordon, R. K. *Anglo-Saxon Poetry.* London, 1927. *Ev. Lib.*, 794.
[A sound and usually reliable prose translation.]

Gummere, F. B. *The Old English Epic: Beowulf, Finnsburg,
Waldere, Deor, Widsith* and the German *Hildebrand.* New York,
1909. [In the original metre.]

Hall, J. L. *Judith, Phoenix and Other Anglo-Saxon Poems.* London,
1902. [Verse form.]

Kennedy, C. W. *Old English Elegies. Translated into Alliterative
Verse with a Critical Introduction.* London, 1936.

Spaeth, J. D. *Old English Poetry.* Princeton, 1922. [In alliterative
verse, with useful bibliography, introduction and notes.]

Williams, M. *Word-Hoard.* London, 1946. [Contains useful
translations of many passages of O.E. literary monuments,
as well as much background material presented agreeably
and simply.]

3. HISTORY AND CRITICISM

Chadwick, H. M. *The Heroic Age.* Cambridge, 1912.

Dixon, W. M. *English Epic and Heroic Poetry.* London, 1912.

Hanscom, E. D. "*The Feeling for Nature in O.E. Poetry*" in
J.E.G.Ph., 5.439–63. 1905.

Keiser, A. *The Influence of Christianity on O.E. Poetry.* Urbana, 1918.

Kennedy, C. W. *The Earliest English Poetry: A Critical Survey of the Poetry written before the Norman Conquest, with Illustrative Translations.* O.U.P., 1943. [Scholarly and indispensable.]

Ker, W. P. *Epic and Romance. Essays on Mediaeval Literature.* 2nd ed. Oxford, 1908, etc.

Marquardt, H. *Die altenglischen Kenningar: ein Beitrag zur Stilkunde altgermanischer Dichtung.* Halle, 1938. [An original survey of the whole corpus of O.E. poetry.]

Mead, W. E. "*Color in O.E. Poetry*" in *P.M.L.A.*, 14.169–206. 1899.

Pons, E. *Le Thème et le Sentiment de la Nature dans la Poésie Anglo-Saxonne.* Strasbourg, 1925.

Rankin, J. W. "A Study of the Kennings in A.S. Poetry" in *J.E.G.Ph.*, 8.357–422, 9.49–84. 1909–10.

Routh, H. V. *God, Man and Epic Poetry.* 2 vols. Cambridge, 1927.

Scholz, H. v.d. M. *The Kenning in A.S. and O.N. Poetry.* Utrecht, 1927.

Sieper, E. *Die altenglische Elegie.* Strassburg, 1915.

Skemp, A. R. "The Transformation of Scriptural Story, Motive and Conception in A.S. Poetry" in *M.Ph.*, 4.423–70. 1906–7.

Smithson, G. A. *The O.E. Christian Epic: a Study of the Plot Technique of the Juliana, the Elene, the Andreas and the Christ, in comparison with the Beowulf and with the Latin Literature of the Middle Ages.* Berkeley, 1910.

Thomas, W. *L'Epopée Anglo-Saxonne.* Paris, 1924.

Wyld, H. C. "Diction and Imagery in A.S. Poetry" in *Essays and Studies*, XI.49–91. 1925.

4. VERSIFICATION

Bright, J. W., "Anglo-Saxon Versification", Appendix II, pp. 229–40, in *A.S. Reader.* [An excellent guide.]

Kaluza, M. *Der altenglische Vers: eine metrische Untersuchung.* Berlin, 1894. [Part I reviews the various theories and endeavours to "reconcile the four-accent theory with Siever's types" (Klaeber); Part II deals with the metre of *Beowulf* and scans the first 1,000 lines.]

Kaluza, M. *A Short History of English Versification.* Translated by A. C. Dunstan. London, 1911. See pp. 1–126. [Contains a useful summary of existing theories. Translates the author's *Englische Metrik in historischer Entwicklung dargestellt.* Berlin, 1909.]

Schipper, J. *A History of English Versification.* Oxford, 1910. [Comprehensive and extremely detailed, with abundant illustrative material. Indispensable. Translates author's *Grundriss der englischen Metrik.* Vienna, 1895.]

Setzler, E. B. *On Anglo-Saxon Versification from the Standpoint of Modern English Versification.* Baltimore, 1904. [A simple explanation of Siever's system intended for students.]

Sievers, E. *Zur Rhythmik des germanischen Alliterationsverses.* Anastatic reprint, New York, 1909. [S. here explains his system of verse types. Of fundamental importance.]

Sievers, E. *Altgermanische Metrik.* Halle, 1893. [A standard work. An abridgment is contained in Paul's *Grundriss*, 2nd ed., Vol. IIb, 1–38, 1905.]

Note.—Useful short accounts of O.E. verse are accessible in Flom. *O.E. Reader*, Krapp and Kennedy, *A.S. Reader*, Sedgefield, *Beowulf*, Spaeth, *O.E. Poetry*, and Sweet, *A.S. Reader*, see above. pp. 152–3.

Two of the undermentioned items explain in German the newer ideas on Anglo-Saxon (and Old Teutonic) versification more recently elaborated by E. Sievers and A. Heusler in Germany. These differ considerably from those that have resulted in the widely accepted "Five-Types" scheme earlier proposed by Sievers himself. More recently still, J. C. Pope's *The Rhythm of Beowulf* has been published reviewing these newer theories, and proposing still another. Until, however, these new theories gain sufficient acceptance to appear in English handbooks, the student who knows no German may well content himself with the older system of scansion.

Sievers, E. "Zu Cynewulf" in *Neusprachliche Studien, Festgabe für Karl Luick*, Marburg, 1925, pp. 60–81. [Sievers "recognizes the musical element of regularly recurring measures, rejects the dynamic basis of alliteration, admits deviations from the normal (prose) accentuation, relies on his feeling for speech melody. The theory that alliteration is not confined to rhythmically accented syllables, raises serious doubts", see Klaeber, *Beowulf and the Fight at Finnsburg*, 3rd ed., Boston, 1941, p. clxxiv.]

Heusler, A. *Deutsche Versgeschichte mit Einschluss des altenglischen und altnordischen Stabreimverses.* 2 vols. Berlin and Leipzig, 1925. ["The different forms of verse (half-line) are viewed as variations of the general *rhythmical* type of two bars . . . | x́xx̀x | x́xx̀x, freely admitting, however, pauses in place of speech material. The 'swelling' lines are not 'hypermetrical' ", cf. Klaeber, *ibid*. Later, on p. 282, Klaeber gives a few specimens of Heusler's system of scansion.]

Pope, J. C. *The Rhythm of Beowulf*. O.U.P., 1942. [An important and elaborate study setting out a new theory for reading O.E. poetry, though it accepts the descriptive part of Sievers' work as being fundamentally sound.]

Daunt, M. "Old English Verse and Speech Rhythm" in *Trans. of the Philological Society*, 1946. [Suggests a new approach to the question of O.E. verse, which may be regarded as "conditioned prose", i.e. spoken language specially arranged with alliteration.]

Baum, P. F. "The Meter of the Beowulf" in *M. Ph.*, 46. 73–91 and 145–162. 1948–9. [Advocates greater freedom of interpretation and admits occasional half-lines of three stresses.]

5. AUTHORS, TEXTS, MANUSCRIPT COLLECTIONS

Almost all the extant O.E. poems are contained in the following four MSS. collections, the *Exeter Book* (*Codex Exoniensis*), the *Junius MS.* (*Junius XI*), the *Vercelli Book* (*Codex Vercellensis*), and the *Beowulf MS.* (*MS. Cotton Vitellius A* 15). A brief account of each is given below in alphabetical order (pp. 173ff, 199ff, 210ff, 156ff, respectively). Their contents are treated separately, under the relevant MS. title and according to their position in the MS. The poems of the *Anglo-Saxon Chronicle* are dealt with chronologically under this title. The other texts are arranged in alphabetical order of titles. Each item is followed by a separate bibliography. When using this, reference should also be made to the bibliography under the group heading, if any.

BEDE'S DEATH SONG

The 5 ll. of this simple *Death Song*, on caring for the needs of the soul, have the additional interest of being the only surviving example of Bede's English compositions. The text, in the Northumbrian dialect, is found solely in Cuthbert's letter to Cuthwin, describing Bede's last moments, of which there are apparently three closely similar recensions, contained in several continental and English MSS. of the Latin text of Bede's *Ecclesiastica Historia*, the oldest being the ninth-century St. Gall Codex 254, as well as in Symeon of Durham's *Historia Dunelmensis* (written 1104–9).

Bibliography.
C.B.E.L., 1.80.
H. & B., 55.
Smith, A. H.   *Three Northumbrian Poems.* London, 1933. *Methuen's O.E. Library.* [Pp. 48–50. An excellent ed. with full apparatus.]

Facsimile.
Brotanek, R.   *Texte und Untersuchungen zur altenglischen Literatur und Kirchengeschichte.* Halle, 1913.

Editions.
Sedgefield, *Bk. A.S. V.P.*, 81; Smith (above).

Translations.
Sedgefield, Bk. *A.S. V.P.*, 174; Wardale 28.

Discussion.
Dobbie, E. v. K.   *The Manuscripts of Cædmon's Hymn and Bede's Death Song.* New York, 1937.
Smith (above).

BEOWULF MS. (*COTTON VITELLIUS A XV*)

This vellum MS., forming part of the Cotton Collection in the British Museum, comprises two separate codices, which were arbitrarily bound together in the sixteenth century. The first codex, fol. 4a–93b (present numbering), written by two main hands in the twelfth century, contains four prose works only, viz., *Alfred's Blooms* (fol. 4a–59), *Gospel of Nicodemus* (60a–84a), *Dialogue between Salomon and Saturn* (84b–93a) and a fragment on martyrs (93b). The second codex (fol. 94a–209b), in the handwriting (c. 1000) of only two scribes, preserves five texts, the last two being in verse. These are:—(fragmentary) *Life of St. Christopher* (fol. 94a–8a), *Wonders of the East* (98b–106b), *Letter of Alexander the Great to Aristotle* (107a–31b), *Beowulf* (132a–201b) and the *Judith* fragment (202a–9b).

At the top of the first page of the MS. is the name Lawrence Nowell (a pioneer student of O.E.) and the date 1563. In 1731, the MS. suffered much damage from the disastrous fire that injured or destroyed many MSS. of Sir Robert Cotton's (see *D.N.B.* s.n.) Collection at Ashburnham House, Westminster.

Bibliography.
C.B.E.L., 1.63.
H. and B., 47–48.

Discussion

Förster, M. *Die Beowulf-handschrift. Berichte über die Verhand-lungen der Sachsischen Akademie der Wissenschaften.* Vol. 71, No. 4. Leipzig, 1919. [Full investigation.]

Klaeber. *Beow.*, xcvii–civ; cxxiii; clv; 413. [Special reference to *Beowulf* text.]

Rypins, S. I. (i) "The Beowulf Codex" in *M.Ph.*, 17.13–9, 1920. (ii) "A Contribution to the Study of the Beowulf Codex" in *P.M.L.A.*, 36.167–85, 1921. [Investigation of Beowulfian scribes' orthography.]

Rypins, S. *Three Old English Prose Texts in MS. Cotton Vitellius A XV.* E.E.T.S., 1924. [For Rypins' latest opinions on the orthography of the two Beowulfian scribes, see pp. i–xxix.]

Sisam, K. "The Beowulf Manuscript" in *M.L.R.*. 11.335–7, 1916. [Note on scribes and articles.]

Zupitza. *Beow.*, below.

1. BEOWULF

Beowulf, a poem of 3182 ll., is the most valuable literary document in any early Germanic language. Although the main story is fantastic fiction—pure folk-tale—most of the principal characters are historical and are Scandinavians known to us from Scandinavian and Continental records; but the chief personage, Beowulf, remains unidentified. Many of the events as well have an historical foundation. The scene is laid in Denmark and Southern Sweden; England is never mentioned. Yet despite all this, the author was undoubtedly an Englishman, one that probably wrote c. 700. As might be expected, the genesis of the poem presents many interesting, but bewildering problems. So, too, does the Christian element, for it is remarkable that while the sentiment is largely Christian, the customs and ceremonies are consistently pagan. The language is predominantly L.W.S., with a sprinkling of Non-W.S., chiefly Anglian forms.

Briefly the poem relates the deeds of Beowulf, a valiant warrior of the people of the Geats in Southern Sweden, who sails from his homeland to help the King of the Danes, Hrothgar, whose royal hall, Heorot, is being regularly ravaged by a murderous, cannibalistic, human monster named Grendel. This fiend is overcome by Beowulf in a memorable encounter, but escapes, only to die from his grievous injuries in his mother's cave-dwelling under the waters of a lake. The mother carries on the depredations, but is pursued to her lair and there slain by the hero. Then Beowulf returns home to Sweden and is subsequently proclaimed King of the Geats. After a glorious reign of fifty years, he is mortally wounded in his successful attack upon the guardian of a treasure-hoard, a fire-breathing dragon that had been devastating the countryside. The poem ends with the burning of Beowulf's body and the treasure on a funeral pyre on a headland, where, amid the lamentations of his people, a monumental barrow is built to perpetuate his memory.

The text, probably complete, is extant in a unique copy on fol. 132a–201b (present foliation) of the MS. and was written by two scribes, the second beginning at *moste*, l. 1939, and writing a thicker, rougher [though clear] and old-fashioned hand. Following current practice, the text, in the main quite legible, is written continuously like prose and divided, sometimes arbitrarily, into forty-three sections. The punctuation is "meagre and unreliable", the spelling inconsistent, vowel length indicated only some 120 times, and the hyphen is never used.

Before anyone had transcribed it, the MS. was damaged in the Cottonian fire of 1731. The edges and margins were charred by the heat and have often subsequently crumbled away. It was first described by H. Wanley in the *Librorum Septentrionalium . . . Catalogus* which he contributed to G. Hickes' *Linguarum veterum septentrionalium thesaurus grammatico-criticus et archaeologicus*, Oxford, 1703–5. But Wanley thought that the poem was an account of a war waged by Beowulf, a Dane, against the Kings of Sweden.

Bibliography.
C.B.E.L., 1.63–8.
Chambers. *Beow. Introd.* [Very full.]
H. and B., 56–61.
Klaeber. *Beow.* (below.) [Very full.]
Lawrence.. *Beow. Ep. Trad.*, 295–301. [Specially selected for beginners.]

Manuscript.
Thorkelin, G. J. (A) *Poema anglosaxonicum de rebus gestis Danorum ex membrana bibliothecae cottonianae . . . fecit exscribi* Londini A.D. 1787 Grimus Johannis Thorkelin, L.L.D. (B) *Poema anglosaxonicum . . . exscripsit* Grimus Johannis Thorkelin. Londini anno 1787. [These are the famous Thorkelin transcripts. Both copies, which, because made when the edges of the parchment were better preserved than they are to-day, have enhanced value, are in the Royal Library at Copenhagen. Thorkelin spent some twenty years on

preparing an edition of the poem, but, when nearing completion in 1807, his translation and notes were destroyed during the English bombardment of Copenhagen. Not till 1815 did his edition finally appear.]

Facsimile.

Zupitza, J. *Beowulf. Autotypes of the Unique Cotton MS. Vitellius A XV in the British Museum with a Transliteration and Notes.* E.E.T.S., 77. London, 1882. ["Almost of equal value with the MS." The transliteration aims at reproducing the probable text of a century earlier and must therefore be used cautiously.]

Editions.

Heyne, M. *Beowulf. Mit ausführlichen Glossar hrsg.* Bearbeitet von L. L. Schücking. 13th ed. Paderborn, 1929. [Reliable.]

Holthausen, F. *Beowulf nebst den kleineren Denkmälern der Heldensage, mit Einleitung, Glossar und Anmerkungen. Teil I: Texte und Namenverzeichnis, 6. verbesserte Auflage. Teil II: Einleitung, Glossar, und Anmerkungen, 5. verbesserte Auflage.* Heidelberg, 1929. [Glossary excellent. Brief introd. and notes.]

Klaeber, F. *Beowulf and the Fight at Finnsburg, edited with Introduction, Bibliography, Notes, Glossary and Appendices.* London, 1922. 2nd ed., 1928. 3rd ed., 1936, 1941 (with Supplement). [The introd. discusses the argument of the poem, the fabulous or supernatural elements, the historical colouring, the structure, tone, style and metre, the language and manuscript, and the genesis of the poem. The very valuable bibliography, which is slightly annotated and mentions reviews, is selective, but very comprehensive to date. The notes are excellent. The appendices contain Parallels (viz., analogues and illustrative passages), Antiquities (index of subjects pertaining to Old Germanic life), textual criticism (specific grammatical and metrical notes), and the text of *Waldere, Deor,* and selected passages from *Widsith.* Includes two pages of facsimiles, five plates, and a sketch map showing the geography of *Beowulf.* The best working edition of the poem. The Glossary is excellent.]

Sedgefield, W. J. *Beowulf, edited with Introduction, Bibliography, Notes, Glossary and Appendices.* 3rd ed., Manchester, 1935. [Also contains the *Finnsburg Fragment, Widsith, Waldere* and *Deor.* The excellent introd. discusses the MS., language, tone, style and vocabulary, composition and structure, subject-

162

matter, origin, authorship and date, and the relationship of *Beowulf* to other Old English poetry. Glossary invaluable.]

Wyatt, A. J. *Beowulf and the Finnsburg Fragment. Revised with Introduction and Notes*, by R. W. Chambers. Cambridge, 1914. 3rd impression, 1925. [Contains, besides facs. of two pages of MS. illustrating the handwriting of each scribe, a facs. page of each of Thorkelin's transcripts. The text is very conservative, the textual notes at the foot of each page are excellent and there is a most useful index of persons and places. A fine edition.]

Translations.

Child, C. G. *Beowulf and the Finnsburg Fragment Translated.* London. 1904. [A good prose translation, with useful introd. and notes.]

Crawford, D. H. *Beowulf, translated into English Verse, with an Introduction, Notes and Appendices.* London, 1926. [Apparatus good.]

Gordon, R. K. *Anglo-Saxon Poetry.* London, 1927. *Ev. Lib.*, 794. Pp. 4–70. [A useful, working, prose translation.]

Gummere, F. B. *The Oldest English Epic.* New York, 1909. ["Translated in the original metres." Good notes and introd.]

Hall, J. R. Clark. *Beowulf and the Finnsburg Fragment. A Translation into Modern English Prose.* New ed. rev. by C. L. Wrenn and prefatory remarks by J. R. R. Tolkien, London, 1940. [An excellent translation with helpful introductions to the study of the poem and its metre.]

Hall, J. R. Clark. *Beowulf, a Metrical Translation into Modern English.* Cambridge, 1914.

Kennedy, C. W. *Beowulf: The Oldest English Epic. Translated into Alliterative Verse, with a Critical Introduction.* O.U.P., 1940.

Leonard, W. E. *Beowulf, a New Verse Translation.* London, 1923.

Strong, A. *Beowulf, translated into Modern English Rhyming Verse, with Introduction and Notes; with a Foreword on "Beowulf and the Heroic Age" by R. W. Chambers.* London, 1925.

Concordance.

Cook, A. S. *A Concordance to Beowulf.* Halle, 1911.

Discussion.

Blackburn, F. A. *"The Christian Coloring in the Beowulf"* in *P.M.L.A.*, 12.205–25, 1897.

Bonjour, A. *The Digressions in Beowulf.* Oxford, 1950.

Bradley, H. " *Beowulf*," in *Encycl. Brit.*, 14th ed.

Chadwick, H. M. *The Heroic Age*. Cambridge, 1912. [Includes a comparison of Germanic and Greek heroic poetry.]

Chambers, R. W. *Widsith: A Study in O.E. Heroic Legend*. Cambridge, 1912. [Invaluable for study of heroic legend and period.]

Chambers, R. W. *Beowulf, An Introduction to the Study of the Poem with a Discussion of the Stories of Offa and Finn*. 2nd ed. Cambridge, 1932. [Comprehensive survey of all the literary and historical problems. Indispensable.]

Chambers, R. W. *Man's Unconquerable Mind*. London, 1939. [Discusses the Heroic Age in England.]

Girvan, R. *Beowulf and the Seventh Century*. London, 1935. *Methuen's O.E. Library, C.I.* [Contains chapters on tne language, the background and the legendary and historical matter. Stimulating.]

Gummere, F. B. *Founders of England*, New York, 1930.

Hamilton, M. P. "The Religious Principle in *Beowulf*" in *P.M.L.A.*, 61.309-330, 1946. [Useful information.]

Hoops, J. *Kommentar zum Beowulf*. Heidelberg, 1932. [A very thorough, conservative and scholarly line-by-line commentary. Excellent in every sense, and indispensable.]

Hoops, J. *Beowulf Studien*. Heidelberg, 1932. [Contains detailed discussions of several difficult problems.]

Hulbert, J. R. "*Beowulf* and the Classical Epic" in *M. Ph.*, 44.65-75, 1946.

Ker, W. P. *Epic and Romance*. London, 1897.

Klaeber, F. "*Die christlichen Elemente in Beowulf*" in *Angl.*, 35. 111-136, 249-270, 453-482 [1911], and 36.169-99 [1912] [Important Survey.]

Lawrence, W. W. *Beowulf and Epic Tradition*. Cambridge (Mass.), 1928. [An excellent summary of modern views on the subject-matter of *Beowulf*, intended for those who have little or no knowledge of O.E.]

Malone, K. "Beowulf" in *English Studies*, *XXIX*, pp. 161-172. [Studies content.]

Morsbach, L. "Zur Datierung des Beowulfepos" in *Nachrichten der K. Gesellschaft der Wissenschaften zu Göttingen, Philologisch-historische Klasse*, 1906. Pp. 251-77. [A linguistic discussion.]

Olrik, A. *The Heroic Legends of Denmark*. Translated and rev. with the Collaboration of the Author, by L. M. Hollander. New York, 1919. [Important for legendary background.]

Phillpotts, B. S. "Wyrd and Providence in Anglo-Saxon Thought" in *Essays and Studies*, 13.7–27. 1928.

Schücking, L. "Das Königsideal im Beowulf" in *E. St.*, 67.1–14. 1932.

Stjerna, K. *Essays on Questions connected with the Old English Poem of Beowulf.* Translated and edited by J. R. C. Hall. Coventry, 1912. [Includes interesting and important articles on archaeological matters in the poem.]

Tolkien, J. R. R. "Beowulf: the Monsters and the Critics" in *Proc. of the British Academy.* London, 1936. [Stimulating article of literary criticism.]

Woolf, H. B. "On the Characterisation of *Beowulf*" in *E.L.H.*, 15.85–92. 1948.

2. JUDITH

Only the concluding portion, totalling 350 ll, and perhaps representing only one quarter of the original, of this late Christian epic has survived. The fragment, divided into Fittes, is found, in the W.S. dialect, on ff. 202a–209b of the MS., and was written by the second scribe of the immediately preceding *Beowulf*. The theme is the slaying (scarcely "murder") of Holofernes, leader of Nebuchadnezzar's Assyrian hosts investing the Jewish city of Bethulia, by the beautiful Jewess, Judith, and the subsequent raising of the siege and defeat of the invaders. The source is the Latin version of the apocryphal *Book of Judith*, but there is much amplification.

Although the subject-matter is Christian (in the Old-Testament sense), the treatment is pagan: no O.E. Christian poem is so essentially heroic. The author is partially successful in his portrayal of character (e.g., Judith and Holofernes), but much more so in point of emotions (e.g., the hesitancy of Holofernes's retinue, ll. 246–84), actions (e.g., the homicide, 73b–121), and scenes (e.g., the carousal, 15–34a). He also clearly reveals his power over his medium, particularly in his effective and contrasting use of passages in long and short lines. End-rhyme, too, is rather frequent. Late as is the date of composition (probably tenth century), the diction compares most favourably with that of the earlier epics. Lastly, the fragment is ably constructed and throughout highly dramatic.

Bibliography.

C.B.E.L., 1.78–9.

H. & B., 83.

Text.

Cook, A. S. *Judith, an Old English Epic Fragment.* Boston, 1904.
[With full apparatus and a tr.]
Grein-Wülker, *Poesie II*, 294–314.

Translations.

Gordon, *A. S. Poetry*, 352–8.

Discussion.

Förster, M. *Die Beowulf-Handschrift.* Leipzig, 1919.
Forster, T. G. *Judith: Studies in Metre, Language and Style.* Strassburg, 1892.
Rypins, S. I. "A Contribution to the Study of the Beowulf Codex" in *P.M.L.A.*, 36.167–85. 1921. [A study of the orthography of the two scribes.]
Sisam, K. "The Beowulf Manuscript" in *M.L.R.*, 11.335–7. 1916. [Important note on the scribes and their work.]
Tupper, F. "Notes on Old English Poems" in *J.E.G.Ph.*, 11.82–9. 1912. [On the home of the *Judith*.]

METRES OF BOETHIUS

The *De Consolatione Philosophiae* (522–5) of Boethius consists of alternate *Prosae* and *Metra*. The latter have come down to us, indirectly, in an A.S. metrical redaction, which, in Krapp's recent edition (below), comprises thirty-one irregular sections, amounting to just over 1750 ll. of verse.

It is generally agreed that Boethius's famous work was translated (with several omissions) by K. Alfred into prose and his rendering is to-day represented by MS. Bodley 180, dating from the beginning of the twelfth century. Later on it appears that those passages which in Alfred's prose translation corresponded to the *Metra* were turned into verse, very probably by Alfred himself, whereupon the verses were introduced into the A.S. translation as substitutes for their prose counterparts. Hence there came into existence a new "composite text of the Anglo-Saxon prose, as in the older version, and the Latin Meters represented by Anglo-Saxon verse" (Krapp, ib., xxxvi). This redaction survives in the B.M. MS. Cotton Otho A.VI (c. 970), which was badly damaged in the Cottonian fire of 1731. Fortunately, however, Junius (p. 205, below), in the seventeenth century made a manuscript copy of the Bodl. MS. that is still extant in the Bodleian and known as MS. Junius 12. Into this he inserted, at the appropriate places, copies of several metres from the Cotton MS. A number of these insertions, all of which were pasted in on odd sheets, now have the additional value of being the sole authority for the text, because many leaves of the Cotton MS. are either in fragments or otherwise illegible.

If the *Metres* were written by Alfred, they may have been composed about 897, or shortly afterwards. Several critics, however, consider they are of too inferior quality to come from the hand of the king.

Bibliography.
C.B.E.L., 1.87.
H. & B., 62.
Krapp, G. P.   *The Paris Psalter and the Metres of Boethius.* London, 1933. Pp. li-lv. [Indispensable ed., with valuable introd. and notes.]

Editions.
Grein-Wülker.   *Poesie IIIb,* 1–57.
Krämer, E.   *Die altenglischen Metra des Boetius. Bonner Beitr. VIII.* Bonn, 1902. [With full apparatus.]
Krapp (above).
Sedgefield, W. J.   *King Alfred's Old English Version of Boethius De Consolatione Philosophiae.* Oxford, 1899.

Translations.
Sedgefield, W. J.   *King Alfred's Versions of the Consolations of Boethius, done into Modern English, with an Introduction.* Oxford, 1900.

Discussion.
Browne, G. F.   *King Alfred's Books.* London, 1920. Pp. 263–390.

CÆDMON (d. 670–80)

The sole original authority for our knowledge of Cædmon, the first English poet, is Bede (*Ecclesiastical History,* translated by A. M. Sellar, Bk. IV, Chap. XXIV; q.v.). Very briefly we are told that Cædmon was an untaught herdsman at the monastery at Streoneshalh (present-day Whitby) under the rule (657–80) of the Abbess Hild, and that one night in his later years he had a dream during which he was divinely inspired to compose a poem on the Creation. Bede then gives us a paraphrase of it. Versions of it still survive. It is universally known as *Cædmon's Hymn.* Hild then received him into the monastery and had him instructed in the Old and New Testaments. All that he here learned, he turned into verse. "He sang the creation of the world, the origin of man, and all the history of Genesis, the departure of the children of Israel out of Egypt, their entrance into the promised land, and many other histories from Holy Scripture; the Incarnation, Passion, Resurrection of our Lord, and His Ascension into Heaven: the coming of the Holy Ghost, and the teaching of the Apostles; likewise he made many songs concerning the terror of future judgment; besides many more about the blessings and the judgments of God, by all of which he endeavoured to draw men away from the love of sin, and to excite in them devotion to well-doing and perseverance therein." Now there exists in the *Junius MS.* a series of four poems, the first three of which (viz., *Genesis, Exodus* and *Daniel*) are certainly not only narratives, but also didactic in tone. The fourth and last, *Christ and Satan*, however, is very different. Whether it be a unity or a group of three distinct poems, all will agree that it is unlike the other pieces in the MS. in point of theme, style and diction; and further, that it is not narrative, but rather lyrical in treatment. In 1655, in the first edition of the *Junius MS.*, Franciscus Junius or Dujon, struck by the correspondence of the subject-matter of its contents with the topics of the (unnamed and unspecified) poems credited to Cædmon by Bede, had no hesitation in allotting all four poems to Cædmon. Although with the exception of Gollancz (*Cædmon Manuscript* [below], lx), modern critics seem unwilling to accept Cædmon's authorship, the MS. is still often referred to as the "Cædmon MS.", and the poems, as the "Cædmon Poems" Indeed, the only poem universally attributed to him to-day is the above-mentioned *Hymn*. For an account of this, see p. 169, and of the four poems of the *Junius MS.*, see pp. 207–10.

M. Förster (*Keltisches Wortgut im Englischen*, Halle, 1921, p. 179) derives Cædmon's name from British *Catumannos*.

Bibliography.
C.B.E.L., 1.73.
H. & B., 63.
Kennedy, C. W. *The Cædmon Poems, translated into English Prose.* London, 1916. Pp. 252–3.

Discussion.
Consult the more recent histories of literature. See also *Encycl. Brit.*, and especially *D.N.B.* (article by H. Bradley) for a summary discussion of the poet and his authorship.
Wrenn, C. L. *The Poetry of Cædmon.* London, 1947.

CÆDMON'S HYMN

Cædmon's *Hymn*, the only poem now universally acknowledged to be the work of the Northumbrian poet (d. 670–80, see further, p. 167), contains only 18 half ll. Although nine of these are recorded elsewhere in O.E. verse, it must be remembered that "in Cædmon's time when Northumbria had been converted to Christianity for only half a century these phrases belonging to Christian poetry could scarcely have become conventional, as they certainly were in later Old English" (Smith, ed. below, 15). Short as it is, the piece contains eight synonyms for God.

The *Hymn* is embodied in the text of nine MSS. of the O.E. version of Bede's *Historia Ecclesiastica*, four of which preserve a Northumbrian version and the other five a later, W.S. version. The seven MSS. (one now lost, and the two earliest dating from c. 740) of the Latin version of the *Historia* do not, however, contain the *Hymn* as an integral part of the text, but only as an entry in the margin or at the foot of the page. The Latin text, indeed, includes only a paraphrase of the *Hymn*, followed by an explanatory note on this paraphrastic rendering and on translation. Naturally this note has been omitted from the O.E. MSS. as being irrelevant.

Bibliography.
C.B.E.L., 1.73.
H. & B., 63–4.
Smith, A. H.   *Three Northumbrian Poems, Cædmon's Hymn, Bede's Death Song, and the Leiden Riddle.* London, 1933. *Methuen's Old English Library A 1.* Pp. 48–50. [Gives both Northumbrian and West Saxon versions, with complete apparatus. Excellent.]

Facsimiles.
Cædmon's Hymn (Moore MS.): Palaeographical Society, First Series, Vol. II, Plate 140. London, 1879.
Dobiache-Rojdestvensky, O. "Cædmon's Hymn (Leningrad MS.)" in *Speculum,* 3.316. 1928.

Editions.
Dobiache-Rojdestvensky (above).
Frampton, M. G. "Cædmon's Hymn" in *M.Ph.,* 22. 1–15. 1924. [Valuable account of relationships of the various versions.]
Gollancz, *Cædmon MS.,* xi.
Sedgefield. *Bk. A.S.V.P.,* 80–1.
Smith (above).

Wuest, P. *Z. f. d. A.*, 48.205 ff. 1904. [With important textual discussion.]

Translations.

Cook and Tinker, *Trans. O. E. Poetry*, 77; Gordon, *A.S. Poetry*, x; Kennedy, *Cædmon's Poems*, 3; Wardale, 113.

Discussion.

Dobbie, E. v. K. *The Manuscripts of Cædmon's Hymn and Bede's Death Song.* New York, 1937.

Pound, L. "Cædmon's Dream Song" in *Studies in English Philology presented to F. Klaeber.* Minneapolis, 1929.

Sievers, E. "Cædmon und Genesis" in *Britannica, Max Förster zum 60. Geburtstage.* Leipzig, 1929.

Note also Frampton, Gollancz, Smith and Wuest, above.

CHARMS

Preserved in unique copies and distributed over several MSS., eight metrical *Charms* constitute the sole relics of the religious poetry of the pagan period. In primitive times, charms were widely used with the intention of promoting fertility and prosperity and of averting evil in any shape or form. The surviving O.E. examples display such a remarkable confusion of Christian and heathen elements—in the main the procedure is heathen and the incantation Christian—that they can only have been written down late in the O.E. period. Their contents, not their literary qualities, render them valuable.

Bibliography.
C.B.E.L., 1.98.
H. & B., 67–8.

Text.

Cockayne, *Leechdoms*, 1.384–405, 3.286–91 and 294–5. [With translation.]

Grein-Wülker. *Poesie I*, 312–30.

Grendon, F. *Anglo-Saxon Charms.* New York, 1931. [With Bibliography, Introduction and critical apparatus. Authoritative and indispensable.]

Storms, G. *Anglo-Saxon Magic.* The Hague, 1948. [Pt. I discusses general problems; Pt. II contains texts of 86 charms, with translation and detained analysis.]

Translations.

Cook and Tinker, *Trans. O. E. Poetry*, 164–71; Gordon, *A.S. Poetry*, 94–104; Gummere, *O.E. Epic.*

Discussion.

Payne, J. F. *English Medicine in the Anglo-Saxon Times.* Oxford, 1904.

Skemp, A. R. *"The Old English Charms"* in *M.L.R.*, 6.289–301. 1911. [Interpretative, textual and metrical notes.]

Singer, C. *From Magic to Science.* London, 1928. [See Chaps. II–IV.]

ANGLO-SAXON CHRONICLE

Embedded in the annals of the various MSS. of the *Chronicle* are seven commemorative poems or lays of varying length. By far the most successful is the stirring piece known as the *Battle of Brunanburh*, which in respect of diction is occasionally reminiscent of the *Judith* fragment (p. 165). Of the others, all unpretentious, some are noteworthy as evidencing the growing interest in rhythmical verse linked by rhyme and assonance.

It should be noted that the *Chronicle* also contains several passages of "sung verse", the first, and best, of these occurring in the *Laud MS.*, *s.a.* 959. They may, however, be more suitably regarded as pieces of "poetical prose". See further Sedgefield, *Maldon*, xx–xxi, *C.H.E.L.*, 1.137–41, and Brandl §§ 86–8.

The poems dealt with below comprise the *Battle of Brunanburh* (*s.a.* 937), *Liberation of the Five Boroughs* (942), *Coronation of Edgar* (973), *Death of Edgar* (975), *Alfred's Capture and Death* (1036), *Death of Edward the Confessor* (1065), *and William the Conqueror* (1087).

1. THE BATTLE OF BRUNANBURH

In 937, at *Brunanburh*, possibly the modern Burnswark, near Dumfries, King Athelstan and all the might of England won a notable victory over Anlaf and Olaf Guthfrithson, King of Dublin and claimant to the throne of York, and his allies, Constantine II, King of the Scots, and Owen, King of the Strathclyde Britons. Shortly afterwards, an anonymous poet, perhaps a native of the Danelaw, composed this spirited song of triumph. The poem, 74 ll. in all, is preserved in 5 MSS. of the *Anglo-Saxon Chronicle* under the year 937, and is the first of its seven versified annals. Curiously, perhaps, the writer names none of the warriors, only the leaders; neither does he report the details of the battle or any speeches. Presumably he was not an eye-witness. Nor in this connexion is there any significance in the specific reference to the presence of the raven, the eagle and the wolf, which feed upon the slain: these are the conventional attendants of the battlefield in A.S., as well as in O.N., poetical literature. Another traditional feature is the diction: "nearlv one-half of its half-lines have been found in earlier A.S. poetry" (Wyatt, 277). A new note, however, is struck by the element of patriotism (cf. *The Battle of Maldon*, p. 212, below), as well as the depth of feeling.

Controversy still centres round the site of the battle-ground.

Bibliography.
C.B.E.L., 1.84.
H. & B., 63.

Editions.
Campbell, A.   *The Battle of Brunanburh*. London, 1938. [With full critical apparatus.]
Crow, C. L.   *Maldon and Brunanburh*. Boston, 1897.
Kershaw, 66–70 (with translation, as well as useful introductory matter and bibliography, pp. 59–65).
Sedgefield, W. J.   *The Battle of Maldon and Short Poems from the Saxon Chronicle*. London, 1904. [Full apparatus.]
N.B.   Several anthologies include the text and useful notes.

Translations.
Gordon.   *A.S. Poetry*, 359–60; Hall, *Jud. Phoen. Mald.*, 57–9.

Discussion.
Angus, W. S.   "*The Battlefield of Brunanburh*" in *Antiquity*, 11.283–93. 1937. [Assigns to Brunswark.]
Klaeber, F.   "A Note on the Battle of Brunanburh" in *Palaestra*, Vol. CL, pp. 1–7. 1925. [Literary criticism.]
Smith, A. H.   "The Site of the Battle of Brunanburh" in *London Medieval Studies*. Vol. I, Part I, 56–9. [Presses claims of Bromborough in Cheshire, but does not rule out Brunswark.]

2. LIBERATION OF THE FIVE BOROUGHS

In 14, metrically correct, but mainly unpoetical lines, this poem with patriotic fervour celebrates the over-running of Mercia by Edmund, *Engla peoden*, and his (only temporary) relief of the Five Boroughs from the oppression of the Norsemen. The text forms part of the entry for 942.

Bibliography.
C.B.E.L., 1.84.
H. & B., 80.

Text.

Classen-Harmer, 46–7.

Craigie. *Specimens III*, 30.

Earle-Plummer. *Sax. Chron.*, 1.110.

Grein-Wülker. *Poesie I*, 380–1.

Mawer, A. "The Redemption of the Five Boroughs" in *E.H.R.*, 38.551–7. 1923. [With translation and important historico-linguistic discussions.]

Sedgefield. *Maldon*, 20–1. [An ed. with full apparatus.]

Translations.

Chambers, *Engl. Norm. Con.*, 240; Mawer (above).

3. CORONATION OF EDGAR

Under the year 973, the *Chronicle* commemorates King Edgar's Coronation at Bath with a poem of 20 ll. What seemed to give the author most pleasure, however, was the presence there of a large body of clerics and the fact that with the lapse of 27 years. it would be A.D. 1000 (the expected end of the World).

Bibliography.

C.B.E.L., 1.84.

H. & B., 77.

Text.

Craigie. *Specimens III*, 30.

Earle-Plummer. *Sax. Chron.*, 1.118.

Grein-Wülker. *Poesie I*, 381–2.

Sedgefield. *Maldon*, 21–2. [Full apparatus.]

Translation.

Wardale, 228.

4. DEATH OF EDGAR

The whole of the entry for 975 in the Parker MS. is made up of 37 ll. of verse, which, though undoubtedly from a monkish pen, preserve several reminiscences of the traditional epic diction. The poem records the deaths of King Edgar and Bishop Cyneweard (ll. 1–15), the decline of religion in Mercia, the banishment of Earl Oslac, the appearance of a comet, and lastly the prevailing famine. Lines 16 to the end form the more spirited portion of the poem.

Bibliography.

H. & B., 77.

Text.

Classen-Harmer, 50; Craigie, *Specimens III,* 31; Earle-Plummer,

> *Sax. Chron.*, 1.118–22; Sedgefield, *Maldon*, 22–4 (with apparatus).

Translations.
Thorpe, *A.S.C.*, 2.97–8.

5. ALFRED'S CAPTURE AND DEATH

The 20 ll. of this poem forming part of the entry for 1036 and notable for the absence of alliteration and the frequency with which the half-lines are linked by rhyme and assonance—conclusive evidence of the growing interest in rhymed verse—tell of Godwine's savage treatment, and the subsequent death, of Alfred, the son of King Aethelred.

Bibliography.
C.B.E.L., 1.84.
H. & B., 54.

Text.
Classen-Harmer, 70–1; Craigie, *Specimens III*, 32; Earle-Plummer, *Sax. Chron.*, 1.158–60; Grein-Wülker, *Poesie I*, 384–5; Sedgefield, *Maldon*, 24–6 (full apparatus).

Translations.
Chambers, *Engl. Norm. Con.*, 286–7; Thorpe, *A.S.C.*, 2.129–30.

6. DEATH OF EDWARD THE CONFESSOR

This poem of 34 ll. is the last example in the *Chronicle* of the old alliterative measure. It records the death of Edward the Confessor, lauds his glorious reign and tells of his exile (necessitated by King Cnut) and welcome return, the loyalty of his subjects, and finally of how he had settled the kingdom upon his trusty subject, Harold.

Bibliography.
C.B.E.L., 1.84.
H. & B., 77–8.

Text.
Classen-Harmer, 84–5; Craigie, *Specimens III*, 32–3; Earle-Plummer, *Sax. Chron.*, Vol. I, 192–5; Grein-Wülker, *Poesie I*, 386–8; Sedgefield, *Maldon*, 26-7, (with apparatus); Sedgefield, *Bk. A.S. V.P.*, 121-2.

Translations.
Thorpe, *A.S.C.*, Vol. II, 164.

7. WILLIAM THE CONQUEROR

This poem tells of William's greed and his cruel game-laws. Its main interest, however, lies in the author's employment of a "rugged metre" for his 22 ll., which, while here and there interrupted by one or two lines of prose, rhyme in pairs.

Bibliography.
H. & B., 93.

Text.
Earle-Plummer, *Sax. Chron.*, Vol. I, pp. 220–1; Sedgefield, *Bk. A.S. V.P.*, pp. 123–4; Sedgefield, *Maldon*, pp. 30–1.

Translations.
Thorpe, *A.S.C.*, 2.189–90.

CYNEWULF

Very little is known of the poet Cynewulf apart from either what he himself tells or what can be deduced from his four signed poems. None of these, like the earlier Christian poetry (e.g., *Genesis*, *Exodus and Daniel*), are mere metrical narratives based on the Bible, but rather connected with events celebrated in the Church Calendar. The poems comprise in the probable order of composition, *Juliana*, the *Fates of the Apostles*, *Elene*, and the *Ascension*, the middle one of the 3 poems often conveniently called *Christ*. All of these are extant in unique (predominantly W.S.) transcripts (see further pp. 183, 219, 223, 179 respectively).

At one time or another, almost all the notable O.E. poems that could not reasonably be ascribed to Cædmon, have been allotted to Cynewulf. The proof of his authorship, however, is contained in the personal passages at the conclusion of all four poems. Into each of these epilogues he has introduced a set of runes which together spell out *Cyn(e)wulf*. From the authographical form of the name it has been inferred that its owner wrote in the ninth century. Again, metrical (evidence of rhyme in *Elene*, 1241) and linguistic considerations presuppose that he was an Anglian. His Latin sources, as well as his religious themes, adequately testify to competent scholarship, and also to his ecclesiastical vocation. From the longest and much the most informative of all the personal passages, viz., *Elene*, 1237–57, we learn of "his conversion to a life of religious contemplation, his learning which he employs in searching out and piecing together the true tale of the cross, which he has just narrated,

175

his poetic powers which find their spring in religious thought, and finally old age pressing hard upon him with sorrow and decay" [Kennedy, *Cædmon*, 11–12].

Although his poems are structurally loose and never sustained upon a high level, he often writes with fine imaginative power: he excels in portraying scenery, especially (though perhaps without actual experience) sea and storm. On the other hand, his battle scenes are only conventional. "The subjective note is everywhere prominent and the poet is interested, first and foremost, in ideas and emotions" (Thomas, *Engl. Lit.*, 22). The style is that of a "man trained to read and write Latin, to admire the orderly progress of a Latin sentence, and to prefer its clarity to the tangled profusion of the native style" [Sisam (below), 15].

Bibliography.
C.B.E.L., 1.75–6.
H. & B., 68–9.

Discussion.
Brown, C. F. "Cynewulf and Alcuin" in *P.M.L.A.*, 18.308–34. 1903.
Brown, C. F. "The Autobiographical Element in the Cynewulfian Rune Passages" in *E.St.*, 38.196–233. 1907.
Brown, C. F. "Irish-Latin Influence in Cynewulfian Texts" in *E.St.*, 40.1–29. 1909.
Das, S. K. *Cynewulf and the Cynewulf Canon.* Univ. of Calcutta, 1942.
Jansen, K. *Die Cynewulf-forschung von ihren Anfängen bis zur Gegenwart.* Bonn, 1908. [Discussion of Cynewulfian studies. Bibliography to date excellent.]
Kennedy, C. W. *The Poems of Cynewulf, translated into English Prose.* London, 1910. [Includes both signed poems and allegedly Cynewulfian poems, together with a valuable introductory account of each and their authorship. Full, but selective bibliography.]
Sisam, K. "Cynewulf and his Poetry" in *Proc. of Brit. Acad.*, Vol. XXVIII, 1932. [An excellent survey of the canon and of the runic signature. Indispensable.]
Trautmann, M. *Kynewulf, Der Bischof und Dichter.* Bonn, 1898.
Tupper, F. "The Philological Legend of Cynewulf" in *P.M.L.A.*, 26.235–79. 1911.

IN PRAISE OF DURHAM

Specially noteworthy as the latest surviving example (composed shortly after 1104 and before 1109, hence, in point of time, M.E.) of the traditional alliterative poetry, this poem of 21 ll. (preserved in 2 MSS.) firstly (ll. 1–8) praises Durham's lofty site, encircled by the Wear, and the abundance both of fish in the river and of wild animals in the neighbouring forests and, secondly, mentions that in the monastery are preserved relics of the Northern saints, Cuthbert, Aidan, Eadberht, Eadfrith, Aethelwold, Bede and Boisil. The author was certainly a monk.—See also Wells, X [25].

Bibliography.
C.B.E.L., 1.84.
H. & B., 77.

Text.
Craigie. *Specimens III*, 42.
Grein-Wülker. *Poesie* I, 389–92.

Discussion.
Schlauch, M. "An O.E. Encomium Urbis" in *J.E.G.Ph.*, Jan., 1941. [Refers back to classical prototypes and discusses parallels.]
Oakden, *Allit. Poetry*, 41-2, 136. [Metre.]

THE EXETER BOOK

The *Exeter Book* (or *Codex Exoniensis*, or *Liber Exoniensis*), the largest of the four great MSS. collections of O.E. poetry, is preserved in the Library at Exeter Cathedral, to which, so we may believe, it was presented, with others, by Leofric, the first bishop of Exeter, who died in 1072. It now consists of 131 parchment leaves, but the first eight (for contents see *The Exeter Book of Old English Poetry* [below] 44–54), were added not earlier than the sixteenth century. The folios were numbered 1 to 130, the first, on which there is no text, not being counted. The last fourteen folios have been damaged by a long diagonal burn, which, beginning on the last folio, where there is a resultant gap almost three inches across at its widest point, is traceable as far forward as fol. 117a. As a consequence lacunæ begin to appear in the text at 117b, and become increasingly numerous towards the end of the MS. Folios 8–130 contain the *Exeter Book* proper. It was written (without ornamentation of any kind) in a monastery "in the West Country early in the period 970–90" (ib., 90), perhaps by only one scribe. The dialect is L.W.S. with an Anglian colouring. The magnificent photographic facs. of the *Book* published (1933) by the Dean and Chapter of Exeter Cathedral (see below), provides the student with an excellent opportunity of studying a noble Old English "manuscript".

The texts included in the *Book* comprise the following, the titles as well as the line references below being taken from the recent edition of Krapp and Dobbie (below):—Christ, Guthlac, Azarias, The Phoenix, Juliana, The Wanderer, The Gifts of Men, Precepts, The Seafarer, Vainglory, Widsith, The Fortunes of Men, Maxims I, The Order of the World, The Riming Poem, The Panther, The Whale, The Partridge, Soul and Body II, Deor, Wulf and Eadwacer, Riddles 1–59, The Wife's Lament, The Judgment Day I, Resignation, The Descent into Hell, Alms-Giving, Pharaoh, The Lord's Prayer I, Homiletic Fragment II, Riddle 30b, Riddle 60, The Husband's Message, The Ruin, Riddles 61–95. All these texts are anonymous unless a statement is made to the contrary in the discussions below.

Bibliography.
C.B.E.L., 1.62.

Krapp, G. P., and Dobbie, E. v. K. *The Exeter Book*. London, 1936. Pp. lxxxix-cxvii. [The Bibliography is to some extent selective, but entirely adequate. Text based on facs. ed. (below). Also contains valuable introds. and notes. Indispensable.]

The Exeter Book of Old English Poetry, with Introductory Chapters, by Chambers, R. W., Förster, M., and Flower, R. Printed and published for the Dean and Chapter of Exeter Cathedral. London, 1933. [For a bibliography of the standard editions in which the various poems are to be found, see 37–43. Chapters:—*The Exeter Book* and its Donor Leofric, by Chambers, 1–9; The Donations of Leofric to Exeter, by Förster, 10–32; Modern Study of the Poetry of *The Exeter Book*, by Chambers, 33–43; The Preliminary Matter of *The Exeter Book*, by Förster, 44–54; General Description of the Manuscript, by Förster, 55–67; Transcription of the Damaged Passages of *The Exeter Book*, by Chambers and Flower, 68–82; The Script of *The Exeter Book*, Notes on the Sixteenth-Century Glosses, and on The Strips from the Binding, by Flower, 83–94.]

Complete Editions.

Gollancz, I. *The Exeter Book—edited from the Manuscript with a Translation*, etc. Part I. Poems I–VIII. London, 1895. E.E.T.S., 104. [Continued by Mackie's ed. (below). No apparatus.]

Krapp and Dobbie (above). [Also lists anthologies containing separate poems and partial texts, xc–xcvi.]

Mackie, W. S. *The Exeter Book. Part II. Poems IX–XXXII*. London, 1934. E.E.T.S., 194. [With two reduced facs., translation facing each page of text. Text based on MS., collated with facs., ed., above. No apparatus.]

Thorpe, B. *Codex Exoniensis*. London, 1842. [With translations. Omits Riddles 67, 78, 82, 89, 92, 94.]

Translations.

Gollancz (above); Gordon, *A.S. Poetry, passim*; Mackie (above); Thorpe (above).

Discussion.

See especially the introductory chapters by Chambers, Förster and Flower in *The Exeter Book of Old English Poetry* (above). Consult, too, the excellent bibliography in Krapp and Dobbie's ed. (above), pp. xcix–cxvii.

1. CHRIST (fol. 8a–32a)

Christ is the conventional title of the first 1664 ll. of *The Exeter Book* proper. The first folio of the original text has apparently been lost. The MS. seems to divide the text intentionally into three parts, viz., ll. 1–439, 440–866 and 867–1664.

Part I comprises twelve short passages, hymnic in tone, on the Nativity and chiefly based on a series of ecclesiastical Antiphons for Advent; Part II is a narrative of the Ascension, founded in the main on a sermon on the Ascension by Pope Gregory the Great; Part III, derived from a variety of sources, is concerned with the Day of Judgment. Hence the respective titles: *Advent, The Ascension*, and *Judgment Day*.

Whether we have here to deal with three poems or one, and with triple or single authorship, is still in dispute. Since, however, Cynewulf's runic signature occurs in ll. 800–7 in Part II, the authorship of at least this section seems beyond doubt. Note that Sisam is fully convinced that the Parts form separate poems, and that Cynewulf may possibly be the author of *Advent*, but certainly not of *Judgment Day*.

There are many first-rate passages, e.g., ll. 604–11 on the gifts of Nature and ll. 850–66 on the perils of the sea.

Bibliography.

C.B.E.L., 1.76.

Cook, A. S. *The Christ of Cynewulf, with Introduction, Notes and Glossary*. Boston, 1900. Pp. 295 ff.

H. & B., 70.

Separate Editions.

Cook (above). 1–64.

Gollancz, I. *Cynewulf's Christ, with a Modern Rendering.* London, 1892.

Grein-Wülker. *Poesie III*, 1–54.

Translations.

Gordon, *A. S. Poetry*, 147–81; Kennedy (above), 153–204; Whitman, C. H., *The Christ of Cynewulf*, Boston, 1900.

Discussion.

Blackburn, F. A. "Is the *Christ* of Cynewulf a single poem?" in *Angl.*, 19.89–98. 1897. [Believes that the three parts are separate poems.]

Gerould, G. H. "Studies in the Christ" in *E.St.*, 41.1–19. 1909 [Not convinced that there are three separate poems. Ascribes the whole to Cynewulf.]

Jansen, 70–7.

Kennedy. *Cynewulf*, 27–34.

Mildenberger, K. "The Unity of Cynewulf's *Christ* in the Light of Iconography" in *Speculum*, 23.426–431. 1948. [Claims unity of the three parts.]

Moore, S. "The O.E. *Christ*. Is it a Unit?" in *J.E.G.Ph.*, 14. 550-67. 1915. [Considers Parts I and II are integrants, but is doubtful of unity of II and III.]

Philip, A. "The Exeter Scribe and the Unity of the *Christ*" in *P.M.L.A.*, 50.903–909. 1940. [Believes the three parts are separate poems.]

Sisam, K. *Cynewulf and His Poetry*, Oxford, 1932. 9–11.

2. GUTHLAC (fol. 33a–52b)

Guthlac, the life of the Mercian saint, Guthlac, in 1,379 ll. of verse, is usually regarded as being two poems by different authors. though this is still disputed. The first twenty-nine lines may be part of the *Christ*, which precedes it in the MS., or even a separate work, and editors' line-numbers vary accordingly. The next section of 789 ll., telling of Guthlac's adventurous youth, conversion, and life in his hermitage at Croyland, is apparently by a contemporary and based on oral tradition, though it may be from the Latin *Life* written (747–9) by Felix, monk of Croyland, used by the author of Part II, the theme of which is the death of Guthlac. This begins at line 819 and is defective at the end. It may be Cynewulf's, and is in any case a more artistic poem—

note especially the description of night, ll. 1278–95, and Guthlac's entry into heaven, 1305–30. The eleventh century W.S. prose *Life*, edited by P. Gonser, Heidelberg, 1909, derives also from Felix, but not from the poem or poems.

Bibliography.
C.B.E.L., 1.78.
H. & B., 72–3.

Edition.
Grein-Wülker. *Poesie IIIa*, 55–94.

Translations.
Gordon, *A.S. Poetry*, 284–309; Kennedy, *Cynewulf*, 264–305.

Discussion.
Forstmann, H. *Untersuchungen zur Guthlac-legende*. Bonn, 1902. [Pp. 1–40.]
Gerould, G. H. "The Old English Poems on St. Guthlac and their Latin Source," in *M.L.N.*, 32.77–89. 1917.
Jansen, 99–105.
Kurtz, B. P. *From St. Anthony to St. Guthlac. A Study in Biography*. Berkeley (U.S.A.), 1925–6.

3. AZARIAS (fol. 53a–55b)

In its present version, *Azarias* (191 ll.) contains the *Prayer of Azariah* and the *Song of the Three Children* set in a narrative framework. One or more sections at the beginning are missing. The first 75 ll. (i.e., the initial portion) of the Prayer correspond fairly closely with ll. 279–356 (also containing *Azariah's Prayer*) of the *Daniel* (p. 209), thus giving rise to various conjectures about their mutual relationship.

Bibliography.
C.B.E.L., 1.74.
H. & B., 55

Separate Editions.
Grein-Wülker. *Poesie II*, 491–7, 516–20.
Schmidt, W. *Die altenglischen Dichtungen "Daniel" und "Azarias"*. Bonn, 1907. Pp. 40–8. [Bibliography, text and notes.]

Translations.
See editions of *Ex. Bk.*

Discussion.
Brandl, §41.

Craigie, W. A. *Philologica*, 2.11 ff.
Gollancz, *Cædmon MS.*, lxxxvi–lxxxvii.
Hofer, O. "Über die Entstehung des angelsächsischen Gedichtes *Daniel*" in *Angl.*, 12.158–204. 1889. [Pp. 184–91 analyse in detail the relationship of *Azarias* to *Daniel*.]

4. THE PHOENIX (fol. 55b–65b)

The Phoenix, a complete poem of 677 ll. without problems of transposition or interpolation, divides naturally at l. 381. Part I freely paraphrases the Latin poem *De Ave Phoenice* (of 170 hexameters) attributed to Lactantius (early Christian writer, *ob.* c. 340). It first tells of the Happy Land, the home of the Phoenix (ll. 1–84—a memorable passage), after which the poet describes the bird's beauty, its journey, in old age, to Syria in order to renew its youth, and the actual process of its rebirth. Part II is a homiletic interpretation (source unknown) of the theme of Part I, in which the Phoenix is made to symbolise, firstly, the life of the Christian and his preparation for the Life Eternal, and secondly, the figure of Christ. The concluding eleven lines are macaronic, each combining half a line of O.E. with half a line of Latin, linked by alliteration conventionally. The authorship is often, though purely on stylistic grounds, attributed to Cynewulf or to one of his school.

Bibliography.
C.B.E.L., 1.77–8.
H. & B., 73–4.

Editions.
Bright, *A.S. Reader*, 165–88.
Cook, A. S. *The Old English Elene, Phoenix and Physiologus*. New Haven, 1919. Pp. 47–73.
Grein-Wülker. *Poesie IIIa*, 95–116.
Schlotterose, O. *Die altenglische Dichtung "Phoenix"*. Bonn, 1908. [With German translation and full apparatus.]

Translations.
Cook and Tinker, *Trans. O.E. Poetry*, 144–63; Hall, *Jud. Phoen. Mald.*, 19–42; Gordon, *A.S. Poetry*, 265–79; Kennedy, *Cynewulf*, 312–32.

Discussion.
Cook (above), xxv–lvi. [Assigns preferably to Cynewulf, or else to one of his school.]

Emerson, O. F. "Originality in O.E. Poetry", in *R.E.S.*, 2. 18–31. 1926. [Careful and authoritative study of poet's treatment of his sources.]

Jansen, 105–8

Schlotterose (above), 78–92.

5. JULIANA (fol. 65b–76a)

Juliana is a poem on the life of the saint in 731 ll. Owing to the loss of certain folios, there are two large gaps at ll. 288 and 558. It is usually regarded as an early, if not the earliest, work of Cynewulf's—his runic signature is contained in ll. 703–09. The source is identical with, or similar to, the Latin life in the Bollandist (see *Encycl. Brit.*, s.v.) *Acta Sanctorum*.

The story in brief is as follows. In the reign of Maximilian (308–14), Juliana, a maiden of Nicomedia and a daughter of Africanus, a persecutor of Christians, is wooed by the Roman Prefect Eleusius. When she rejects his love because of his refusal to accept Christianity, Eleusius, with her father's approval, endeavours to break down her opposition by incredible tortures. But Juliana's faith and fortitude are proof against all such persuasion, as well as sundry temptations by the devil. She is therefore slain with the sword. Shortly after, Eleusius is drowned at sea with all his retinue, thus receiving his due reward.

The poem is a good example of O.E. religious poetry in that it applies to sacred and saintly personages the old warlike epithets of the earlier heroic poetry. The treatment is undramatic and bookish, and the dialogue is dull.

Bibliography.

C.B.E.L., 1.76–7.

H. & B., 73.

Editions.

Grein-Wülker. *Poesie IIIa*, 117–39.

Strunk, W. *Juliana*. Boston, 1904. [Excellent apparatus. Includes the Latin *Acta S. Julianae*.]

Translations.

Gordon, *A.S. Poetry*, 182–96; Kennedy, *Cynewulf*, 129–152; Murch, H. S., *J.E.G.Ph.*, 5.303–19 (1904).

Discussion.

Kennedy, *Cynewulf*, 21–7.

Smithson, *Christian Epic*, passim.

6. THE WANDERER (fol. 76b–78a)

The theme of the first part of this very fine, elegiac poem of
111 ll. is the sorrow and sufferings of a homeless man who has
been deprived of his lord. The remainder, beginning at l. 58 and
gnomic in tone, is mainly concerned with the vicissitudes of life,
suggested by contemplation of a ruined building. Both the first
and last sections of 5 ll. (the latter are long) have a distinctly
Christian flavour.

Structurally, the poem invites comparison with the *Seafarer*
(p. 185): both begin with the treatment of a specific topic and conclude with sententious moralising on human life in general. The
old theory of composite origin now seems to be in disfavour.

Bibliography.
C.B.E.L., 1.70.
H. & B., 91

Editions.
  In various books of selections.
Grein-Wülker. *Poesie I*, 284–9.
Kershaw, 7–15. [With tr., also an excellent introd., 1–7.]
Sedgefield. *Bk. A.S. V.P.*, 28–31.
Wyatt. *A.S. Reader*, 144–7.
      NOTE.—An edition by J. R. R. Tolkien and the late E. V.
  Gordon is to appear in *Methuen's O.E. Library* series.

Translations.
Cook and Tinker, *Trans. O.E. Poetry*, 50–5; Gordon, *A.S. Poetry*,
  81–3.

Discussion.
Lawrence, W. W. "The Wanderer and the Seafarer," in
  J.E.G.Ph., 4.460–80. 1902.
Williams, B. C. *Gnomic Poetry in Anglo-Saxon Verse*. New York,
  1914. Pp. 42–7.

7. THE GIFTS OF MEN (fol. 78a–80a)

This poem of 113 ll. opens with a passage (1–29) on God's
bountifulness in so richly and circumspectly conferring his gifts
upon men, and thereupon proceeds to the enumeration of the
various gifts in considerable, but haphazard, detail. Though of
no particular literary merit, the wide range of its vocabulary is a
point in its favour. In connexion with the *Gifts of Men*, the student

should note the existence, in different parts of *The Exeter Book*, of the four following short poems :—*Vainglory*, the *Fortunes of Men*, the *Order of the World* and the *Judgment Day I* (see below). Some authorities regard these five as forming "a highly homogeneous collection of didactic or homiletic verse" (Krapp and Dobbie, above, xxxix). In each case, metre and language presuppose an early date of composition, either the end of the eighth, or at latest the beginning of the ninth century (ib., xlii).

Bibliography.
C.B.E.L., 1.81.
H. & B., 61.

Editions.
Craigie. *Specimens*, III, 64–6.
Grein-Wülker. *Poesie IIIa*, 140–3.
Sedgefield. *Bk. A.S. V.P.*, 106–9.

Translation.
Gordon. *A.S. Poetry*, 348–9.

8. PRECEPTS (A FATHER'S INSTRUCTIONS ; fol. 80a–81a)

This poem of 94 ll. comprises a series of ten admonitions on morals and manners addressed by a father to his son. A possible source is the *Proverbs* of Solomon. Essentially Christian in mood, the poem may have been written with didactic intentions by a cleric.

Bibliography.
C.B.E.L., 1.81.
H. & B., 78.

Editions.
Craigie. *Specimens III*, 51–3.
Grein-Wülker. *Poesie I*, 353–7.
Sedgefield. *Bk. A.S. V.P.*, 109–11.

9. THE SEAFARER (fol. 81b–83a)

The Seafarer (124 ll.) resembles *The Wanderer* (p. 184) in structure: both begin by treating a single theme and conclude with a moralising epilogue that is Christian in tone; and both have provoked critics to doubt their structural homogeneity. In vocabulary and phraseology, too, there are resemblances; but in matter and style they are very different—the atmosphere of *The Wanderer* is one of unrelieved gloom, whereas *The Seafarer* "breathes the true spirit of adventure" (Wardale, 43).

The first 64 ll. of *The Seafarer*—it contains passages of rare beauty—contrasts the hardships of the seafaring life with its joys. Some regard this part as a dialogue between an old sailor and a young one, but are unable to agree about the division of the speeches. Others, again, consider it a monologue spoken by an old sailor. From 64b to the end, the poem is concerned both with the transitoriness of earthly life and the vanity of its glories, and with the "eternal rewards of religion". Although it was formerly widely assumed that this second part was a later addition, modern opinion is inclined to the view that except for the last 21 ll., which is an undoubted Christian appendage, the poem as it now stands is essentially preserved in its original form.

Bibliography.
C.B.E.L., 1.70–1.
H. & B., 89.

Editions.
Craigie, *Specimens III*, 45–7.
Grein-Wülker. *Poesie I*, 290–5.
Kershaw, 20–6. [With tr.]
Sedgefield. *Bk. A.S. V.P.*, 32–4.
An edition by the late E. V. Gordon and J. R. R. Tolkien will appear in *Methuen's Old English Library* series.

Translations.
Bone, G., *The Seafarer*, in *Medium Aevum*, Vol. III (1934); Gordon, *A.S. Poetry*, 84–6.

Discussion.
Anderson, O. S. *The Seafarer: an Interpretation.* Lund, 1937. [An important and stimulating study, with translation and notes.]
Ferrell, C. C. "Old Germanic Life in the A.S. Wanderer and Seafarer" in *Z.f.d. Ph.*, 35.1–28. 1894.
Kershaw. 16–19.
Lawrence, W. W. *The Wanderer and the Seafarer*, in *J.E.G.Ph.*, 4.460–80. 1902.
Williams. *Gnomic Poetry*, 47–9.

10. VAINGLORY (A WARNING AGAINST PRIDE ; fol. 83a–84b)

This is a short poetical homily of 84 ll. against arrogance, and partly against drunkenness. It has an autobiographical introduction of 8 ll. No single source for the poem has been detected. Additional variant titles are *The Spirit of Men*, *The Mind of Man* and *Bi Manna Mode*.

Bibliography.
C.B.E.L., 1.82.
H. & B., 61.

Editions.
Craigie. *Specimens III*, 53–5.
Grein-Wülker. *Poesie IIIa*, 144–7.

11. WIDSITH (fol. 84b–87a)

Widsith, apparently composed in the later part of the seventh century, is probably the oldest poem in English. A relic of heathendom, it is a lyric based upon epic tradition. Critics no longer consider it an autobiography, but rather an account of the wanderings of the ideal *scop*, Widsith (i.e., "Far-way", or "Far-travelled"). The gleeman here catalogues both the peoples he has visited—some seventy in all, inhabitants of territory stretching from Britain to India—and the (sixty-nine, mostly Germanic) chieftains he has known. Between them, the latter cover a period extending from the third to the sixth century. Short as it is (143 ll.), the poem bristles with ethnological, historical and structural problems. For the history of the migration period, it is a document of the utmost value. So too is it as a revelation of "the stock-in-trade of the old Anglian bard". But the many allusions to the heroes and peoples of the distant past— formerly no doubt the chief attraction of the poem—render it difficult for the modern reader to appreciate its intrinsic poetic merit. Nevertheless the tale is told simply and straightforwardly.

Structurally the poem is highly complex. Earlier critics have therefore been prone to detect in it numerous interpolations; but the theory that the chronological discrepancies arise from extensive interpolation has now fallen into disfavour. Its most recent editor, K. Malone (see below), whose analysis is at once elaborate and ingenious, as well as rather flattering to the (unknown) poet, believes that only eight ll. (as against Chambers 46, cf. ed., below, p. 152) are not original.

Bibliography.
C.B.E.L., 1.67–70.
Chambers, R. W. *Widsith: A Study in Old English Heroic Legend.*
C.U.P., 1912. [A monumental study of the poem in all its
aspects. Includes text based on the MS. with very full notes
and translation. Indispensable. Bibliography, 225–35.]
H. & B., 92–3.
Malone, K. *Widsith.* London, 1936. *Methuen's Old English
Library*, A. 5. [An excellent ed., with copious notes and a
particularly valuable Glossary of Proper Names. Text based
on own typescript, collated with facs. ed., as well as previous
printed edd. For a very fine bibliography (exhaustive of
treatises devoted specifically to *Widsith*), see pp. 98–113.]

Editions.
Chambers (above), 187–224.
Flom, *O.E. Reader*, 1–56.
Grein-Wülker, *Poesie I*, 1–6.
Malone (above), 61–97.
Sedgefield, *Bk. A.S. V.P.*, 1–5.

Translations.
Gordon, *A.S. Poetry*, 75–8; Gummere, *O.E. Epic*, 191–200.

Discussion.
Hoops, J. *Waldbäume und Kulturpflanzen im germanischen Altertum.*
Strassburg, 1905. See pp. 566–89.
Jordan, R. "Widsith" in Hoops's *Reallexikon*, 4.520–6. 1918.
Langenfelt, G. "Notes on the Anglo-Saxon Pioneers" in *E.St.*,
66.101–248. 1931. [Important section on Widsith Folk-
names, pp. 213–316.]
Van Grienberger, T. "Widsið" in *Angl.*, 46.347–82. 1922.
[Valuable line by line commentary.]

12. THE FORTUNES OF MEN (FATES OF MEN; fol. 87a–8b)

This short poetical homily of 98 ll. falls into two main sections,
the first of which (ll. 10–63) is a gloomy and realistic account
of the dangers that may beset a man during his lifetime, and the
second (ll. 64–92), strongly reminiscent of the *Gifts of Men*,
surveys the happier destinies of men. In ll. 85–92 there is an
interesting reference to a method of taming the hawk.

Bibliography.
C.B.E.L., 1.82.
H. & B., 62.

Editions.
Craigie. *Specimens III*, 67–9.
Grein-Wülker. *Poesie IIIa*, 148–51.
Sedgefield, *Bk. A.S. V.P.*, 45–48.

Translations.
Gordon, *A.S. Poetry*, 350–1.

13. MAXIMS I (Gnomic Verses ; fol. 88b–92b)

Maxims I, so titulated in order to distinguish them from a
similar though less diverse series in the B.M. Cott. Tib. B.I.
entitled *Maxims II*, sometimes, is a set of 204 ll. of verse
usually arranged, following indications in the MS., in three
sections, viz., 1–70, 71–137 and 138–204, comprising a hetero-
geneous collection of trite sayings, expressing moral truths, and
commonplace facts about nature and everyday life. "The entire
text gives the impression of a mass of unrelated materials gathered
from a number of sources [including Christian and pagan],
and assembled by the compiler more or less mechanically, with
no attempt at selection or logical arrangement" (Krapp and
Dobbie, xlvi–xlvii). Not only attractive on account of the
proverbial wisdom it contains, the poem (or poems) is of special
interest because it sheds light upon earlier beliefs and practices.

Bibliography.
C.B.E.L., 1.83.
H. & B., 80–1.

Editions.
Craigie. *Specimens III*, 57–63.
Grein-Wülker. *Poesie I*, 341–52.
Williams, B. C. *Gnomic Poetry in Anglo-Saxon.* New York. 1914.
    [Indispensable. Contains a good general introd. to the
    genre, text and a detailed analysis of the subject-matter.]

Discussion.
Krüger, C. *Beiträge zur gnomischen Dichtung der Angelsachsen,*
    Halle, 1924.

Translation.
Gordon, *A.S. Poetry*, 341–7 (selections only).

14. THE ORDER OF THE WORLD (fol. 92b–4a)

Better known as *The Wonders of Creation*, this loosely constructed
poem (102 ll.), comprises four sections: an autobiographical

passage of 37 ll. serving "merely to indicate a fictitious situation or occasion for the material which follows", a description of the Creation (ll. 38–89), a brief allusion to the joys of the saints in Heaven (ll. 90–7), and, finally, a moralising passage of 4 lines. In ll. 76–81, there is a reference to one of the shortcomings of current astronomical knowledge.

Bibliography.
C.B.E.L., 1.80.
H. & B., 94.

Edition.
Grein-Wülker. *Poesie IIIa*, 152–5.

15. THE RHYMING POEM (RHYMING SONG; 94a–5b)

Unique in O.E. poetry because of its rhyming scheme, which is superimposed upon the conventional alliterative line, the *Rhyming Poem* of 87 ll., probably written in the eighth century, resembles the *Wanderer* and the *Seafarer* in point of its melancholic themes, namely the speaker's regret for former happiness, his present misery, the transitoriness of human life and the bliss of Heaven. The two halves of each line normally rhyme, and many of the imperfect rhymes of the extant text become regular if they are switched into their cognate Anglian forms. In addition, and especially at the beginning of the poem, four, and sometimes even eight, successive half-lines rhyme. Not unexpectedly, meaning is occasionally sacrificed to metrical requirements. Nevertheless, since rhyme in O.E. (and in old Germanic) poetry was a rarity, the poem must be acclaimed as a distinct achievement. Whether the author found his model in O. Norse or in Latin verse, or whether, again, he was merely experimenting, are unsolved problems; but O. Norse influence seems extremely unlikely.

Bibliography.
C.B.E.L., 1.84–5.
H. & B., 87.

Editions.
Craigie. *Specimens III*, 73–5.
Grein-Wülker. *Poesie IIIa*, 156–63.
Mackie, W. S. "The Old English Rhymed Poem" in *J.E.G.Ph.*, 21.507–19. 1922. [With bibliography, translation and notes.]
Holthausen, F. "Das altenglische Reimlied" in *E.St.*, 65.181–9. 1931.

16. THE PANTHER (PHYSIOLOGUS I ; fol. 95b–6b)

This is a poem of 74 ll. containing a description of the panther's appearance and habits, the latter then being allegorically interpreted, with Christ as the panther. Together with the *Whale* and the *Partridge* (see below), which immediately follow it in that order, it was formerly thought to represent merely a small part of an extensive O.E. Physiologus (on the *genre*, see *Encycl. Brit.*, s.v.). Yet modern opinion, relying upon the evidence of the MS., is inclined to regard the trilogy as constituting the entire cycle, although, be it noted, the major portion (all of one folio) of the third poem is now lost.

Bibliography.
C.B.E.L., 1.78.
H. & B., 74–5.

Editions.
Cook, A. S. *Elene*.
Grein-Wülker. *Poesie IIIa*, 164–6.

Translations.
Cook, A. S. *The Old English Physiologus*. New Haven, 1921. Yale Studies, 63. [Includes text.]
Gordon, *A.S. Poetry*, 280–2.

Discussion.
Peebles, R. J. "The Anglo-Saxon Physiologus", in *M.Ph.*, 8.571–9. 1911.
Tupper, F. "The Physiologus of the Exeter Book", in *J.E.G.Ph.*, 11. 89–91. 1912.
Wellman, M. *Der Physiologus. Eine religionsgeschichtlichnaturwissenschaftliche Untersuchung*. Leipzig, 1930.

17. THE WHALE (PHYSIOLOGUS II ; fol. 96b–7b)

In the 89 ll. of this interesting poem, the habits of the whale, here depicted as a particularly deceitful creature, are described and then interpreted allegorically with reference to the Devil.

Edition.
Grein-Wülker. *Poesie IIIa*, 167–9.

Translation.
Gordon. *A.S. Poetry*, 282–3.
For other bibliographical items, see the *Panther* (above).

191

18. THE PARTRIDGE (PHYSIOLOGUS III; fol. 97b–8a)

Only 16 ll., the beginning and end, of this poem now survive, a complete folio apparently having been lost from the MS. Very likely the original totalled some 80 ll. The identity of the bird, the theme of the poem, cannot be determined from the extant text, which in the main comprises merely the concluding part of the allegorical section. But the evidence of the corresponding Latin *Physiologus* suggests the Partridge.

Ed., Grein-Wülker, *Poesie IIIa*, 170. Bibliographical material as for the *Panther* (above).

19. SOUL AND BODY II (ADDRESS OF THE SOUL TO THE BODY; fol. 98a–100a)

Following Krapp and Dobbie, the above title is here used to differentiate this macabre piece from the similar, but longer, *Soul and Body I* of the *Vercelli Book* (see p. 220). In 79 of the 121 ll. of the poem, the Body is fiercely denounced by the Soul for failing during this earthly life to safeguard its eternal welfare. The earlier lines inform us that the Soul will continue to do this every seventh night for 300 years, unless in the meantime God should bring the World to an end. The source of both *Exeter* and *Vercelli* poems is apparently the full Latin version of the Apocalypse of St. Paul as represented by MS. Nouv. acq. Lat. 1631 of the Bibliothèque Nationale in Paris (see Willard below). The theme of the Soul and the Body has been frequently treated in our early literature. For M.E. examples, see pp. 333–4.

Bibliography.
C.B.E.L., 1.79.
H. & B., 89.

Edition.
Grein-Wülker. *Poesie II*, 92–107. [Prints *Ex. Bk.* and *Verc. Bk.* texts on opposite pages.]

Discussion.
Willard, R. "The Address of the Soul to the Body" in *P.L.M.A.*, 50.957–983 (1935). [Prints two hitherto unpublished specimens, and discusses the nature and sources of the genre.]

20. DEOR (DEOR'S LAMENT; fol. 100a–100b)

This poem of 42 ll. in 7 unequal sections is one of two (the other being *Wulf and Eadwacer*, the next item in the MS.), with a stanzaic structure and a refrain (occurring 6 times). The stanzas are unequal in length, which is dependent upon matter, not form.

Very briefly, the poem, besides animadverting on adversity generally (ll. 28–34; yet they are often condemned as an inter-polation), mentions six examples of misfortune outlived, the last being attributed to himself. "After each example he points the moral: that passed; this will pass too. The first five examples are taken from heroic tradition, and the sixth, the misfortune which befell the poet himself, is given an heroic setting. In other words, the poem, though lyric in form and tone, depends on the Heroic Age for its matter" (K. Malone, ed. [below], p. 1).

Some authorities believe that the poem was written to cheer up someone burdened by depression and that the tale of the poet's own trouble is to be regarded as fictitious (ib., p. 16 and ref.). In the section concerned, Deor, the *scop* of the Heodenings, laments that after many years in the service of a lord, he was supplanted by another bard named Heorrenda (ll. 35–42). Again, others consider it the (misplaced) introduction to the poem, which is "possibly autobiographical" (cf. Wardale, 32–3). The poem is a document of very great historical interest, but still presents several unsolved problems.

Bibliography.
C.B.E.L., 1.68–9.
H. & B., 76.
Malone, K. *Deor.* London, 1933. *Methuen's Old English Library*,
    A.2. Pp. 28–31. [The first complete ed. Contains a com-
    prehensive account of the historical background, and several
    new interpretations.]

Editions.
Craigie. *Specimens III*, 5–6.
Dickins, B. *Runic and Heroic Poems of the Old Teutonic Peoples.*
    Cambridge, 1915. Pp. 70-7. [With translation and full notes.]
Grein-Wülker. *Poesie I*, 278–80.
Sedgefield, *Bk. A.S. V.P.*, 8–9.
Wyatt, *A.S. Reader*, 140–1.

Translation.
Gordon, *A.S. Poetry*, 79–80.

Discussion.
Clarke, M. G. *Sidelights on Teutonic History.* Cambridge, 1911.
    Pp. 188–208.

Lawrence, W. W. "The Song of Deor" in *M. Ph.*, 9.23–45. 1911.
Norman, F. " 'Deor'; A Criticism and an Interpretation" in *M.L.R.*, 32.374–81. 1937.

21. WULF AND EADWACER (EADWACER; fol. 100b–101a–)

This very controversial, and rather obscure poem of only 17 ll. (though the last two are abnormally long ones, and are often printed as 4) has been variously interpreted as a riddle (and even called the *First Riddle* – note that it immediately precedes the *Riddles*), a lyric fragment, and a dramatic lyric. The last interpretation seems to secure widest acceptance. The piece, which was formerly, though only on somewhat fanciful evidence, attributed to Cynewulf, is cast in the form of a monologue, in which a woman, apparently the wife of Eadwacer, and a captive in some foreign land, speaks of the plight of herself and of her absent, outlawed lover, Wulf, for whom she expresses her longing. A refrain (compare in this respect *Deor*, p. 192), *Ungelic(e) is us.* "Our lots are different", occurs twice.

Bibliography.
C.B.E.L., 1.72.

Editions.
Craigie. *Specimens III*, 50.
Grein-Wülker. *Poesie IIIa*, 183–4.
Sedgefield, *Bk. A.S. V.P.*, 39–40.
Tupper, F. *The Riddles of the Exeter Book.* Boston, 1910.
Trautmann, M. *Die altenglischen Rätsel.* Heidelberg, 1915.
Wyatt, A. J. *Old English Riddles.* London, 1912. P. xxi.
    [Pp. xx–xxviii contain a valuable historical summary and criticism of the theories about the authorship of this "Quondam First Riddle".]

Translations.
Gordon, *A.S. Poetry*, 91; Wyatt (above), xxi–xxii.

Discussion.
Bradley, H. See *Academy*, 33.197 ff.
Imelmann, R. *Die altenglische Odoaker-Dichtung.* Berlin, 1907.
    ["Proposes the theory that the 'First *Riddle*', *Wife's Lament* and *Husband's Message* form a trilogy connected with the Odoaker Legend", H. & B., 50.]

Imelmann, R. *Forschungen zur altenglischen Poesie*. Berlin, 1920. [Elaborates the theory proposed above.]

Lawrence, W. W. "The First Riddle of Cynewulf" in *P.M.L.A.*, 17.247–61. 1902. [Suggests that the poem is a translation from O.Norse. An important article on the poem's structure, refrain, and peculiarities of diction.]

Schofield, W. H. "Signy's Lament" in *P.M.L.A.*, 17.262–95. 1902. [Supports Lawrence's opinion above, and identifies the poem with an ancient Norse lay of the Volsungs, which may properly be entitled "Signy's Lament".]

Sieper, E. *Die altenglische Elegie*. Strassburg, 1915. Pp. 169–82.

Whitbread, L. "A Note on Wulf and Eadwacer" in *Medium Ævum*, 10.150–4. 1941. [Interpretation.]

22. RIDDLES 1–59 (fol. 101a–115a)

Under this heading it is convenient also to treat *Riddles* 30b and 60, and *Riddles* 61–95 (items 31 and 34 respectively, below). These poems, of very unequal quality, though some are first-rate, vary in length from 1 to 108 ll., the average length being about 15. Each personifies some object, which describes itself, though often deliberately and tantalisingly obscurely. Since the themes include birds, beasts, animals, the elements, musical instruments, weapons and armour, as well as tools and implements used in daily life, we sometimes obtain intimate glimpses of life in Anglo-Saxon times. The *Riddles*, however, are not "riddles in the modern sense of the word, but enigmas, descriptions of an object which are intended to be once accurate and misleading; the more misleadingly accurate and accurately misleading, the better" (Wyatt, ed. below, xxviii). The authorship of the three groups is still unascertained: no longer are they regarded as a "single and homogeneous collection", the work of Cynewulf; they are, it appears, a very miscellaneous collection, written by several authors, including perhaps Cynewulf.

The sources are diverse, and a "general statement is hardly possible. Many of the riddles show strong resemblances, both in subject matter and in style of treatment, to the Latin riddles of the Middle Ages, especially to the hundred Latin riddles of uncertain date, associated with the names of Symphosius (see *Encycl. Brit.* s.v.) and to the three collections of Latin riddles ascribed to Aldhelm, bishop of Sherborne (640?-709), to Tatwine, archbishop of Canterbury (d. 734), and to one Eusebius, who has been generally identified with Hwætberht, abbot of Wearmouth

THE BEGINNINGS OF ENGLISH LITERATURE

(c. 680–c. 747), a friend of Bede. But in most cases it is impossible to tell whether similarity between an Exeter Book riddle and a Latin riddle, rests upon conscious imitation of the Latin riddle, or upon the use of the same traditional material" (Krapp and Dobbie, lxvi–lxvii).

Many of the *Riddles* may perhaps date from the early eighth century "when Englishmen were most active in the composition of Latin riddles" (*ib.*), but in view of the doubt attending their unity and authorship, as well as of the mystery of their occurrence and grouping in the MS., the date of composition is still obscure.

Bibliography.
C.B.E.L., 1.72.
H. & B., 75.

Editions.
Grein-Wülker. *Poesie IIIa*, 184–218.
Trautmann, M. *Die altenglischen Rätsel*. Heidelberg, 1915.
Tupper, F. *The Riddles of the Exeter Book*. Boston, 1910. [Standard ed., the apparatus and introd. being excellent.]
Wyatt, A. J. *Old English Riddles*. London, 1912. [A reliable ed.]

Discussion.
Trautmann, M. "Quellen der altenglischen Rätsel. Sprache und Versbau der altenglischen Rätsel. Zeit, Heimat und Verfasser der altenglischen Rätsel," in *Angl.*, 38.349–73. 1914.

Translation.
Gordon. *A.S. Poetry*, 320–40. [Many not included.]

23. THE WIFE'S LAMENT (THE WIFE'S COMPLAINT; fol. 115a–115b)

Certain difficulties in point of structure, matter and interpretation are provided by this touching lyric of 53 ll. Several critics consider it complete in itself, while others have attempted to connect it with the poem entitled *The Husband's Message* (p. 200) from which it is separated in the MS. by 7 fols. But the relationship is by no means established. Others again regard it as an incident in some cycle of Germanic legend, but disagree about the cycle.

The one speaker in the poem, a woman, complains of her misfortune in being parted from her husband (or lover) who has left the country, and subsequently, through the action of his kinsmen, become estranged from her. In the rather obscure

196

final portion beginning at line 42, she roundly curses a young man, who is perhaps the cause of her present misery.

Bibliography.
C.B.E.L., 1.71.
H. & B., 93.

Editions.
Craigie. *Specimens III*, 47–8.
Grein-Wülker. *Poesie I*, 302–5.
Kershaw, 32-4. [With translation. Note also the valuable introd., pp. 28–31.]
Sedgefield. *Bk. A.S. V.P.*, 35–6.

Translations.
Cook and Tinker. *Trans. O.E. Poetry*, 64–6.
Gordon. *A.S. Poetry*, 87–8.

Discussion.
Imelmann, R. *Die altenglische Odoaker-dichtung.* Berlin, 1907. [Regards *Wulf and Eadwacer*, *The Wife's Lament* and *The Husband's Message* as a trilogy connected with the Odoacer legend.]
Imelmann, R. *Forschungen zur altenglischen Poesie.* Berlin, 1920. [Elaborates theory proposed in preceding item.]
Lawrence, W. W. "The Banished Wife's Lament" in *M.Ph.*, 5.387–405. 1908.
Schücking, L.L. "Das angelsächsische Gedicht von der Klage der Frau" in *Z.f.d.A.*, 48.436 ff. 1906.
Sieper, E. *Die altenglische Elegie.* Strassburg, 1915.
Stefanović, S. "Das angelsächsische Gedicht 'Die Klage der Frau' " in *Angl.*, 32.399–433. 1909.
Trautmann, M. "Zur Botschaft des Gemahls" in *Angl.*, 16. 207–25. 1894. [Argues for unity of *Wife's Lament* and *Husband's Message*.]

24. JUDGMENT DAY I (THE LAST JUDGMENT; fol. 115b-17b)

This is a somewhat dull, homiletic poem of 119 ll., also called *Doomsday.* It foretells what is to happen at the end of the world, and describes the Second Coming, the terrors of the damned and the joys of the blessed. It has been confused with the infinitely superior poem on the same subject variously entitled *Judgment Day II*, *Be Domes Dæge* and *Doomsday*, extant in the Cambridge C.C.C. MS. 201 (see p. 204).

Bibliography.
C.B.E.L., 1.79.
H. & B., 83.

Separate Edition.
Grein-Wülker. *Poesie IIIa*, 171–4.

Translation.
Thorpe, *Cod. Ex.*, 445–52.

Discussion.
Deering, R. W. *The Anglo-Saxon Poets on the Judgment Day.* Halle, 1890.
Menner, R. J. "The Vocabulary of the O.E. poems on Judgment Day" in *P.M.L.A.*, 62.583–597. 1947. [Claims Anglian origin.]

25. RESIGNATION (A PRAYER; fol. 117b–19b)

This is a poem of 118 ll. in which a penitent sinner first prays to God for forgiveness and then expresses resignation to his lot. In it "we find a subjectivity and a preoccupation with abstract ideas which is quite foreign to the older lyrics" (Krapp and Dobbie [above], x). Judging by the extent of the Biblical influence observable in it, as well as its versification and diction, the poem is a late composition, dating perhaps from the late ninth or tenth century.

This is the first text to exhibit lacunae resulting from the burn which damaged the last 14 folios of the MS.

Edition.
C.B.E.L., 1.80.
Grein-Wülker. *Poesie II*, 217–23.

Discussion.
Sieper, E. *Die altenglische Elegie.* Strassburg, 1915. Pp. 253–7.

26. THE DESCENT INTO HELL (CHRIST'S DESCENT INTO HELL; fol. 119b–21b)

This somewhat uninspiring poem of 137 ll., probably compiled about 800, falls naturally into two parts. The first, ll. 1–23a, deals with the visit of the two Marys to the Sepulchre of Jesus, and the Resurrection, and the second, ll. 23b to the end, comprises a description of Christ's Descent into Hell and His reception there by John the Baptist and Patriarchs, as well as Adam's welcoming speech. There are several lacunae in four separate passages. No precise literary source has been traced; but the first part corresponds in general with the New Testament accounts, particularly St. Matthew's, and the second ultimately derives from the apocryphal Gospel of Nicodemus (a (?) tenth-century version of which is edited by W. H. Hulme, *P.M.L.A.*, 13.457–542). Most likely, however, the author, apparently not Cynewulf himself, though one of his school, relied entirely upon Christian tradition.

Bibliography.
C.B.E.L., 1.78 (sub *Harrowing of Hell*).
H. & B., 76.

Editions.
Cramer, J. "Quelle, Verfasser und Text des altenglischen Gedichtes 'Christi Höllenfahrt'" in *Angl.*, 19.137–74. 1897. [Detailed Study.]
Crotty, G. "The Exeter *Harrowing of Hell*" in *P.M.L.A.*, 54.349–58. [Sources and identity of speaker in latter part of poem.]
Grein-Wülker. *Poesie IIIa*, 175–80.

27. ALMSGIVING (ALMS; fol. 121b–2a)

Amounting to only 9 ll. on the subject of the Christian's reward for generous giving of alms, this is the first of a sequence of four short, simple, religious poems of no special literary merit.

Bibliography.
C.B.E.L., 1.82.
H. & B., 54.

Edition.
Grein-Wülker. *Poesie IIIa*, 181.

28. PHARAOH (fol. 122a)

The theme of this dialogue poem of 8 ll. (in part mutilated) is the size of Pharaoh's army destroyed whilst pursuing the Children of Israel.

Bibliography.
C.B.E.L., 1.82.
H. & B., 85.

Edition.
Grein-Wülker. *Poesie IIIa*, 182.

29. THE LORD'S PRAYER I (PATERNOSTER; fol. 122a)

This poetic rendering of the Lord's Prayer in 11 lines is the shortest and perhaps earliest of three A.S. versions, the others being extant in C.C.C. Cambridge MS. 201 and the Junius MS. (see p. 205) respectively. For a bibliography of all three, see H. and B., 85.

Bibliography.
C.B.E.L., 1.81.
H. & B., 85.

Edition.
Grein-Wülker. *Poesie II*, 227–8.

30. HOMILETIC FRAGMENT II (FRAGMENTS OF MAXIMS; fol. 122a–122b)

This (?) tenth-century poem of 20 ll., its opening apparently missing, and at the end certainly incomplete, constitutes a consolatory admonition addressed to someone in trouble. It contains a gnomic passage; and the concluding mutilated portions treat of the Nativity. For *Fragment I*, see p. 221.

Bibliography.
C.B.E.L., 1.82.

Edition.
Grein-Wülker. *Poesie II*, 280–1.

31. RIDDLE 30b, RIDDLE 60 (fol. 122b–3a)

The first of the above (9 ll. in all) is another version with but unimportant differences, of *Riddle 30* and of the same length. A satisfactory solution has still to be suggested. *Riddle 60*, amounting to 17 ll. (on the Reed-pipe), in the opinion of some, is to be regarded as the opening of *The Husband's Message* (q.v.), the next piece in the MS. (see F. A. Blackburn, *J.E.G.Ph.*, 3.1–13 [1901]).
For discussion and bibliography, see item 22 above.

Edition.
Grein-Wülker. *Poesie IIIa*, 202, 218–19.

32. THE HUSBAND'S MESSAGE (fol. 123a–123b)

Taken at its face value, this piece is a charming love message evidently delivered by a staff upon which it is carved, from a man, apparently in exile across the sea, to a royal lady who is either his wife or lover. In it he recalls their former vows of devotion to each other, bids her, now that his troubles are past, join him as soon as she hears the sad notes of the cuckoo in the wood, and goes on to promise happiness and wealth in his new abode.

The alleged organic connexion between this poem and the *Wife's Lament* (item 23 above) resting chiefly upon the similarity of theme and situation and their presence in the same MS., still requires substantiation.

In its usual printed form, the poem amounts to just over 50 ll., the numbering varying in existing editions according to their authors' different estimates of the length of the two passages, at the beginning and middle, mutilated by the burn. Several scholars, however, regard the 17 ll. of *Riddle 60*, the preceding item in the MS., as the real opening portion of the poem (cf. Blackburn below). Yet the theory is not without serious objections. The last few lines, too, present difficulty because of the doubtful interpretation of the five runes at ll. 49–50.

Bibliography.
C.B.E.L., 1.82.
H. & B., 82.

Editions.
Blackburn, F. A. "*The Husband's Message* and the accompanying Riddles of *The Exeter Book*," in *J.E.G.Ph.*, 3.1–13. 1901. [Includes a tr. Integrates the poem with *Wulf and Eadwacer*, item 21 above.]
Craigie. *Specimens III*, 49–50.
Grein-Wülker. *Poesie I*, 306–11.
Kershaw. 44–9. [With tr. Note the useful introductory matter. pp. 37–43.]
Sedgefield. *Bk. A.S. V.P.*, 36–9.
Wyatt. *A.S. Reader*, 142–3. [Mutilated passages omitted.]

Translation.
Cook and Tinker, *Trans. O.E. Poetry*, 62–3; Gordon, *A.S. Poetry*, 89–90.

Discussion.
Imelmann, R. *Die altenglische Odoaker-dichtung.* Berlin, 1907. [Suggests *Wulf and Eadwacer*, the *Wife's Lament* and *The Husband's Message* form a trilogy belonging to the Odoacer legend.]
Imelmann, R. *Forschungen zur altenglischen Poesie.* Berlin 1920. [Elaborates theory proposed in preceding item.]

Sieper, E. *Die altenglische Elegie*. Strassburg, 1915. [Opposes Blackburn's unity-theory. Includes text.]

Trautmann, M. "Zur Botschaft des Gemahls" in *Angl.*, 16.207–25. 1894. [Supports unity of *Husband's Message* and *Wife's Lament*.]

33. THE RUIN (fol. 123b–4b)

Unlike other A.S. poems, the 49 ll. of this elegy, much mutilated in two passages, are concerned with the concrete: the subject is a scene. The author here contemplates the ruins of an ancient stone-built city, and contrasts its former splendour with its existing desolation. Its mention of baths and hot springs has inevitably prompted critics to identify the derelict buildings with the former Roman city of Bath, without, however, obtaining general approval. Maybe the poet had no particular ruin in mind.

The reader will note several internal rhymes, many peculiar words, some of which are not elsewhere recorded, two or three unusual compounds, and certain references to specific colours, the latter feature being rare in A.S. poetry.

Bibliography.
C.B.E.L., 1.71.
H. & B., 87–8.

Editions.
Craigie. *Specimens III*, 76–7.
Earle, J. *An Ancient Saxon Poem of a City in Ruins supposed to be Bath*. Bath, 1872.
Grein-Wülker. *Poesie I*, 296–301.
Kershaw. 54–6. [With brief discussion and bibliography, 51–3, and tr.]

Translation.
Cook and Tinker, *Trans. O.E. Poetry*, 56–7 (obscure lines omitted); Gordon, *A.S. Poetry*, 92–3.

Discussion.
Sieper, E. *Die altenglische Elegie*. Strassburg, 1915. Pp. 226–33.

34. RIDDLES 61–95 (fol. 124b–30b)

This group of riddles forms the last entry in the MS. As a result of the burn, the text contains very many lacunae.

Edition.
Grein-Wülker. *Poesie IIIa*, 219–38. [Riddles 62–85 only.] See further item 22 above.

THE FIGHT AT FINNSBURG

In his *Linguarum Veterum Septentrionalium Thesaurus* (1705), the antiquary Hickes, from a single leaf of a MS. (now lost) in the Lambeth Library, printed a very corrupt text of a metrical fragment of 48 ll. connected with the tale recited by the minstrel in *Beowulf*, ll. 1069–1159a, and now known as the *Finn Episode*. Lacking both beginning and end, this tragic *Fragment* tells how a young king at night in a hall rouses his sixty warriors to warn them of the approach of an enemy, and bids them be resolute. Thereupon five of them, all named, man the two doors. One of the foes coming near, inquires who guards the door and receives a reply, couched in the accepted epic style, giving the speaker's name and lineage as well as a challenge. The fight then begins, and continues for five days. But the attackers are driven off, with the loss of their leader. The *Fragment* then breaks off with the (?)attackers' leader asking for a casualty report.

The narrative itself is told briskly and dramatically, and in the main fairly clearly. Yet the lay as a whole only begins to be really intelligible when considered along with the *Episode*, which is much the more informative. Even then, however, critics disagree both about the identity of the personages and the course of events prior to, during, and after the fight. Indeed the relationship of the *Fragment* to the *Episode* is the crucial problem of the lay. In the past, perhaps because there are no discrepancies in subject-matter between them, they have often been looked upon as a sequence. The prevailing tendency, however, is to regard them as independent versions, the *Fragment* as a portion of a short heroic lay, and the *Episode* as an abbreviated account of such a lay (cf. Klaeber, *Beow.*, 224, and Hoops, *Kommentar*, 134).

Bibliography.
C.B.E.L., 1.63–8.
H. & B., 78–80.
Chambers. *Beow.*, 387–413, *passim*. [Annotated.]
Klaeber. *Beow.*, 227–30. [Standard edition with full and excellent apparatus, and Hickes' text.]

Text.
Dickins. *Run. Poems*, 64–9. [With bibl., introd., notes and tr.]
Klaeber (above).
Mackie, W. S. "*The Fight at Finnsburg*" in *J.E.G.Ph.*, 16.250–73. 1917. [With introductory and textual notes.]
Note.—The text is printed in many anthologies.

Translations.

Dickins (above); Gordon, *A.S. Poetry*, 71–2; Gummere, *O.E. Epic*, 160–3; Hall, *Beow.*, 156–9.

Discussion.

Ayres, H. M. "The Tragedy of Hengest in Beowulf" in *J.E.G.Ph.*, 16.282–95. 1917. [Valuable.]

Brandl, § 23.

Chambers. *Beow. Introd.*, 245–89. [Full survey of *Finn* legend. Indispensable.]

Girvan, R. "Finnsburuh" in *Proc. of Brit. Acad.*, 26. 1942. [Interpretation and date.]

Klaeber (above), 219–26. [Indispensable.]

Klaeber, F. "Beowulfiana" in *Angl.*, 50. 1926. See pp. 224–33.

Lawrence, W. W. "Beowulf and the Tragedy of Finnsburg" in *P.M.L.A.*, 30.372–431. 1915. [Indispensable.]

Lawrence. *Beow. Ep. Trad.*, 107–28.

Mackie (above).

Malone, K. "The Finn Episode in Beowulf" in *J.E.G.Ph.*, 25.157–72. 1926.

Trautmann, M. *Finn and Hildebrand. Bonner Beitr. VII.* 1903. Pp. 3–64.

JUDGMENT DAY II

This poem (MS. C.C.C. Camb., 201), which should be distinguished from the very inferior *Judgment Day I* (119 ll.) treated above (p. 197) translates, and at the same time expands, the 157 ll. of the Latin poem *De Die Judicii*, attributed to either Bede or Alcuin. "The translation is one of the finest in Old English" (*C.H.E.L.*, 1.146). Alternative titles are *Doomsday* and *Be Domes Dæge*.

In the opening lines—a beautiful nature passage—the author tells how he sat in a woodland bower by murmuring streams, reflecting upon Death and Doomsday. The bulk of the poem is taken up with his musings on the events of that Day. Judging from the alliterative licences and end-rhymes, the poem must be a latish composition, but not later than the beginning of the eleventh century, because its diction is closely similar to and often identical with that of a Homily attributed to Wulfstan and extant in a MS. dating from the middle of that century (cf. Brandl., § 98).

Bibliography.
C.B.E.L., 1.78.
H. & B., 55–6.

Text.
Grein-Wülker. *Poesie II*, 250–72. [Gives relevant text of the Wulfstanian Homily.]
Löhe, H. *Be Domes Dæge. Bonner Beitr. XXII*, 1907. [Text, German translation, Latin original, notes on text, metre, account of relationship to Latin source and Homily, and a glossary with German meanings. Valuable.]
Lumby, J. R. *Be Domes Dæge*. E.E.T.S., 65. 1876. [Text, tr., Latin source and Notes.]

Translation.
Gordon, *A.S. Poetry*, 314–19; Lumby (above).

Discussion.
Deering, R. W. *The Anglo-Saxon Poets on the Judgment Day*. Halle, 1890.
Menner, R. J. "The Vocabulary of the O.E. poems on Judgment Day" in *P.M.L.A.*, 62.583–597. 1947. [Claims Saxon origin.]

THE JUNIUS MANUSCRIPT

This MS. takes its name from its former owner, the pioneer A.S. scholar, Franciscus Junius or Dujon (b. 1589 at Heidelberg, d. 1678). Brought up in Holland, Junius in 1620 crossed to England and became Librarian to the Earl of Arundel. Receiving the MS. from Archbishop Ussher (1581–1656), the Irish Primate, Junius had it printed at Amsterdam in 1655, attributing, without any MS. authority whatsoever, all the contents to Cædmon (q v.) —hence the variant title the *Caedmon MS.*—and later bequeathed it to Oxford University. It is now preserved in the Bodleian Library as MS. Junius XI.

Although controversy has since raged round the question of the authorship of the four poems, the sole contents of the MS., Cædmon's claim seems to rest merely upon this perhaps flimsy basis: these authorless poems correspond in theme, a biblical one, to those that Bede credited to Cædmon. With the exception of Gollancz (*Cædmon MS.*, lx), modern critics seem inclined neither to accept them as Cædmon's nor to regard them as the work of only a single poet.

The text of this West-Saxon MS., which contains 116 folios

numbered 1–229 by a later hand beginning at 2a, was written c. 1000 by four different scribes. The first wrote the whole of pp. 1–212, i.e., the first three poems, *Genesis* (pp. 1–142), *Exodus* (pp. 143–71), and Daniel (pp. 173–212); the other three copyists were responsible for the fourth and last poem, *Christ and Satan* (pp. 213–19), the task being broken up as follows:—pp. 213–15, 216–18, and 219. There is MS. authority for calling the portion written by the three scribes *Liber II.* The first three poems presumably form *Liber I.* "Besides these scribes, account must be taken also of other hands which appear in many corrections, additions and alterations in the MS., in the drawing of ornamental capitals, in the drawing of numerous illustrations accompanying the text, and in comments on these, and in a few marginal notations of a casual nature (Krapp, *Junius Manuscript* (below), x). The crude illustrations (conveniently accessible in Kennedy, *Caedmon Poems* [below], 197–248) are numerous up to p. 96, after which there is only one more (p. 225), though it is unfinished and apparently wholly irrelevant to the text.

Bibliography.

C.B.E.L., 1.62–3.

H. and B., 46–7.

Krapp, G. P. *The Junius Manuscript*. London, 1931. Pp. xlv–lviii. [Standard ed., with excellent introds., bibl. and notes. Indispensable.]

Manuscripts and Reproductions.

Gollancz, I. *The Cædmon Manuscript of Anglo-Saxon Biblical Poetry, Junius XI in the Bodleian Library*. Oxford, 1927. [Full-sized facs. ed. with invaluable introd. Indispensable.]

Stoddard, F. H. "The Cædmon Poems in MS. Junius XI" in *Angl.*, 10.157–67. 1888. [Full description of MS.]

Kennedy, C. W. *The Cædmon Poems, translated into English Prose*. London, 1916. [See pp. 197–248 for facs. of illustrations, which are discussed in a separate chapter by C. R. Morey, pp. 177–95.]

Editions.

Grein-Wülker. *Poesie II*, 318–562.

Krapp (above; also lists anthologies containing poetical texts, xlvii–xlix).

Translations.

Kennedy (above). Note also refs. under separate items below.

1. GENESIS

Genesis is the title assigned to a metrical paraphrase in 2936 ll. of Chaps. I–XXII of the *Book of Genesis*. At least two poets contributed to the existing version. As long ago as 1875 the German scholar Sievers, impressed not only by certain peculiarities in point of metre (viz., long lines), style and diction (viz., rare, or otherwise [except in O.S.] unknown words), but also by several resemblances to the ninth century O.S. poem (on the New Testament) now entitled *Heliand* ("Redeemer"), expressed his conviction that ll. 235–851 in reality constituted an interpolation that was a translation from an O.S. original. In 1894 his opinion was adequately substantiated by the discovery in the Vatican Library of an O.S. fragment (25 ll.) of a poem on Genesis that corresponded closely to ll. 791–817 of the A.S. text. This interpolation is regularly known as *Genesis B*, and the remaining portions as *Genesis A*. The former is usually thought to date from the early part of the ninth century, and the latter, possibly composed by a monk in a Northern monastery, from the period about 700.

Genesis A opens with a prologue on the Revolt and Fall of the Angels and then fairly closely follows the biblical account from the Creation up to the Sacrifice of Isaac. A typical A.S. religious poem, attractive but never inspired, it reveals the customary blend of heathen and Christian ideas. On the other hand, *Genesis B*, which repeats the narrative of the previous sections on the Fall, is in parts magnificent: e.g., the character of Satan, portrayed as a hero, and the resounding call to action (ll. 356–440) addressed by Satan to his followers. [Readers will note the similarities between the B-portion and Milton's *Paradise Lost.*] In addition to his biblical source, the poet derived ideas from a Latin poem by Alcimus Avitus, bishop of Vienne, c. 500.

Bibliography.
C.B.E.L., 1.74.
H. & B., 66–7.

Editions.
Grein-Wülker. *Poesie II*, 318–444.
Holthausen, F. *Die altere Genesis.* Heidelberg, 1914. [An ed. of *Genesis A*, with full apparatus and Latin source. Addenda and errata in *Angl.*, 46.60–2. (1922).]
Klaeber, F. *The Later Genesis and Other Old English and Old Saxon*

Texts relating to the Fall of Man. Heidelberg, 1913. New ed. (with supplement), 1931. [Ed. of *Genesis B*, with complete apparatus.]

Translations.

Gordon, *A.S. Poetry*, 105–22; Kennedy, *Cædmon Poems*, 7–96; Mason, L., *Genesis A, translated from the Old English*, New York, 1915.

Discussion.

Berthold, L. "Die Quellen für die Grundgedanken von V. 235–851, der altsächsisch-angelsächsischen Genesis," in *Germanica, Edward Sievers zum 75. Geburtstage*, Halle, 1925, pp. 380–401.

Bradley, H. The "Cædmonian" Genesis, in *Essays and Studies*, 6.7–29. 1920. [Appreciation of *Gen. B*.]

Gerould, G. H. "The Transmission and Date of Genesis B," in *M.L.N.*, 26.129–33, 1911.

Jovy, H. *Untersuchungen zur altenglischen Genesisdichtung. Bonner Beitr.* V, 1–32. 1900. [With discussion of author, locality and date. Textual notes, 22–32.]

Kennedy. *Cædmon Poems*, xxiii–l. [Good literary criticism.]

Sievers, E. "Cædmon und Genesis" in *Britannica, Max Förster, zum 60. Geburtstage*, Leipzig, 1929, pp. 57–84. [On authorship.]

2. EXODUS

Unlike *Genesis A, Exodus* is no mere biblical paraphrase, but rather an epic narrative (in 590 ll., but incomplete) of the Departure of Israel from Egypt, their passage of the Red Sea, and the Destruction of the Host of the Egyptians. In the main it is based on Chaps. XIII and XIV of the *Book of Exodus*. Certain of its passages have given the critics cause for speculation. Some condemn, as an interpolation, ll. 362–446, which contain a brief reference to Noah and the Flood, followed by a lengthy account of the Sacrifice of Isaac. Others, again, would rearrange the final portion, beginning at l. 515, because of its alleged inconsequentiality. However, Krapp (*Junius Manuscript*, above, xxvii–xxxi), ably defends the unity of the present version.

The poem appears to have been composed about 700 by an unknown author, who, though certainly a churchman, was steeped in the old pre-Christian tradition. Possessed of a good eye for detail, he obviously revels in battle scenes. His description of the Drowning of the Egyptians (ll. 447–515) is a tremendously

powerful piece of composition, as vigorous and realistic as anything in O.E. Literature.

Bibliography.
C.B.E.L., 1.74–5.
H. & B., 65–6.

Editions.
Blackburn, F. A. *Exodus and Daniel*. London, 1907. [Reliable,
and with good apparatus.]
Grein-Wülker. *Poesie II*, 445–75.

Translations.
Gordon. *A.S. Poetry*, 123–32 (omits ll. 307–446).
Johnson, W. S. "Translation of the Old English Exodus" in
J.E.G.Ph., 5.44–57 (1903).
Kennedy. *Cædmon Poems*, 99–118.

Discussion.
Bright, J. W. "On the Anglo-Saxon Poem Exodus" in *M.L.N.*,
27.13–19. 1912. [Textual notes.]
Clubb, M. D. "The Second Book of the *Cædmonian Manuscript*"
in *M.L.N.*, 43.304–6. 1928.
Kennedy. *Cædmon Poems*, i–ix. [Structural and literary
criticism.]
Klaeber, F. "Concerning the Relation between Exodus and
Beowulf" in *M.L.N.*, 33.218–24. 1918. [Considers *Exodus*
older than *Beowulf*.]
Moore, S. "On the Sources of the Old-English Exodus" in
M.Ph., 9.83–108. 1911.
Mürkens, G. *Untersuchung über das altenglische Exoduslied. Bonner
Beitr.* II, 62–117. 1899.

3. DANIEL

This homiletic, episodic, metrical narrative of 764 ll. is based,
excluding, however, the introductory matter, on Chaps. I–V of
the Vulgate *Book of Daniel*. Prefaced by an account of the Jews
of Jerusalem, and of that city's fall, the poem tells of Nebuchadnezzar's first dream and its interpretation, the Three Hebrews in
the Fiery Furnace, Nebuchadnezzar's second dream and its
interpretation, his consequent exile and subsequent return, and
Belshazzar's Feast. Here it breaks off. Naturally Daniel is the
central theme of each episode.

Ll. 279–439, however, seem to be an interpolation involving

peculiar difficulties. This portion of the poem comprises two lyrical passages, which are conventionally known as the *Prayer of Azarias* (ll. 279–356) and the *Song of the Three Children* (ll. 362–408), together with their several links. Now in *The Exeter Book* we find in the poem called *Azarias* (see p. 181) another version of the *Prayer*, the first 75 ll. of which correspond so closely to the *Daniel* text as to warrant the supposition that we have actually to deal with variants of the same original. Nevertheless, the precise nature of their mutual relationship, and the explanation of the presence of the *Prayer* in Daniel, still remain unsolved problems. Further, the second part of *Azarias* in *The Exeter Book* also contains a version of the *Song of the Three Children* (see p. 181). But the important differences between this and the *Daniel* text clearly imply that they are separate renderings of the same material. Once again the problems of relationship and date are unsolved. Both *Songs*, however, depend upon a Canticle version of the *Benedicite* that to some extent differed from the Vulgate version. (A Latin copy of this Canticle, with an O.E. interlinear gloss., is printed by Sweet, *Oldest English Texts*, 414–15.) The *Song* in *Daniel* is undoubtedly the best part of the poem.

Bibliography.
C.B.E.L., i.75.
H. & B., 65.

Editions.
Blackburn, F. A. *Exodus and Daniel*. London, 1907. [Standard.]
Grein-Wülker. *Poesie II*, 476–515.
Schmidt, W. *Die altenglischen Dichtungen Daniel und Azarias.* Bonner Beitr. Vol. XXIII, 1–84. 1907. [With full apparatus].

Translations.
Gordon. *A.S. Poetry*, 133–9 [omits ll. 46–223 and 489–end.]
Kennedy. *Cædmon Poems*, 121–45.

Discussion.
Hofer, O. "Über die Entstehung des angelsächischen Exodus" in *Angl.*, 12.158–204. 1889.
Kennedy. *Cædmon Poems*, lx–lxiv.

4. CHRIST AND SATAN

Although this somewhat unimportant piece of 729 ll. is often thought to comprise three poems in one, viz., ll. 1–364, *The Lament of the Fallen Angels* (with Satan depicted as a miserable self-pitying wretch), ll. 365–662, *The Harrowing of Hell*, and ll. 663–729, *The Temptation* (incomplete), the assumption is confirmed neither by the arrangement of the text in the MS. nor by any differences in style or diction detectable throughout the poem. The chief reason for suspecting its unity is the "vague continuity of the narrative or structural interest" (Krapp, *Junius Manuscript* [above], xxxiv). It is "not primarily a narrative poem . . . (but) . . . a set of lyric and dramatic amplifications of a number of Biblical and legendary themes of a familiar character" (ib., xxxiv–xxxv). Other modern critics, however, seem content to regard it as a "unity with three divisions" and the work of a single author writing in the Cynewulfian tradition.

No basis for the poem as a whole has been discovered. The source of Part I seems to be legendary matter and certain hints from the Old Testament; of Part II, perhaps an Easter homily; and of Part III (ll. 689–709 of which are majestic), the writer's own, but not specially accurate knowledge of the Bible. The poem may have been written in the eighth century.

Bibliography.
C.B.E.L., 1.75.
H. & B., 64.

Editions.
Clubb, M. D. *Christ and Satan: an Old English Poem.* New Haven, 1925. [With full apparatus. Excellent.]
Grein-Wülker. *Poesie II*, 521–62.

Translations.
Kennedy, *Cædmon Poems*, 149–73; Gordon, *A.S. Poetry*, 140–6 (ll. 1–223, 265–467 only.)

Discussion.
Frings, T. "Christ and Satan" in *Z.f.d.Ph.*, 45.216–36. 1913. [On date and authorship.]
Kennedy. *Cædmon Poems*, lxiv–lxx. [Literary criticism.]

LEYDEN RIDDLE

The Latin Riddle *De Lorica* of Bishop Aldhelm (c. 639–708; see further, p. 195) has come down to us in two independent O.E. versions, the later, in the W.S. dialect, being found on fol. 109a and b of the *Exeter Book* (see No. 35 in Wyatt's *Old English Riddles*). The earlier version, written in the Northumbrian dialect, is preserved in a unique copy in the ninth century MS. Voss 106 in Leyden University Library. Hence the name "Leyden Riddle".

Separate Edition.

Smith, A. H. *Three Northumbrian Poems.* London, 1933. *Methuen's O.E. Library.* [Prints both versions. An excellent edition with complete apparatus. Bibliography, 48–50.]

THE BATTLE OF MALDON (BYRHTNOTH'S DEATH)

This very fine, though incomplete, poem of 325 ll. (with beginning and ending lost) celebrates the death of the famous Alderman Byrhtnoth at the historically unimportant battle that was fought on Aug. 11th, 991, at Maldon, between the *fyrd* of the East Saxons under Byrhtnoth, accompanied by his household troop, and the Vikings, who were mainly Norwegians. Hitherto the latter were supposed to have been led by the great Ōlaf Tryggvason, but modern opinion disagrees (cf. e.g., Gordon. ed. below, 10–15).

The (late 11 c.) MS. of the poem was almost completely destroyed by the fire in the Cotton Library in 1731, only a few charred fragments now surviving. Fortunately some few years before it had been transcribed by the Library's under-keeper, John Elphinston. This transcript, which has only recently been found by N. R. Ker, passed into the hands of Thomas Hearne, who in 1726 printed it as an appendix to his edition of John of Glastonbury's *Chronicle.* Up to 1937, when Professor E. V. Gordon published his excellent edition (below) of the poem, Hearne's print was the sole authority for the text. Gordon believes that Elphinston, though knowing little O.E., was a fairly accurate copyist, and also that Hearne's copy is remarkably correct.

The poem was composed soon after the battle while the events were still fresh in the memory; but the poet (still unidentified) seems to have been writing from hearsay. "The aristocratic quality of *Maldon* is evident both in the glorification of the military ideals of the *comitatus* and in the close kinship in art and sentiment with other Old English court poetry. *Maldon* is of the same school as *Beowulf* and nearer to *Beowulf* in heroic art and social feeling than any other Old English poem" (Gordon, ed., p. 23). Again it is even "more directly in the heroic tradition than *Beowulf*; it is indeed the only purely heroic poem extant in Old English, since *Finnesburh* and *Waldere* are too fragmentary for their general scope and quality to be gauged. *Beowulf*, usually accounted primarily heroic and epic, is in its ultimate aim elegiac" (ib., 24).

After years of controversy, the site of the battle was finally determined by E. D. Laborde in 1925 (see article below). It was the mainland immediately opposite Northey Island in the estuary of the River Blackwater in Essex. The *bricg* and *ford* of the poem refer to the causeway some eighty yards long that still links the mainland with the island.

Bibliography.

Ashdown, M. *English and Norse Documents relating to the Reign of Ethelred the Unready.* Cambridge, 1930. *Passim.* [A valuable ed. with a serviceable tr. Contains appendices on the metre and language, and much excellent material in the indexes of personal names, place-names and names of people.]

C.B.E.L., 1.83–4.

Gordon, E. V. *The Battle of Maldon.* London, 1937. *Methuen's O.E. Library,* A, 6. Pp. 63–5. [An excellent ed. of Elphinstone's transcript, with full apparatus, photograph of the causeway at Northey and a sketch map of the battlefield.]

H. & B., 84.

Laborde, E. D. *Byrhtnoth and Maldon.* London, 1936. Pp. 162–6. [Comprehensive, but much stronger historically than linguistically. See especially pp. 9–49 (on persons mentioned in the poem, the site of the battle, Olaf Tryggvason and the "Wickings"). Includes photographs of the causeway and the battlefield, as well as a map of the latter.]

Editions.

Ashdown (above), 22–37. [Tr. facing each page. Very full notes, 72–90.]

Gordon (above).

Laborde (above).

Sedgefield. *Bk. A.S. V.P.,* 70–9.

Wyatt. *A.S. Reader,* 188–97.

Translations.

Ashdown (above).

Gordon. *A.S. Poetry,* 361–7.

Ker, W. P. On pp. 260–7 of R. W. Chambers' *England before the Norman Conquest.* Tr. 1887.

Discussion.

Gordon, E. V. "The Date of Aethelred's Treaty with the Vikings: Olaf Tryggvason and the Battle of Maldon," in *M.L.R.,* 32.24–32. 1937.

Ker, W. P. *Epic and Romance.* London, 1922. Pp. 55–7.

Laborde, E. D. "The Style of the Battle of Maldon" in *M.L.R.*, 19.401–17. 1924. [Detailed study.]

Laborde, E. D. "The Site of the Battle of Maldon" in *Engl. Hist. Rev.*, 40.161–73. 1925.

Phillpotts, B. S. "The Battle of Maldon; some Danish Affinities" in *M.L.R.*, 24.172–90. 1929. [Assumes the *Maldon* poet knew Danish poems and was under their influence. See, however, Gordon (ed. above), 25.]

MENOLOGIUM

Prefixed to the Abingdon MS. of the *Anglo-Saxon Chronicle* is a versified calendar of 231 ll., probably composed towards the end of the tenth century. It is a "survey of the progress of the year, with special mention of the Saints' days observed by the church . . . and retaining traces of heathen times, though the whole is Christian in basis" (*C.H.E.L.*, 1.145). Happily several poetical passages referring to nature relieve this somewhat drab piece of verse.

Bibliography.
C.B.E.L., 1.79.
H. & B., 85.

Text.
Earle-Plummer. *Sax. Chron.*, 1.273–80.
Grein-Wülker. *Poesie II*, 282–93.
Imelmann, R. *Das altenglische Menologium*. Berlin, 1902. [With comprehensive discussion.]

METRICAL PSALMS (PARIS PSALTER)

A West-Saxon metrical version of Ps. 51, v. 7, to Ps. 150, v. 3, is preserved with the corresponding Latin text on fol. 64a–175b of the early eleventh century *Paris Psalter*, where it follows a prose version of Ps. 1–50 in the same hand (see p. 257). Apparently the poetical and prose versions originated independently. Possibly, too, the original *Versified Psalter* included all the psalms.

Bibliography.
C.B.E.L., 1.80.
H. & B., 86–7.
Krapp, G. P. *The Paris Psalter and the Meters of Boethius*. London, 1933. Pp. xxxiii–xxxv. [An indispensable ed., with excellent introd. and notes.]

Editions.
Grein-Wülker, *Poesie IIIb*, 86–230; Krapp (above).

Discussion.
Bartlett, H. *The Metrical Division of the Paris Psalter.* Baltimore, 1896.

Bruce, J. D. "The Anglo-Saxon Version of the Book of Psalms commonly known as the Paris Psalter" in *P.M.L.A.*, 9.43–164. 1894.

Brüning, E. *Die altenglischen metrischen Psalmen in ihrem Verhältnis zur lateinischen Vorlage.* Königsberg, 1921. [Abstract of dissertation.]

Cook, A. S. *Biblical Quotations in Old English Prose Writers.* London, 1898. [See xxxiv–xliii.]

Förster, M. "Die altenglischen Texte der Pariser Nationalbibliothek," in *E.St.*, 62.113–31. 1927.

RUNIC POEM

The MS. (eleventh century or later) of the 94 ll. of this (?) mnemonic poem was destroyed in the Cotton Fire of 1731, but happily the text had been printed earlier by Hickes in his *Thesaurus* (1705). Each of the twenty-nine runes is here mentioned in turn and the animate or inanimate object of which it is the name is then described in usually 3 or 4 ll. Naturally the poem, which has Scandinavian analogues, is of value for its information upon the O.E. runic alphabet.

Bibliography.
C.B.E.L., 1.84.
H. & B., 88.
Arntz, H. *Handbuch der Runenkunde.* Halle, 1935. Pp. 114–6. [With German tr.]

Text.
Dickins. *Run. Poems*, 12–22. [With bibl., introd., notes and tr.]

Discussion.
Dickins, *ibid.*
Keller, W. "Zum altenglischen Runengedicht" in *Angl.*, 60.141–9. 1936. [On the origin of the rune names.]

Von Grienberger, T. "Das angelsächsische Runengedicht" in *Angl.*, 45.201–20. 1921. [Textual notes.]

DIALOGUE OF SALOMON AND SATURN

This *Dialogue* is extant in two metrical versions, both found in the same tenth-century MS. in C.C.C. Library, Cambridge. The first version, containing 179 ll., exclusive of the first thirty which are now illegible, is interrupted at l. 170 by a lengthy passage in prose. Happily ll. 1–94 are also preserved in a fragmentary version in another MS. (late eleventh century) in the same Library. This version deals with the efficacy of prayer. The much more interesting second version (325 ll.), gnomic and riddle-like in treatment, is concerned with moral and theological subjects. It also more clearly represents a literary *genre* that was widespread in Europe and may be very old. This literary form is essentially a contest of wits between Salomon representing Christianity and another disputant representing the wisdom of the East. Both dialogues were probably composed in the Anglian area in the tenth century. Note the alliterative licences in both and the occasional rhymes in the first.

Bibliography.
C.B.E.L., 1.82–3.
H. & B., 88.

Text.
Grein-Wülker. *Poesie IIIb*, 58–82.
Kemble, J. M. *The Dialogue of Salomon and Saturnus, with an Historical Introduction*. London, 1848. [With tr.]

Discussion.
Menner, R. J. "The *Vasa Mortis* passage in the Old English Salomon and Saturn" in *Studies in English Philology, A Miscellany in Honor of F. Klaeber*. Minneapolis, 1929. Pp. 240–57. [Study of genesis of story.]
Menner, R. J. *The Poetical Dialogues of Solomon and Saturn*. O.U.P., 1941. [With full apparatus. Authoritative edition.]
Von Vincenti, A. R. *Die altenglischen Dialoge von Salomon und Saturn*. Leipzig, 1904. [Study of relationship to Oriental legend and to later mediaeval versions.]

THE VERCELLI BOOK

This well-preserved, well-written and easily legible West-Saxon MS. is now in the Chapter Library of the Cathedral at Vercelli in Northern Italy. Hence its titles, *Vercelli Book* or *Codex*, and *Codex Vercellensis*. How and when it found its way there is a mystery. Most likely the MS. was a compilation of the tenth century (second half), written and produced in England, and the work of a single scribe. It contains 137 folios, without ornamentation, except for a small animal figure on fol. 49a. The first is now illegible on both sides, the last two are blanks, and several are missing. Many of the leaves are only partly filled up.

The *Book* seems to be no haphazard collection: it was apparently designed to contain in one volume a number of prose homilies and legendary and homiletic poems that could be used "to supplement and lighten the formal offices of the service" (Krapp, *The Vercelli Book* [below] Preface). The contents are as follows the several titles.

Contents of the Vercelli Book (after Krapp, ib., xviii–xx).

fol.	1a–9a	Homily on the Passion.
fol.	9b–12a	Homily on the Last Judgment.
fol.	12b–16a	Homily on Christian Virtues.
fol.	16b–24b	Homily on Penance.
fol.	25a–29a	Homily on Birth of Christ.
fol.	29b–52b	*Andreas.*
fol.	52b–54a	*The Fates of the Apostles.*
fol.	54b–56a	Homily on the Miracles preceding the Birth of Jesus and the Flight into Egypt.
fol.	56b–59a	Homily on Extravagance and Gluttony.
fol.	59a–61a	Homily on the Last Judgment and Hell Torment.
fol.	61a–65a	Homily on the Terrors of Death.
fol.	65a–71a	Homily on the Transitoriness of the World and its Joys.
fol.	71b–73b	Homily for the First Rogation Day.
fol.	73b–75b	Homily for the Second Rogation Day.
fol.	75b–76b	Homily for the Third Rogation Day.
fol.	76b–80b	Homily (for general use).
fol.	80b–85b	Homily on the Day of Judgment.
fol.	85b–90b	Homily on the Epiphany.
fol.	90b–94b	Homily on the Purification.
fol.	94b–101a	Homily on St. Martin.
fol.	101b–103b	*Soul and Body I.*
fol.	104a–104b	*Homiletic Fragment I.*
fol.	104b–106a	*Dream of the Rood.*
fol.	106b–109b	Homily on the Creation.
fol.	109b–112a	Homily on the Deadly Sins.
fol.	112a–116b	Homily on Duty to God.
fol.	116b–120b	Homily on the Christian Virtues.
fol.	121a–133b	*Elene.*
fol.	133b–135b	Prose Life of St. Guthlac.

Bibliography.
C.B.E.L., 1.63.
H. & B., 47.

Krapp, G. P. *The Vercelli Book*. London, 1932. [Contains only the poems. An excellent ed., the text being based on the photographic reprints of Wülker and Förster (below). The introductory matter, bibliography (lxxxi–xciv) and notes are first-rate. Standard ed. Indispensable.]

Manuscript and Reproductions.

Förster, M. *Der Vercelli-Codex CXVII nebst Abdruck einiger altenglischen Homilien der Handschrift.* In *Fest-schrift fur Lorenz Morsbach*, Halle, 1913, pp. 20–179.

Förster, M. *Il Codice Vercellese con Omelie e Poesie in Lingua Anglosassone.* Rome, 1913.

Wülker, R. *Codex Vercellensis. Die angelsachsische Handschrift zu Vercelli in getreuer Nachbildung.* Leipzig, 1894. [Contains only the poetry.]

Editions.

Grein-Wülker. *Poesie II*, 1–201.

Kemble, J. M. *The Poetry of the Codex Vercellensis*, with an English tr. Published for the Aelfric Society. London, 1843–56.

Krapp (above; with list of edd. of poetical texts, lxxiii–lxxxiv).

Translations.

Gordon. *A.S. Poetry.* [Contains all except *Homiletic Fragment 1*.] N.B.—See below for tr. of the individual poems.

1. ANDREAS (fol. 29b–52b)

Closely similar to *Beowulf* in point of structure and diction, the *Andreas*, "The Christian *Beowulf*", is a stirring romantic poem of 1722 ll. recounting legendary episodes in St. Andrew's missionary life in Mermedonia. While owing all these various incidents to the source-book, viz., a lost Latin version of the Greek *Acts of Andrew and Matthew* (ed. Bonnet, *Acta Apostolorum Apocrypha*, 1.2, 65–116 [1898]), the poet has greatly elaborated upon them, especially in his depiction of scenes. This "romance of the seas" is in fact notable for the magnificence of its descriptions of the raging storms (cf. ll. 369 ff., 435 ff., 489 ff., 511 ff.). Also the poem affords an excellent illustration of the blend of the old and the new: the relationship of Christ and His Apostles is simply that of *lord and comitatus*. Indeed the whole background is permeated with heroic ideas. (The existence of an independent A.S. prose version [2 MSS.] of the life of St. Andrew, from the same ultimate origin, may also be noted, see pp. 243–4 below.)

In the past, critics have been tempted to regard the *Andreas* and the next poem in the MS., viz., the *Fates of the Apostles* (below), as forming a single poem, but Krapp (q.v. below) opposes the full weight of his immense authority to this supposition, pointing out that there is no MS. justification for it, and that the *Fates* is clearly based upon an entirely different, though undiscovered, source.

Bibliography.
C.B.E.L., 1.77.
H. & B., 69.

Editions.
Baskervill, W. M. *Andreas : A Legend of St. Andrew.* Boston, 1885. [2nd ed., 1891.]
Krapp, G. P. *Andreas and the Fates of the Apostles.* London, 1906. [Excellent in every way. Standard.]

Translations.
Gordon, *A.S. Poetry*, 200–33; Hall, *Jud. Phœn. Mald.*, 62–119.
Kennedy. *Cynewulf*, 211–63. Also Root, R. K., *Andreas: The Legend of St. Andrew, translated from the Old English, with an Introduction. (Yale Studies*, VII, 1899.)

Discussion.
Bourauel, J. *Zue Quellen und Verfasserfrage von Andreas, Crist und Fata.* Bonn, 1901.
Cook, A. S. "The Authorship of the O.E. Andreas" in *M.L.N.*, 34.418–19. 1919.
Cook, A. S. "The Old English Andreas and Bishop Acca of Hexham" in *Trans. Connecticut Academy*, 26.245–332. 1924.
Hamilton, G. L. "The Sources of the Fates of the Apostles and Andreas" in *M.L.N.*, 35.385–95. 1920.
Kennedy. *Cynewulf*, 42–51. [Summary of theories of authorship.]
Smithson. *Christian Epic*, passim.

2. THE FATES OF THE APOSTLES (fol. 52b–4a)

This (superficially complete) poem of 122 ll. briefly tells of the lives and deaths of the Twelve Apostles, the source apparently being some undiscovered "Latin list of the Apostles, their missions and passions, of a type commonly current at the time the Anglo-Saxon poem was written, and possibly of Irish origin" (Krapp

Vercelli Book [above], *xxxvii*). Several critics have (unconvincingly) connected it with the preceding poem in the MS., viz., the *Andreas* (q.v.), while yet others would detach from it the last 27 ll. beginning at l. 96. This part not only comprises all of the text on fol. 54a, but contains Cynewulf's runic signature. The supposition is that the poem as it stands is too slight to be the work of such a practised hand and that the folio in question is out of its proper place, viz., the end of the *Andreas*. While the inferiority is readily admitted, apart from the fact (a mere coincidence) mentioned above, the evidence of the MS. points entirely to the unity of the existing version of the poem.

Bibliography.
C.B.E.L., 1.77.
H. & B., 72.

Editions.
Grein-Wülker. *Poesie II*, 87–91.
Krapp, G. P. *Andreas and the Fates of the Apostles.* London, 1906.
Translations.
Gordon, *A.S. Poetry*, 197–9; Kennedy, *Cynewulf*, 205–8.
Discussion.
  See under the *Andreas.*
Jansen, K. *Die Cynewulf-forschung von ihren Anfängen bis zur Gegenwart.* Bonn, 1908. See pp. 77–90.
Kennedy. *Cynewulf*, 40–2, and refs.
Perkins, R. "On the Sources of the Fates of the Apostles" in *M.L.N.*, 32.159–61.
Sisam, K. "Cynewulf and his Poetry" in *Proc. of the Brit. Acad.*, Vol. XXVIII, 1932. Pp. 8–9.

3. SOUL AND BODY I (fol. 101b–3b)

The *Soul and Body I*, so called in order to distinguish it from the shorter and very similar *Soul and Body II* of *The Exeter Book* (see p. 192), now has 166 ll., but suddenly breaks off in the middle of a sentence at the bottom of fol. 103b. It contains two distinct parts, ll. 1–126, and ll. 127 to the end. In the first, a former sinful body is angrily reviled by its soul, which may repeat the reproaches every seventh night for 300 years, unless the end of the world should intervene. It is a grim denouncement. The second part, however, comprises the address of a soul in bliss to its body but the quality of the poet's exultation scarcely equals the ferocity of his castigation. Possibly we should have come to some other opinion after reading the concluding parts of the poem that have been lost with one or two folios now missing from the MS. between fol. 103 and fol. 104. For M.E. examples see pp. 333–4.

Text.

Grein-Wülker. *Poesie II,* 92–107. [Prints both *Vercelli* and *Exeter Book* texts.]

Translation.

Gordon. *A.S. Poetry,* 310–13.

Discussion.

Willard, R. "The Address of the Soul to the Body" in *P.M.L.A.,* 50.957–983. 1935. [On nature and sources of the genre.]

4. HOMILETIC FRAGMENT I (fol. 104b–6a)

This *Fragment* (for *Fragment II,* see Item 30 of *Ex. Bk.*) of 47 ll. is a rather loose expansion of the last 7 of the 9 verses of Psalm 28. The initial portion, doubtless corresponding to the first two verses, has been lost with the preceding folio, presumably missing.

Bibliography.
C.B.E.L., 1.82.
H. & B., 61. (See *Bi Manna Lease.*]

Text.

Grein-Wülker. *Poesie II,* 108–10.
Williams, O. T. *Short Extracts from Old English Poetry.* Bangor, 1909.

Translation.
Kemble. *Poetry of Cod. Verc.* above, 79–82.

5. THE DREAM OF THE ROOD (fol. 104b–6b)

The most complete text of this lovely dream-poem, unique in pre-Conquest poetry, is contained in the *Vercelli Book* and totals 156 ll. A shorter mutilated (North Northumbrian) version, comprising three passages, corresponding to perhaps 15 ll. in the Vercelli text, is also carved in runes on the famous Ruthwell Cross (which Dickins and Ross [ed. below] assign to the eighth century, see 1–13), but its precise relationship to the longer text is still controversial: "it might (herewith) be suggested that an original poem, selections from which appear on the Ruthwell Cross, was later expanded and added to. From this expanded version of sporadic Anglian forms in the latter .... we may assume that this expanded version was written in an Anglian dialect" (ib., 18). Further, two lines (in late West Saxon) inscribed on the silver work of the Brussels Cross, a supposed fragment of the True Cross now preserved in Brussels Cathedral, appear to be reminiscent of the poem (ib., 13–15). The source and authorship of the poem are both unknown. The older ascription to Cynewulf (cf. e.g. Cook, ed. below, xvii–xli), based on general and circumstantial evidence, is unacceptable to recent editors.

Very briefly, the theme is the Crucifixion, the story of which is told by the Cross to the poet as he dreamt at midnight. Peculiarly interesting is the representation of Christ as a native chieftain, and of his disciples as his thanes. Similarly striking, because reminiscent of primitive burial custom, is the singing of a dirge by the disciples before leaving the sepulchre in the evening (ll. 67–8). Although the critics have not failed to regard the poem as an object worthy of dissection (e.g. most would willingly dispense with the last 10 ll. as an accretion), all accord it the very highest praise.

Bibliography.
C.B.E.L., 1.78.
Dickins, B., and Ross, A. S. C. *The Dream of the Rood.* London, 1934. *Methuen's O.E. Library*, A. 4. Pp. 36–9. [A first-rate ed. Note the description of the Ruthwell Cross, with figures showing the runes in situ and the fuþorc (runic alphabet) used thereon. Reproduces the text of all three sources.]
H. & B., 71.

Facsimiles.
Bütow, H. *Das altenglische "Traumgesicht vom Kreuz", textkritisches, literaturgeschichtliches, kunstgeschichtliches.* Heidelberg, 1935. Pp. 4–38. [Full, annotated bibliography. An excellent ed., containing a comprehensive survey of all the problems, including the text of the Ruthwell Cross.]

Editions.
Bütow (above).
Cook, A. S. *The Dream of the Rood.* Oxford, 1905. [Partly superseded by ed. of Dickins and Ross (above). See, however, pp. xli–lvii on the poem's literary characteristics. Very full notes.]

Dickins and Ross (above).

Sweet. *A.S. Reader* (ll. 1–94, 131–48 and 154–8 only).

Wyatt. *A.S. Reader*, 170–2 (ll. 88–129 only).

Translations.

Brooks, H. F. *The Dream of the Rood.* Dublin, 1942.

Gordon. *A.S. Poetry*, 261–4.

Kennedy. *Cynewulf*, 306–11.

Discussion.

Brandl, A. "On the Early Northumbrian Poem 'A Vision of the Cross of Christ'" in *Scottish Hist. Rev.*, 9.139–47 [1912]. [Summary and discussions of date and occasion of poem.]

Brown, G. Baldwin. *The Arts in Early England:* Vol. 5, *The Ruthwell and Bewcastle Crosses*, London, 1921. [Chaps. IV–XII (pp. 102–317). Indispensable.]

Collingwood, W. G. *Northumbrian Crosses of the Pre-Norman Age.* London, 1927. *Passim.*

Cook, A. S. "The Date of the Old English Inscription on the Brussels Cross" in *M.L.R.*, 10.157–161. 1915.

Kennedy. *Cynewulf*, 62–8.

Logeman, H. *L'Inscription anglo-saxonne du reliquaire de la vraie Croix au trésor de l'église des SS. Michel-et-Gudule à Bruxelles.* 1891.

Patch, H. R. "Liturgical Influence in the Dream of the Rood" in *P.M.L.A.*, 34.233–57. 1919.

Ross, A. S. C. "The Linguistic Evidence for the Date of the Ruthwell Cross" in *M.L.R.*, 28.146–55. 1933.

Vietor, W. *Die nordhumbrischen Runensteine: Beiträge zur Text-kritik: Grammatik und Glossar.* Marburg, 1895. Pp. 2–13.

6. ELENE (fol. 121a–33b)

The theme of this long and complete poem of 1321 ll., universally acknowledged as Cynewulf's masterpiece, is the successful search for the True Cross by St. Helena undertaken at the instigation of her son, Constantine the Great. So far the source remains untraced, but it may have been a Latin version, which, differing but slightly from that in the *Acta Sanctorum* for May 4th, was made in Ireland from a Greek original.

The poem contains 15 numbered Sections. But the narrative properly ends with Section 14 at l. 1235, the last word of which is *Finit.* The remaining Section, which contains Cynewulf's runic signature as well as autobiographical information of the highest importance, constitutes an appendix so different stylistically from the earlier portions that it "would seem to have been composed as an entirely independent effort" (Krapp, *Vercelli Book*, xl). Nevertheless, the unity of the whole is in no doubt.

Like the *Andreas*, the *Elene* is cast in the heroic mould. "It is written in a simple, dramatic style, interspersed with imaginative and descriptive passages of great beauty. The glamour and pomp of war, the gleam of jewels, the joy of ships dancing on the waves, give life and colour to a narrative permeated by the deep and serious purpose of the author (*C.H.E.L.*, 1.56). Some of the notable passages are ll. 109–37 (battle-scene), 225–55 (sea-voyage), and the whole of Section 15.

Bibliography.
C.B.E.L., 1.76.
H. & B., 71–2.

Editions.
Cook, A. S. *The Old English Elene, Phoenix and Physiologus.* New Haven, 1919.
Holthausen, F. *Cynewulf's Elene.* 3rd ed. Heidelberg, 1914. [Excellent.]
Kent, C. W. *Elene, an Old English Poem.* 2nd ed. London, 1903.

Translations.
Gordon. *A.S. Poetry*, 234–60.
Kennedy. *Cynewulf*, 87–128.

Discussion.
Holthausen, F. "Zur Quelle von Cynewulfs Elene" in *Z.f.d. Ph.*, 37.1–19. 1905.
Holthausen, F. "Zur Quelle von Cynewulfs Elene" in *Archiv.*, 125.83–8. 1910.
Kennedy. *Cynewulf*, 34–40.
Smithson. *Christian Epic, passim.*

WALDERE

All that survives of this epic poem is found on two separate vellum folds, conveniently termed Fragments I and II, that were discovered in 1860 in the Royal Library at Copenhagen. They were apparently written about 1000, or possibly earlier, maybe by a Northumbrian scribe who was attempting to write "Standard" Old English, cf. p. 7 of F. Norman's excellent ed. (below), upon which the following account relies. The folds, each of which has had most of one leaf cut away leaving a narrow strip containing only parts of words, can be shown to be adjacent folds (II being the outer) in the original MS., and further, to have occurred in the order I, II (not II, I, as many earlier scholars have supposed). Between them, there is a gap of one whole leaf—i.e., at least 30 ll. The whole poem probably totalled over 1,000 ll. Only some 53 ll. now remain.

In Fragment I (32 ll.), a hero, Waldere, is encouraged by somebody, apparently his betrothed, Hildegyð (though she is nowhere mentioned in the text), to continue a fight. In II (31 ll.), somebody else (Norman argues that it was Waldere—earlier authorities suggest Guðhere or Hagena) praises a sword, Waldere extols his armour and challenges another hero, Guðhere, to battle.

A fuller, but later, and in several respects different version of the epic is extant in a Latin poem *Waltharius*, written about 930 by Ekkehard (d. 973), a monk of St. Gall, Switzerland (for a résumé, see Norman, p. 7). (Still later allusions occur in O.H.G., M.H.G., Norwegian and Polish texts, ib., 8–12.) Probably both O.E. and Latin poems originate from the same source, which may have been a lay created shortly after 600 by an unknown Bavarian poet (ib., 34).

Both the author and the date of composition are still undetermined, but Norman considers that the poem was very likely a "book-epic" written by a cleric not earlier than the middle of the eighth century.

Bibliography.
C.B.E.L., 1.69.
H. & B., 90.
Norman, F. *Waldere*. London, 1933. *Methuen's Old English Library*, A. 3. Pp. 44–8. [Very valuable ed., with excellent accounts of the manuscript and its foliation, as well as of the story in all its various forms.]

Facsimiles.
Holthausen, F. *Die altenglischen Waldere-Bruchstücke. Mit vier Autotypien.* Gothenburg, 1899.

Editions.
Dickins, B. *Runic and Heroic Poems.* Cambridge, 1915. [Text, with notes, pp. 56–63. Translation facing each page of text.]
Sedgefield. *Bk. A.S. V.P.*, 6–8.
Wyatt. *A.S. Reader*, 148–9.

Translations.

Clarke. *Sidelights*, 219 ff.

Dickins (above), 57–63.

Gordon. *A.S. Poetry*, 73–4.

Gummere. *O.E. Epic*, 167–70.

Discussion.

Chadwick. *The Heroic Age, passim.*

Clarke. *Sidelights*, 209 ff.

Dickins (above), 37–43.

Heusler, A. "Walther und Hildegund" in Hoops's *Reallexikon*, 4.476–7. 1919. [Summary survey of the legend.]

Schücking, L. "Waldere und Waltharius" in *E.St.*, 60.17–36. 1925–6. [On relationship of the two stories.]

Wolff, L. "Zu den Waldere Bruchstücken", in *Z.f.d.A.*, 62. 81 ff. 1925.

CHAPTER VI

OLD ENGLISH LITERATURE—PROSE

1. MODERN COLLECTIONS.

Cockayne, *Leechdoms*. [For list of contents, see p. 253 below.]

Craigie, W. A. *Specimens of Anglo-Saxon Prose*. Edinburgh, 1923–9. [Handy, cheap collections of extracts, with short vocabularies.]

Grein, C. W. M., and Wülker, R. *Bibliothek der angelsächsischen Prosa*. Cassel, 1872-. [Now under the editorship of H. Hecht. To date 13 vols. of this excellent series have been issued.]

Sedgefield, W. J. *Anglo-Saxon Prose Book*. Manchester, 1928. Series of extracts, with notes and vocabulary, also published in the ed.'s *Bk. A.S. V.P.*]

NOTE. Prose extracts are included in the various anthologies and *Readers* listed on pp. 152–3 above.

2. TRANSLATIONS

Chambers. *Engl. Norm. Con.* [Includes translations of much A S. prose of historical interest.]

Cook, A. S., and Tinker, C. B. *Select Translation from O.E. Prose*. Boston, 1908.

Sampson, G. (ed.). *The Cambridge Book of Prose and Verse*. C.U.P., 1924. [Designed to illustrate *C.H.E.L.*, Vol. I, for the ordinary reader.]

3. HISTORY AND CRITICISM

Chambers, R. W. *On the Continuity of English Prose from Alfred to More and his School*. London, 1932. [An extract from the Introduction to Nicholas Harpsfield's *Life of Sir Thomas More*, edited by E. V. Hitchcock and R. W. Chambers.]

Earle, J. *English Prose, its Elements, History and Usage*. 1890, 1903.

Krapp, G. P. *The Rise of English Literary Prose*. Oxford, 1916.

Smith, C. A. "The Order of Words in Anglo-Saxon Prose"

227

in *P.M.L.A.*, 8.210–42. 1893. [Based on a study of Alfred's *Orosius* and Aelfric's *Homilies*.]

Saintsbury, G. *A History of English Prose Rhythm*. London, 1912. [Reprinted, 1922.]

Tupper, J. W. *Tropes and Figures in Anglo-Saxon Prose*. Baltimore, 1897.

See also the books of literary criticism mentioned above, pp. 150–1.

4. AUTHORS AND TEXTS
AELFRIC (c. 955–c. 1020)

One of the most prominent literary figures of his time and undoubtedly the most accomplished prose writer of the O.E. period, Aelfric, now often called Grammaticus (note his *Latin Grammar*) thus distinguishing him from several other ecclesiastics of the same name, including e.g. his pupil Aelfric Bata (fl. 1005) and especially Aelfric, Archbishop of Canterbury (d. 1005), was educated at the famous monastic school at Winchester under the care of Bishop Aethelwold (c. 908–84), and then in 987, as a priest, became novice-master at the restored Benedictine monastery at Cernel (Cerne Abbas) in Dorsetshire. In 1005 he became the first abbot of Eynsham Abbey, Oxfordshire.

A good classical scholar, equally facile in both Latin and O.E., Aelfric wrote homilies, legends, theological commentaries, translations from the Old Testament, pastoral letters, works on monastic customs, grammar and mathematics, as well as a Latin life of his best friend, Bishop Aethelwold. His theological writings, though chiefly derivative, are of special interest because they shed much light upon contemporary Christian beliefs and practices (see Gem [below], 66–165). In particular, he vigorously opposed the doctrine of transubstantiation (see "A Sermon on the Sacrifice on Easter Day", Thorpe [below], 2.263–83), for which reason several of his writings were printed as early as the sixteenth century (cf. *D.N.B.*). Right from the first Aelfric proved himself able to write clearly and attractively (e.g., the first series of *Homilies*), but he soon developed an ornateness (alliteration and rhythm) that is over-elaborate (cf. e.g., *The Lives of Saints;* but this feature is already observable in the second series of *Homilies*). Gerould (below) convincingly argues that Aelfric was here "following and adapting what he must have believed the best Latin style" and that "he was trying to give his English readers the equivalent of the rhymed [Latin] prose in which men of taste found pleasure for a great many centuries".

228

Bibliography.
C.B.E.L., 1.89–92.
H. & B., 96–102.

Discussion.

Dietrich, E. *Abt Aelfric. Zur Literaturgeschichte der angelsächsischen Kirche* in *Zeitschrift für die historische Theologie*, 25.487–594 [1855], and 26.163–256 [1856]. Gotha. [A standard work. "Much of it is translated in White", H. & B.; summarised by Skeat (below). Contains four sections on Aelfric's writings, the doctrine of the A.S. Church according to Aelfric, his education and character, and his life.]

Dubois, M.-M. *Ælfric, Sermonnaire, Docteur et Grammarien.* Paris, 1943. [Indispensable.]

Gem, S. H. *An Anglo-Saxon Abbot: Aelfric of Eynsham.* Edinburgh, 1912. [Useful survey of life and doctrines intended for the general reader. With translations of the *Life of St. Aethelwold* and the *Colloquium.*]

Gerould, G. H. "Abbot Aelfric's Rhythmic Prose" in *M. Ph.*, 22.353–66. 1925.

Skeat, W. W. *Aelfric's Lives of the Saints, being a set of Sermons on Saints' Days formerly observed by the English Church.* 2 vols. E.E.T.S., 76, 82, 94, 114. 1881–1900. [With translation facing text. Vol. II gives an account of the MSS. of the *Lives* and of Aelfric's life and authorship, the latter being a useful summary of Dietrich (above).]

White, C. L. *Aelfric: A New Study of his Life and Writings.* Boston, 1898. [Based on Dietrich's monumental work (above), parts being simply translations, and supplemented by results of investigation to date. Includes a full chronological bibliography. Appendices summarise important Aelfrician studies. Indispensable.]

Aelfric's writings fall into two groups, those he wrote while still a monk, and those he wrote after becoming an abbot (i.e. from 1005 onwards). The following is a chronological list of his chief works, the most important being discussed in some detail. All are in English unless the contrary is stated.

1. CATHOLIC HOMILIES (991–2).

These homilies consist of two series, each provided not only with a Latin Preface addressed to Sigeric, Archbishop of Canterbury 989–95, but also with an English preface (composed after 1016) stating, in the first, Aelfric's reason for translating them from

Latin into English and, in the second, the plan and (broadly) the sources. Aelfric's intention was that each series should contain forty sermons, to cover the whole of the church year. The first actually does so, but until recently the second was commonly assumed to contain forty-five, the last six being supposedly a later accretion. But Sisam's brilliant studies of the Bodley MSS. 340 and 342 (refs. below) have disposed of the difficulty: the sermons are to be reckoned not according to the items, but, as in the first series, according to the days which they were designed to serve. "Thus Thorpe's 39 sermons before the Apology [giving reasons for omitting the story of St. Thomas of India] cover only 34 feast-days and when the 6 sermons after the Apology are added we get the exact number 40 that Aelfric promised" (Sisam, ib.). The "issue of both [series] may be assigned to the years 991–2" (Sisam, ib.). The first are "simple, doctrinal and instructive, the second discursive, historical and more elaborate, with much narrative" (*C.H.E.L.*, 1. 117).

In his Latin Preface to the first series, Aelfric mentions several sources, the better-known being St. Augustine, St. Jerome, St. Gregory and Bede. But he must have used others, including Alcuin, Gregory of Tours and Rufinus. St. Gregory, however, seems to be the principal source.

For excellent illustrations of Aelfric's lucid style, see the English Prefaces. A masterly exposition of a difficult theme will be found in the "Sermon on the Sacrifice on Easter Day" (Thorpe, below, 2.263–83). This, perhaps the most notable of all, has given rise to considerable theological controversy.

The MSS. seem to fall into three groups, the chief differences being the following. In the first (represented by Thorpe's ed. (below) of Camb. Univ. Lib., MS. Gg. 3. 28), the two series of homilies are kept distinct and the prefaces retained. In the second (cf. C.C.C.C. MS. 188, ? 1007–20), the second series and all the prefaces are omitted. The third group comprises several MSS. "in which both [series] are recast together in the order of the church year" (*C.H.E.L.*, 1.117).

Bibliography.
C.B.E.L., 1.89–90.
H. & B., 99–101.
White, 211–12.

Text.
Assman, B. *Angelsächsische Homilien und Heiligenleben.* Cassel, 1889. [*Prosa, III.*]

Sweet, H. *Selected Homilies of Aelfric.* Oxford, 1885, etc. [Texts from Thorpe's ed., below.]

Thorpe, B. *The Homilies of the Anglo-Saxon Church.* 2 vols. London, 1844–6. [Containing both series. this is a complete ed., with notes and translation, but no glossary, of Camb. Univ. Lib. MS. Gg. 3. 28. The precise significance of "Part I" of the sub-title is obscure; no Part II was ever published.]

Warner, R. D–N. *Early English Homilies from the Twelfth Century MS. Vesp. D. XIV. Part I, Text.* E.E.T.S., 152. 1917. [Mainly Aelfric's. Part II containing an Introd., Notes and Glossary promised, but not yet issued. An admirable description of the contents of this MS. has been given by M. Förster in *E.St.*, 54. 46–68.]

Note.—The E.E.T.S. promise another ed. of Aelfric's *Homilies* by Dr. A. Pope.

Discussion.

Förster, M. *Ueber die Quellen von Aelfrics Homiliae Catholicae, I Legenden.* Berlin, 1892. [Continued in *Angl.*, 16.1–61 (1894), under the title of "*Uber die Quellen von Aelfrics exegetischen Homiliae Catholicae*".]

Sisam, K. "MSS. Bodley 340 and 342: Aelfric's *Catholic Homilies*" in *R.E.S.*, 7.7–22 (1931), 8.51–68 (1932) and 9.1–12 (1933). [A most valuable and definitive article on date, composition, and arrangement.]

2. DE TEMPORIBUS ANNI (992)

Extant in several MSS., four being in the Cotton Collection (B.M.), this scientific treatise, recently assigned unquestioningly to Aelfric by Sisam (*R.E.S.*, 8.52) and variously entitled *De Temporibus, De Computo* and *De Primo Die Saeculi*, discusses firstly and secondly the division of time and of the solar year, and lastly astronomy and the phenomena of the atmosphere. While claiming dependence upon Bede (viz., *De Temporibus Ratione, De Temporibus* and *De Natura Rerum,* the first two being manuals on the calculation of respectively ecclesiastical festivals and Easter, and the third a text-book of cosmography) it apparently includes much original information.

Bibliography.
C.B.E.L., 1.91.
H. & B., 99.

Text.

Cockayne. *Leechdoms*, 3.232–83. ["A Treatise on Astronomy and Cosmogony"; with tr.]

Henel, H. *Aelfric, De Temporibus Anni.* E.E.T.S., 213. London, 1942 (for 1940). [Authoritative.]

Wright, T. *Popular Treatises on Science written during the Middle Ages.* London, 1841; Pp. 1–19. [With tr.]

3. LATIN GRAMMAR (995)

Extant in fifteen MSS., pointing to its popularity, the *Grammar* is a tr. from the Latin *Grammar* of Priscian (fl. 500), the favourite class-book of the mediaeval schools. Edited by J. Zupitza: *Aelfrics Grammatik und Glossar*, Berlin, 1880.

4. LIVES (PASSIONS) OF SAINTS (996–7)

The *Lives* comprise a third series of homilies, arranged according to the church calendar and intended for reading to laymen at monastic services. They include two prefaces, one in Latin stating the purpose and source (*Vitae Patrum*) of the book, the other in English and cast in the form of a letter to Alderman Aethelweard[1], stating that the series had been specially written at the request of himself and of his son Aethelmaer (founder of Cerne Abbey). Though in the Latin Preface Aelfric quotes *Vitae Patrum* as his sole source, in the text he mentions several of the Early Fathers as his authorities (see further Skeat, above, 2.xlvii–xlviii, and 446–56). The best MS. (B.M. Cotton Julius E. VII) "contains thirty-three lives, six general homilies and a narrative without title on the legend of Abgarus, thus, like the two previous series [*Homilies*, v.p. 229], comprising forty sermons in all", *C.H.E.L.*, 1.20—all the extant MSS. are mentioned by Skeat, above, 2.445.

Except for the first on the Nativity—in ordinary prose—these homilies illustrate Aelfric's characteristic alliterative, rhythmical prose at its best. At the same time, being narratives, they are all intrinsically interesting, especially so the accounts of the English saints, Oswald, Swithin and Edmund. The *Life* of the latter is of particular importance as a revelation of the ardour of Aelfric's patriotism and of his conception of the ideal king.

[1] On Aethelweard and Aethelmaer, see White, 47–50, *et passim*. It was Aethelweard who appears to have inspired Aelfric to write the *Catholic Homilies* and to begin his version of the Bible. Certainly *Joshua and Judges* were written at his request. Aethelmaer, too, promoted Aelfric's work. See further *The Exeter Book of Old English Poetry*, London, 1933, pp. 87–90.

Bibliography.
C.B.E.L., 1.89.
H. & B., 101.

Text.
Skeat, W. W. (above).

5. INTERROGATIONS (QUESTIONS) OF SIGEWULF THE PRIEST

This work is appended to the best MSS. of the *Lives of the Saints*, of which it probably forms a part. It consists of a series of catechetical answers to questions on *Genesis* and is based on the Latin *Handbook upon Genesis* written at the end of the eighth century by the celebrated English scholar Alcuin (735–804) and dedicated to his inseparable pupil and friend, the priest *Sigewulf*. Edited by Maclean, G. E. ,"Aelfric's Version of Alcuini Interrogationes Sigewulfi in Genesin" in *Angl.*, 6.425–73 (1883), 7.1–59 (1884), with Latin and O.E. texts.

6. LATIN-ENGLISH GLOSSARY (997–9)

Seven of the fifteen MSS. of the *Grammar* contain the *Glossary* as an appendix to the *Grammar*. It consists of an English dictionary of Latin nouns and adjectives classified according to subject. Bibl.: H. & B., 99. Edited by T. Wright: *Anglo-Saxon and Old English Vocabularies*, 2 vols., 2nd ed., edited and collated by R. P. Wülcker, London, 1884; see 2.306–36. Do not confuse this *Glossary* with the text called "Archbishop Aelfric's Vocabulary", ib., pp. 104–91, which is apparently not the work of Aelfric, cf. White above, 121.

7. COLLOQUIUM (995–1005)

A Latin dialogue intended to help the novices at Winchester to speak correct Latin. Extant in two MSS., it consists of entertaining conversations between a teacher, a novice, and single representatives of various occupations and trades. Each describes his daily duties. The work therefore adds considerably to our knowledge of A.S. daily life, especially that in the monastery. MS. Cott. Tib., A. 3 is furnished with a running O.E. interlinear gloss, of unknown authorship. The MS. in St. John's College, Oxford, contains only a few glosses.

Bibliography.
C.B.E.L., 1.92.
H. & B., 98.

Editions.

Thorpe, B.   *Analecta Anglo-Saxonica*, 2nd ed. London.1846. Pp. 18–36.

Wright, T.   *Anglo-Saxon and Old English Vocabularies*. 2 vols. 2nd ed. Edited and collated by R. P. Wülcker. London, 1884. See 1.89–103.

Stevenson, W. H.   *Early Scholastic Colloquies*. Oxford, 1929. [Prints the glosses of the Cotton MS., and occasional ones, at the foot of the page, from the Oxford MS.]

Garmonsway, G. N.   *Aelfric's Colloquy*. London, 1939. *Methuen's O.E. Library*. [With full critical apparatus.]

Translation.

Gem (above), 183–95.

Discussion.

Schroeder, E.   "Colloquium Aelfrici" in *Z.f.d.A.*, 41.283–90. 1897.

Zupitza, J.   "Die Ursprungliche Gestalt von Aelfric's Colloquium" in *Z.f.d.A.*, 31.32–45. 1887.

8. PENTATEUCH AND JOSHUA (c. 997)

These are partly translated and partly abridged from the books of the *Pentateuch* and of *Joshua*, and are apparently not all from Aelfric's hand. First printed by Thwaites (1698), who added Aelfric's translations from the books of *Judges* and of *Job*. As a convenient name for the *Pentateuch*, together with the books of *Joshua* and *Judges*, Thwaites invented the term *Heptateuch*, which is used by its most recent editor, S. J. Crawford (*The Old English Version of the Heptateuch*, E.E.T.S., 160. [1922]. With Latin text of the Vulgate). Also edited by C. W. M. Grein, *Aelfrik de vetere et novo Testamento Pentateuc. Isua, Buch der Richter und Hiob*, Cassel, 1872. (*Prosa I.*). Crawford (above) points out that this is a reprint, with emendations, of the edition of the *Heptateuch* by E. Thwaites (Oxford, 1698) and of W. L'Isle's edition (1623) of Aelfric's treatise, *On the Old and New Testaments*. Apparently Grein never kept the promise made in his Preface to publish a collation of his editions with the MSS. Nor was it included in the 1921 anastatic reprint of Grein, despite the existence of such a collation prefixed to J. Wilke's *Lautlehre zu Aelfric's Heptateuch und Buch Hiob*, Bonn, 1905. Aelfric's version of the Bible was "essentially meant to be preached rather than read; he wrote for those who should teach the as yet unlettered people", *C.H.E.L.*, 1.122. See also White (above), 146-9.

9. JUDGES (997-8)

A translation from the biblical book of that name. Skeat (above, p. xxix) regards this as "a distinct work . . . to be considered as a metrical (or alliterative) Homily". It was arranged by Grein as verse (480 ll.) and printed after his death by R. Wülcker, *Angl.*, 2.141-5.

10. JOB, ESTHER AND JUDITH (997-8)

The first is an epitome of the *Book of Job*, the others are translations of the biblical books of the same names. *Job* is edited by Grein (*Prosa I*, 265-72); for *Esther* and *Judith*, see B. Assmann, *Prosa III*, 92-101 and 102-16 respectively.

11. HEXAMERON (possibly 991-8)

In the main this is translated from the Latin *Hexameron* of St. Basil, and partly from Bede's *Commentary on Genesis*. It "contains an introductory address to the reader; an account of the works of each of the six days of creation; of the fall of the angels before the creation of man; of the seventh day of rest; of the temptation and sin of man; of his expulsion from Paradise; and of his redemption through Christ", cf. White, above, 116-17. Edited by S. J. Crawford: *Exameron Anglice or the Old English Hexameron. With an Introduction, a Collation of all the Manuscripts, a Modern English Translation, Parallel Passages from the Other Works of Aelfric and Notes on the Sources*, Cassel, 1921 (*Prosa X*). Also edited (with tr.) by H. W. Norman: *The Anglo-Saxon Version of the Hexameron of St. Basil*, London, 1849.

12. CANONS (? 998)

This work consists of a pastoral letter written at the request of Wulfsige, Bishop of Sherbourne (993-1001), for the use of the clergy in his diocese. Prefaced with a short personal letter to Wulfsige, its subject is priestly duties. A summary of its thirty-five sections (in two parts) is given by White, above, 135-9. It has been edited, with tr., by B. Thorpe, *Ancient Laws and Institutes*, London, 1840 (pp. 441-51).

13. BENEDICTINE RULE (c. 1005)

This is a Latin abridgement of the *De Consuetudine Monachorum* by

Bishop Aethelwold of Winchester. It was specially written for the monks of Eynsham (Oxfordshire), of which monastery Aelfric had become Abbot in 1005 or the previous year. Edited by A. Schröer, "De Consuetudine Monachorum" in *E. St.*, 9.294–6 (1886).

14. ADVICE TO A SPIRITUAL SON (after 1005)

This incomplete and unique version of St. Basil's *Admonitio ad Filium Spiritualem* was written for Benedictine monks. Edited by Norman with tr. (see item 11 above).

15. HOMILY ADDRESSED TO WULFGEAT (1005–6)

This is "a discourse in two parts, which is in substance, first, a summary of Christian doctrine, and second, a sermon". Wulfgeat was, until disgraced in 1006, a favourite thane of Æthelred II. Edited by Assmann, *Prosa III*, 1–12.

16. LIFE OF ST. AETHELWOLD (1006)

This work is in Latin and dedicated to Kenwulf, Bishop of Winchester, edited by J. Stevenson, *Chronicon Monasterii de Abingdon*, 2 vols., Rolls Series, London, 1858 (see 2.255–66). Translated Gem (above), 166–80.

17. INTRODUCTION TO THE OLD AND NEW TESTAMENTS
(?1006–8)

This was written at the request of a certain Sigwerd. "The work as a whole is a practical, historical introduction to the Holy Scriptures" and is designed for laymen, the chief sources being St. Augustine's *De Doctrina Christiana* and Isidore's *In Libros Veteris ac Novi Testamenti Proemia* (itself based on the former), cf. White (above), 66–7, 152–5. Edited (with tr.) by S. J. Crawford, *The Old English Version of the Heptateuch*, E.E.T.S., 160 [1922], pp. 15–75.

18. HOMILY FOR THE BIRTHDAY OF A CONFESSOR (c. 1008)

Shows the "forbearance of God by many instances", see White (above), 108–10. Edited by Assmann [*Prosa III*, 49–64].

19. A HOMILY ON THE SEVENFOLD GIFTS OF THE HOLY SPIRIT (1000–8)

For text, see Napier, A.S., *Wulfstan*, Berlin, 1883, pp. 56–60.

20. PASTORAL LETTERS (1015)

Written for Wulfstan (Archbishop of York, 1003–23), the themes being clerical chastity and the use of holy oil. Edited, with tr., by B. Thorpe, *Ancient Laws and Institutes of England*, London, 1840, pp. 452–65.

21. HOMILY ON THE BIRTH OF THE VIRGIN
(date undetermined)

This is an elaborate plea for celibacy. Edited by Assmann, *Prosa III*, 24–48.

22. A LETTER (after 1005)

Written to Sigferth on the celibacy of the clergy (*C.H.E.L.*, I. 126); but entitled "Of Holy Chastity" by White (above; p. 110), and "Purity" by Skeat (above; p. xxxix). Extant in 4 MSS. Edited by Assmann, *Prosa III*, 13–23.

ALEXANDER'S LETTER TO ARISTOTLE

Immediately preceding, and in the script of the first hand of, the *Beowulf MS.* (Cotton Vitell. A XV, c. 1000) is this unique prose version of the famous, though spurious, Latin *Epistola Alexandri* describing the wonders of India. The *Epistola* circulated independently in the Middle Ages, but was ultimately based on the early Greek work (c. A.D. 200) of an unknown author commonly called Pseudo-Callisthenes.

The O.E. version, in W.S. tinged by Anglian, contains many rare words. Historically it is important because it shows that long before the Conquest the Anglo-Saxons found entertainment in the exotic romanticism of the East. [Cf. in the same respect *Wonders of the East* (p. 259) and *Apollonius of Tyre* (p. 244).]

Bibliography.
C.B.E.L., 1.94.
H. & B., 102–3.

Text.
Rypins, S. *Three Old English Prose Texts in MS. Cotton Vitellius A XV, edited with an Introduction and Glossarial Index.* E.E.T.S., 161. London, 1924. [With one facs. page and Latin text. Contains also *Wonders of the East* and *Life of St. Christopher*, pp. 259, 247.]

ALFRED (849–901)

Alfred's literary activities arose out of his determination to restore education to his kingdom of Wessex. Almost all of his known writings are translations from notable Latin books, which were either philosophical or else purely factual. In the main their chronology can be determined only from internal evidence, from their literary style or the closeness of the reproduction.

His first work, the *Handbook*, begun in 887, is untraced. It was apparently a mere collection of extracts from the Latin Bible and the Early Fathers. His next was a close translation of the *Cura Pastoralis* of Gregory the Great. In his Preface—the first important piece of English prose—written, so it seems, as an introduction to the whole series of his translations, Alfred notes the decline of learning in England and announces his intention of reforming the system of public education. Following upon this, and with the idea of providing his people with a compendium of world history, he translated the famous *Historia adversus Paganos* of Orosius. Into this, he incorporated an account of Germania, as well as the narratives of the celebrated voyages of Ohthere to the White Sea and Wulfstan to the Baltic. The latter are accessible in most *Readers*. How far Alfred composed the O.E. version of Bede's *Historia Ecclesiastica* is still undetermined. External evidence, including the testimony of Aelfric, certainly points to his authorship. The translation is far too close to be entirely successful. In addition there are numerous omissions.

Alfred next turned his attention to the law, and produced, perhaps c 893, a legal code of a rather composite character. Besides elements from the Mosaic law, it contained material from the laws of earlier A.S. Kings, viz., Ine, Offa and Aethelred. Some time after 897, Alfred completed a somewhat free rendering of Boethius's *De Consolatione Philosophiae*, to which he made many additions. He seems to have ended his translating career with a version of St. Augustine's *Soliloquiae*, which becomes freer as the book proceeds.

The above probably represent the sum total of Alfred's own literary productions. He also partly inspired the literary achievements of others, including the writers of the *Anglo-Saxon Chronicle*. It was at his command, too, that Bishop Werferth translated Gregory's *Dialogues* (see p. 258).

Bibliography.
C.B.E.L., 1.85–8.
H. & B., 103–8.

General.

Borenski, L. *Der Stil König Alfreds. Eine Studie zum Psychologie der Rede.* Leipzig, 1934. [See especially pp. 288–310 for a discussion of the special characteristics of Alfred's style. An important book on the psychology of literary expression.]

Bowker, A. (ed.). *Alfred the Great, containing Chapters on his Life and Times.* London, 1899. [Contains essays by various authors of repute.]

Hodgkin, R. H. *History of Anglo-Saxons.* [See Vol. II, Chaps. XIV–XX, particularly XVII (on "Restoration of Order and of Learning") and XX (on "Alfred the Man and his Message").]

Lees, B. A. *Alfred the Great, the Truthteller, Maker of England.* New York, 1915. [An excellent biography. Contains some fifty illustrative plates. Very useful for the history of the period.]

Plummer, C. *The Life and Times of Alfred the Great.* Oxford, 1902. [See especially 140–96. Authoritative and indispensable.]

Stevenson, W. H. (ed.). *Asser's Life of King Alfred, together with the Annals of St. Neots erroneously ascribed to Asser.* Oxford, 1904. [Standard ed. of the Latin text. A tr. with valuable introd. and notes by L. C. Jane was pub. (London, 1908) under the title of *Asser's Life of Alfred.*]

Thorpe, B. *The Life of Alfred the Great, translated from the German.* Bohn Library, London, 1902. [Tr. from R. Pauli's famous *König Alfred.* Berlin, 1851.]

Translation.

Giles, J. A. (ed.). *The Whole Works of King Alfred the Great, with Preliminary Essays illustrative of the History, Arts and Manners of the Ninth Century.* Jubilee Ed. Oxford and Cambridge, 1858.

1. GREGORY'S CURA PASTORALIS

The following MSS. are extant:—(i) Bodl. Hatton 20. Contemporary. (ii) B.M. Cotton Tiberius B. 11. Contemporary. Injured in the Cotton Fire and now a collection of fragments. (iii) Bodl. Junius 53. Copied from preceding MS. Cott. Tib. (iv) B.M. Cotton Otho B.2, and 3 MSS. at Cambridge in C.C.C. Trin. and the Univ. Lib. There is also a leaf out of another at Cassel.

Editions,

Sweet, H. (ed.). *King Alfred's West-Saxon Version of Gregory's Pastoral Care, with an English translation, the Latin Text, Notes and an Introduction.* E.E.T.S., 45, 50. 1871–2. [Contains full text of Hatton and Cott. Tib. MSS., the latter from Junius's copy in the Bodleian [MS. Jun. 53]. Variant readings are supplied from Cott. Otho B. 21. The Latin text is not included.]

Discussion.

Klaeber, F. *"Zu König Alfreds Vorrede zu seiner Übersetzung der Cura Pastoralis"* in *Angl.,* 47.53–65. 1923. [Throws light on Alfred's personality and reading.]

2. OROSIUS'S HISTORIA

The extant MSS. comprise:—(i) Lauderdale (Helmingham Hall, Suffolk). Contemporary but defective. (ii) Cotton Tiberius B.I. Tenth or eleventh century. (iii) Transcript of Cotton MS. by Junius. (iv) Transcript of Junius by Elstob and Ballard.

Edition.

Sweet, H. *King Alfred's Orosius.* E.E.T.S., 79. London, 1883. [Contains the Latin original. Standard.]

Selections.

Schram, O. K. *The Old English Orosius.* In preparation for *Methuen's Old English Library* series.

Sweet, H. *Extracts from Alfred's Orosius.* Oxford, 1885, etc. 80 pp. [Contains selections from Lauderdale MS. and is intended to supplement the editor's *A.S. Reader.*]

Discussion.

Ekblom, R. "Alfred the Great as Geographer," in a *Philological Miscellany presented to E. Ekwall.* Uppsala, 1942. [Shows that Alfred used two systems of orientation.]

Geidel, H. *Alfred der Grosse als Geograph.* In *Münchener Geographische Studien,* No. 15. 1904.

Hampson, R. T. "On the Geography of King Alfred the Great" in Giles's *The Whole Works of King Alfred* (above), 3.11–63. See also 2.10–17, by J. Bosworth.

Hübener, G. *König Alfred und Osteuropa* in *E.St.,* 60.35–57. 1925.

Malone, K. "King Alfred's Geographical Treatise" in *Speculum,* [Jan.] 1933.

Markham, C. *"Alfred as a Geographer"* in Bowker's *Alfred the Great* (above), 151-67. [Mainly summarises Alfred's three original contributions to the *Orosius*, viz., the account of Central and Northern Europe, and the voyages of Ohthere and Wulfstan.]

Nansen, F. *In Northern Mists. Arctic Exploration in Early Times.* Translated by A. G. Chater. 2 vols. New York, 1911. See 1.169-81. [A geographical study of Ohthere's narrative.]

Ross, A. S. C. *The "Terfinnas" and "Beormas" of Ohthere.* Leeds School of English Language. Kendal, 1940.

3. BEDE'S ECCLESIASTICAL HISTORY

The text is extant in the following MSS.:— (i) Oxford Bodl. Tanner 10. Oldest and best. (ii) Corpus Christi College 41, Cambridge. (iii) Otho, B. II, Brit. Mus. Fragments only. (iv) Corpus Christi College 279, Oxford. (v) Cambridge Univ. Library kk. 3.18.

Editions.

Miller, T. *The Old English Version of Bede's Ecclesiastical History of the English People.* E.E.T.S., 95, 96, 111. 1890-8. [Standard. With translation.]

Schipper, J. *König Alfreds Übersetzung von Bedas Kirchengeschichte.* Leipzig, 1879. (*Prosa* 4.)

Discussion.

Hart, J. M. *"Rhetoric in the Translation of Bede"* in *An English Miscellany.* Oxford, 1901.

Potter, S. *On the Relation of the O.E. Bede to Werferth's Gregory and to Alfred's Translations.* Prague, 1930.

Thompson, A. H. [ed.]. *Bede: his Life, Times and Writings, Essays in Commemoration of the Twelfth Centenary of his Death.* Oxford, 1935. [Contents: The Life of the Venerable Bede, the Age of Bede, Northumbrian Monasticism, Monkwearmouth and Jarrow, Bede as Historian, Bede as Exegete and Theologian, Bede's Miracle Stories, The Manuscripts of Bede, The Library of the Venerable Bede.]

van Draat, P. F. "The Authorship of the Old English Bede" in *Angl.*, 39.319-47. 1916. ["A Study in Rhythm." Argues against Alfredian authorship.]

4. LAWS

For complete list of the MSS., see Liebermann, F., *Die Gesetze der Angelsächsen*, 1.xviii-lxii.

Editions.

Attenborough, F. L. *The Laws of the Earliest English Kings.* Cambridge, 1922. pp. 62–93. [With translation opposite each page of text.]

Liebermann. *Gesetze*, 1.16–88.

Turk, M. H. *The Legal Code of Alfred the Great.* Halle, 1893. [With full critical apparatus.]

Translation.

Attenborough (above).

Discussion.

Liebermann. *Gesetze*, 3.30–86.

Pollock, F. "English Law before the Norman Conquest" in Bowker's *Alfred the Great*, 209–39.

5. BOETHIUS' DE CONSOLATIONE PHILOSOPHIAE

The text is preserved in the following MSS.:—(i) B.M. Cotton, Otho A. vi. Early 10th C. or 906–70. Injured in Cotton Fire of 1731. *Metra* in Verse. (ii) Bodl. MS. 180, Oxford. Early twelfth century. The most complete. *Metra* in prose. (iii) Fragment forming the last leaf of Bodl. MS. 86, from second half of tenth century. A transcript of the Cotton MS. was made by Junius.

Edition.

Sedgefield, W. J. *King Alfred's Old English Version of Boethius de Consolatione Philosophiae, edited from the MS. with Introduction, Critical Notes and Glossary.* Oxford, 1899. [Standard].

Translation.

Sedgefield, W. J. *King Alfred's Version of the Consolations of Boethius. Done into Modern English, with an Introduction.* Oxford, 1900. [A handy literal rendering. "The passages . . . which do not occur in the Latin original are printed in italics", (Preface). The *Metra* are translated into the metre of O.E. verse, without, however, sacrificing literalness.]

Discussion.

Fehlauer, F. *Die englischen Übersetzung von Boethius' De Consolatione Philosophiae.* Berlin, 1909.

James, H. R. *The Consolation of Philosophy.* London, 1907. [Translation of Latin text into English prose and verse.]

Patch, H. R. *The Tradition of Boethius: A Study of his Importance in Medieval Culture.* Oxford, 1935.

Schmidt, K. H. *König Alfreds Boethius-Bearbeitung*. Göttingen, 1934. [Considers that Alfred was much indebted to the commentary on the *Consolation* by his contemporary Remigius of Auxerre (d. 908). Analyses the prose and metrical versions and provides notes on commentary.]

Stewart, H. F. *Boethius, An Essay*. Edinburgh, 1891. [Pp. 170–8.]

6. ST. AUGUSTINE'S SOLILOQUIAE [THE BLOOMS]

There are two MSS., viz.:—(i) Cotton Vitellius A. 15, B.M., twelfth century, and (ii) transcript of same by Junius, Jun. 70. I. Oxford.

Editions.

Cockayne, T. O. *The Shrine. A Collection of Occasional Papers on Dry Subjects*. London, 1864–9.

Endter, W. [ed.]. *König Alfred der Grosse: bearbeitung der Soliloquien des Augustines*, Hamburg, 1922. [*Prosa* 11. The best ed. A conservative text with good notes. Introd. brief but useful; good bibliography. A Latin version is printed on lower half of each page.]

Hargrove, H. L. *King Alfred's Old English Version of St. Augustine's Soliloquies, edited with Introduction, Notes and Glossary*. New York, 1902. [Though the best ed. in English, is far from satisfactory, see Holthausen's review, *Angl. B. Bl.*, 15.321–8.]

Hulme, W. H. " 'Blooms' von König Alfred" in *E.St.*, 18.332–56. 1893. [Corrections in *E.St.*, 19.470, 1894. A much criticised ed.]

Translation.

Hargrove, H. L. *King Alfred's Old English Version of St. Augustine's Soliloquies, turned into Modern English*. New York, 1904.

Discussion.

Hubbard, F. G. "The Relation of the Blooms of King Alfred to the Anglo-Saxon translation of Boethius" in *M.L.N.*, 9.321–42. 1894. [Demonstrating identity of authorship.]

Jost, K. "Zu Textkritik der altenglischen Soliloquienbearbei-tung" in *Angl. B. Bl.*, 31.259–72 and 280–90 (1920), and 32.8–16 (1921). [An important article on textual criticism and interpretation.]

LEGEND OF ST. ANDREW

This short and unpretentious version of the legendary adven-tures of St. Andrew found both in C.C.C.C. MS. 198, and as the nineteenth homily of the *Blickling Homilies* (see p. 245), recounts the saint's missionary activities in Mermedonia. Like the infinitely superior metrical rendering known as the *Andreas* (see p. 218), it is based upon a lost Latin redaction of the Greek *Acts of Andrew and Matthew.*

Bibliography.
H. & B., 108.

Editions.
Bright. *A.S. Reader*, 113–28.
Craigie. *Prose Specimens II*, 32–42.
Goodwin, C. W. *The Anglo-Saxon Legends of St. Andrew and St. Veronica*. London, 1851. [With translation.]
Morris, R. *The Blickling Homilies*. E.E.T.S. London, 1880. Pp. 228–49. [With translation.]

Discussion.
Krapp. *Andreas and the Fates of the Apostles*. London. 1906. [See pp. xxi–xxix. On source.]

APOLLONIUS OF TYRE

The story of *Apollonius of Tyre* seems to have been put together by a Greek author in the third century. However the eleventh century O.E. version (C.C.C.C. MS. 18), unfortunately only extant in a fragment containing the first half and the concluding portion, is directly based upon a lost (undated) Latin recension. "It tells of the wooing of the King of Antioch's daughter by Apollonius of Tyre, and how her father, to prevent her marriage, required her suitor to solve a riddle or to be beheaded," *C.H.E.L.*, 1.135.
Two reasons make this very readable narrative specially noteworthy: its evidence of A.S. interest in legends of the East; and again, it is prose fiction unprompted by clerical didacticism.

Bibliography.
C.B.E.L., 1.94–5.
H. & B., 108–9.

Text.
Thorpe, B. *The Anglo-Saxon Version of the Story of Apollonius of Tyre*. London, 1834. [With translation.]
Zupitza, J. "Die altenglische Bearbeitung der Erzählung von Apollonius von Tyrus" in *Archiv.*, 97.17–34. 1896.

Selection.
Cook. *First Bk. O.E.*, 164–88. [With apparatus.]

Translation.
Thorpe (above).

BLICKLING HOMILIES

In a much mutilated MS. (written by two hands) formerly preserved at Blickling Hall, Norfolk, is a collection of 19 homilies composed about the seventies of the tenth century. Some of them are incomplete, and several only fragmentary. The earlier ones are genuine sermons, the later, narratives concerned with Christian legend.

In style, these Homilies occupy a position intermediate between Alfred and Aelfric. While the syntax is often awkward, the descriptions are usually meritorious, and several, excellent (cf. e.g., the description of the [fictitious] church on Mt. Olivet in No XI [*On Ascension Day*] and the picture of Doomsday in No. VII [*On Easter Day*]. Noteworthy, too, is the frequent use of similies, many poetical.

Bibliography.
C.B.E.L., 1.93.
H. & B., 110–1.

Edition.
Morris, R. *The Blickling Homilies of the Tenth Century.* E.E.T.S., 58, 63, 73. London, 1874–80. [With translation opposite text, and glossary.]
Note.—Homily XIX, on St. Andrew, is treated above, p. 243.

BYRHTFERTH'S MANUAL

This *Manual*, also called *Enchiridion, pæt ys manualis on Lyden*] *handbóc on Englisc* [Crawford, *infra*, 132] is found in a single late-tenth century Bodl. MS. (Ashmole, 328), with numerous and often intricate illustrations. The author was Byrhtferth (fl. 990–1000), a monk of Ramsey Abbey and head of its school, who also wrote Latin commentaries on four of the writings of his hero, *pæs eadigan weres . . . Bedan, pæs æðelan boceres* (ib. 72). This scientific manual is sure to appeal to students of early astronomy, which subject, together with mathematics, receives the bulk of the attention. It "treats, for instance, of the signs of the zodiac and the length of the sun's course through each; of the

method for finding Easter; the symbolic properties of certain
numbers and the correspondence between the four ages of man,
the four seasons, the four elements, the four humours (choler,
melancholy, etc.), and the four qualities, dry, moist, cold and
hot" (Wardale, 288–9). Despite the inherent difficulties of the
subject, Byrhtferth's lucid, stimulating and intimate handling
of his themes will not fail to impress the reader.

Bibliography.
C.B.E.L., 1.97.
H. & B., 111.

Text.
Crawford, S. J. *Byrhtferth's Manual* (*A.D. 1011*). Vol. I (contains
 text and an excellent translation). E.E.T.S., 177, 1929.
 [A second vol., containing an introd. and a vocabulary, is
 promised for the same series.]

Discussion.
Classen, K. M. *Über das Leben und die Schriften Byrhtferths, eines
 angelsächsischen Gelehrten und Schriftstellers um das Jahr 1000.*
 Dresden, 1896.
Forsey, G. F. "Byrhtferth's *Preface*" in *Speculum*, 3.505–22.
 1928. [General discussion.]
Singer, C. & D. *An Unrecognised Anglo-Saxon Medical Text.*
 New York, 1921.

CHARTERS

Under this heading may be conveniently grouped a great
variety of most interesting and historically invaluable documents
that shed a flood of light upon life in Anglo-Saxon times. Some
of them are muniments relating to grants of land—some for-
geries—which are of the greatest assistance to students of place-
names. Others are wills, heriots, marriage settlements, leases,
mortgages, market and toll rights. Others again concern constitutional law and the law of the courts. There are manumissions too.
The Charters are in fact the documentary annals of Pre-Conquest
England.

Bibliography.
C.B.E.L., 1.96–7.
H. & B., 134–5.

Text.
Birch, W. de G. *Cartularium Saxonicum.* 3 vols. London, 1885–93.

Earle, J. *A Handbook to the Land Charters and other Saxonic Documents*. Oxford, 1888.

Harmer, F. E. *Select English Historical Documents of the Ninth and Tenth Centuries*. C.U.P., 1914. [With translation and notes.]

Kemble, J. M. *Codex Diplomaticus Aevi Saxonici*. 6 vols. London, 1839–48.

Napier, A. S. and Stevenson, W. H. *The Crawford Collection of Early Charters and Documents now in the Bodleian Library*. Oxford, 1895.

Robertson, A. J. *Anglo-Saxon Charters, edited with Translation and Notes*. C.U.P., 1939. [Prints 135 documents, with comprehensive apparatus. A first-rate source book for historical studies.]

Thorpe, B. *Diplomatorium Anglicum Aevi Saxonici*. London, 1865. [With translation.]

Whitelock, D. *Anglo-Saxon Wills*. C.U.P., 1930. [Wills from middle of tenth century to end of A.S. period, edited with translations and notes.]

LIFE OF ST. CHRISTOPHER

This unique text, opening defective and much mutilated through the Cotton Fire, forms the beginning of the second codex of the *Beowulf MS.* and is in the handwriting of the first scribe of the *Beowulf*. It translates, in the main fairly closely, the *Acta Sanctorum* for July 25th (Vol. XXXIII, pp. 148 ff.).

Bibliography.
H. & B., 112.

Edition.
Rypins. E.E.T.S., 161. [With introd., Latin text, and glossary.]

ANGLO-SAXON CHRONICLE

This *Chronicle*, the greatest prose work of the O.E. period, was probably initiated by King Alfred about 890, perhaps at Winchester. It was almost certainly copied from an earlier W.S. chronicle, which in its turn was based upon records made at various times by monks in order to distinguish the passing years by events of note. Copies of the Alfredian redaction then appear to have been dispatched to monasteries in various parts of the country, where they were first revised to include incidents of regional importance and thereafter kept up to date with material supplied from some official source, supplemented by local information.

In one version or another, the *Chronicle* records matters of fact right from the beginning of the Christian era and continues for 250 years after Alfred's death. It is accordingly one of our primary sources of historical knowledge. Because original and uninfluenced by any Latin prototype, its narratives, almost wholly impersonal, enable us to obtain a complete conspectus over the development of O.E. prose from Alfred's period onwards. In view of the circumstances governing its composite authorship, literary inequalities are only to be expected. There are several notable passages—accessible in most *Readers*—e.g., the annals for 755 (Murder of Cynewulf), 893–7, and 994–1010. In the middle quarters of the tenth century, the unusually arid entries are relieved by several poetical and patriotic passages, one, the spirited *Battle of Brunanburh*, being an undoubted achievement, see further pp. 171–5 above.

Four distinct recensions of the *Chronicle*, differing only in matters of detail, have come down to us in seven different MSS., as follows.

MS. A. Corpus Christi College, Cambridge. The "Parker" MS. Written by one scribe to A.D. 891; thereafter (? at Winchester) by seven scribes in succession to 923; so also from 955–1001; then at Canterbury, 1005 to 1070. Bequeathed to C.C.C. by Archbishop Parker in 1575. A copy made c. 1025 was burned in the fire which damaged the Cotton Collection (1731); but a transcript (abbreviated) made by Lambard in 1564, is in Trinity College, Dublin; and it had been printed by Wheloc in 1643.

MS. B. Brit. Mus. Cotton Tiberius A. 6. Written c. 1000; stops at 977.

MS. C. Brit. Mus. Cotton Tiberius B. 1. Written by various scribes c. 1055 at Abingdon. Copied from B. down to 977 and continued to 1066. Contains also copy from Mercian Chronicle of events in years 902–24.

MS. D. Brit. Mus. Cotton Tiberius B. 4. The "Worcester Chronicle". Written c. 1100; closes 1079. Includes some Northumbrian annals of 733–806 and excerpts from Bede, also the Mercian annals.

MS. E. Bodl. Laud Misc. 636. The "Peterborough Chronicle". Written in various hands, 1121–54. Close to D. with local interpolations, copy of a Canterbury original.

MS. F. Brit. Mus. Domitian A. 8. Written in Canterbury c.

1090. Copy of archetype of E, abbreviated, with local interpolations and translations into Latin.

The following table from *C.H.E.L.*, 1.112, shows the relationship of the various MSS.

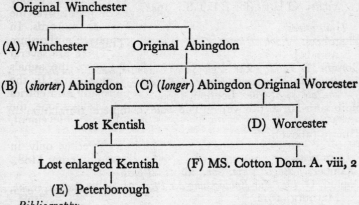

Original Winchester

(A) Winchester   Original Abingdon

(B) (*shorter*) Abingdon   (C) (*longer*) Abingdon Original Worcester

Lost Kentish   (D) Worcester

Lost enlarged Kentish   (F) MS. Cotton Dom. A. viii, 2

(E) Peterborough

Bibliography.

C.B.E.L., 1.88–9.

H. & B., 112–13.

Hoffmann-Hirtz, M. *Une Chronique Anglo-Saxonne traduite d'après le Manuscrit 173 de Corpus Christi College, Cambridge.* Strasbourg, 1933. Pp. 133–43.

Smith (below) 53–5.

Editions.

Classen, E., and Harmer, F. E.   *An Anglo-Saxon Chronicle from the British Museum, Cotton MS. Tiberius B. IV, edited with a Glossary,* Manchester, 19 . [MS. D.]

Earle, J.   *Two of the Saxon Chronicles Parallel, with Supplementary Extracts from the Others, edited with Introduction, Notes and a Glossarial Index.* Oxford, 1865. (The introd. is still valuable.]

Plummer, C.   *Two of the Saxon Chronicles Parallel, with Supplementary Extracts from the Others: a Revised Text edited with Introduction, Notes, Appendices and Glossary, on the Basis of an Edition by John Earle.* 2 vols. Oxford, 1892–9. [Standard ed. Indispensable.]

Thorpe, B.   *The Anglo-Saxon Chronicle.* 2 vols. [Rolls Series], 1861. [Vol. I, text; Vol. II (composite) tr.]

Note.—Selections are printed in many *Readers* and anthologies. Note especially the ed. (with tr.) of the annals for 978–1017

(M.S. C.) in M. Ashdown's *English and Norse Documents*, Cambridge, 1930. Pp. 38–71.

Facsimile.

Flower, R., and Smith, H. *The Parker Chronicle and Laws. A Facsimile.* O.U.P. (for E.E.T.S.), 1941.

Translations.

Chambers. *Engl. Norm. Con.*, *passim*. [Translates numerous annals.]

Gomme, E. E. C. *The Anglo-Saxon Chronicle, edited from the Translation in Monumenta Historica Britannica and Other Versions by the late J. A. Giles.* London, 1909.

Hoffmann-Hirtz (above). [The sole complete translation of MS. A.]

Thorpe (above).

Discussion.

Chambers. *Engl. Norm. Con.*, xii-xx, *et passim*.

Donald, G. C. *Zur Entwicklung des Prosastils in der Sachsenchronik.* Marburg, 1914.

Galbraith, V. H. *The Historia Aurea of John, Vicar of Tynemouth* in *Essays . . . presented to Reginald Lane Poole.* Oxford, 1927.

Mawer, A. "Some Place-name Identifications in the Anglo-Saxon Chronicles", *Palaestra* 147. Berlin, 1925.

Poole, R. L. *Chronicles and Annals: A Brief Outline of their Origin and Growth.* Oxford, 1926. [Attempts to "trace in outline the manner in which the elements of the medieval chronicle were inserted in tables designed for the calculation of the date of Easter and to show how, in course of time, they developed". See especially pp. 41–9.]

Smith, A. H. *The Parker Chronicle* [832–900]. London, 1935. *Methuen's O.E. Library, B.I.* [An excellent ed. with full apparatus. Valuable introd. and bibl.]

Stenton, F. M. "The South-Western Element in the Old English Chronicle" in *Essays in Medieval History presented to T. F. Tout.* Manchester, 1925.

GOSPELS

The four Gospels have been preserved in a W.S. version extant in six MSS. These are (1) C.C.C.C. 160, c. 1000; (2) Camb. Univ. Lib. MS. Ii. 2. 11, c. 1050; (3) Bodl. MS. 441, after 1000; (4) B.M. Cotton Otho C. I, c. 1000; (5) Bodl. Hatton MS. 38, *temp.* Henry II, and (6) B.M. Royal MS. I, A. xvi, *temp.* Stephen. No. 5 is copied from 6, which itself is a copy of 3. Nos. 1, 2, 3 and 4 are all from the same lost original.

Besides the above W.S. version, two separate interlinear glosses of the four Gospels have been preserved, one (c. 950), in the North Northumbrian dialect of Durham, in the magnificently illuminated Lindisfarne MS. (B.M. Cotton Nero, D. 4), and the other (latter half of tenth century), written by two glossators, in the Rushworth MS. (Bodl. MS. Auct. D. ii. 19). The first glossator wrote St. Matthew and St. Mark up to Chap. II, v. 15, in the Mercian dialect. These glosses are of the highest importance to philologists.

Bibliography.
C.B.E.L., 1.95.
H. & B., 115–16.

Text.
Bright, J. W. *The Gospel of St. Luke in Anglo-Saxon.* Oxford, 1893.
Bright, J. W. *The Gospels of St. Matthew, St. Mark and St. John in West Saxon.* 3 vols. Boston, 1904.

Discussion.
Harris, L. M. *Studies in the Anglo-Saxon Version of the Gospels.* Baltimore, 1901.
Skeat, W. W. *The Holy Gospels in Anglo-Saxon, Northumbrian, and Old Mercian Versions, synoptically arranged.* C.U.P., 1871–87. [Standard. Note important introds.]
The Lindisfarne Gospels. Printed by Order of the Trustees of the British Museum. London, 1924. [Contains reproductions of the decoration of the MS., also an introd. on the history of the MS., and a description of its contents and writing.]

LAWS

In the main, A.S. law was purely Teutonic, owing nothing to Celtic practice. Although a considerable amount has come down to us, the earliest codes being preserved in late MSS., this can only represent a small part of the whole. What has been committed to writing really implies a mass of oral custom. Its historical importance cannot be over-estimated.

The actual laws themselves can be grouped into three main codes:—

(1) The laws of the Kentish kings, viz., Aethelbert (596), Hlothere and Eadric (685–6) and Wihtred (690–6).

(2) The W.S. codes. The earliest are the laws of Ine (688–725), and the most important, those of Alfred (v. p. 241 above). The latter were added to by later kings of Wessex as the need arose.

(3) Laws of Cnut. These formed a comprehensive code for Saxon and Dane. Cnut was the last great law-giver of the A.S. kings.

Bibliography.
C.B.E.L., 1.96–7.
H. & B., 120–1.

Text.

Attenborough, F. L. *The Laws of the Earliest English Kings.* C.U.P., 1922. [With (brief) introductory notes, tr., and textual and historical notes.]

Liebermann. *Gesetze.* [Indispensable for complete study. But the complementary edd. of Attenborough (above) and Robertson (below) are sufficient for ordinary purposes.]

Robertson, A. J. *The Laws of the Kings of England from Edmund to Henry I.* C.U.P., 1925. [With (brief) introd., tr., and textual and historical notes.]

Translation.
Attenborough and Robertson (above).

Discussion.

Bethurum, D. "Stylistic Features of the O.E. Laws" in *M.L.R.*, 27.263–9. 1932.

Whitelock, D. E. "*Wulfstan and the Laws of Cnut*" in *Engl. Hist. Rev.*, 63.433–452. 1948. [Favours Wulfstan's authorship.]

MARTYROLOGY

Amateur hagiologists will know how to appreciate this interesting *Martyrology*, a calendar of lives of saints and martyrs intended to perpetuate their memory among, and inculcate their example upon, the faithful. Monastic custom in the A.S. period was that the appropriate extract from such a collection should be read to the monks assembled in the Chapter-house after Prime.

The text is preserved in four MSS., viz. (A) B.M. Addit. 23211, a mere fragment of two leaves from the latter half of the ninth century; (B) B.M. Cott. Julius A X, fol. 44–175, from the second half of the tenth century; (C) C.C.C.C. 196, fol. 1–110, from the beginning of the tenth century; and (D) C.C.C.C 41, fol. 122b–32a. MS. A is nearest to the archetype, then B.

The O.E. version, which was perhaps composed about 850, derives, whether it be a translation or an abridgement, from an unknown Latin original. It covers the period from Dec. 25th to Dec. 21st, and as a rule gives only an outline of the various legends. The author of the Latin original used various sources including Bede, who himself compiled a (Latin) martyrology, Aldhelm, Gregory, Adamnan and other early Fathers.

Bibliography.
C.B.E.L., 1.88.
H. & B., 123–4.

Edition.
Herzfeld, G. *An Old English Martyrology.* E.E.T.S., 116. London, 1900. [With full critical apparatus and tr.]

MEDICAL LITERATURE

About a score of MSS. containing medical, or rather pseudo-medical, literature, survive from the period 900–1100, most of the documents being printed in Cockayne's *Leechdoms* (below). There is no separate work on surgery, although there were probably surgeons in England from the seventh century onwards (Payne, *English Medicine*, 83, below). The chief documents, discussed below, are collections of prescriptions, of which herbs and the parts of animals form the main ingredients. Depending largely upon Latin source-books, these works cannot be uncritically relied upon to provide evidence as to the life and thought of the period. Nevertheless as human documents they are of very considerable interest and ought certainly to be examined. Moreover, they make a valuable contribution to the stock of O.E. words, especially plant-names. The following books should be consulted:

Bibliography.
C.B.E.L., 1.97.

Texts.
Cockayne, O. *Leechdoms, Wortcunning and Starcraft of Early England.* 3 vols. Rolls Series, London, 1864–6. [Vol. I:—(Introductory) Preface, *Herbarium, Medicina de Quadrupedibus, Leechdoms from Fly-Leaves of MSS., Charms.* Vol. II:—(Introductory) Preface, *Leechbooks I–III.* Vol. III:—*Lacnunga, Remedies Birth-forecasts, Prognostics, De Temporibus, Cherins, Durham Glossary of Plant Names, Collection of Saxon Names of Plants and*

Trees, and *Historical Fragments*. Translations face each page of text.]

Leonhardi, G. *Kleinere Angelsächsische Denkmäler I*. Hamburg, 1905. (*A.S. Prosa*, 6.) [Contains *Leechbook, Lacnunga, Lorica Hymn*, and *Lorica Prayer*. To each monument, there is a bibl. and brief notes on contents, dialect and MSS., but no glossary.]

Discussion.

Cockayne (ib.). [See prefaces.]

Payne, J. F. *English Medicine in the Anglo-Saxon Times*. Oxford, 1904. [Note especially the chapters entitled *History of A.-S. Medicine, The A.-S. Medical Literature, The Herbarium of Apuleius, A.-S. Surgery, Charms and Superstitious Medicine*. A valuable book, with excellent illustrations reproduced from the MSS., as well as translations of excerpts from the texts.]

Singer, C. *From Magic to Science, Essays on the Scientific Twilight*. London, 1928. [In particular, see pp. 133–67 on "Early English Magic and Medicine" (this being a "somewhat abbreviated" rearrangement of the author's chapter "Early English Magic and Medicine" in *Proc. of the British Academy, 1919–20*, 9.341–74).]

1. LEECH BOOK

As printed by its first editor, Cockayne, the *Leech Book* consists of three sections or books, all from a single B.M. MS., Reg. 12, D, XVII (second half of tenth century). The first two, forming a whole, often nowadays referred to as the *Leech Book of Bald* (the owner, apparently an A.S. leech who authorised a certain *cild* to copy or write the MS.), constitute a treatise on medicine in altogether 155 chapters, each devoted to a particular malady. The third part, a scribal addition of similar content, but having really nothing to do with the former (Payne [above], 36) contains seventy-three chapters of leechdoms or prescriptions. The original exemplum apparently dates from 900–50. Bald's "text-book of medicine" seems to include a certain amount of original knowledge of native plants and herbs, classical lore chiefly from Latin versions of Greek authors, superstitious matter (charms and rites) from Greek and Latin medicine, ecclesiastical formularies and possibly Teutonic and Celtic folklore (Payne [above], 61–2).

Bibliography.
H. & B., 121.

Text.
Cockayne. *Leechdoms*, 2.2–364.
Leonhardi (above), 1–112.

Discussion.
Cockayne. *Leechdoms*, 2.xx–xxxiii.
Payne (above), 39–62, 154–7. (Excerpts in translation.)

2. THE HERBARIUM

Extant in 4 MSS., the *Herbarium*, a pseudo-scientific treatise on the medicinal properties and uses of 185 plants, consists of two parts: the first, a translation of the (very popular) Latin *Herbarium* of Apuleius (an unidentified Latin naturalist apparently of the fourth or fifth century A.D.), while the second is based on the *On Materia Medica* of Dioscorides, a Greek physician (fl. c. A.D. 60), whose work, translated into Latin in the sixth century, is assumed to be the primary source of that of Apuleius. The earliest and best MS., B.M. Cotton Vitellius C III (1000–50), "though sadly damaged (by the fire in the Cotton Library) must have once been a splendid volume, beautifully written, and decorated with a large number of coloured figures of plants and animals" (Payne [above], 62). But the figures themselves are merely traditional (ib., 76). Of little value, because derivative, as a guide to A.-S. customs and folklore, the *Herbarium* is mainly of interest, apart from its vocabulary, as evidence of the astonishing claims and beliefs of Pre-Conquest drug-mongers. For a M.E. version, see Wells X [15].

Bibliography.
H. & B., 117.

Text.
Cockayne. *Leechdoms*, 1.2–325.

Discussion.
Cockayne. *Leechdoms*, 1.ix–cv.
Flom, G. T. "The O.E. Herbal of Apuleius Vitellius C III" in *J.E.G.Ph.*, (Jan.) 1941. [Contents and state of MS.]
Payne (above), 62–82.
Singer (above), 164, 168–98.

3. LACNUNGA (HEALINGS)

A further series of prescriptions, conventionally designated
255

(though without textual justification) *Lacnunga*, survives in B.M.
MS. Harl. 585 (late eleventh century). It includes several charms
in verse as well as nostrums and prayers in Latin. Some of its
formulas include Greek and Hebrew words.

Bibliography.
H. & B., 120 (who state that a new ed., with notes and transla-
tions, by C. Singer and J. H. G. Grattan, is promised).
Leonhardi (above), 157.

Editions.
Cockayne. *Leechdoms*, 3.2–80.
Leonhardi (above), 122–55. [With an analysis of the phonology,
160–74.]

4. PERI DIDAXEON (OF SCHOOLS OF MEDICINE)

Another series of Leechdoms is contained in *Peri Didaxeon*,
which in the main translates the works of certain eleventh-century
Salernitan writers, in particular the *Practica* of Petrocellus or
Petronius. (For a brief account of the Medical School at Salerno,
see Payne [above], 144 ff.) Actually the title is relevant only to the
first chapter, the other sixty-five being prescriptions. These differ
from all other A. S. nostrums in being wholly free from magic
and superstition.—AM.E. version is noted by Wells, X [3].

Bibliography.
H. & B., 126.

Editions.
Cockayne. *Leechdoms*, 3.82–145.
Löweneck, M. *Peri Didaxeon, eine Sammlung von Rezepten in
englischen Sprache aus dem 11/12 Jahrhundert.* Erlangen, 1896.

Discussion.
Payne (above), 143–57.
Singer (above), 148.

5. MEDICINA DE QUADRUPEDIBUS OF SEXTUS PLACITUS

This work, extant in the same 4 MSS. as the *Herbarium*, is a
translation of the Latin treatise on remedies obtainable from
animals that is attributed to Sextus Placitus, a shadowy figure of
either the fourth or the sixth century. Incredible curative virtues
are claimed for the parts of thirteen quadrupeds, but astonish-
ment is soon replaced by pity for the wretches who may have had
to swallow such nauseating nostrums. The ultimate source is Pliny.

An E.M.E. version from MS. Harleian 6258 (c. 1150) was edited with introduction, notes, translation, and glossary by J. Delcourt. (*Medicina de Quadrupedibus*. Heidelberg, 1913.) See also Wells, X [4].

Bibliography.
H. & B., 124.

Text.
Cockayne. *Leechdoms*, 1.326–73.

Discussion.
Cockayne. *Leechdoms*, 1.lxxxix ff.
Payne (above), 64–5.

NICODEMUS, GOSPEL OF

The complete form of this gospel, which can be traced back to A.D. 400, comprises the *Acti Pilati* and the *Descensus Christi ad Inferno*, is notable for its tremendous influence upon mediaeval religion, art and drama. For M.E. versions, see pp. 342–3.

Bibliography.
C.B.E.L., 1.93.
H. & B., 125.

Editions.
Crawford, S. J. *The Gospel of Nicodemus*. Edinburgh, 1927.
Hulme, W. H. "The O.E. Version of the Gospel of Nicodemus" in *P.M.L.A.*, 13.457–542. 1898. [Text of MS. Cbg. Univ. Lib. Ii, 2, 11, and B.M. Cott. Vitell. A, XV, with apparatus.]
Hulme, W. H. "The O.E. Gospel of Nicodemus" in *M.Ph.*, 1.579–614. 1904. [Text of a L.O.E. version from Cott. Vitell. A, XIV.]

PROSE PSALMS (PARIS PSALTER)

A West-Saxon prose rendering of Ps. 1 to 50, v. 8, is the first entry (fol. 1a–63b), and immediately precedes a metrical version of Ps. 51, v. 7, to 150, v. 3 (fol. 64a–175b; see p. 214), in the *Paris Psalter*, a manuscript of 186 folios, all written by the one hand in the first half of the eleventh century, and to-day preserved in the Bibliothèque Nationale in Paris. The MS. is written in double columns with the O.E. text on the right and the corresponding Latin text on the left. The prose version may be connected with King Alfred, who, according to William of Malmesbury, began but did not complete a translation of the Psalter.

Bibliography.
C.B.E.L., 1.95–6.
H. & B., 129–30.

Editions.
Bright, J. W., and Ramsay, R. L. *Liber Psalmorum: The West Saxon Psalms.* Boston. 1907. Grein-Wülker, *Prosa 7.*

Discussion.
Bruce, J. D. "The Anglo-Saxon Version of the Book of Psalms commonly known as the Paris Psalter" in *P.M.L.A.*, 19.43–164. 1894.
Cook, A. S. *Biblical Quotations in Old English Prose Writers.* London, 1898. [Pp. xxxiv–xliii.]
Förster, M. "Die altenglischen Texte der Pariser National Bibliothèque" in *E.St.*, 62.113–31. 1927.
Krapp. *Paris Psalter*, vii–xxi. [Discussion of MS.]

The first eight of these homilies were edited (with variant readings from the other MSS., and textual notes) by M. Förster in the first volume of his *Die Vercelli-Homilien.* Hamburg, 1932 (Grein-Wülker, *Prosa 12*). A complete edition is also in course of preparation by R. Willard.

WERFERTH'S TRANSLATION OF GREGORY'S DIALOGUES

It was probably between 880 and 885 that Werferth, bishop of Worcester 873–915, at the king's request translated the *Dialogues* of Pope Gregory the Great (590–604). This famous work, actually only partly in dialogue form, is a series of legends about martyrs and saints in Italy, told by Gregory to Peter the Deacon in order to distract his own mind from the burden of his pastoral duties. Containing four books, the second being wholly concerned with St. Benedict, it is certainly an entertaining collection of stories, fully meriting its mediaeval popularity that led to translation into almost every European language. Werferth's rendering is rugged and simple, and will be read with ease.

Three texts have come down to us, all in MSS. of the earlier half of the eleventh century, viz. (C) C.C.C.C. MS. 332; (O) B.M. Cotton Otho C I, and (H) Bodleian Hatton 76. All are from a common source, MS H being closest to the original version. Both C and H begin with a short prose preface by King Alfred, while O has a slightly longer metrical preface. This was written, so it states, by Bishop Wulfstan—possibly the cleric consecrated to the See of Worcester in 1063.

Bibliography.
C.B.E.L., 1.88.
H. & B., 132.

Text.
Hecht, H. *Bischofs Wœrferth von Worcester Übersetzung der Dialogue Gregors des Grossen.* Leipzig, 1900–7. [*A.S. Prosa 5.* Standard ed. of all three texts, with valuable introd.]

Discussion.
Potter, S. *On the Relation of the O.E. Bede to Werferth's Gregory and to Alfred's Translations.* Prague, 1930.

Timmer, B. J. *Studies in Bishop Werferth's Translation of the Dialogues of Gregory the Great.* Wageningen, 1934. [On word-order and use of prepositions.]

WONDERS OF THE EAST

Of special importance because it testifies to the interest of the Anglo-Saxons in the Orient, the *Wonders of the East* is preserved in two short O.E. versions, one, the briefer, in the second part, and in the same hand as the first scribe, of the *Beowulf MS.* (Cott. Vitell. A, XV; c. 1000) and the other, somewhat later, in MS. Cotton Tiberius B.V. The latter also contains, in parallel, the unique Latin recension, though this is the source of neither. The remote ancestor seems to be a lost Latin compilation of the fabulous elements in classical literature.

Bibliography.
C.B.E.L., 1.94.
H. & B., 133

Text.
Rypins: E.E.T.S. 161. [With introd., Latin text, and glossary. Standard.]

WULFSTAN (d. 1023)

Wulfstan was Archbishop of York from 1002–23 and part of this time (1002–16) was Bishop of Worcester as well. During his tenure of the Sees, the ravages of the Vikings were at their worst.

Of the fifty-three homilies preserved in Bodl. MS. Jun. 99 (after 1050) and attributed to Wulfstan in an entry at the beginning of the first, only four are undoubtedly his. All these contain his Latin signature *Lupus.* Parts of a fifth are also allotted to him.

The most important and impressive of the acknowledged four is that which is described in one of the other four extant MSS. as *Sermo Lupi ad Anglos* and dated 1014. In it Wulfstan vehemently denounces the depravity of the English, vividly portrays the affliction caused by the Danes and regarded by him as divine punishment for the sins of his countrymen, and scourges his hearers for their cowardice in face of the invaders. He ends with a moving call to repentance. It is easily the most forceful piece of prose in O.E. Yet it is scarcely prose. It is oratory, and all the artifices of the accomplished orator are employed: rhythm, repetition of ideas by synonyms, enumeration, balanced epithets and clauses, startling and effective diction, as well as rhyme within the phrase, assonance and alliteration. The whole homily is skilfully calculated to rouse his hearers by appealing to their hearts rather than their heads; and no doubt its purpose was achieved.

Lastly, there are certain correspondences in phraseology between this homily and the O.E. version of the laws of Aethelred drawn up at Eynsham in 1014. Since Wulfstan admitted to the authorship of the extant Latin text of these laws, very likely he wrote the English one too.

Bibliography.

Becker, R.   *Wulfstans Homilien.* Leipzig, 1910. ["A very good bibliography. Gives a brief statement of the content of each homily," H. & B., 133.]

C.B.E.L., 1.92.

H. & B., 133.

Editions.

Napier, A. S.   Wulfstan. *Sammlung der ihm zugeschriebenen Homilien nebst Untersuchungen über ihre Echtheit.* Berlin, 1883. [Standard.]

Whitelock, D.   *Sermo Lupi ad Anglos.* London, 1939. *Methuen's O.E. Library.* [Includes discussion of the canon of W's works.]

Discussion.

Jost, K.   "Wulfstan und die angelsächsische Chronik" in *Angl.*, 47.105–23. 1923. [Assigns poetical entries for 959 and 975 in MS. D to Wulfstan.]

Kinard, J. P.   *A Study of Wulfstan's Homilies; their Style and Sources.* Baltimore, 1897.

Napier, A. S.   *Über die Werke des altenglischen Erzbischofs Wulfstan.* Weimar, 1882.

Whitelock, D. E.   "Archbishop Wulfstan, Homilist and Statesman", in *Trans. of Royal Hist. Soc.*, 1942.

Whitelock, D. E.   "Wulfstan and the Laws of Cnut" in *Engl. Hist. Rev.*, 63. 433–452. 1948.

CHAPTER VII

MEDIAEVAL PERIOD—PEOPLE, INSTITUTIONS, LANGUAGE

1. PEOPLE AND INSTITUTIONS

A. GENERAL BIBLIOGRAPHY

See the items mentioned under this heading on p. 135 above.

B. POLITICAL HISTORY

Adams, G. B. *The Political History of England (1066–1216)*. Rev. ed. London, 1935.

Bense, J. F. *Anglo-Dutch Relations*. Oxford, 1925.

Davis, H. W. C. *England under the Normans and Angevins, 1066–1272*. London, 1905, etc. [Students of literature will be specially interested in Chaps. II, VI, and XIX, entitled respectively, *The Reorganisation of England*, 1072–1087; *The Old Order and the New*, 1000–1154; and *England in De Montfort's Day*, 1216–1271.]

Haskins, C. H. *The Normans in European History*. London, 1916. [Chap. III: Normandy and England.]

Oman, C. *The Political History of England (1377–1485)*. London, 1906.

Stenton, F. M. *The First Century of English Feudalism*. Oxford, 1932.

Tout, T. F. *The Political History of England (1216–1377)*. London, 1905.

Vickers, K. H. *England in the Later Middle Ages (1272–1485)*. Sixth ed. London, 1938.

C. SOCIAL HISTORY

Abram, A. *Social Life in the Fifteenth Century: a Study of the Effects of Economic Conditions*. London, 1909.

Abram, A. *English Life and Manners in the Later Middle Ages.* London, 1913.

Bateson, M. *Medieval England, 1066–1350.* London, 1903. [A brief but valuable account of all classes of society in mediaeval England, illustrated from contemporary accounts. Note especially Chap. IV entitled *Learning, Art and Education,* and Chap. X on the *Church, Education and Learning.*]

Bennett, H. S. *The Pastons and their England.* C.U.P., 1922.

Bennett, H. S. *Life on the English Manor. A Study of Peasant Conditions,* 1150–1400. C.U.P., 1937.

Chadwick, D. *Social Life in the Days of Piers Plowman.* Cambridge, 1922. [On peasant life and agricultural conditions. A sort of digest of *Piers Plowman* considered as a document for contemporary society.]

Chambers, E. K. *The Medieval Stage.* 2 vols. Oxford, 1903. [Minstrelsy and the Drama.]

Coulton, G. G. *Chaucer and his England.* London, 1908, etc.

Coulton, G.G. *Medieval Studies.* Rev. ed. London, 1915.

Coulton, G. G. *Social Life in Britain from the Conquest to the Reformation.* Cambridge, 1918. Rev. ed., 1921. [Source book, containing extracts from contemporary writers.]

Coulton, G. G. *The Mediæval Village.* Cambridge, 1925. [On agricultural conditions and life of peasants. Contains extracts from contemporary writers to the Reformation, not chosen to represent the Middle Ages as a Golden Age; full of queer information.]

Coulton, G. G. *Life in the Middle Ages.* 4 vols. Cambridge, 1928–30. [1: *Religion, Folklore, Superstition.* 2: *Chronicles, Science and Art.* 3: *Men and Manners.* 4: *Monks, Friars and Nuns.* A source-book.]

Coulton, G. G. *Medieval Panorama: the English Scene from Conquest to Reformation.* C.U.P., 1938.

Cutts, E. L. *Scenes and Characters of the Middle Ages.* Fifth ed. London, 1925. [A most interesting and well illustrated book containing a "series of sketches of medieval life and medieval characters, looked at especially from the artist's point of view".]

Davis, H. W. C. *Mediæval England. Being a new ed. of Barnard's Companion to English History.* Oxford, 1924. [The chapter headings alone suffice to show the value of this excellent book. They are: Ecclesiastical Architecture; Domestic Architecture; War; Costume, Civil; Costume, Military; Heraldry; Shipping; Town Life; Country Life; The Monks, the Friars and the Secular Clergy; Learning and Education; Art; Coinage; Trade and Commerce. Indispensable.]

Davies, R. T. *Documents Illustrating the History of Civilisation in Mediaeval England* [*1066–1500*]. London, 1926.

Gretton, R. H. *The English Middle Class*, 1917. [Chaps. II to V give a useful summary of the rise in power of the merchants.]

Hall, H. *Court Life under the Plantagenets*. Second ed. 1899. [A description of English country life and the court of Henry II in the form of a narrative. An appendix contains a full discussion of the court's organisation.]

Hartley, D. and Elliot, M. M. *Life and Work of the People of England. A Pictorial Record. The eleventh to the thirteenth Centuries*. London, 1931.

Holmes, M. R. *Mediæval England*. London, 1924.

Homans, G. C. *English Villagers of the Thirteenth Century*. Harvard U.P., 1942. [A picture of social life in the open-field villages.]

Hunt, W. *Medieval Studies*. London, 1933. [A popular account of various aspects of English life and institutions between the eleventh and fifteenth centuries.]

Jusserand, J. J. *Wayfaring Life in the Middle Ages*. Translated by L. T. Smith. London, 1889, etc. Often reprinted.

Mead, W. E. *The English Mediæval Feast*. London, 1931. [Concerned with the distinctive features of the mediaeval cuisine, based upon contemporary material. Good reading-matter, illustrated with photographic reproductions from MSS.]

Power, E. *Medieval People*. London, 1924. (Pelican Books, 1937.) [Designed to illustrate various aspects of social life in the Middle Ages.]

Powicke, F. M. *Medieval England, 1066–1485*. Home Univ. Lib. London, 1931.

Quennell, M., and C. H. B. *Everyday Things in England from 1066–1499*. London, 1918, etc.

Rickert, E., and others. *Chaucer's World*. Ed. by C. C. Olson and M. M. Cross. Illustrations selected by M. Rickert. New York, 1948. [An anthology of excerpts from documents illustrating the life of a typical fourteenth-century person.]

Salzman, L. F. *English Life in the Middle Ages*. London, 1926. [Contains many excellent (chiefly contemporary) illustrations. Deals with life in country, town and the home; with the church and religion, education, literature (though only cursorily), art and science, warfare, law and order, industry,

trade and finance, women, and warfaring. With a good
selective bibliography.]

Seebohm, F. *The English Village Community*. C.U.P., 1896.

Traill, H. D., and Mann, J. S. (eds.). *A Record of the Progress of
the People in Religion, Laws, Learning, Arts, Industry, Commerce,
Science, Literature and Manners*. 6 vols. London, 1912.

Trevelyan, G. M. *England in the Age of Wycliffe*. London, 1899.

Trevelyan, G. M. *English Social History: Chaucer to Queen Victoria*.
London, 1944.

Tupper, F. *Types of Society in Medieval Literature*. New York,
1926.

Vinogradoff, P. *The Growth of the Manor*, 2nd rev. ed. London,
1911, etc. [Pp. 291 ff. Feudal period.]

Wright, T. *The Homes of Other Days. A History of Domestic Manners
and Sentiments in England*. London, 1871.

D. ECONOMIC HISTORY

Ashley, W. J. *An Introduction to English Economic History and
Theory*. 2 vols. London, 1888–93.

Ashley, W. *The Bread of our Forefathers*. Oxford, 1928.

Bland, A. E., Brown, P. A., and Tawney, R. H. *English Economic
History: Select Documents*. London, 1914. [Illustrates various
aspects of the economic structure.]

Cunningham, W. *The Growth of English Industry and Commerce
during the Early and Middle Ages*. Cambridge, 1890–3, etc.
[Standard.]

Fisher, H. A. L. (Mrs.). *Life and Work in England. A Sketch of Our
Social and Economic History*. London, 1934.

Gibbins, H. de B. *The Industrial History of England*. Completely
revised by J. F. Rees. London, 1926.

Gras, N. S. B. and Gras, E. C. *The Economic and Social History of
an English Village (Crawley Hampshire) A.D. 909–1928*. Cambridge, 1930.

Knoop, D. and Jones, G. P. *The Medieval Mason. An Economic
History of English Stone Building in the Later Middle Ages and
Early Modern Times*. Manchester, 1934.

Lipson, E. *An Introduction to the Economic History of England*.
Vol. I. *The Middle Ages*. London, 1915, etc.

Rogers, J. E. T. *A History of Agriculture and Prices in England,
1259–1793*. 7 vols. Oxford, 1866–1902. [Economists have
abandoned the conclusions, but the facts are there, and are
more useful to us.]

Orr, J.   *A Short History of British Agriculture.* Oxford, 1922.

Salzman, L. F.   *English Industries of the Middle Ages.* London, 1923.

Salzman, L. F.   *English Trade in the Middle Ages.* Oxford, 1931.

Waters, C. M.   *An Economic History of England.* O.U.P., 1925.

E. LAW AND CONSTITUTION

See "Law and Constitution" for the O.E. period, p. 140
    Note also the following:—

Jenks, E.   *Law and Politics in the Middle Ages.* 2nd ed. London, 1913.

Treharne, R. F.   *A Constitutional History of England from 1066–1399.* In preparation.

F. THE CHURCH

Bland, C. C. S.   *Miracles of the Blessed Virgin Mary.* London, 1928.

Byrne, M.   *The Tradition of the Nun in Mediæval England.* Washington, 1932.

Capes, W. W.   *The English Church in the Fourteenth and Fifteenth Centuries.* London, 1900. [Standard.]

Coulton, G. G.   *Five Centuries of Religion.* Vol. II: *The Friars and the Dead Weight of Tradition.* 1200–1400. Cambridge, 1927.

Cranage, D. H. S.   *The Home of the Monk. An account of English Monastic Life and Buildings in the Middle Ages.* 3rd ed. C.U.P., 1934.

Crossley, F. H.   *The English Abbey. Its Life and Work in the Middle Ages.* London, 1935. [Beautifully illustrated with photographs, and sketches. Indispensable.]

Cutts, E. L.   *Parish Priests and their People in the Middle Ages in England.* London, 1898. [A mine of interesting information, copiously illustrated with photographic reproductions of manuscript illuminations. A useful, popular book.]

Cutts, E. L.   *A Dictionary of the Church of England.* New ed. London, 1913.

Deanesly, M.   *History of the Mediæval Church, 590–1500.* London, 1925, etc.

Gasquet, F. A.   *English Monastic Life.* 6th ed. London, 1936.

Gasquet, F. A.   *Parish Life in Mediæval England,* 6th ed. London, 1936.

Gwynn, A.   *The English Austin Friars in the Time of Wyclif.* London, 1940.

Jessop, A. *The Coming of the Friars.* London, 1889, etc. [A good popular account of the friars.]

Jessop, A. *Before the Great Pillage.* London, 1901.

Kempe, Marjory. *The Book of Marjory Kempe* is a unique autobiography of a fifteenth-century woman of religious type, pub. in modern form; an ed. of the original has been edited for E.E.T.S. by S. B. Meech and H. E. A. Allen (No. 212, 1940).

Knowles, D. *The Religious Houses of Medieval England.* London, 1940.

Makower, F. *The Constitutional History and Constitution of the Church of England.* London, 1895, etc.

Ollard, S. L., and Crosse, G. *A Dictionary of English Church History.* London, 1912.

Owst, G. R. *Preaching in Medieval England.* C.U.P., 1926. [Based upon the study of the more important sermon MSS. of the period c. 1350–1450.]

Owst, G. R. *Literature and Pulpit in Medieval England.* C.U.P., 1933. [Full of interesting material connected with mediaeval preaching.]

Power, E. *Mediæval English Nunneries.* Cambridge, 1922.

Stephens, W. R. W. *The English Church*, 1066–1272. London, 1901. [Standard.]

Thompson, A. H. *English Monasteries.* C.U.P., 1913. [With a useful selective bibliography, 143–8.]

Wakeman, H. O. *An Introduction to the History of the Church of England.* London, 1908, etc.

Wall, J. C. *Shrines of British Saints.* London, 1905.

Wood-Leigh, K. L. *Studies in Church Life in England under Edward III.* C.U.P., 1934.

G. SCIENCE

Dampier-Whetham, W. C. D. *A History of Science and its Relations with Philosophy and Religion.* C.U.P., 1929, etc. [See especially Chaps. II and III on, resp., "The Middle Ages" and "The Renaissance".]

Steele, R. *Medieval Lore from Bartholomew Anglicus.* (Medieval Library 20.) King's Classics. London, 1905. [Gives a useful sample of Bartholomew's *De Proprietatibus Rerum* (1220–50) in modernised form.]

Steele, R. (ed.). *The Earliest Arithmetics in English.* E.E.T.S., 118.

Steele, R. "Roger Bacon and the State of Science in the Thirteenth Century", being Chap. III of Vol. II of *Studies in the History & Method of Science*, edited by C. Singer, Oxford, 1921.

Moore, N. *History of the Study of Medicine in the British Isles.* Oxford, 1908.

Payne, J. F. *English Medicine in the Anglo-Saxon Times.* Oxford, 1904. [Authoritative.]

Read, J. *An Outline of Alchemy, its Literature and Relationships.* London, 1936.

Riesman, D. *The Story of Medicine in the Middle Ages.* New York, 1935.

Rohde, E. S. *The Old English Herbals.* London, 1922. [Illustrated.]

Singer, C. *A Review of the Medical Literature of the Dark Ages.* London, 1917. [Valuable.]

Singer, C. (ed.). *Studies on the History and Method of Science.* Oxford, 1921.

Singer, C. *Early English Magic and Medicine.* Proc. of Brit. Acad., 1919–20. 9.341–74. London, 1924.

Singer, C. *From Magic to Science. Essays on the Scientific Twilight.* London, 1928.

Singer, C. *A Short History of Medicine.* Oxford, 1928. [See particularly the first 3 chapters dealing with Greece, Rome and the Middle Ages.]

Sarton, G. *Introduction to the History of Science.* 2 vols. Baltimore, 1927–36. [A complete guide to early, universal, scientific knowledge.]

Thorndike, L. *A History of Magic and Experimental Science during the First Thirteen Centuries of our Era.* See Vols. 3 and 4, publ. Oxford, 1934.

Walsh, J. J. *Medieval Medicine.* London, 1920.

Wedel, T. O. *The Mediaeval Attitude towards Astrology, particularly in England.* New Haven, 1921.

2. HISTORY OF THE LANGUAGE

Books relating to the Mediaeval Period will be found in the lists on pp. 143–8, above.

3. GRAMMARS, PHONOLOGY

Huchon   *Hist. Lang. Angl.* See Tome 2.

Jordan, R. *Handbuch der mittelenglischen Grammatik.* I Teil:

Lautlehre. 2nd ed. revised by H. C. Matthes. Heidelberg, 1934. [Phonology only.]

Luick. *Hist. Gram. d. engl. Sprache.*

Sisam, K. *Fourteenth Century Verse & Prose.* Oxford, 1921. [The Appendix, pp. 264–92, on "The English Language in the Fourteenth Century" is excellent.]

Wardale, E. E. *An Introduction to Middle English Grammar.* London, 1937.

Wright, J. and E. M. *An Elementary Middle English Grammar.* 2nd ed. Oxford, 1928.

Wyld. *Short Hist.* [Phonology.]

4. DICTIONARIES

Most editions of M.E. texts have Glossaries.

Mayhew, A. L. and W. W. Skeat. *A Concise Dictionary of Middle English from A.D. 1150–1580.* Oxford, 1888.

Oxford English Dictionary. 13 vols. Oxford, 1933.

Stratmann, F. H. *A Middle-English Dictionary.* Revised and enlarged by H. Bradley. Oxford, 1891.

A Middle English Dictionary is being prepared by the Modern Language Association of America.

CHAPTER VIII

MEDIAEVAL ENGLISH LITERATURE—GENERAL

A. HISTORY AND CRITICISM

Atkins, J. W. H. *English Literary Criticism: The Mediaeval Phase.* C.U.P., 1943.

Baldwin, C. S. *Three Mediæval Centuries of Literature in England 1100–1400.* Boston (U.S.A.), 1932. [Intended as a compact guide book for those who wish to study the period for themselves. Useful, especially for the romances, which have received most attention. Supersedes the same writer's *Introduction to English Mediæval Literature,* New York, 1914.]

Bennett, H. S. *Chaucer and the Fifteenth Century.* (Oxford History of English Literature, Vol. II, Pt. I.) Oxford, 1947. [Indispensable.]

Brown, C., and Robbins, R. H. *The Index of Middle English Verse.* New York, 1943.

Brandl, A. *Mittelenglische Literatur,* in Paul's *Grundriss der Germanischen Philologie.* 1st ed. Strassburg, 1893. Vol. II (1), 609–736. Index, Vol. II (2), pp. 345 ff.

C.H.E.L., Vols. I and II.

Chambers, Sir E. K. *English Literature at the Close of the Middle Ages.* (Oxford History of English Literature, Vol. II, Pt. II.) Oxford, 1945; 1947 (with corrections). [An erudite compendium. Each essay has an excellent bibliography.]

Chambers, *Cont. Engl. Prose.*

Courthope, W. J. *A History of English Poetry.* 6 vols. London, 1895–1910. [See Vol. I.]

Craik, G. L. *A Compendious History of English Literature and of the English Language from the Norman Conquest.* 2 vols. 1869. [A compact working manual in chronological order. Contains interesting sections on topics not usually found in histories of literature (e.g., Arabic learning, scholastic philosophy). An abridgment is included in Everyman's Library, entitled *Manual of English Literature.* London, 1909.]

Elton, O. *The English Muse*. London, 1933. [See Chaps. I–V. Good descriptions.]

Encyclopaedia Britannica, 14th ed.

Jusserand, J. J. *Literary History of the English People, from the Origins to the Renaissance*. London, 1895. [A standard work, trans. of *Histoire Littéraire du Peuple anglais*. Vol. I. *Des Origines à la Renaissance*. 2e éd. Paris, 1896.]

Ker, W. P. *English Literature, Medieval*. London, 1912. Home Univ. Lib. 43. [A stimulating introductory book.]

Krapp, G. P. *The Rise of English Literary Prose*. O.U.P., 1916. [See particularly the Introduction (on fourteenth century prose), and the chapters on Wiclif, Controversy and Free Speech and the Pulpit. Krapp considers that O.E. prose is "in no sense the source from which modern English prose has sprung", and, further, that Wiclif was not only "the first Englishman clearly to realise the broad principles which underlie prose expression", but also the first intelligent writer of English prose, a discovery in the truest sense of the word" (Preface). These opinions have been controverted, however, by R. W. Chambers, *On the Continuity of English Prose*. London, 1932.]

Lawrence, W. W. *Mediæval Story*. Rev. ed. New York, 1926.

Lewis, C. S. *The Allegory of Love: a Study in Medieval Tradition*. O.U.P., 1936.

Oakden, J. P. *Alliterative Poetry in M.E.: the Dialectal and Metrical Survey*. Manchester Univ. Press, 1930. [Invaluable.]

Oakden, J. P., with the assistance of E. R. Innes. *Alliterative Poetry in M.E.: A Survey of the Traditions*. Manchester U.P. 1935. [Pt. I, publ. separately as *The Poetry of the Alliterative Revival* (1937) is a valuable *seriatim* account of the M.E. alliterative texts.]

Russell, J. C. *Dictionary of Writers of Thirteenth-Century England*. London, 1936. [Emphasis on lives, rather than writings.]

Saintsbury, G. *A History of English Prosody*. Vol. I. London, 1906.

Saintsbury, G. *The Flourishing of Romance and the Rise of Allegory*. Edinburgh and London, 1907. [Concerned with European Literature.]

Saintsbury, G. *A Short History of English Literature*. London, 1897.

Schofield, W. H. *English Literature from the Norman Conquest to Chaucer*. London, 1906. [An excellent survey of the period, comprehensive and reliable. Noteworthy are the chapters on Anglo-Latin literature, and Anglo-Norman and Anglo-French Literature.]

Snell, F. J. *The Fourteenth Century*. London, 1899.

Snell, F. J. *The Age of Chaucer* [1346–1400], with an introd. by J. W. Hales, London, 1901, etc.

Stephen, L., and Lee, S. *Dictionary of National Biography*. London, 1885–. [Indispensable.]

Ten Brink, B. *Early English Literature*, translated by H. M. Kennedy. London, 1883. [Excellent criticism.]

Warton, T. *History of English Poetry*. Ed. W. C. Hazlitt. London, 1871. [Useful criticism.]

Wells. *Manual*. [The references to Wells under the heading *Discussion* in the book-lists of Chapters IX and X are intended to direct the reader not only to the "Text" of the *Manual*, but also to the invaluable "Bibliographical Notes". Strictly speaking, such references should have been repeated under the heading *Bibliography*.]

Wilson, R. M. *Early Middle English Literature*. London, 1939. [A valuable handbook for the student of the literature composed between 1066 and 1300.]

Note also the items on pp. 150–1.

B. BOOKS OF SELECTIONS

Brandl, A., and O. Zippel. *Mittelenglische Sprach- und Literaturproben, mit etymologischem Wörterbuch*. Berlin, 1917, etc. [A valuable collection of specimens predominantly in rhymed verse and often with parallel texts from several MSS. Good glossary with meanings in English and German. Designed for philological study.]

Cook, A. S. *A Literary Middle English Reader*. Boston, 1915. [A good collection of representative texts designed for the reader's literary enjoyment and profit. Contains no separate vocabulary or corpus of notes, but the meanings of difficult words are provided in abundance at the foot of each page.]

Dickins, B., and Wilson, R. M. *An Early Middle English Reader*. Cambridge, 1951. [This excellent reader, which bridges the gap between O.E and Sisam's *Fourteenth Century Verse and Prose*, contains a wide variety of representative texts collated with the manuscripts and carefully edited. The notes and glossary are first-rate. The book is an invaluable introduction to a close study of the literature and language of the period.]

Emerson, O. F. *A Middle English Reader, edited with grammatical Introduction, Notes and Glossary*. New York, 1905, etc. [Intended "to serve as an introduction to the language and literature of the period . . . between 1100 and 1500", the book is designed for those who are already acquainted with O.E. The Notes (pp. 247–318) and the Glossary (319–468) are good. There is a useful account of M.E. (chiefly Midland) grammar.]

French, W. H., and Hale, C. B. (edd.). *Middle English Metrical Romances*. New York, 1930. [Specially intended for classroom use, contains a most comprehensive selection of texts. Each piece is furnished with a brief introductory note on MS., dialect, theme, etc. Difficult words and phrases are glossed at the foot of the page, where too, are provided explanations of the more obscure allusions. The vocabulary includes only the commoner words, with etymologies.]

Hall, J. *Selections from Early Middle English, 1130–1250*, edited with Introduction and Notes. Oxford, 1920. [Part I: Texts. Part II (pp. 223–675), contains the Notes, which provide invaluable material for the understanding and elucidation of the texts. The editor here gives full information about the MSS., facsimiles, editions, literature, sources and illustrations, phonology, accidence, vocabulary, dialect, and metre or style, and an introduction to each text, as well as copious notes, with a wealth of illustration, on passages containing difficulties or topics of peculiar interest. A monument of scholarship, although it lacks a glossary.]

Morris, R. *Specimens of Early English, with Introduction, Notes and Glossarial Index*. Part I, 1150–1300. 2nd ed., revised by A. L. Mayhew and W. W. Skeat. Oxford, 1898. [Contains a grammatical introduction to M.E., and 17 selections. The whole book requires thorough revision.]

Morris, R., and Skeat, W. W. *Specimens of Early English with Introduction, Notes and Glossarial Index*. Part II, 1298–1393. 4th ed. Oxford, 1898. [Contains a brief grammatical introduction to the language of the period and 22 selections. The apparatus is out of date.]

Mosse, F. *Manuel de l'anglais du moyen âge des origines au XIVe siècle. II, Moyen anglais. Tome premier: Grammaire et Textes. Tome second: Notes et Glossaire*. Paris, 1949. [An excellent manual, with an instructive account (in 50 pp.) of ME syntax.]

Sampson, G. *The Cambridge Book of Prose and Verse, in Illustration*

of English Literature from the Beginnings to the Cycles of Romance.
Cambridge, 1924. [Contains a selection of passages illustrating *C.H.E.L.*, Vol. I. As the book is primarily intended for the "plain man who wants to read" rather than the philologist, all except two of the pre-thirteenth century specimens are represented by translations. Each extract is prefaced by an introductory note on its literary interest, and at the foot of each page is a running glossary. Excellent for the purposes in view.]

Segar, M. G. *Some Minor Poems of the Middle Ages.* London, 1917.

Sisam, K. *Fourteenth Century Verse and Prose.* Oxford, 1921. A Vocabulary to same, by J. R. R. Tolkien, Oxford, 1922, pub. separately and combined. [A fine collection of representative texts. The book also includes an Introduction to the period, copious notes on the texts, and Appendix on the English Language in the Fourteenth Century. A model book of selections.]

Skeat, W. W. *Specimens of Early English.* Part III, 1394–1579. 6th ed., Oxford, 1892.

C. COLLECTIONS OF TRANSLATIONS

Adamson, M. R. *A Treasury of Middle English Verse, selected and rendered into Modern English.* London, 1930.

Benham, A. R. *English Literature from Widsith to the Death of Chaucer.* O.U.P., 1916.

Darton, F. J. H. *Wonder Book of Old Romance.* New York, 1907.

Gerould, G. H. *Old English and Mediæval Literature.* Rev. and enlarged ed. New York, 1934.

Loomis, R. S., and Ward, R. (eds.). *Medieval English Verse and Prose in Modernised Versions.* New York, 1948.

Neilson, W. A., and Webster, K. G. T. *Chief British Poets of the Fourteenth and Fifteenth Centuries. Selected Poems, edited with Explanatory and Biographical Notes.* Boston, 1916.

Pancoast, H. S., and Spaeth, J. D. E. *Early English Poems.* New York, 1911.

Reinhard, J. R. *Medieval Pageant.* New York, 1939.

Segar, M. G. *A Mediæval Anthology, being Lyrics and Other Short Poems, Chiefly Religious.* London, 1916.

Rickert, E. *Early English Romances in Verse: Romances of Friendship,* Vol. I; *Romances of Love,* Vol. II. London, 1908.

Schlauch, M. *Mediæval Narrative. A Book of Translations.* New York, 1928.

Shackford, M. H. *Legends and Satires from Medieval Literature.* Boston, 1913.

Weston, J. L. *Romance, Vision and Satire, English Alliterative Poems of the Fourteenth Century.* Boston, 1912.

Weston, J. L. *The Chief Middle English Poets. Selected Poems newly rendered and edited, with Notes and Bibliographical References.* Boston, 1914.

D. EARLY MODERN ENGLISH

See Tucker and Benham, *A Bibliography of Fifteenth Century Literature*, Univ. of Washington Publ., Vol. II, No. 3, Seattle, 1928.

The most representative selections are: W. W. Skeat, *Specimens of Early English*, Vol. III, 6th ed., 1892; Eleanor P. Hammond, *English Verse from between Chaucer and Surrey*, Durham, N. Carolina, 1927, limited deliberately to "conventional secular poetry" and so less interesting, but with thorough notes and full bibliography; W. A. Neilson and K. G. T. Webster, *The Chief British Poets of the 14th and 15th Centuries*. Boston, 1936, an anthology whose scope is indicated in the title: the apparatus is small. A. F. Pollard, *Fifteenth Century Prose and Verse*, in the re-issue of Arber's Scholar's Library, 1903, gives good mixed reading in modernised spelling. Percy's *Reliques* is of course to be seen, especially ed. H. B. Wheatley, 1891, the Percy Folio MS., ed. F. J. Furnivall and J. W. Hales, 3 vols. and supplement, 1867. W. C. Hazlitt, *Remains of the Early Popular Poetry of England*, 1864, is a valuable collection of material of all sorts. Other collections are mentioned in their places—e.g., Lyric, Political Poetry, etc.

R. W. Chambers and Marjorie Daunt, *A Book of London English*, 1384–1425, Oxford, 1931, is a text-book for the study of London English. An appendix, "a descriptive list of English MSS. in the Public Record Office", catalogues most of the documents written in English up to 1425. This is better reading than some more pretentious literature.

CHAPTER IX

MEDIAEVAL PERIOD—INDIVIDUAL AUTHORS AND TEXTS

The authors and texts discussed below comprise the under-mentioned:—

Ancren Riwle.
Andrew of Wyntoun.
Ayenbite of Inwyt.
Hector Boece.
Nicholas Bozon.
Charles d'Orleans.
Geoffrey Chaucer.
Sir Thomas Clanvowe.
Cursor Mundi.
John Gower.
Robert Grosseteste.
Handlyng Synne.
Stephen Hawes.
Walter Hilton.
John Hoccleve.
John Lydgate.
Sir Thomas Malory.
Sir John Mandeville's Travels.
Laurence Minot.
John Mirk.
The *Pearl* Poet.
Reginald Pecock.
The Vision Concerning Piers Plowman.
Poema Morale.
Prick of Conscience.
Richard Rolle.
Sir Richard Ros.
John Skelton.
William of Shoreham.
John Wycliffe.

ANCREN RIWLE (*The Nuns' Rule*)

The most important prose work of its period and moreover one of the most charming pieces in the whole of M.E. literature, the *Riwle* must certainly be read. It is a devotional manual, originally composed, perhaps c. 1200, for the guidance and profit of three young ladies who had withdrawn from the world in order to live as anchoresses close by a church. Two MSS., viz., Cott. Nero A. 14 (1230–50) and Cott. Tib. D 18 (1230–50), preserve the text in full, whilst extracts are contained in MS. Caius Coll. Cbg. 234 (thirteenth century). About 1250, however, the *Riwle* was revised for more general application, which version is now customarily referred to as *Ancrene Wisse* ("The Nuns' Guide"). This revised recension is preserved in only one MS., viz., C.C.C.C. 402 (1230–50). "All our other manuscripts, and the Latin and French versions, go back to the older stage of the Rule as written for three recluses only" (Chambers, *Cont. Engl. Prose*, xcvii).

After long neglect by critics, this treatise is now being intensively studied by some of our foremost scholars, and we may look forward to receiving precise information about the problems of authorship, date and occasion of composition, the identity of the ladies, and the dialect of the various texts. Meanwhile the reader may to some extent follow the course of these interesting investigations by consulting the articles of Miss Allen and Professors Chambers and Tolkien mentioned below.

Bibliography.
C.B.E.L., 1.179–80.

Editions.
Morton, J.   *The Ancren Riwle*. Camden Soc. 1853. [An ed. of MS. Cott. Nero, with translation. The latter, with slight changes, and prefaced by an introd. by Abbot Gasquet, was issued in book-form as Vol. XVIII of the *Medieval Library*, under the title of *The Nuns' Rule*. London, 1926.]

Påhlson, J.   *The Recluse: A Fourteenth-Century Version of the A.R.* Lund, 1918. [Ed. of Magd. Coll. Cbg. Pepys 2498 (fourteenth century).]

N.B.—E.E.T.S. has edd. of all extant texts at Press.

Discussion.
Allen, H. E.   (1) "The Origin of the A.R." in *P.M.L.A.*, 33.474–546. 1918. [Identification of the three ladies.] (2) "The

'A.R.' and Kilburn Priory" in *M.L.R.*, 16.316–22. 1921.
(3) "Some Fourteenth Century Borrowings from the A.R."
in *M.L.R.*, 18.1–8. 1923. [Showing the popularity of the A.R.
during the period.] (4) "Further Borrowings from A.R." in
M.L.R., 24.1–15. 1929. [Concludes that the A.R. enjoyed a
prodigious popularity in mediaeval England for at least 300
years.] (5) "On the Author of the *Ancren Riwle*" in *P.M.L.A.*,
44.635–80. 1929. [Identifies the author with Godwin, hermit
of Kilburn, and master of the anchoresses.]

Bethurum, D. "The Connexion of the Katherine Group with
O.E. Prose" in *J.E.G.Ph.*, 34.553 ff.

Bøgholm, N. "Vocabulary and Style of the M.E. Ancren Riwle"
in *English Studies*, 19.133 ff.

Chambers. *Cont. Engl. Prose*, xcvi ff.

Chambers, R. W. "Recent Research upon the A.R." in *R.E.S.*,
1.4–23. 1925. [Accepts the theory of an English original.]

Dymes, D. M. E. "The Original Language of the A.R." in
Essays and Studies, 9.31–49. 1923. [Argues that the original
language was English, not French.]

Hall. *Sels.*, 354–407. [MSS., bibl., language, style, authorship.]

Macaulay, G. C. "The A.R." in *M.L.R.*, 9.63–78, 145–60, 324–
31, 463–74. 1914. [Collation of C.C.C.C. with Morton's
text; discussion of relationship of A.R. to existing French and
Latin versions.]

Tolkien, J. R. R. "Ancrene Wisse and Hali Meiðhad" in *Essays
and Studies*, 14.104–26. 1929. [Linguistic survey.]

Wells. VI [40].

ANDREW OF WYNTOUN, c. 1350–c. 1425

Wyntoun, an Augustinian Canon of St. Andrew's and prior of
St. Serf's monastery in Lochleven, wrote *The Oryginall Cronycle*
—"original" because it begins at the beginning—in ten Books.
With Bk. VI he arrives at reasonably historical times, and continues the history of Scotland down to James I. His use of the
8-syllable couplet indicates his affiliation, and he cites Barbour
frequently. He is not an emotional romancer, but a serious and
cultivated person interested in history, of some value as evidence
for the later times. Nine MSS. exist, representing three recensions
of the text. The first ed. was by David Macpherson, 1795; it was
revised by Laing for the *Historians of Scotland* series, 1872–9. The
best ed. is by F. J. Amours, in 6 vols., S.T.S., 50, 53–4, 56–7, 63,
1902–5, 1914. In Vols. II–VI the text of the MS. in Wemyss

Castle, supplemented by MS. T.T.6.6. in St. Andrew's University Library, is printed parallel with that of MS. Cotton Nero D.XI. in the British Museum. Vol. I contains life, bibliography, etc., and notes. See also Sir Herbert Maxwell, *The Early Chronicles relating to Scotland*. Glasgow, 1912, and F. Brie, *Die Nationale Literatur Schottlands*, Halle, 1937.

AYENBITE OF INWIT ("*Remorse of Conscience*")

The chief merit of this long and dreary moral treatise, which the Canterbury monk, Dan Michel of Northgate, despite his inadequate French scholarship translated—fairly closely but with innumerable errors—from Friar Lorens' *Le Somme des Vices et des Vertues*, is this: it survives in the author's own MS., Arundel 57, is dated 1340, and claims to be written in the Kentish dialect. Hence, philologically, the document is priceless.

Its contents include expositions of the Commandments and the Creed, an interpretation of St. John's Vision, and expositions of the *Pater Noster* and of the Seven Gifts of the Holy Ghost.

Bibliography.
C.B.E.L., 1.184–5.

Edition.
Stevenson, Roxburgh Club, 1855.
Morris, R. *Dan Michel's Ayenbite of Inwyt.* E.E.T.S., 23.

Discussion.
Wallenberg, J. K. *The Vocabulary of Dan Michel's Ayenbite of Inwyt. A Phonological, Morphological, Etymological, Semasiological and Textual Study.* Uppsala, 1923. [Invaluable.]
Wells. VI [4].

HECTOR BOECE (?1465–1536).

A Scot of Angus, professor in Paris and Principal of King's College, Aberdeen, is to be mentioned, since it was his chronicle that more than any other gave form and currency to the legends of the early Scottish people and kings. It was published in Paris, 1526, translated by John Bellenden (?1490–1550) and again by Harrison in Holinshed's Chronicle, where Shakespeare found it.

Chroniklis of Scotland with the cosmography and dyscription thairof. Compilit be the noble clerk maister Hector Boece, channoun of Aberdene. Translatit laitly in our vulgar and common language be maister John Bellenden, Archdene of Murray. Originally published. Edinburgh, ?1540. *Edition:* Chambers, R. W., Batho, E., and Husbands, W. S.T.S. 1938–41. See F. Brie, *Die nationale Literatur Schottlands*, Halle, 1937. He wrote also an ecclesiastical history: *Episcoporum Murthlacensium et Aberdonensium per Hectorem Boetium Vitae.* Paris, 1522. Bannatyne Club, 1825.

NICHOLAS BOZON

Nothing is known of him, except that he was a Franciscan and lived round about 1300. His Anglo-Norman *Contes Moralisés*, ed. from two MSS. by Lucy Toulmin Smith and Paul Meyer, Soc. des Anciens Textes Francais, 1889, are drawn from Bartholomeus Anglicus and the Aesopic tradition, and though written down in French have a perceptible background of English anecdote, phrase, and detail. Besides this collection of *exempla* for sermons some scattered poems remain; see the introd. to ed. above, and Vising, *Anglo-Norman Language and Literature*.

CHARLES D'ORLEANS, 1391–1455.

Nephew of Charles VI of France, he was captured at Agincourt, 1415 and remained prisoner in England till 1440. He learned English—with a slight Northern accent, and, according to courtly tradition, from a lady—and among his French poems are some in English. His poetry is slight, elegant and charming. For his life, see P. Champion, *Vie de C. d'O.*, Paris, 1911. Two editions of his complete works appeared in Paris, 1842, by L. Champollion-Figeac and J. M. Guichard. The ed. by P. Champion, *Classiques Français du Moyen Age*, Paris, 1923, lacks the English poems, which may be found in Miss Hammond, *English Verse*. The illumination in MS. Royal 16. F. II (B.M.), showing Charles in the Tower, is often reproduced, though it was made c. 1500. There are also English versions of 77 of Charles's French poems in MS. Harleian 682, of which Miss Hammond prints a selection: see P. Sauerstein, *C. d'O. und die englische Übersetzung seiner Dichtungen*, Halle, 1899. Dr. Steele believes them to be Charles's own, and credits him with 121 English poems; which makes him much more important than he seemed.

Edition.
Steele, R. E.E.T.S. 1941.

GEOFFREY CHAUCER, 1340?–1400

Life

The documents are collected in the Chaucer Society's *Life Records*, 1875–1900: Parts I and III by W. W. Selby, Part II by F. J. Furnivall, Part IV by R. E. G. Kirk (with a good summary prefixed); index by E. P. Kuhl in *Mod. Phil.* X (1913). Besides the usual encyclopaedias, see the Lives in Ward, French, Hadow, Legouis and Ten Brink below, and in the editions. For later additions and criticisms see Brusendorff (below), Chap. I, J. R. Hulbert, *Chaucer's Official Life*, 1912, and especially J. M. Manly, *Some New Light on Chaucer*, New York, 1926. M. H. Spielman, *The Portraits of Chaucer*, Ch. Soc. 31, 1900, may be noted here. A. A. Kern, *The Ancestry of Chaucer*, 1906 and R. Krauss, *Chaucerian Problems* (concerned especially with his descendants) in *Three Chaucer Studies*, New York, 1932, shed little light on Chaucer, but include useful references to contemporary figures: see also J. M. Manly's criticism of the latter in *R.E.S.* X, 1934. For Chaucer's literary life, see G. A. Plimpton, *The Education of Chaucer*, O.U.P., 1935; J. S. P. Tatlock, *The Development and Chronology of Ch.'s Works*, Ch. Soc. 37, 1907; W. W. Skeat, *The Chaucer Canon*, Oxford, 1900; and Brusendorff, Chap. I and *passim*. There are, of course, still differences of opinion as to the dates and occasions of some poems: for a useful summary of the various attempts, see Wells, *Manual*, p. 623–8.

Bibliography

Eleanor P. Hammond, *Chaucer, a Bibliographical Manual*, New York, 1908 (reproduced 1933), is the necessary basis for solid study, not only as an indispensable list of publications up to its date, but as a summary collection of facts. Continuations to 1924, by D. D. Griffith, Univ. of Washington Press, 1926, and from 1924 to 1933 by W. E. Martin, Duke Univ. Press, 1935, are more strictly lists of books and papers. J. Koch, *Der gegenwärtige Stand der Chaucerforschung*, in *Anglia* 49 (n.f. xxxvii, May, 1925) reviews work between 1908 and 1925. These, or Wells, *Manual*, Chap. XIV, the Mod. Hum. Annual Bibliographies, the Year's Work in English Studies, and Kennedy, will enable the student to trace general and special studies, but he may find enough in the lists in French, *Handbook* (below) and the edd., notably Robinson's. Charlotte F. E. Spurgeon, 500 *Years of Chaucer Criticism and*

Allusion, 3 vols., 1925 (collecting work in Ch. Soc. 48–56), more inclusive and more "literary", gives an interesting survey of Chaucer's reputation; her conclusions being drawn in *Chaucer devant la critique*, Paris, 1911. There is a *Concordance* by J. S. P. Tatlock and A. G. Kennedy, Carnegie Institute, Washington, U.S.A., 1927, and an *Index to Proper Names, etc.*, by H. Corson, New York, 1911.

Chaucerian Studies

The beginner will do well to possess A. W. Pollard's *Chaucer*, 1893, and reprints, in Macmillan's series of Primers; though it requires revision and supplement, and stereotypes the unhappy division into "periods", the gist of the matter is there. R. D. French, *A Chaucer Handbook*, 2nd ed., New York, 1947, has the advantage of recent research, but wastes time on analysis of poems which the student reads for himself. Other useful introductions are: G. H. Cowling, *Chaucer*, 1927; D. Martin, *A First Book about Chaucer*, 1927; Grace E. Hadow, *Chaucer and his Times* (Home Univ. Lib.), 1927, and reprints; A. W. Ward, *Chaucer*, English Men of Letters Series, 1880 and reprints; N. Coghill, *The Poet Chaucer* (Home Univ. Lib.), 1949. More advanced works are: R. K. Root, *The Poetry of Chaucer*, revised edition, 1934, and G. L. Kittredge, *Chaucer and his Poetry*, 1925: both excellent. M. Kaluza, *Chaucer Handbuch für Stüdierende*, 2nd ed., Leipzig, 1927, is still more complete. Advanced study will be based on Hammond's *Manual* (above). B. Ten Brink, *Chaucer Studien*, Munster, 1870, was a great contribution. T. R. Lounsbury, *Studies in Chaucer*, 3 vols., 1892, contains much sound and valuable stuff, somewhat smothered in words. J. Livingston Lowes' *Geoffrey Chaucer*, 1934, is admirable for those who already know something about Chaucer, especially in the brilliant Chapters I–III, on Backgrounds and Horizons, The World of Affairs, and The World of Books, and for its good sense throughout. Aage Brusendorff, *The Chaucer Tradition*, Copenhagen and London, 1925, is decidedly not for beginners, but contains good mixed matter and a correct critical attitude to uncertain and difficult questions. G. G. Coulton, *Chaucer and His England*, will help with "background". Hérancourt, W., *Die Wertwelt Chaucers, die Wertwelt einer Zeitwende*, Heidelberg, 1939, is a dull but valuable examination of C.'s ethical ideas.

Such collections as O. F. Emerson, *Chaucer Essays and Studies*. Cleveland, Ohio, 1930, and the Essays published by the Chaucer

Soc. are very variable, and each paper must be taken on its merits.

Of more specifically literary studies Dryden's Preface to the Fables (edited by Ker, Vol. II) is the backbone of all, and Lowell's essay in *My Study Windows* is still worth reading. G. K. Chesterton, *Chaucer*, 1932, and reprints, is refreshing and characteristic. J. Livingston Lowes, *The Art of G.C.*, Proc. British Academy, 1931, J. M. Manly, *Chaucer and the Rhetoricians*, British Academy Warton Lecture, 1926, and John Masefield's Leslie Stephen Lecture, Cambridge, 1931, are brief but admirable. L. Cazamian, *The Development of English Humour*, Vol. I, New York, 1930, Chap. IV., E. F. Shannon, *Ch. and the Roman Poets*, Cambridge, Mass., 1929; W. C. Curry, *Ch. and the Mediaeval Sciences*, New York, 1926, and C. S. Lewis, *The Allegory of Love*, Oxford, 1936, Chap. IV, attack from special angles, but such as contribute importantly to general views. But Chaucer's best modern critics are E. Legouis, whose *Chaucer* (translated by L. Lailavoix, 1913 and 1928, but best in the original French) contains true "genial" criticism and is also corrective of the over-emphasis on Italian noticeable, e.g., in Miss Hammond; and W. P. Ker, whose ripe understanding illuminates his *English Literature, Mediaeval* (Home Univ. Lib.), Chap. IX, Essays on *Mediaeval Literature*, 1905, and *Form and Style in Poetry*, 1928, pp. 49–79. Thomas Warton's *History of English Lit.*, Vol. I, sect. xii ff., as purged by W. C. Hazlitt, is not to be neglected, nor J. J. Jusserand, *Literary History of the English People*, I, ii. Courthope, Saintsbury, and the historians will naturally be consulted, and Saintsbury's chapter in C.H.E.L., Vol. II, Chap. VII

The Chaucer Society was founded by the indefatigable Furnivall in 1868, and has completed its task, which was in two parts: first, to print texts as they appear in the MSS., and second, to publish certain studies. The most important are noted in their places here; for a complete list see the catalogue of the Oxford Univ. Press.

Language and Metre

The standard work is B. ten Brink, *Chaucers Sprache und Verskunst*, Leipzig, 1884, and reprints, revised by F. Kluge, translated by M. Bentinck Smith, 1901. Good brief outlines are given in French, *Handbook* (above), in Skeat's ed. of *C.T.* in the school editions which see under *C.T.* below, and in S. Moore, *Historical*

Outlines of English Phonology and Morphology, Ann. Arbor, Mich., 1925, Part V. J. Mersand studies an important aspect in *Chaucer's Romance Vocabulary*, New York, 1939. For metre, see Schipper, *Englische Metrik*, Bonn, 1888; Ten Brink, Chap. III; Saintsbury, *History of English Prosody*, 1906, Vol. I, and the apparatus in editions.

Collective Editions

The first was edited by William Thynne, 1532 (facs. ed. W. W. Skeat, Oxford, 1905), and was reprinted in 1542, 1546, 1555 and 1561, the last being edited by John Stowe. In 1598 Thomas Speght produced an ed. with brief glossary and notes criticised by Francis Thynne (son of William) in *Animadversions*, ed. from MS. by F. J. Furnivall, E.E.T.S. 9, 1865, and Chaucer Soc. 13, 1875. Thynne helped with Speght's second ed., 1602, which was the basis for editions until John Urry's, 1721. Tyrwhitt (see under *C.T.*) showed the need for a new approach, but no ed. matters until W. W. Skeat's in 7 vols., Oxford, 1894–7, and this is still the most fully-annotated ed. Vol. I contains Life of G.C.; II–V, texts and apparatus; VI, notes on *C.T.*; VII, non-Chaucerian poems printed in early editions. One-vol. editions are edited by Skeat, Oxford, 1895, and since; Pollard, Heath, Liddell and McCormick, the "Globe" ed., 1898, and reprints; H. M. Mac-Cracken, "College Chaucer", Yale Univ. Press, 1913, a very useful ed.; and F. N. Robinson, Boston and Oxford 1933, with good introd. and excellent notes, full of bibliographical help, and a rather less satisfactory account of G.C.'s language. Besides profiting by another generation of scholarship, the American editions have the advantage of more legible printing. There are editions also in the World's Classics (Skeat's text), Everyman Lib., etc.

The Canterbury Tales

Some eighty-three MSS. exist: see the complete list in Robinson's ed., p. 1001, and descriptions (though the list is incomplete) in Hammond, *Chaucer Manual*, p. 163. Eight, the most important, are printed by the Chaucer Soc. In the Six-Text Edition, edited by Furnivall, with Index by H. Corson, are parallel texts of the Ellesmere (now in the Huntington Library, California), Hengwrt (now in the National Library of Wales), Cambridge Univ. Lib. Gg. 4.27, Corpus Christi Coll. (Oxford), Petworth (privately owned), Lansdoune (B.M.). The separate texts are also available. The Society also printed Harleian 7334 (B.M.) and C.U.L. Dd. 4.24 completed by Egerton 2726 (B.M.); and, as specimens, the

Doctor-Pardoner Link and Pardoner's Prologue and Tale from forty-three MSS. and Caxton's (two) and Thynne's prints, the Pardoner's Prologue and Tale from Hodson 39 (now John Rylands Lib., Manchester, Engl. 113), and the Clerk's Tale from 8 MSS., with separate introd. by J. Koch, No. 97. See also notes and corrections, Nos. 47 and 49. For the physical appearance of MSS., see the *Autotype Facsimiles*, Ch. Soc. 48, 56, 62, 74 (1876–85): that of the Ellesmere MS., which is the basis of all modern texts, and notable for its illustrations, is No. 74: a better facs. was publ., Manchester, 1911. For descriptions and discussion see, besides editorial matter in the above, Brusendorff, 11.2, and especially W. S. MacCormick and J. Heseltine, *The MSS. of the Canterbury Tales*, Oxford, 1933. All known MSS. are collated in *The Text of the Canterbury Tales*, by J. M. Manly and Edith Rickert, Chicago, 1940. Muriel Bowden, *A Commentary on the Canterbury Tales*, New York, 1948, is valuable.

Printed texts begin in 1478 with Caxton (see p. 432), whose second edition (1484) was reprinted by de Worde and Pynson, and incorporated in the tradition of the collected works until Thomas Tyrwhitt began the modern study of Chaucer in his edition of the *Tales*, 1775–8, reprinted 1798, 1822, and in later collective editions. The (separate) edition by J. M. Manly, Chicago, 1929, is bowdlerised, or, rather, selected, but contains most valuable introd., notes, glossary, etc. There are many school editions of the Prologue and various tales, of which note M. Bentinck Smith, *Prol. and Knight's Tale*, Cambridge, with lucid introd. based on Ten Brink; A. J. Wyatt, *Prol. and Nuns' Priest's Tale*, Univ. Tutorial Press, 1930; K. Sisam, *Nuns' Priest's Tale* and *Clerk's Tale;* A. J. Wyatt, *The Links of the C.T.*, unexpectedly interesting by themselves.

The question of the order of the tales, which imposes itself for both textual and critical reasons, is discussed by C. Robert Kase in *Three Chaucer Studies*, New York, 1932, wherein are references to earlier discussions: see J. M. Manly on this in R.E.S. x, 1934. Modern editors accept the order of the Ellesmere MS., since it is clear that Chaucer had not revised certain discrepancies out of his unfinished book. Henry Littlehales, *Some Notes on the Road from London to Canterbury in the Middle Ages*, Ch. Soc. 30 (1898) helps the broad understanding of the plan. The reader will find enough guidance as to sources and studies thereon among Robinson's notes, but may be amused by *Originals and Analogues of some of Chaucer's Canterbury Tales*, ed. Furnivall, Brock, and Clouston, Ch. Soc. 7, 10, 15, 20, 22 (1872–87; index in Part V).

Troilus and Criseyde

There are 16 MSS. and some fragments: see R. K. Root, *The Troilus MSS.*, Ch. Soc. 98 (1914) for descriptions and fac-similes. The text-material is given in *Three Parallel-Texts* and *Three More Parallel-Texts*, Ch. Soc. 63, 64, 87, 88 (1881–95), and *Specimen Extracts*, ed. McCormick and Root, Ch. Soc. 89 (1914); for discussion, see Root, *The Textual Tradition of Troilus*, Ch. Soc. 99 (1916), Brusendorff, Ch. III, sect. 3, and the editions.

The relation of *T. and C.* to its source, Boccaccio's *Il Filostrato* can be grasped from W. M. Rossetti's comparison, Ch. Soc. 44, 65 (1875–83) and is traced in detail by Karl Young, *The Origin and Development of the Story of T. and C.*, Ch. Soc. 40 (1914). See also N. E. Griffin and A. B. Myrick's translation, *The Filostrato of Boccaccio*, Philadelphia, 1927, with introd. There is valuable material in G. L. Kittredge, *The Date of Chaucer's Troilus and other Chaucer Matters*, Ch. Soc. 42 (1909); C. S. Lewis, *The Allegory of Love*, Oxford, 1936, pp. 176–97 and *What Chaucer Really did to Il Filostrato*. Engl. Ass. Essays and Studies, xvii, 1932; and W. P. Ker's brilliant appreciation in *English Literature: Medieval* (Home Univ. Lib.), Ch. IX.

Minor Poems in Alphabetical order

For discussion of provenance of texts, etc., see A. Brusendorff, *The Ch. Tradition*, Chaps. III and IV; Skeat, *The Ch. Canon* and editions. The number of MSS. is mentioned, to suggest the relative circulation before the printed collective editions.

An ABC: 13 MSS.: an early work, translated from a passage in G. Deguileville, *Pèlerinage de la Vie Humaine*, being a prayer to Our Lady, each stanza beginning with a letter of the alphabet in sequence.

Anelida and Arcite: 8 MSS. and 4 partial MSS.: printed by Caxton, 1477–8. A court poem after the French manner, with suggestions from Boccaccio's *Teseide* (cf. *Knight's Tale*), being a *complainte* with a story-setting in quasi-epic style. Unconvincing attempts have been made to prove a personal allegory. Ch. *may* have thought of an elaborate sequence— a story with elaborate lyrical passages inset, and left it unfinished, like others.

The Book of the Duchess: 3 MSS. An elegy on Blanche, First wife of John of Gaunt, who died 1369, in courtly allegory.

A Complaint to Pity: 9 MSS.; *A Complaint to his Lady:* 2 MSS. These are early exercises in a fashionable French form.

The Complaint of Mars: 8 MSS.; printed by Julian Notary, ?1500. A proem, astronomical story, second proem and 5 lyrical pieces. Allegorical explanations have been suggested even by Shirley, the early fifteenth-century copyist; but none are sure.

The Complaint of Venus: 8 MSS.; and Julian Notary's print. This set of ballads is not connected with *Mars*, is much later, and a version of a poem by Otes de Granson.

A Complaint to his Purse: 8 MSS.; printed by Caxton, 1477–8. This is not a conventional poem like the above, but a personal address to Henry IV, and therefore to be dated in 1399, at the end of Ch.'s life.

The Former Age: 2 MSS.; a moral ballade perhaps on a suggestion from Boethius, but on a theme that goes back to Ovid and further.

Fortune: 10 MSS.; printed by Caxton, 1477. Three "ballades de visage sanz peinture": the third a "debate". Written ?1390.

Gentilesse: 9 MSS.; printed by Caxton. A moral ballade, on the theme developed by the Wife of Bath.

The House of Fame: 3 MSS.; printed by Caxton, 1483. Unfinished. The attempts to find personal allegories may be disregarded. See W. O. Sypherd, *Studies in Ch.'s H. of F.*, Ch. Soc. 39, 1907; Brusendorff, Ch. III, I.

Lak of Stedfastness: 12 MSS. A ballade, with envoy to Richard II, on the times.

The Legend of Good Women: 12 MSS. There are two versions of the Prologue; most editors print both. Ed. W. W. Skeat, Oxford. See Amy, *The Text of Ch.'s L.G.W.*, Princeton, 1918; Brusendorff, Chap. III, I.

Lenvoy to Scogan: 3 MSS. A friendly epistle to Henry Scogan, poet and disciple, tutor to Henry IV's sons. Written ?1393.

Lenvoy to Bukton: 1 MS.; printed by Julian Notary. A letter of advice to Sir Peter or Sir Robert B.—opinion is divided, and it might be to either: a late work, on internal evidence.

Lines to Adam Scriveyn: 1 MS. Admonition to his copyist.

The Parliament of Fowls: 3 MSS.; printed by Caxton, 1483, under title of *The Temple of Bras*. There is much controversy about the occasion of composition, for it looks like a courtly allegory: a late specimen, containing full references to earlier views, is by Haldeen Braddy, No. III in *Three Chaucer Studies*, New York, 1932. J. M. Manly (Kittredge Anniv. Vol.)

denies all allegory. We may agree with J. L. Lowes (*Chaucer*, p. 125) that results have not justified the expense of argument and research.

The Romaunt of the Rose: 1 MS. In *L.G.W.*, prol. 328–31, Ch. avows a translation of *Le Roman de la Rose*, by G. de Lorris and J. de Meung; much argument has been expended on whether this is it. M. Kaluza broke it in three (see *Ch. und der Rosenroman*, Berlin, 1893), and the conclusion at present, if any, is that A is Ch.'s, B is not, C may be. Its importance is symbolic: the *Rose* was one of the great influences in his work: see D. S. Fansler, *Ch. and the R. de la R.*, New York, 1914. The best ed. of the original is by Langlois, Soc. des Anciens Textes Français; there is a good verse translation by F. S. Ellis, Temple Classics, 1900.

Truth: 22 MSS.; printed by Caxton, 1477. A "balade de bon conceyl", addressed to Sir Peter de la Vache, according to Miss Edith Rickert, *Mod. Phil.*, XI.

Womanly Noblesse: 1 MS. A complaint to a lady.

Prose Works

Boece: 10 MSS.; printed by Caxton, 1475. This is a free translation of the *Consolatio Philosophiae* of A. M. S. Boethius (c. 470–525), one of the capital books throughout the Middle Ages. Ch. translates both *prosae* and *metra* into prose. For the original, the Loeb ed. and translation by H. F. Stewart and E. K. Rand, 1918, are convenient. See H. F. Stewart, *Boethius*, Edinburgh, 1891; B. L. Jefferson, *Ch. and the Consolation of Philosophy of B.*, Princeton, 1917.

A Treatise of the Astrolabe: 22 MSS. Skeat's notes are most helpful. See R. T. Gunther, *Early Science in Oxford*, Oxford, 1921–3.

Poems of Uncertain Attribution.

Usually included by modern editors: their relation in kind to accepted poems is clear.

Against Women Unconstant: 3 MSS.
Compleynt d'Amours: 3 MSS.
Merciles Beauty: 1 MS.
A Balade of Complainte: 1 MS.
Proverbs: 3 MSS.

SIR THOMAS CLANVOWE, fl. 1394–1404

A Hereford man, and one of the society centring in Prince Hal, he is credited with *The Cuckoo and the Nightingale* (see p. 333), one of the prettiest things in Mediaeval English, in the *estrif* or disputation form. There are six MSS., and Thynne printed it in his ed. of Chaucer, 1532. Wordsworth modernised it pleasantly in 1801. It it most accessible in Skeat's *Chaucer*, Vol. VII.

CURSOR MUNDI

The text of this metrical "encyclopædia" of Bible stories, comprising some 30,000 ll. and composed in the North c. 1300–25, is preserved in seven MSS.; Cott. Vesp. A III (c. 1340; 29,547 ll.); Göttingen Univ. Lib. Theol. 107 (14th c.; 25,766 ll.); Trin. Coll. Cbg. R, 3, 8 (15th c.; 23,898 ll.); Fairfax 14 (15th c.; 27,899 ll.; with many gaps); B.M. Add. 36,983 (15th c.; 22,004 ll.); Laud 416 (15th c.; 23,898 ll.); College of Arms 57 (c. 1450; ll. 153–23,898). Moreover, fragments are found in several others.

Chiefly in octosyllabic couplets, the poem consists of a prologue and seven parts, as well as four appendices, with, all told, four appendages, not all of which occur in the same MS. Apparently designed both to instruct and to entertain, its many merits (in point of diversity of contents [betokening wide reading], its structure and writing, the regularity of its verse, its direct language, and the author's sympathetic attitude) clearly achieved its purpose—witness the number of extant MSS.

Bibliography.
C.B.E.L., 1.182.

Text.
Morris, R. The "*Cursor Mundi*". E.E.T.S., 57, 59, 62, 66, 68, 99. [With apparatus.]

Discussion.
Hupe, H. *Cursor Mundi.* E.E.T.S., 101. [Essay on the MSS., their dialects.]
Wells. VI [1].

JOHN GOWER, c. 1330–1408

A Kentish squire, he seems to have lived in London and in touch with the court, was a partizan of Henry IV, died in the Priory of St. Mary Overy and was buried in its church (now

Southwark Cathedral) where his tomb still is. For bibliography see Wells, Ch. XV. 2. For life, MSS., etc., Macaulay's introds. (below) are standard. For criticism, see the histories, and W. P. Ker, *Essays*, and *Eng. Lit. Med.*; W. G. Dodd, *Courtly Love in Gower and Chaucer*, Boston, 1913; and especially C. S. Lewis, *The Allegory of Love*, 1936, Ch. V. The one collective ed. is by G. C. Macaulay, 4 vols., Oxford, 1899–1902: Vol. I, French works; II–III, English; IV, Latin; with introd. and apparatus in each, Life in Vol. IV.

(*a*) French works: *Speculum Meditantis* (the title in a Latin note in some MSS. of *V.C.*, below) or *Le Mirour de l'Omme* (the title in the MS.) is a moral work, in some 30,300 lines in 12-line stanzas, written 1376–9, on the effects of sin on society. Long lost, a MS. was found in 1895, now Addit. 3035 in Univ. Lib., Cambridge. See R. Elfreda Fowler, *Une Source Française des Poèmes de G.*, Paris, 1905; the analysis is useful, and relates G. to the body of *Summae* of virtues and vices which took the place of ethical philosophy. *Traitié pour essampler les amantz mariez*, written 1397, before his marriage late in life; 10 MSS. *Cinkante Ballades*, 51 attractive love poems, one to the B.V.M. and two of dedication to Henry IV, probably collected 1399 but may include early work; 1 MS.

(*b*) Latin works: *Vox Clamantis*, in some 10,000 Latin elegiacs, first written c. 1382 but altered later, denouncing political and social conditions under Richard II; 10 MSS., of which Cotton Tiberius A. iv (in B.M.) and Hunterian T. 2.17 (Glasgow Univ.) contain "portraits" of G. aiming an arrow at the globe. *Cronica Tripartita*, in leonine hexameters, describes the last 12 years of Richard II from a hostile position; 1 MS., printed by T. Wright in *Political Poems*, Rolls Ser., 1859–61. Macaulay adds 10 minor poems, mainly political, in Vol. IV.

(*c*) English works: *Confessio Amantis*, Prologue and 8 Books in 33, 444 8-syllable lines, written 1390 and revised 1393, is a treatise on love, morality, and learning. The scheme is a religious parody, a confession to Venus's priest Genius on the lines of a *summa* (see *S.M.* above) and illustrated with over 100 tales; but general morality and learning through the last 4 Books out of proportion. There are some 40 MSS., a print by Caxton, 1483, and two by Berthelet. Ed.: R. Pauli, 1857, from Berthelet's print of 1532; G. C. Macaulay, E.E.T.S. LXXXI–II, 1900–1. Macaulay ed. an ample selection, Oxford, 1903. *In Praise of Peace*, addressed to Henry IV on his accession, was included in Thynne's Chaucer, 1532 (Skeat, Vol. VII), T. Wright, *Political Poems*, Vol. I; 1 MS.

ROBERT GROSSETESTE, d. 1253

A Suffolk man of humble origin, an Oxford scholar acquainted with Greek and Hebrew, science and medicine, the first Chancellor of the University, 1214, and Bishop of Lincoln, 1235, he was often called Saint Robert after his death. For this most remarkable man, see F. S. Stevenson, *R.G.*, 1899. He left many sermons, and treatises on theology, mathematics, estate management (see under Agriculture, p. 441). His *Epistolae*, ed. H. R. Luard, Rolls Ser., 1861, show his emphasis on scripture against tradition and his opposition to foreign prelates. *Le Chasteau d'Amour*, a mystical-homiletic work in irregular 8-syllable verse, (ed. J. Murray, Paris, 1918) was influential; there are some 15 MSS., and must have been many more. There are several translations, for which see F. K. Haase in *Anglia*, XII, 1890, and Hupe, ib., XIV, 1892, who prints a fifteenth-century verse translation from MS. Egerton 927 in the *B.M.*

HANDLYNG SYNNE

Despite its somewhat repellent title, Robert Mannyng's (see p. 324) most interesting poem of 12,630 four-beat ll. in couplets, with its wealth of illustrative stories, will amply repay the reader's time and attention. Preserved in four MSS., viz., Harley 1701 (c. 1360) and Bodley 415 (c. 1400), the fifteenth-century Cbg. Univ. Lib. Ii IV 9 (lacks prologue), and Dulwich Coll. XXIV (2,897 ll.), the poem was adapted from William of Wadington's A.N. *Manuel des Péchiez*, with liberal additions from Mannyng's own store of knowledge. It was specially designed for the common people by one who was familiar with their lives and conditions, as a counter attraction to the pleasures of the inn—hence the great variety of anecdotes.

The poem treats of the Ten Commandments, the Seven Deadly Sins, the Seven Sacraments and Shrift—all well illustrated with stories. (Compare Gower's *Confessio Amantis* for a similar, but later use of the story.)

Bibliography.
C.B.E.L., 1.183–4.

Editions.
Furnivall, F. J. *Robert of Brunne's Handlyng Synne (1303) and its French Original.* E.E.T.S., 119, 123. Also by the same editor, Roxburgh Club, 1862.

Discussion.
Robertson, D. A., Jr. "The Cultural Tradition of Handlyng
Synn" in *Speculum*, 22.162–185. 1947.
Wells. VI [2].

STEPHEN HAWES (?1474–?1523)

An Oxonian (according to Anthony à Wood) who, after some
travel, became a Groom of the Chamber to Henry VII, and a
devout follower of the antiquated allegorical school of court
poetry that derived from the *Romance of the Rose*, content to play
disciple to Lydgate and to parade the learning and the morality
of the days before 1450. His minor poems are naught; the
Passetyme of Pleasure can be read on the principle of Lamb's
friend George Dyer, that in a poem of such length there must
be some good lines—which happens to be true, for the thing has
an occasional mild suffusion of poetry in it. The minor works
were published by W. de Worde:—

> *The convercyon of swerers,* 1509.
> *The example of virtue,* ?1510.
> *A joyfull medytacyon of the coronacyon of Henry the eyght,* 1509.

His largest work was:
> *The historie of graunde Amoure and la belle Pucel, called the
> pastime of pleasure,* 1509, 1517 (W. de Worde), 1554 (from
> which the descriptive title comes), 1555 (two editions).
> 5,816 lines in rime royal, except for Chaps. XXIX and
> XXXII, which are partly in ten-syllable couplets. This has
> been edited by W. E. Mead, E.E.T.S., 174 (1927).
> Extracts and a notice are in Miss Hammond's *Chaucer to
> Spencer.* See Whitney Wells, *Stephen Hawes and "The Court of
> Sapience",* R.E.S., VI, 1930.

For what can be said about Hawes see Warton, Jusserand
and Courthope, W. Murison in C.H.E.L., II.ix, and Berdan
Early Tudor Poetry (1920), Chap. II. He should be looked at, not
only as a sample of aureate vocabulary and uncertain metre,
but for his awkward elegance and for his mixture of romantic
love with the exposition of the Seven Liberal Arts, and because
he is the formal link between Lydgate and Spenser. In Chaps.
XXIX and XXXII he introduces a comic character who brings
in some traditional satire against women; but he has stated his
usual position for himself in Chap. XIV, and more shortly
in his epilogue.

for to eschewe the synne of ydlenes
To make suche bokes I apply my besynes

Besechynge god for to gye me grace
Bokes to compyle of morall vertue
Of my mayster lydgate to followe the trace
His noble fame for to laude and remeue
Whiche in his lyfe the slouthe dyde eschewe
Makynge grete bokes to be in memory
On whose soule I pray god have mercy

WALTER HILTON (d. 1396)

Of the life of Hilton very little is known beyond the date of
his death (March 24, 1396) and the fact that he was a canon of
the Augustinian house at Thurgarton, near Newark. He had,
however, a considerable influence upon the spiritual life of the
late fourteenth century, as well as later. His merits as a writer
of prose have recently been emphasized by Professor Chambers,
Cont. Engl. Prose, ciii ff. In addition, note that research upon the
canon of Hilton's works is being actively pursued.

Discussion.

Deanesly, M. "Vernacular Books in England in the 14th and
   15th Centuries" in *M.L.R.*, 15.349-58. 1920. ["Hilton's
   works seem to have been most popular after those of Rolle."]

Gardner, H. L. "W. Hilton and the Authorship of 'The Cloud
   of Unknowing'" in *R.E.S.*, 9.129-47. 1933. [Does not
   accept Hilton's authorship.]

Gardner, H. L. "W. Hilton and the Mystical Tradition in
   England" in *Essays and Studies*, 22.103-127. 1936. [Man,
   teaching, works.]

Jones, D. *Minor Works of Walter Hilton.* London, 1929. [Modern-
   ised text.]

Wells. XI [53].

The Scale of Perfection is universally assigned to Hilton. It
is an extensive prose work, preserved in many MSS., and possibly
written for the recluse, treating of Contemplation, its several
types, its aims and methods.

Bibliography.

C.B.E.L., 1.194.

Horstmann, C. *Yorkshire Writers*, Vol. I. Pp. 104-6. [Parts only.]
Wells. XI [54].

Edition.

Underhill, E. *The Scale of Perfection*. London, 1923. [Modernised text.]

Other writings assigned to Hilton are *An Epistle on Mixed Life* (7,500 words of prose), *Of Angels' Song* (2,000 words of prose), *Proper Will* (1,000 words of prose), *Encomium Nominis Jesu* (1,800 words of prose), *Of Deadly and Venial Sin* (600 words of prose); and *The Cloud of Unknowing*, a didactic prose treatise of seventy-five chapters on the contemplative life (ed. P. Hodgson, E.E.T.S., 218, who does not admit Hilton's authorship).

JOHN HOCCLEVE (or OCCLEVE), 1370?–1450?

He was a clerk in the Privy Seal Office, as he tells us along with much else about himself, and a follower of Chaucer, much less prolific than Lydgate, less scholarly, but less conventional. His one long work, *The Regement of Princes*, exists in two MSS. in B.M., Royal 17. D. VI, printed by T. Wright, Roxburgh Club, 1860, and Harl. 4866, printed by F. J. Furnivall, E.E.T.S., ex. ser. LXXII, 1897. It consists of 2,016 lines of proem, full of personal details and complaints; 147 lines of address to Prince Henry (later Henry V), including an elegy on Chaucer; 3,276 ll. of good counsel, drawn from *Secreta Secretorum* (cf. ed. Steele, E.E.T.S., ex. ser. LXVI and LXXIV) and other sources duly noted by Hoccleve himself; and 24 ll. of envoy. The stanza is rime royal, except in the envoy, which is in 8-line stanzas on two rhymes.

The *Minor Poems* appear in many MSS., and were edited by F. J. Furnivall and I. Gollancz, 2 vols., E.E.T.S., E.S., LXI and LXXIII, 1892 and 1897. Miss Hammond, *English Verse between Chaucer and Surrey*, prints four poems and two extracts, including the often-quoted praise of Chaucer from the *Regement*.

A fair idea of Hoccleve's easy, slipshod style can be seen in his *Complaint*, which illustrates also the literary complication that betrays the fifteenth-century men so readily into dullness. He states, directly and personally, the difficulty of re-establishing himself after a bout of temporary insanity, and his feelings thereon:

> ". . . for ofte when I/in Westmynster hall[e],
> and eke in London/amonge the prese went[e],
> I se the chere abaten and apalle
> of them that weren wonte me for to calle

293

to companye/her heed they caste a-wry[e],
when I them mette/as they not me sye . . .

Thus spake many one/and seyde by me:
"all-thoughe from hym/his siknesse savage
with-drawne and passyd/as for a tyme be,
Resorte it wole/namely in suche age
as he is of"/and thanne my visage
bygan to glowe/for the woo and fere;
Tho wordis, them unwar/cam to myn ere . . .

But to express his resignation to God's will, he has to report
a dialogue, which he read in a book, between Reason and a
mourner; and so the personal directness is clouded. These
personal poems—*La Male Regle* in which he confesses his feeble
iniquities, *The Complaint* and its sequel the *Dialogue* with a
Friend—are to be read, along with the "club" poems like the
Balade to Sir Henry Somer and such dedicatory poems as the *Balade
to my Gracious Lord of York*. The two tales of Jerislaus and Jonathas
are pleasant in their dilatory fashion, and the *De Regimine
Principum* may be dipped into for glimpses of a fifteenth-century
life as well as of a fifteenth-century mind. A life of Hoccleve
by Furnivall is appended to his edition of the Minor Poems,
noted above.

JOHN LYDGATE (?1370–1452)

"The Monk of Bury" is a correct designation, since he spent
all his life in the great monastery of Bury St. Edmunds, except
for eleven years when he was seconded for duty as prior of Hat-
field in Essex. (For the Bury monastery see the chronicle of
Jocelyn of Brakeland [in the King's Library series], and Carlyle's
commentary thereon in *Past and Present*.) His poetic practice
extended to London, and he had a pension from the Crown.
For his life, see J. Schick, in his edition of *The Temple of Glas*
(see below), and Kingsford, *English Historical Literature in the
15th Century*.

The canon of Lydgate's works is discussed by H. N. Mac-
Cracken in his edition of the Minor Poems (see below), but there
is still room for argument, and always will be. His popularity
is proved not only by the admiring references of later writers
but by the number of MSS. Caxton printed 7 works (*The Churle
and the Bird, Medicina Stomachi, Duodecim Abusiones, The Horse,*

the Goose and the Sheep, The Life of our Lady, Stans Puer ad Mensam, The Temple of Glas), W. de Worde printed 3 more, besides reprints, and Pynson 4, including the formidable Fall of Princes and Troy Book.

The Fall of Princes, 36,365 lines, in nine Books, mainly in rime royal, translated and versified from Laurent de Premierfait's second French version of Boccaccio de Casibus Virorum Illustrium. Bergen (below) describes 30 MSS. and four prints: Pynson's of 1494 and 1527, Tottel's of 1554 and Wayland's, ?1554.

The one modern edition is by Henry Bergen, four vols., E.E.T.S., E.S., CXXI–CXXIV, 1918–19, and the Carnegie Institute of Washington, 1923 and 1927. Vol. I contains a note on the book and one on the metre as well as text; Vol. IV, bibliographical introduction, notes and glossary. Miss Hammond's *English Verse between Chaucer and Surrey* contains the preface and sufficient specimens of the tragic tales. The wordy weakness of fifteenth century writers is plainly stated by Lydgate, who thinks it a virtue:

> a story which is not pleynli told,
> But constreynyd vnder woordes fewe
> For lak off trouthe, wher thei be newe or old,
> Men bi report kan not the mater shewe;
> These ookes grete be not doun ihewe
> First at a stroke, but bi long processe,
> Nor longe stories a woord may not expresse.

The Troy Book, 29,626 lines in 5 Books, in ten-syllable couplets, with 384 lines of prologue in ten-syllable couplets and 107 of envoy in rime royal, amplified from the *Historia Destructionis Troiae* of Guido delle Colonne (c. 1287). Bergen (below, Part IV) describes 19 MSS. and 2 printed editions; Pynson's of 1573, and Marshe's of 1555.

The one modern edition is by Henry Bergen, in four Parts, E.E.T.S., E.S., XCVII, CIII, CVI, CXXVI, 1906–35, Part IV containing bibliographical introduction, notes on Guido, and a full glossary.

The Pilgrimage of the Life of Man, a version of Guillaume de Deguileville's *Pélérinage de la Vie Humaine* (1330–50) a moral vision-allegory of the *Rose* type, in 24,648 eight-syllable lines rhyming in couplets, with 184 ten-syllable lines of prologue. Three MSS. are described in the edition by F. J. Furnivall and K. B. Locock, E.E.T.S., E.S., LXXVII, LXXXIII, XCII, 1899, 1901, 1904, with apparatus in Part I.

The Temple of Glass, a love-vision in 1,403 ten-syllable lines rhymed in couplets. Ed.: J. Schick, E.E.T.S., E.S., LX, 1891, with an important and valuable introduction.

Reson and Sensuallyte, an unfinished vision-poem of 7,042 lines in eight-syllable couplets, taken from French sources. Chess, Nature, and various goddesses are introduced in the usual garden, to preach chastity. Ed.: E. Sieper, E.E.T.S., E.S., LXXXIV and LXXXIX, 1901–3, Part II containing studies on the poem.

The Siege of Thebes, 4,716 lines of (approximately) ten-syllable couplets, comes from a French prose version of the twelfth century *Roman de Thebes*. It is designed as a supplement to the Canterbury Tales, with a prologue of 176 lines to link it with the original, and was printed in the early editions of Chaucer. Some 24 MSS. exist, and a print by W. de Worde, 1500 (?). Ed.: A. Erdmann, E.E.T.S., E.S., CVIII, CXXV, 1911–30: Part I, text, Part II, bibliography, sources, language, metre, etc. The Prologue is in Miss Hammond's collection.

Secrees of old Philisoffres, a version in rime royal of the Latin *Secreta Secretorum*, a treatise on government, medicine and science popularly attributed to Aristotle. Lydgate died before finishing it, and Benedict Burgh (died 1483) continued from line 1,491 to the end in line 2,730. Ed.: R. Steele, E.E.T.S., E.S., LXVI, 1894. This should be examined by anyone who wishes to gather a general notion of the mediaeval mind. Compare the three prose versions of *Secreta Secretorum* edited by R. Steele, E.E.T.S., E.S., LXXIV, 1898.

THE MINOR POEMS

The E.E.T.S. edition (E.S., CVII, 1910, and O.S. 192, 1934) by H. N. MacCracken and M. Sherwood, contains 69 religious poems in Vol. I, and 77 secular poems in Vol. II. The essay in Vol. I on the Lydgate canon is important if not final. These poems are very variable in quality; the student will get an idea of Lydgate in his better moments by beginning with, say, in Vol. I, nos. 15 (singing God's Praise), 33 (saint's lives), 38 (a legend of St. Austin, on tythe-paying), 63 (a valentine, as an example of court poetry spiritualised), 65 (The legend of Dan Joos, a monkish tale) and 68 (The Testament of Dan John Lydgate, really prayers to Jesus, with courtly material in Part II and personal reminiscences and confession in Part IV).

In Vol. II, 3, (*The Complaint of the Black Knight*), 11 (*Bycorne and Chichevache*, a satire), 18 and 19 [satires on the times], 38 (*Horns Away*, on women's dress), 55 (*Stans Puer ad Mensam*, manners for children), and the various *Mummings* and *Soteltyes*. These, and the minor poems generally, should precede any examination of the longer works.

Otto Glauning edited "The Two Nightingale Poems", E.E.T.S., E.S., LXXX, 1900. The first is spurious, the second is No. 43 in MacCracken's first Vol. above.

The following are contained in Miss Hammond's collection: *The Churl and the Bird*, *Horns Away*, *Bycorne and Chichevache*, *The Dance Macabre*, (also in Bergen's *Fall of Princes*, Vol. III), *Epithalamium for Gloucester*, and *Letter to Gloucester*.

To the studies of Lydgate's life, canon, language, metre, etc., in the apparatus appended to the above editions, add Miss Hammond's general introduction and her useful introduction to her selections from Lydgate. Gray left notes on Lydgate, the only extant fragment of his projected History of English poetry. It was a sound instinct that led him to make sure of Lydgate first, since he is the clue to much later mediaeval poetry. All histories of English literature discuss Lydgate perforce, with results varying from the usual boredom to Churton Collins's extravagant praise; the truth being in the midst as usual—for there is much in Lydgate to attract the curious and supple mind.

SIR THOMAS MALORY

The best identification is (according to Vinaver) with Sir Thomas Malory of Newbold Revel, c. 1408–71; but the name was fairly common and the identification cannot be considered absolutely certain. The book, however, bears its date in the colophon: "This book was ended the IX yere of the reygne of kyng edward the fourth by syr Thomas Mallore knyght"—i.e., March 1469–March 1470.

The MS. recently discovered in Winchester College Library is being edited for the Oxford University Press by Professor E. Vinaver. The first edition is Caxton's, "by me devyded in to xxi bookes chapytred and enprynted/and fynysshed in thabbey westmestre the last day of Juyl the yere of our lord/M/CCCC IXXXV/". Caxton's division into books and chapters is convenient but not very adequately performed. His edition was reprinted by Wynkyn de Worde in 1498 and (with some verbal alterations) in 1529, by Copland in 1557, by East in 1585(?), and by Stansby for J. Bloom in 1634.

The best edition is still that of H. Oskar Sommer, 1889; a page reprint of Caxton's. Vol. II contains prolegomena. There are many editions, of which we may note Southey's (1816) and Wright's, from the 1632 edition, 1858. The Globe edition (ed.: Strachey) is abridged and modernised. Routledge's edition, modernised by A. W. Pollard, is good and has a useful name-index. The "Everyman" edition is out of print.

The indispensable book on Malory is Eugene Vinaver, *Sir Thomas Malory*, Oxford, 1929. Note the appendix on materials for the life of Malory; the bibliography is valuable. See also W. P. Ker in *Essays on Mediaeval Literature*, 1905; E. K. Chambers, English Association Pamphlet, No. 51, 1922, reprinted in *Sir Thomas Wyatt and Some Collected Studies*, 1933, and *English Literature at the Close of the Middle Ages*, Chap. IV. The sources are studied by Sommer in his second Vol., by Vida K. Scudder, *Le Morte Darthur of Sir Thomas Malory and its Sources*, 1921, and by Vinaver in his second appendix.

SIR JOHN MANDEVILLE'S TRAVELS

This book of travels, ostensibly by Sir John Mandeville of St. Albans, was designed as a pilgrims' guide-book for the routes to Jerusalem, but, extending its scope to include travel in the Orient, it ultimately became a book of entertainment. That it entirely succeeded herein, is attested by the existence both of some 300 MSS. and of printed versions as late as 1725. Wells notes that before 1500 it had been printed in German, Dutch, Italian, Latin and French.

There are three distinct English versions, as represented by: (1) MS. Cott. Titus C 16 (?1410–20), (2) MS. Egerton 1982 (?1410–20) and (3) certain defective MSS. The two first are written in excellent prose.

Though plausibly presented, and containing a wealth of convincing detail, the book is not an account of actual travel by the Englishman Mandeville or even by any one person, but is a compilation originally written in French, perhaps 1356–7, from various source-books of travel and of natural history. It may have been made by John de Bourgoyne (fl. 1313–65), a French physician at Liège. But the problem of the authorship is notoriously difficult.

Bibliography.
C.B.E.L., 1.191.

Editions.
Hamelius, P. *Mandeville's Travels.* E.E.T.S., 153, 154. [Cotton text, with critical apparatus.]
Warner, G. F. Ed. of Egerton, with the French text, and an excellent apparatus, for Roxburghe Club, 1889.

Reprint.
The Voiage and Travaile, etc. O.U.P., 1932. [Reprint of 1568 text.]
Bramont, J. Ev. Lib., 812. 1928.

Discussion.
Jackson, I. "Who was Sir J. M.?" in *M.L.R.*, 23.466–8. 1928.
Sisam, 94–6 (authorship), 238–42 (relationship of versions).
Wells, X [31].

LAURENCE MINOT

Minot, of whom nothing is really known, though he was possibly a Norfolk man, between 1333 and 1352 wrote eleven poems of no special literary merit, on the wars of Edw. III. They are characterised by fervid patriotism and intense scorn for the Scots and French. Each was written soon after the occasion celebrated. About 1352 Minot revised them and united them all by providing each with a metrical title of one couplet. Excluding these links, there are 923 ll. Nos. 2, 5, 9, 10, and 11 are written in the long alliterative line, the rest, in various metres. The text is preserved in MS. Galba E 9 (c. 1425), in an E. Midl. dialect.

Bibliography,
C.B.E.L., 1.270–1.

Edition.
Hall, J. *The Poems of Laurence Minot.* 3rd rev. ed. Oxford, 1914.

Discussion.
Oakden. *Allit. Poetry*, 106–7, 201–16, 239.
Wells. IV [12].

JOHN MIRK (OR MYRC)

Sometime after 1400 John Mirk (Myrc), Prior of the Monastery at Lilleshall in Shropshire, wrote his so-called *Instructions for Parish Priests*. This is a versified translation of the *Oculus Sacerdotis* of William de Pagula, a Berkshire vicar. The text survives in six MSS., of which MS. B. M. Cotton Claudius A2, written in the W. Midland dialect, has been edited by E. Peacock (below).

Bibliography.
C.B.E.L., 1.175.

Edition.
Peacock, E. E.E.T.S. O.S., 31 (revised 1902).

Selections.
Cook, A. S. *Literary M.E. Reader*, 287–93.
Emerson, O. F. *M.E. Reader*, 119–25.

Discussion.
Pfander, H. G. "Some Medieval Manuals of Religious Instruction" in *J.E.G.Ph.*, 35.243–58, 1936. [On the nature of the genre. See p. 252.]
Wells, VI [38].

Besides his *Instructions*, Mirk wrote a *Festial* (see Wells, V [20]), a collection of sermons—virtually a fusion of Homily Cycle and Legendary—for Church festivals. This is mainly based on the extremely popular medieval source-book, *Legenda Aurea*, written by the Dominican preacher, Jacobus a Voragine (Archbishop of Genoa, 1292; died 1298), as well as on local oral tradition.

THE PEARL POET

Preserved in the same (unique) MS., viz., Cotton Nero A X+4 (c. 1400; W. Midl. dialect), are *Sir Gawayne and the Grene Knight*, *Pearl*, *Patience*, and *Purity*. Struck by the resemblance between all of them in point of dialect, diction, style, parallels and poetic achievement, several critics have assumed identity of authorship, and accordingly style the (anonymous) writer the Gawain or Pearl poet. The question is involved, but each may study it for himself; the bibliography under the next item may be consulted for the purpose.

1. *The Pearl*

The poem, the structure of which is the "most elaborate and

ingenious in M.E." has 101 stanzas (apparently in error for 100), arranged with one exception of six, in groups of five and each containing twelve four-stress ll. rhyming abababababbcbc, with two or three instances of alliteration in every line. In addition, subtle devices are used to link section with section and stanza with stanza.

Briefly, the poem, one of the loveliest in English, is cast in the form of a vision in which the poet, sleeping near the grave of his two-year-old daughter, Pearl, sees his dead child on the opposite bank of a river, in Paradise, as he imagines. But she is no longer a child. They converse about her present state and various aspects of Christian faith regarding Paradise. The inner meaning of this conversation is so obscure as to suggest various interpretations, and to lead critics to divergent conclusions about the poet's purpose. Some consider the piece an elegy, others a religious allegory (with various sub-divisions), others a combination of both.

Bibliography.
C.B.E.L., 1.201–203.

Editions.
Chase, S. P., and others. *Pearl: the Text of the Fourteenth Century Poem.* The Bowdoin Edition. Edited by Members of the Chaucer Course in Bowdoin College, Boston, 1932.
Gollancz, I. *Pearl . . . with Modern Rendering.* Rev. ed. London, 1907.
Gollancz, I. *Pearl, Cleanness, Patience, Sir Gawain (in facsimile).* E.E.T.S., 162.
Osgood, C. G. *The Pearl.* London, 1906. [With full apparatus. Handy ed.]

Translation.
Chase, S. P. *The Pearl.* O.U.P., 1932. [In verse. Valuable introductory essay.]
Gollancz (above).
Gollancz, I. *Pearl.* Medieval Library, XIII. London, 1921.
Neilson and Webster. *Ch. Brit. Poets,* 7–18.
Osgood, C. G. *The Pearl rendered in Prose.* Princeton, 1907.
Weston. *Rom. Vi. Sat.,* 187–237. [Verse.]

Discussion.
Brown, C. F. "The Author of the Pearl" in *P.M.L.A.*, 19.115–53. 1904.

Cargill, O., and Schlauch, M. "Pearl and its Jeweler" in *P.M.L.A.*, 43.105–23, 1928. [Identification of child of Author.]

Chapman, C. O. "The Authorship of the Pearl" in *P.M.L.A.*, 47.346–53. 1932.

Coulton, G. G. "In defence of Pearl" in *M.L.R.*, 2.39–43. 1907.

Emerson, O. F. "Some Notes on the Pearl" in *P.M.L.A.*, 53–93, 1922. [Valuable interpretative and linguistic notes.]

Garrett. *The Pearl: An Interpretation*. Seattle, 1918.

Greene, W. K. "The Pearl—A New Interpretation" in *P.M.L.A*. 40.814–27. 1925.

Gordon, E. V., and C. T. Onions. "Notes on the Text and Interpretation of Pearl" in *Med. Aevum*, I and II. 1932–3.

King, R. W. "A Note on *Sir Gawayne and the Green Knight*" in *M.L.R.* 29.435–6. 1934.

Koziol, H. "Zur Frage der Verfasserschaft einiger me. Stabreimdichtungen" in *E.St.*, 67.165–73. 1932–3.

Madelava, M. *Pearl. A Study in Spiritual Dryness*. London, 1925.

Menner, R. J. "*Sir Gawain and the Green Knight* and the West Midland" in *P.M.L.A.*, 37.503–26. [Linguistic.]

Northup, C. S. "Study of the Metrical Structure of the Pearl" in *P.M.L.A.*, 12.326–40. 1897.

Oakden. *Allit. Poetry. passim.* [Metre, dialect and author.]

Schofield, W. H. "Nature and Fabric of the Pearl" in *P.M.L.A.*, 19.154–215. 1904.

Schofield, W. H. "*Symbolism, Allegory and Autobiography in the Pearl* in *P.M.L.A.*, 24.585–675. 1909.

Wells. XV [2].

Note also the introductions to the editions of the other poems in the group.

2. *Patience*

This homiletic poem is concerned with the virtue of patience and (vividly) paraphrases the biblical story of Jonah and the Whale to illustrate the evil of impatience. It consists of 531 long alliterative lines, possibly in short sequences and varying from 3 to 5 ll. according to the sense.

Bibliography.
C.B.E.L., 1.202.

Editions.
Bateson, H. *Patience*. 2nd rev. ed. Manchester, 1918.

Gollancz (above). E.E.T.S., 162.
Gollancz, I. *Patience*. 2nd ed. rev. O.U.P., 1924.

Translation.
Weston. *Rom. Vis. Sat.*, 173–83. [Part only.]

Discussion.
On authorship, see refs. above.
Day, M. "Strophic Division in M.E. Alliterative Verse" in
    E.St., 66.245–8.
Oakden. *Allit. Poetry, passim*. [Metre, dialect, author.]
Wells. XV [3].

3. *Purity* (Cleanness)

The author of this homiletic poem of 1,812 long alliterative
lines, divided into thirteen irregular sections, inculcates the virtue
of purity. By way of emphasis he relates biblical *exempla* of over-
whelming destruction, including the Fall of the Angels, the Flood,
Sodom and Gomorrah and the fate of Nebuchadnezzar. By way
of contrast he tells of the purity of Christ and the Virgin and of
their power to save. The sources also include the French *Mandeville's Travels*, the *Cursor Mundi*, and *Le Livre du Chevalier de la Tour
Landré*.

Bibliography.
C.B.E.L., 1.202–3.

Editions.
Day, M. *Cleanness*. London, 1933.
Gollancz (above). E.E.T.S., 162.
Menner, R. J. *Purity*. Yale, 1920.

Discussion.
Bateson. *Patience*, 67.
Day, M. "Strophic Division in M.E. Alliterative Verse" in
    E.St., 66.245–8.
Oakden. *Allit. Poetry, passim*.
Wells. XV [4].

4. *Sir Gawayne and the Grene Knight*

See under Romances, p. 365 ff below.

REGINALD PECOCK, ?1395-?1460

This great scholar wrote against the Lollards, but was indiscreet enough to prefer argument to burning, was found heretical, deprived of his bishopric of Chichester, and confined in Thorney Abbey. He solved the problem, as nearly as could be, of arguing of theology in set academic form, in English; his language and style are thus most interesting, and might have been influential had his superiors permitted his works to circulate.

The Repressor of Overmuch Blaming of the Clergy, 1455, is his greatest work, ed. from Kk. 4. 26 in Univ. Lib. Cambridge, by C. Babington, 2 vols. 1860, with a standard introd.

The Book of Faith, 1456, printed in part by H. Wharton, 1688, is edited by J. L. Morison, Glasgow, 1909.

The Donet and *The Follower to the Donet*, are ed. E. V. Hitchcock, E.E.T.S., 156 and 164, 1921 and 1924.

The Reule of Crysten Religion is edited by W. C. Greet, E.E.T.S., 171, 1927.

THE VISION CONCERNING PIERS PLOWMAN

Despite being open to criticism in point of structure, clarity, elegant diction, metre, selection of isolated themes, *Piers Plowman* is rightly accounted one of the greatest achievements in M.E. literature and second only to the *Canterbury Tales*. It is a vision poem, though not visionary: it is allegorical and satirical, though realistic and reformative: it preaches true Christianity.

One of the most popular works up to the sixteenth century, the poem has survived in some 60 MSS. These represent 3 successive versions of unequal length, termed respectively the A-, B-, and C-texts. The inter-relationship of these texts and their authorship, whether the work of several writers or of the obscure cleric, William Langland, still form the subject of animated dispute, but cannot be discussed here. Note however, the several items concerned with these problems, especially those by R. W. Chambers, in the bibliography (but a small selection) below. For a full bibliography, see Wells V [51].

The three versions, all in the long alliterative line, are constituted as follows:—

(1,) A-text. Written 1362-3 and containing 2,567 ll., has a Prologue and 12 Passus, and consists of 2 parts: (*a*) a Prologue and 8 Passus, dealing with the Vision of the Fair Field full of Folk, Holy Church and Lady Meed, and the Vision of Piers Plowman, 1,833 ll.; (*b*) 4 Passus concerning the Vision of Dowel, Dobet and Dobest, 734 ll.

(2) B-text. Written 1376-7, as a revision of A, in 7,242 ll. It contains both the Vision of Piers Plowman (in a Prologue and 7 Passus), and of Dowel, Dobet and Dobest (in 3 Prologues and 10 Passus, divided up as follows:— Dowell: Prologue and 6 Passus: Dobet: Prologue and 3 Passus; and Dobest: Prologue and 1 Passus).

(3) C-text. Written 1393-8, is a much re-arranged and amplified revision of the B-text in 7,357 ll. It has 23 Passus, 10 being concerned with Piers Plowman, 7 with Dowel, 4 with Dobet and 2 with Dobest.

Apart from its undoubted and universally acknowledged literary merits, the poem is of considerable importance histori-cally, because of the flood of light it sheds upon the political and social life of ordinary people. Langland, if indeed he is the author, and Chaucer between them give us a complete picture of the social life of the age in which they lived.

Bibliography.
C.B.E.L., 1.197–200.

Editions.
Skeat, W. W. *The Vision of William concerning Piers the Plowman.*
2 vols. Oxford, 1896. [Standard ed. of all three texts.]
Skeat, W. W. E.E.T.S., 28, 38, 54, 81. [Separate editions of A, B and C, with notes and glosses.]
Skeat, W. W. *The Vision of William concerning Piers the Plowman.*
9th rev. ed. Oxford, 1906.
N.B. Editions by Prof. Knott of Chicago Univ. and by R. W. Chambers and J. H. Grattan for E.E.T.S., in preparation.

Translations.
Burrell, A. *Piers Plowman.* Ev. Lib. 571, London, 1912, etc. [Prose.]
Neilson and Webster. *Ch. Brit. Poets,* 47–78. [Verse. A-text, Prol. and 8 Pass.]
Skeat, W. W. *The Vision of Piers Plowman.* London, 1905.
Warren, K. M. *The Vision of Piers the Plowman.* London, 1913. [Prose. Prol. and Passus of B.]
Weston. *Rom. Vi. Sat.,* 241–327. [Verse. A-text, and Prol. of B.]
Wells, H. W. *The Vision of Piers Plowman newly rendered into Modern English.* New York, 1935. [Whole poem.]

Discussion.
The Piers Plowman Controversy. E.E.T.S., 139. Extra issue, 1910.

[Indispensable series of essays by Jusserand, Manly, Chambers and Bradley.]

Bennett, J. A. W. The Date of the B-text of *Piers Plowman* in *Medium Ævum*, XI, 55–64. 1943. [Assigns to 1377–9.]

Bright, A. *New Light on Piers Plowman*. London, 1928. [On author's identity.]

Carnegy, F. A. R. *The Relations between the Social and Divine Order in William Langland's Vision*. Breslau, 1934.

Chadwick, D. *Social Life in the Days of Piers Plowman*. C.U.P., 1922.

Chambers, R. W. "The Original Form of the A-Text" in *M.L.R.*, 6.302–23, 1911; with J. H. G. Grattan, "Text of *Piers Plowman*: Critical Methods" in *M.L.R.*, 11.257–75, 1916; "The Three Texts of P.P. and their Grammatical Forms" in *M.L.R.*, 14.129–51, 1919; "Long Will, Dante, and the Righteous Heathen", *Essays and Studies*, 9.50–69, 1923; with Grattan, "The Text of 'Piers Plowman'" in *M.L.R.*, 26.1–51, 1926; "Poets and their Critics: Milton and Piers Plowman" in *Proc. Brit. Acad.* (Warton Lecture), 1942; *Man's Unconquerable Mind*, London, 1939. [See especially Chapters 4 and 5.]

Coghill, N. K. "The Character of Piers Plowman considered from the B-Text" in *Medium Ævum*, 2.108–135, 1933; *The Pardon of Piers Plowman*, London, 1946. [Brilliantly interpretative.]

Dunning, T. P. *Piers Plowman: An Interpretation of the A-text*. London, 1937.

Gerould, G. H. "The Structural Integrity of *Piers Plowman*" in *Studies in English Philology*, 45.60–75, 1948. [Claims organic unity of B-text.]

Hort, G. *Piers Plowman and Contemporary Religious Thought*. London, 1938.

Hulbert, J. R. "Piers the Plowman after Forty Years" in *M.Ph.*, 45.215–225, 1948. [Argues against unity of authorship.]

Huppé, B. F. "Piers Plowman: the Date of the B-Text Reconsidered" in *Studies in English Philology*, 46.6–13, 1949. [Assigns to 1377–9.]

Knott, T. A. "Observations on the Authorship of *P.P.*" in *M.Ph.*, 14.531 ff., 15.23 ff. "Essay Toward a Critical Text of the A-Version" in *M.Ph.*, 12.

Manly, J. M. *Piers the Plowman and its Sequence*, E.E.T.S., Extra Issue, 135 b.

Stone, G. W. "In Interpretation of the A-Text" in *P.M.L.A.*, 53.656–77, 1938.

Wells, H. W. "The Construction of *Piers Plowman*" in *P.M.L.A.*, 44.123–40, 1929.

Wells, IV [51]. [Includes a summary of the various controversies.]

POEMA MORALE ("*A Moral Ode*")

Although the poem enjoyed great popularity in the period, it is to-day important more for its metrical form than its contents. The author surveys his long life, notes his shortcomings with regret, recommends right and holy living, deplores waste of opportunities, pictures Doomsday and finally describes the Joy of Heaven.

Composed c. 1180, it is the first known example in English of the septenary, a line of seven stresses, with a cæsura after the fourth, and of Latin origin (see further Schipper, *Hist. of Engl. Vers.*, 193 ff.). The text is preserved in MS. Lambeth 487 (end of twelfth century; first 270 ll.), MS. B.M. Egerton 613 (two copies of text, the first and earlier, written 1200–5; 370 ll.), MS. Trin. Coll. Cbg. B, 14, 52 (early thirteenth century; 400 ll.), MS. Jesus Coll. Oxon. 29 (c. 1275; 390 ll.), MS. Cbg. McClean 123 (soon after 1300; 337 ll.), and Bodl. MS. Digby A 4 (beginning 13th c.; 764 ll. in quatrains). All of them are in the Southern dialect.

Bibliography.
C.B.E.L., 1.180.

Editions.
Texts from various MSS. appear in E.E.T.S. 34, 29, 53; Hall, *Sels.*, 1.30, with valuable notes on language, dialect, metre, MSS. in 2.312 ff.; Morris, *Specimens*, 1.194–221 (two texts); Marcus, H., *Das frühmittelenglische "Poema Morale"*, Leipzig, 1934 [Critical ed., with German tr.].

Discussion.
Moore, S. "The MSS. of the *Poema Morale*: Revised Stemma" in *Angl.* 54.269–87. 1930. [Proposes a re-arrangement of texts.]
Wells. VII [25.]

THE PRICKE OF CONSCIENCE

Although over a hundred MSS. (as well as Latin versions) point to the former popularity of this long, introspective, theological poem (in seven parts) on the soul, modern readers scarcely find it alluring. Nevertheless, it has the merits of being based on wide reading and of constituting a compendium of current knowledge upon this particular theme. The best MS., viz., Cotton Galba E IX (Northern; early fifteenth century), preserves the text in 9,624 four-beat ll. rhyming in couplets. The poem was formerly attributed to Richard Rolle (q.v.), but the whole weight of Miss H. E. Allen's unique authority opposes the ascription: in only five of the MSS. is such an assignment made.

Bibliography.
C.B.E.L., 1.185.

Edition.
Horstmann, C. *Yorkshire Writers, Richard Rolle of Hampole.* 2 vols., London, 1895–6. Pp. 2.36 ff., 1.372ff., 1.129 ff.
Morris, R. *The Pricke of Conscience.* Berlin, 1863. [Standard.]

Discussion.
Allen. *Writings Ascribed to R. Rolle.* London, 1927.
Wells. XI [4].

RICHARD ROLLE OF HAMPOLE (c. 1300–49)

Rolle, Yorkshire hermit and mystic, and one of the most important intellectual figures of the fourteenth century, exercised a considerable influence both in his own day and for long afterwards. His works—English and Latin—were frequently copied and imitated, thus rendering it difficult to distinguish authentic from spurious. The writings allowed to him by Miss Allen, his latest biographer, are listed below, with mention of editions, etc. Note especially that these do not include the *Pricke of Conscience*, which was long assigned to him.

Bibliography.
C.B.E.L., 1.191–4.

Discussion.
Allen, H. E. *Writings Ascribed to Richard Rolle, Hermit of Hampole, and Materials for his Biography.* London, 1927. [Standard.]
Comper, F. M. M. *The Life of Richard Rolle.* London, 1928.
Horstmann, C. *Richard Rolle of Hampole and his Followers.* (*Yorkshire Writers.*) 2 vols. London, 1895–6.
Wells. XI. 1.

Texts.

Allen, H. E. *The English Writings of Richard Rolle.* Oxford, 1931.
[The introd. has a useful summary of Rolle's life and writings
based on her earlier book above.]

Hodgson, G. E. *Some Minor Works of Richard Rolle.* London, 1923.
[Contains all the undermentioned except item 4.]

Horstmann (above).

Perry, G. G. *English Prose Treatises of Richard Rolle de Hampole.*
E.E.T.S., 1866, reprinted 1920.

Translation.

Heseltine, G. C. *Selected Works of Richard Rolle.* London, 1930.
[Prose and verse renderings.]

1. The *Form of Perfect Living.* A prose epistle (after 1348) of
some 10,000 words addressed to Margaret Kirkby, who was
a disciple of his and an anchoress living in a neighbouring
hermitage. Preserved in 38 MSS., the two best, both in the
Northern dialect, being MSS. Cbg. Univ. Lib. Dd. V 64 (c.
1400) and Rawlinson C 285 (early 15th c.), it has twelve
chapters, six on the form of living in general and six on Love.

Edition.
Allen. *Engl. Writings R.R.*

Translation.
Heseltine (above); Hodgson, G. E. *"F. of P.L." and other Prose
Treatises of R.R. of H.,* London, 1910.

2. *Ego Dormio et Cor Meum Vigilat.* A prose tract (c. 1343) of
some 3,500 words addressed to a nun on the subject of complete
devotion to the Heavenly Love. Preserved in 12 MSS. Edited by
Allen, *Engl. Writings R.R.* Trans.: Heseltine (above) and Hodgson,
Some Minor Works (above). Wells, XI [6].

3. *A Commandment of Love to God.* A prose tract of some 3,000
words, in 14 MSS. Edited by Allen, *Engl. Writings R.R.* Trans:
Heseltine (above) and Hodgson, *Some Minor Works* (above).
Wells, XI [7].

4. *Commentary on the Psalter.* An epitome (after 1337) of Petrus
Lombardus' *Commentarium in Psalmos,* preserved in some 40 MSS.
and written at the request of Margaret Kirkby as is explained
in the prologue of 60 long alliterative ll. in couplets.

Edition.

Bramley, H. R. *The Psalter translated by Richard Rolle*. Oxford, 1884.

Selection.
Allen. *Engl. Writings R.R.*

Translation.
Hodgson, G. *Penitential Psalms*. London, 1928.

Discussion.
Everett, D. "The M.E. Prose Psalter of R.R. of H." in *M.L.R.*, 17.217–27, 337–50 [1922] and 18.381–93 [1923].
Wells, XI [8].

5. *Meditatio de Passione Domini*. Basis: *The Privity of the Passion*, an abridged prose translation of Bonaventura's *Meditationes Vitae Christi*, Chaps. LXXIV–XCII. Survives in two versions, one of some 5,000 words extant in MS. Cbg. Univ. Lib. Ll. 1, 8 (14th c.), and the other of 7,000 words in MSS. Cbg. Add. 3042, Bodl. e. Musaeo 232 and Uppsala Univ. C 494. Reputed to be one of the most poetical of the M.E. Passion writings. See Wells, XI [9].

Editions.
Allen. *Engl. Writings R.R.* [Ed. of Cbg. Ll., and Bodl. e Mus.]
Lindkvist, H. *R.R.'s M. de P.D., according to MS. Uppsala C 494.*
     Uppsala, 1917.

Translation.
Heseltine (above).

6. *Moralia Richardi Hermite de Natura Apis*. A short prose passage on the nature of the bee claiming (but unjustifiably) reliance upon [the *Historia Animalium* attributed to] Aristotle. Preserved in two MSS., viz., Thornton (1430–40) and Durham Cosin V, i, 12. Wells, XI [28].

Edition.
Allen. *Engl Writings R.R.*; Sisam, *Fourteenth Cent. Verse*.

Translation.
Heseltine (above).

7. *On Foure Maners May a Man Wyt*. Comprises only fifty words

of prose interposed among certain lyrics in MS. Cbg. Univ. Lib. Dd. V 64 (c. 1400). Ed. Horstmann, 1.73. See Wells, XI [50].

8. *Gastly Gladness in IHESU.* Some hundred words of prose in MS. Longleat 29. Ed. Allen, *Engl. Writings R.R.* Trans.: Heseltine (above).

9. Three Short Prose Expositions. (1) The *Commandments*; (2) *Seven Gifts of the Holy Ghost*, and (3) *Delight in Christ.* Ed. Allen, *Engl. Writings R.R.* Trans.: Heseltine (above).

10. Twelve lyrics, over-alliterated, in MS. Cbg. Univ. Lib. Dd. V 64 (Northern: c. 1400), all characterised by intense feeling. Ed.: Allen, *Engl. Writings R.R.*, 294–300.

11. Two lyrics on Christ on the Cross in MSS. Cbg. Univ. Lib. Dd. V 64, and Vernon. Ed. Allen, *Writings Ascribed R.R.*, 294.

SIR RICHARD ROS, 1429–?

A Lancashire squire, he translated Alain Chartier's *La Belle Dame sans Merci* in 8-line stanzas, adding four 7-stanzas at beginning and end. It is a dialogue between lover and lady, with some pleasant descriptive passages, a typical court piece. It was only the title that inspired Keats. There are four MSS., and Thynne printed it. It will be found in Skeat's *Chaucer*, Vol. VII.

JOHN SKELTON, ?1460–1529

A Norfolk man, Oxford and Cambridge bred, tutor to the Prince Henry who became Henry VIII and so somewhat a courtier, took orders in 1498—probably, like some others, in despair of other living—and became parson of Diss in his native county, from which post he was suspended for misbehaviour. His too violent criticism of Wolsey necessitated his taking sanctuary at Westminster, where he died, not in the odour of sanctity but having achieved publicity, which doubtless he preferred. The *Merry Tales* printed by Colwell in 1567 may be apocryphal, but they show what legend he left behind him—a legend that does not entirely conflict with his later life and work, though out of keeping with the academic scholar praised by Caxton in the preface to *Eneydos* in 1490, or the courtly scholar complimented by Erasmus in 1507 as *unum Britannicarum literarum lumen et decus.* The curious will find them in Dyce's edition noted below.

Some of his works exist in more or less fragmentary MSS., but here the printed editions become important.

A Ballade of the Scottysshe Kynge, a song of triumph over Flodden. R. Fawkes, 1573.

The Booke of Phyllyp Sparowe. 844 lines of "Skeltonic" verse, with much Skeltonic charm. R. Kele, 1545?.

The Bowge of Court. 539 lines of court satire, in rime royal. W. de Worde, undated.

Colyn Cloute. 1,270 Skeltonic lines of anti-prelatical satire. Kele, 1545?

The Epitaph of Jasper late duke of Beddeforde. Pynson 1496.

Magnificence, a morality, J. Rastell, 1533. Rather dull and sententious, as if the occasion constrained him. Ed.: R. L. Ramsay, E.E.T.S., ex ser. XCVIII, 1906 (1908), with elaborate introd.

A Replycacion agaynst certaigne yong scolers. Pynson, 152–.

The Garland of Laurell. 1,552 lines, in rime royal and skeltonics, largely in praise of his own poetry. R. Fawkes, 1523.

Agaynste a Comely Coystrowne. Pynson, n.d.

The Tunnyng of Elynour Rummyng. 623 skeltonic lines of coarse, lively, low comedy.

Why Come Ye Not to Courte. 1,248 lines of satire, largely against Wolsey, and (with *Speke, Parrot*) the main cause of his offence. Kele, 1545?

Collections of his verse appeared as under:

Dyuers Balettys and Dyties, Pynson, n.d.

Certayne Bokes, ?1545, ?1560, ?1565.

Litle Works, 1547.

Pithy, Pleasaunt and Profitable Workes, 1568—a fairly full collection.

The standard modern edition is still that of Alexander Dyce, 3 vols., 1843, reprinted several times in America. The edition by Philip Henderson, 1931, is based on Dyce's, but the spelling is modernised, which has its advantages and its awkwardnesses. The bibliography is useful, but there are no notes.

Selections are: W. H. Williams, 1902; R. Hughes, 1924, with a partisan introduction; R. Graves, 1927—modernised text, but a sympathetic edition by a poet who has praised Skelton judiciously in his own verse. Miss Hammond prints The *Garland of Laurell*, the most English-literary but not the most telling of his poems.

The best guide to Skelton is still in Dyce's introduction and notes; thereafter, Berdan, *Early Tudor Poetry*, New York, 1920—a solemn but admirable statement in Chap. III; A. Koelbing in C.H.E.L., III Chap. IV, and F. Brie, *Skelton-studien*, in *Englische Studien* 37 (1907). See also C. H. Herford, *Literary Relations of England and Germany in the 16th Century*, 1886, and Pacher, *Verse Satire in England*, New York, 1908. For his verse, see G. Saintsbury, *English Prosody*, Vol. I. See also H. L. R. Edwards, *J.S.*, *a Genealogical Study* in R.E.S. XI, 1935. L. J. Lloyd's *John Skelton: A Sketch of his Life and Writings*, Oxford, 1938, is to be read; and W. Nelson, *J. S. Laureate* (New York and O.U.P., 1939) for the life.

WILLIAM OF SHOREHAM

William of Shoreham, Kent, who appears to have been vicar of Chart in the same county, is the author of seven pieces of unpretentious religious poetry preserved in MS. B.M. Add. 17376 (c. 1350–1400, or earlier). The lines are short and syllabic, and arranged in various rhyming patterns. Four of the poems, totalling over 3,900 ll., are didactic. The other three, amounting to about 520 ll., are devotional. But one of the latter may not be William's.

Bibliography.
C.B.E.L., 1.271–2.

Text.
Konrath, M. *William of Shoreham's Poems*. E.E.T.S., E.S. 86.

Discussion.
Wells, VI[10].

JOHN WYCLIFFE (c. 1320–84)

Because of Wycliffe's great reputation as a churchman and reformer, many writings have clustered round his name. His main literary achievement, however, is the initiation of the English version of the Bible (ed. Forshall and Madden. 4 vols. Oxford, 1850) that was completed c. 1382. Nevertheless, until his precise contribution to this has been ascertained, the *Sermons* constitute his most important authentic literary work in English, and from these alone must begin any attempt to sort out the various pieces ascribed to him.

Bibliography.
C.B.E.L., 1.203–5.

Discussion.

Deanesly, M. *The Lollard Bible and other Medieval Biblical versions.* C.U.P., 1920.

Lechler, G. V. *John Wycliffe and his English Precursors.* Translated by P. Lorimer. 2nd ed. 1884. Reprinted 1903.

Loserth, J. *Wyclif & Hus.* Translated by M. J. Evans. 1884.

Matthew, F. D. *English Works of Wyclif, hitherto Unprinted.* E.E.T.S., 74. 1880. [With valuable introd. and notes.]

Poole, R. L. *Wycliffe and Movements for Reform.* London, 1899.

Trevelyan, G. M. *England in the Age of Wycliffe.* 3rd ed. 1900.

Workman, H. B. *John Wyclif. A Study of the English Medieval Church.* 2 vols. Oxford, 1926. [Standard.]

Wells. XII.

Editions.

Arnold, T. *Select English Works of John Wycliffe.* 3 vols. Oxford, 1869–71.

Matthew (above).

Selections.

Winn, H. E. *Wyclif: Select English Writings.* O.U.P., 1929.

Wycliffe's accepted English writings come under four heads:— I, Sermons; II, Didactic Works; III, Statements of Belief, etc.; IV, Controversial Works. For a discussion of the individual items, see Wells, XII. Texts of all of them are available in the editions mentioned above.

Sermons

The Sermons include (*a*) 123 on the Gospels for Sunday; (*b*) 116 on the Gospels for Week-days, and (*c*) 55 on the Epistles for Sunday, for the *Commune Sanctorum,* and for the *Proprium Sanctorum.* Nineteen MSS. (containing all or less) are available, but the chief MS., Bodley 788 (end of 14th c.), has them all. They are chiefly concerned with current ecclesiastical conditions, particularly with those which Wycliffe regarded as abuses. Text: see Arnold (above).

CHAPTER X

MEDIAEVAL PERIOD—OTHER TEXTS

The texts described below are classified under the following
heads :—
- Anonymous
- Bible Paraphrases
- Chronicles
- Debates
- Dialogues
- Drama
- Legends
- Lyrical Poetry
- Proverbs
- Romances
- Sermons and Homilies
- Tales
- Some Mediaeval Latin Writers
- A Note on Anglo-Norman

ANONYMOUS

A. COURTLY

The Assembly of Gods has been attributed to Lydgate ever since
the first edition, printed by W. de Worde in 1498. It is a com-
plicated religious allegory of the usual kind, in 2,107 lines of
rime royal. Two MSS. exist, and printed editions, three by W. de
Worde, and one by Redman. Ed.: O. L. Triggs, E.E.T.S., E.S.,
LXIX, 1896, with the usual apparatus.

The Tale of Beryn. An apocryphal addition is found in the
Northumberland MS. of *The Canterbury Tales*, long, unexciting,
but not uninteresting. With it there goes a lively prologue
describing the behaviour of the pilgrims on arrival in Canterbury,
and an unedifying adventure of the Pardoner's.   It is edited by
F. J. Furnivall and W. G. Stone, Ch. Soc. 17, 24 (1876–87),
and E.E.T.S., ex. ser. CV, 1909.

The Flower and the Leaf was printed by Thynne, and long thought to be Chaucer's, but it is the work of a cultivated lady of the fifteenth century. Dryden "translated" it admirably (Fables, 1700). It is a dream-poem in praise of chastity, very prettily done. The text-authority is Thynne's Chaucer, 1532, whence Skeat prints it in his Chaucer, Vol. VII.

The Assembly of Ladies is also by a lady, and Skeat attributes it to the same hand. There are two MSS. besides Thynne's print. Skeat prints it in his Chaucer, Vol. III, collating all three texts. It also is a dream-poem, told by a lady to a squire. This and the above are to be read, as products of cultivated fifteenth-century lay society, well read in English poetry and in French, capable of expressing its pleasure in gardens, clothes and polite conversation, and not without its ideals. Their sedate clarity of feeling and style gives a charm to both.

The Mass of Venus, an erotic parody of the church service, is printed from MS. Fairfax 16 in Bodl. by T. F. Simmond in *The Lay Folk's Mass Book*, E.E.T.S., 71, 1879, and (under the title *The Lover's Mass*) by Miss Hammond.

The Nutbrown Maid is often reckoned among the ballads; it is in fact a lady's reply to the innumerable gibes at the inconstancy of women. The form is a hybrid between disputation, drama, and lyric, in which two persons agree to dramatise a romantic situation. The earliest and best text is in Richard Arnold's Chronicle, printed at Antwerp, in 1502. It is in a volume of the Percy Folio MS., ed. F. J. Furnivall and J. W. Hales, 1867, who add another text from MS. Balliol 354. Percy has it in his *Reliques*, W. C. Hazlitt in *Remains of Popular Poetry*, Vol. II, and it has been reprinted often. For a good text see Skeat, *Specimens*, Vol. III.

B. SATIRICAL

The Plowman's Tale is an anticlerical satire with a strong tincture of Lollardry, in 173 8-line stanzas. After a 52-line prologue to attach it to *The C.T.*, it proceeds with an allegorical disputation between the Pelican and the Griffin, of considerable interest and occasional power. It was added in the 2nd ed. of Chaucer, 1542, and there are separate eds. of li. 1545 and 1606. Wright prints it in *Pol. Poems*, Vol. I, and Skeat in his Chaucer, Vol. VII. (See also *A New Plowman's Tale*, ed. A. Beatty, Ch. Soc. 34, 1902.)

Pierce the Ploughman's Crede is by the same hand (see *Tale*, line 1,065), and is directed against the regular clergy. It consists of

850 alliterative lines in Langland's style. There is a print of 1553. Ed. Skeat, E.E.T.S., 30, 1867, from MS. Trin. Coll., Cambridge, MS. R. 3. 15. He prints a selection in *Specimens*, Vol. III. Whatever the virtues of the friars, they had a bad press: Wright, *Pol. Poems*, prints three poems against them, and a longish prose piece *Jack Upland*, with the verse reply of "Friar Daw Topias" (whose name seems to be John Walsingham) and the rejoinder (in prose, though Wright tries to make verse of it) of Jack. Wright prints it from Speght's Chaucer, 1602, Skeat, in his Chaucer, Vol. VII, from an ed. of c. 1540.

London Lickpenny. Usually ascribed to Lydgate, but denied to him by MacCracken. It is a lively satire on London and the law, in 16 stanzas. Two versions exist, one in 7-line, the other in 8-line stanzas: they are printed side by side by Miss E. P. Hammond, *Anglia*, XX (1898). It has often been printed, in editions of Lydgate and elsewhere. See Miss Hammond's introd. to the poem, in her *English Verse between Chaucer and Surrey*.

The Turnement of Tottenham is a burlesque, with many congeners in French and Scots. It was printed by Bedwell, 1631; T. Wright, 1836; W. C. Hazlitt, in *Remains of the Early Popular Poetry of England*, 1864, Vol. III; and Percy in the *Reliques*, Vol. II— in his ed. of the *Reliques* H. B. Wheatley prints a better text from MS. Harleian, 5396.

The Pilgrim's Sea Voyage, or *The Voyage to Compostella*, a lively, realistic-comic description of the sufferings of the pilgrims at sea, is ed. from Trin. Coll. Cambridge, MS. R. 3. 19 by F. J. Furnivall, E.E.T.S., 25, 1867.

C. POLITICAL POEMS

The great collection is T. Wright, *Political Poems and Songs . . . Edward III to Richard III*, Rolls Series, 2 vols., 1859–61. See also his *Satirical Poets of the Middle Ages* in the same series, and *The Political Songs of England . . . John to Edward II*, Camden Soc. 6, 1839. Ritson, *Ancient Songs and Ballads*, 1829, and F. J. Furnivall, *Political, Religious and Love Songs*, E.E.T.S., 15, new ed. 1903. Wright's texts give no sound basis for philologists, but he collects the material, and his introductions are readable. See his *Essays on the Literature . . . of England in the Middle Ages*, 2 vols., 1846, Vol. II, Chap. XIX; C. L. Kingsford, *English Historical Literature in the 15th Century*, Oxford, 1913, Chap. IX—very reliable; C. H. Firth, *The Ballad History of the Reigns of Henry VII and Henry VIII*, Trans. Royal Historical Soc., Vol. XXII, 1908.

The Libelle of Englyshe Polycye. A serious, able, and interesting treatise on sea-power and international trade, in 1,092 ten-syllable couplets, with prologue of 49 lines in rime royal and 16 lines of epilogue in 8-line stanzas rhyming ababbcbc. There are two "editions", the main difference being in the second stanza of the epilogue, the first form stating that the poem has been seen and vouched for by Lord Hungerford (d. 1449), the second merely addressing it to three lords of the Council. The difference of the editions helps to date the poem, since the first mentions the Emperor Sigismund as living, the second as dead; Sigismund died in December, 1437. Warner (see below) identifies the author as Adam Moleyns (d. 1450), at that time clerk to the Council and later Bishop of Chichester: see *D.N.B.*, s.n. Molyneux. The *Libelle* (i.e., *libellus*, little book) was well known and is often quoted. A dozen or more MSS. still exist. It was printed by Hakluyt, and by T. Wright, *Political Poems and Songs*, Rolls Series, 1861, Vol. II. The best edition is by Sir George Warner, Oxford, 1926, with full introduction and notes. Miss Hammond prints lines 1–563. Compare with it a shorter poem, almost an epitome, printed by Wright, Vol. II, p. 282.

D. BALLADS

The great collection is that of F. J. Child, 5 vols., Boston, U.S.A., 1882–98, of which an excellent abbreviation was made by G. L. Kittredge, *English and Scottish Popular Ballads*, Cambridge, Mass., 1904, with an interesting introduction and a convenient list of "Sources of the Texts". Other good collections are: W. Allingham, *The Ballad Book*, 1864; F. B. Gummere, *Old English Ballads*, Boston, 1894; F. Sidgwick, *Popular Ballads of the Olden Time*, 4 ser.; A. T. Quiller-Couch, *The Oxford Book of Ballads*, 1910. There are many others, of such varying merit that the student is advised to keep to Child—not that Percy's *Reliques* and Scott's *Border Ministrelsy* are to be ignored, whatever their textual value. *A Lytell Geste of Robyn Hode* was printed by W. de Worde before 1519, and odd leaves by him and by Pynson in 1500, so we may judge of their popularity. The very mixed collections of the Ballad Society and the Percy Society contain much seventeenth-century street balladry along with a little early material. E. Flügel, *Zur Chronologie der englischen Balladen*, in Anglia XXI (1899), attempts to place ballads in chronological order; the list is very useful if not quite conclusive.

The "nature and origins" provide one of the grand unending controversies. The theories are discussed, with healthy scepticism, by Louise Pound, in *Poetic Origins and the Ballad*, New York, 1921, where full references will be found. The *loci classici* are: (*a*) the dance theory; W. P. Ker, *English Literature, Mediaeval*, Ch. V, and *Form and Style in Poetry*, 1928; (*b*) the "communal" theory; F. B. Gummere, *The Popular Ballad*, Boston, 1907, and C.H.E.L., Vol. II, Chap. XVII, and Kittredge, introd. to the one-vol. Child (above); (*c*) the "minstrel" theory, Courthope, History, Vol. I, Chap. XI. For criticism of (*b*) see Quiller-Couch, *Studies*, II.

Indeed it has been a well-spring of mystical and sentimental "sociology". All are doubtless correct in their place, and there is room for a "journalism" theory. See also F. Sidgwick, *Ballad*, Art and Craft of Letters Series, and for a brief, sensible statement, R. Graves, introd. to *The English Ballad*, 1927; W. P. Ker, *Spanish and English Ballads*, Collected Essays, Vol. II; Gregory Smith, *The Transition Period*, 1900, Chap. VI; A. Keith, *Scottish Ballads*, in *Essays and Studies*, Vol. XII, 1926; E. K. Chambers, *English Literature at the Close of the Middle Ages*, Chap. III. [See also under Historical Poems, above.]

BIBLE PARAPHRASES

1. *Genesis and Exodus*

Preserved in MS. C.C.C.C. 444, this unpoetical, versified paraphrase of *Genesis* and *Exodus*, supplemented by parts of *Numbers* and *Deuteronomy*, was composed c. 1250 in the S.E. Midlands. Its immediate source appears to be Peter Comestor's *Historia Scholastica*. The metre is the 4-beat couplet, with some alliteration. Ed.: R. Morris, *Genesis and Exodus*, E.E.T.S., 7. See Wells, VIII [1]; *C.B.E.L.*, 1.187–8.

Patience and *Purity*, both metrical, biblical paraphrases in the W. Midl. dialect, are treated under "The Pearl Poet", p. 300.

CHRONICLES

A. ENGLISH

1. *The Anglo-Saxon Chronicle*

The *A.S. Chronicle* was continued into M.E. times at three different places: Canterbury (MS. C.C.C.C., also called the Parker MS.); Worcester (B.M. MS. Cotton Tib. B, IV) and Peterborough (Bodl. Laud MS. 636). But to students of M.E. the last is of greatest importance. At Canterbury, only eleven brief and scattered entries (in O.E.) were made, all referring to local events between 1005 and 1070. The Worcester text carries on to 1079 in W.S., the entries being both regular and well put together. But the Peterborough text, which, up to 1121, was transcribed from a Canterbury version now lost, was continued in E.M.E. up to 1154. At 1132, the first scribe breaks off and all the remainder is the work of another scribe writing shortly after 1153. The first scribe reveals a particular interest in ecclesiastical matters and especially in his own monastery, whereas the second gives us graphic descriptions of the unhappy conditions of the people and of the cruelties of the barons during the troublous times of King Stephen. See Wells, III [1].

For Bibliography, see p. 247 ff., above.

2. Lawman's *Brut*

One of the most important compositions of the period, as well as one of the most entertaining, has come down to us in two British Museum MSS., viz. (A) Cotton Caligula A IX and (B) Cotton Otho C XIII. A, written in the first quarter of the thirteenth century, contains 32,241 short lines in the dialect of N.W. Worcester (according to some in a S.W. dialect). B, however, dates from the third quarter of the thirteenth century, and is a N. Somerset or S. Gloucester text. Seriously damaged in the Cotton Fire (1731), it now contains only some 23,590 complete and about a thousand defective lines out of an estimated original total of 26,960. Moreover B, much the inferior text, is thought to be derived from the same exemplum as A, or else to be based upon A (Wyld).

The poem was probably composed in the N. Worcester dialect at a date which is still controversial, but perhaps between 1173 and 1207.

The author himself tells us that his name was Laȝamon (MS Cotton Caligula A IX, c. 1225, though MS Cotton Otho C XIII, c. 1250, gives it as Laweman) and that he was a priest at *Ernleȝe* (identified as Lower Arley or Arley Regis, nearly Bewdley, Worcester). Although he gives us to understand that he used three source-books, namely, the O.E. translation of Bede's *Historia Ecclesiastica*, a Latin version of the same work, and Wace's *Le Roman de Brut* (an A.N metrical rendering, c. 1155, of Geoffrey of Monmouth's *Historia Regum Britanniae* 1135–1477), Lawman derived most of his material either from Wace's book direct or from a later recension that included elements from another (lost) metrical A.N. translation of Geoffrey's *Historia* by Gaimer entitled *Estoire des Bretons* (1150). Bede's work, despite the claim, was used not at all. Nevertheless, further sources were apparently employed, but have not yet been ascertained. Maybe much of this additional matter is simply contemporary Welsh tradition.

The *Brut* is a history of the Britons from the ancestors of Brutus (grandson of Ascanius, son of Aeneas), the supposed founder of Britain, down to the ejection of the Britons to Wales, ending with 689. It "falls into three chief parts, ll. 1–18,532 dealing with the early history from the fall of Troy to the begetting of Arthur . . . ll. 18,533–28,651 dealing with the story of Arthur . . . ll. 28,652–32,241 dealing with the history from the passing of Arthur to the final expulsion of the Britons by Aethelston" [Wells, 194].

The metre is of special interest because it represents an important transitional stage between the old alliterative poetry and the new syllabic rhymed verse of foreign origin.

Bibliography.
C.B.E.L., 1.165.

Editions.
Brie, F. *The Brut.* E.E.T.S., Nos. 131, 136.
Madden, F. *Laȝamon's Brut.* 3 vols. London, 1847. [Includes both texts, with translation.]
> N.B.—An ed. by M. S. Serjeantson and the late E. V. Gordon is in preparation for the E.E.T.S. Selections are accessible in most *Readers*.

Translation.
Madden (above); Paton, L. A., *Arthurian Chronicles by Wace and Layamon.* Ev. Lib. 578. London, 1912, etc. (parts only); Weston, *Ch. M.E. P.*, 1–20 (parts only).

Discussion.
Bartels, L. *Die Zuverlässigkeit der Handschriften von Layamon's Brut und ihr Verhältniss zum Originale.* Halle, 1913.
Brown, A. C. L. "Welsh Traditions in Laȝamon's Brut" in *M.Ph.*, 1.95–103.
Gillespy, F. L. *Layamon's Brut. A Comparative Study of Narrative Art.* Univ. of California Pub. in Mod. Phil., 3.361–510. [An analysis of Lawman and Wace.]
Hall. Sels., 463–6. [Metre.]
Imelmann, R. *Laȝamon's Versuch über seine Quellen.* Berlin, 1906. [Sources.]

Kaluza. *Sh. Hist. E. Verse*, 132–40.

McNary, S. J. *Studies in Layamon's Verse*. New York, 1904.

Oakden. *Allit. Poetry*, 142–5, 243. [Versification.]

Schipper. *Hist. Engl. Verse*, 67–79.

Tatlock, J. S. "Epic Formulas, especially in Laȝamon" in *P.M.L.A.*, 38.494–529. 1923.

Tatlock, J. S. "Laȝamon's Poetic Style and its Relations" in *Manly Anniversary Studies*. Chicago, 1923.

Wells. III [3].

Wyld, H. C. "Laȝamon as an English Poet" in *R.E.S.*, 6.1–30. 1930. [The "Brut is incomparably the greatest achievement in English poetry between the Anglo-Saxon period and Chaucer". Indispensable.]

Wyld, H. C. "Studies in the Diction of Laȝamon's Brut" in *Language*, 6.1–24 (1930); 9.47–71, 171–91 (1933); 10.149–201 (1934); 13.29–59 (1937). [Indispensable. A model investigation.]

3. Robert of Gloucester's *Rhymed Chronicle of Britain*

Robert's *Chronicle* (from the earliest times to the end of the reign of Henry III) has irregular long lines of six or seven stresses with a cæsura in the middle, and rhyming in couplets. Originally written in the Gloucester dialect, it exists in two versions, X and Y. Both are found in several manuscripts, the earliest of X being MSS. Cotton Caligula A XI (early fourteenth century), Harley 201 (c. 1400; ends at 9,529), B.M. Additional 19,677 (1390–1400; wants beginning to l. 4,683, Brandl-Zippel); and of Y, MSS. Trin. Coll. C. R., 4, 26 (late fourteenth century), Digby 205 (fourteenth or early fifteenth century) and Cbg. Univ. Lib. Ee. IV 31 (c. 1430–40), and Huntington Lib. [California] MS. (c. 1400). X is not only older, but also considerably longer than Y.

The *Chronicle* is assumed to be the work of three authors: A, a monk of Gloucester Abbey, who late in the thirteenth century composed in 9,137 ll. (Wright's ed., below) a metrical history of Britain from the destruction of Troy to the death of Henry I (1135); B, a monk of the same fraternity and named Robert (l. 11,748), who shortly after 1297 wrote a recension of A's poem and added just under 3,000 ll. to complete the history up to the end of Henry III's reign (ll. 9,138–12,046); and C, also a monk of Gloucester, who at the beginning of the fourteenth century similarly wrote up A's poem, interpolating over 800 ll. (Wright, ib., vii) and continued it as far as B, but in only as few as 572 ll. B is therefore the author of X, and C of Y.

In the *Chronicle* an endeavour has been made to be scholarly, accurate and impartial. Various sources were used including Geoffrey of Monmouth, Henry of Huntingdon, William of Malmesbury, Matthew of Westminster, Ailred of Rievaux, the Annals of Winchester, Tewkesbury, and Waverley, the Southern Legend Collection, and possibly Roger of Hoveden (Wells, III [4]). Much space is devoted to Arthur. There is also a large amount of traditional lore, while from the beginning of Henry III's reign there is direct information on contemporary affairs that is of historical importance.

On the whole without any particular literary merit, the choice of verse for a literary medium being purely conventional, the *Chronicle* has several passages of considerable merit, e.g., the vivid descriptions of the town-and-gown riot at Oxford in 1263 and of the Battle of Evesham (1265). Finally, what strikes the reader most of all is the intense nationalism pervading the whole poem.

Bibliography.
C.B.E.L., 1.165–6.

Editions.
Wright, W. A. *The Metrical Chronicle of Robert of Gloucester*. Rolls Series. 2 vols. London, 1887. [Based on Cotton.]

Translation.
Weston. *Ch. M.E. P.* 20 ff. [Parts only.]

Discussion.
Ellmer, W. "Ueber die Quellen der Reimchronik R. v. Gl." in *Angl.* 10.1–37, 291–322. 1888. [Detailed study of sources].
Kaluza. *Sh. Hist. E. Verse*, 186–8.
Wells. III [4].

4. Thomas Castleford's *Chronicle of England*

Comprising some 20,000 short couplets extant in 221 leaves of the unique Göttingen University Library Codex MS. Hist. 740, dated c. 1400, this *Chronicle*, composed between 1327 and 1350, and in the handwriting of two scribes, contains a prologue of 225 lines on the story of Albion and her sisters as the first settlers in England, followed by eleven books recording events from Brutus to Edward III's accession in 1327. While Geoffrey of Monmouth's *Historia* seems to be the source of the first 27,464 ll, the poem reveals a knowledge of Castleford and neighbourhood in the West Riding of Yorkshire, and also of the history of York and its conditions.

Bibliography.
C.B.E.L., 1.165.

Edition.
Behre, F. *Thomas Castleford's Chronicle, edited in part with Comments.* Gothenburg, 1940. [Behre has a complete survey of the language and the orthography in preparation. He locates the text in S. Yks. (? Pontefract).]
An edition is in preparation for the E.E.T.S. by S. Blach and A. McIntosh.

Discussion.
Blach, S. "Ist Thomas Bek der Verfasser der Göttinger Reimchronik" in *Engl. Stud.*, 64.170–173. 1929.
Wells, III [6].

5. Robert Mannyng's *Rhyming Chronicle*

Thirty-five years after completing his important prose treatise *Hendlying Synne* (see p. 290), Robert Mannyng, born May 15th, 1283 (or earlier), at Bourne, Kesteven, Lincs., in 1338 finished his *Rhyming Chronicle of England.* From 1302 to 1317 (or later), Mannyng was a canon at Sempringham Priory, where he may have been Master of the Novices. His *Chronicle* consists of two parts: the first, A, covering the period between the arrival of the legendary Brutus in Britain and the death of Cadwallader in 689; the second, B, from 689 to the close of Edward's I reign [1307]. A has 16,630 [mainly octosyllabic] ll., rhyming in couplets, not 16,730 [Schofield, 361] or "8365 short couplets" (Wells, 199), for though the last line in his edition (below) is 16,730, Furnivall points out on p. 580 that one hundred line-numbers between 12,899 and 13,000 have been omitted. B has some 9,000 ll., chiefly alexandrines, but often pentameters. A is a close translation of Wace's *Brut*, with additions from Dares Phrygius, Bede, Henry of Huntingdon, William of Malmesbury. B is a version of Peter Langtoft's A.N. *Chronicle*, with interpolations based on Bede, Ailred of Riveaux, Henry of Huntingdon, Nicholas Trivet, romances on Havelock and Richard Cœur de Lion, popular songs, contemporary traditions and personal experiences.

The *Chronicle*, which was composed in tne East Midland dialect, survives in the following MSS.:—Inner Temple Lib. Petyt MSS. No. 511, No. 7 (before 1400), MS. Lambeth 131 (c. 1350), MS. Cotton Julius A.V. (end of thirteenth or fourteenth century), a Lincoln Cathedral MS., and (but fragmentarily in only 176 ll.) MS. Rawlinson Misc. 1370 (end of fourteenth century).

Intending his *Chronicle* for the enlightenment and entertainment of unlettered men, Mannyng wrote in simple English so that it would be easily understood when read aloud.

To the modern reader, B is far more stimulating than A, so much of which is rather hackneyed fiction. In B there are certain additions relating to the reign of Edward I that are not only pleasing in themselves, but also historically valuable, since they are apparently from M.'s own knowledge. Further, his bitter remarks about the Scots catch the eye.

Bibliography.
C.B.E.L., 1.165–6.

Editions.
1. Part I [A]. Furnivall, F. J. *The Story of England by Robert Mannyng of Brunne. A.D. 1338.* 2 vols. Rolls Series. London, 1887.
2. Part II [B]. Hearne, T. *Peter Langtoft's Chronicle (as Illustrated and Improved by Robert of Brunne). From the Death of Cadwalader to the End of King Edward I's Reign.* 2 vols. Oxford, 1725.
3. Lambeth MS. (from beginning to birth of Christ only). Zetsche, A. *Chronik des R. v. B.* in *Angl.* 9.43–194. 1886. [A reprint of the text only with several passages interpolated from the Temple MS. Various readings from the latter are given in footnotes.]

Translation.
Weston. *Ch. M.E. P.*, 25 ff.

Discussion.
Crosby, R. "Robert Mannyng of Brunne: a New Biography" in *P.M.L.A.*, 57.15–28. 1942. [Clarifies Mannyng's connexions with Sempringham and his status there.]
Preussner. *R.M. of Br.'s Übersetzung von P. de Langtoft's Chronicle und ihr Verhältniss zum Originale.* Breslau, 1891.
Seaton, E. "Robert Mannyng of Brunne in Lincoln" in *Medium Ævum*, 12.77. [Locates M. in Lincoln in 1327.]
Thümmig, M. *Über die M.E. Übersetzung der Reimchronik Peter*

Langtoft's durch R. M. v. B. Leipzig, 1891. Also in *Angl.*, 14.1–76. 1892. [A careful and detailed analysis of Mannyng's sources.]

Wells. III [7].

6. Trevisa's *Polychronicon*

In 1387 John of Trevisa (1362–1402) completed his translation of the *Polychronicon* of Ranulph Higden. Higden (d. 1364) was a monk of St. Werburg's at Chester and a writer on theology and history. His *Polychronicon*, a huge work of seven books in Latin prose, was a universal history from the Creation down to his own time (1352). It soon became a standard work and over 100 existing MSS. testify to its popularity down into the sixteenth century. Perhaps its special interest to-day lies in the fact that it sheds so much light on fourteenth-century knowledge of history and geography. Two English prose translations have survived, one by Trevisa, the other by an unknown writer of the fifteenth century.

Trevisa, a Cornishman educated at Oxford, whence, because of "unworthiness", he was expelled in 1379 along with the Provost and other members of his college (Queen's), was vicar of Berkeley, and canon of Westbury, both in Gloucestershire. Here he seems to have lived most of his life, spending much of his time in translating various Latin works into English. One of the most notable of these is Bartholomew de Glanville's *De Proprietatibus Rerum*, the "gem of (medieval) scientific compilations" (Thomas, *Engl. Lit.*, 103), which Trevisa finished in 1398. Though blundering occasionally through faulty scholarship, he translated Higden fairly closely and in simple English. He contributed little outside his source, apart from an introductory dialogue on the art of translation and, in addition, the short continuation carrying the narrative down to 1360. The latter includes the memorable passage on the [in 1385] new Oxford method of teaching schoolboys in English instead of French as in the past.

Trevisa's translation, written in the Gloucester dialect, has been preserved in four MSS. Further, it was printed in 1482 by Caxton, who, however, modernised its spelling, vocabulary and idioms. The work is of considerable interest to historians of the language.

Bibliography.
C.B.E.L., 1.167.

Edition.

Babington, C., and Lumby, J. R. *Polychronicon Ranulphi Higden.*
Rolls Series. 9 vols. London, 1865–86. [Gives, besides Higden's Latin, the translations of both treatises and the anonymous fifteenth-century writer.]

Discussion.

Kinkade, B. L. *The English Translations of Higden's Polychronicon.*
Urbana, 1934.

Perry, A. J. *Trevisa's Dialogus,* E.E.T.S., 167. [See pp. lv–cxxxviii on T.'s life and works.]

Wells, III [9].

Wilkins, E. H. (1). *Was John Wycliffe a Negligent Pluralist; also John de Trevisa his Life and Work.* New York, 1915. (2) *An Appendix to John Wycliffe; also John de Trevisa.* London, 1916.

7. Barbour's *Bruce*

See p. 408 below.

8. Capgrave's *Chronicle of England*

John Capgrave (1393–1464), born at Lynn, Norfolk, educated at Oxford, there became a D.D. and perhaps a lecturer on theology, was reputed to be one of the most learned men of his day. He became an Augustine friar, later Provincial of the Order in England, and probably in his last years Prior of the Friary at Lynn. His many writings in Latin and English reveal him as a theologian, hagiologist and historian. His English works include the Life of St. Augustine and of St. Gilbert of Sempringham (both ed. J. Munro, E.E.T.S., 140 [1910]), the *Life of St. Katherine of Alexandria* (ed. C. Horstmann, with "Forewords" by F. J. Furnivall, E.E.T.S., 100 [1893]) and the *Chronicle of England* (ed. F. C. Hingeston, Rolls Series, London, 1858).

Capgrave's *Chronicle* is preserved in two MSS.: his autograph, Camb. Univ. Lib. MS. Cg. IV. 12, and C.C.C. Camb., MS. CLXVII, copied from it. The book, beginning (as usual) with the Creation, deals with the general history of the world, but gradually narrows in scope till 1216, after which it is concerned almost wholly with English history down to 1417, when it suddenly breaks off (apparently with the death of the author). The earlier portions are scanty, but the entries for later reigns are often very full, and also original. While the *Chronicle* is always readable, its first editor, Hingeston, was rather too favourably impressed by Capgrave's apparent honesty of purpose, but Furnivall in his fuller discussion prefixed to Horstmann's ed. of *The Life of St. Katherine*, terms him a "flunkey, with an inordinate reverence for kings and rank".

Note the accounts of the rebellion of Wat Tyler, "a proude knave and malapert", of Sir John Oldcastle, a "strong man in bataile, but a grete heretik, and a gret enmye to the Cherch", and of the "many straunge opiniones" of "Jon Wiclef, Maystir of Oxenforth" In his remarks on the latter, we have an excellent instance of Capgrave's vituperative ability, for Wiclif is "the orgon of the devel, the enmy of the Cherch, the confusion of men, the ydol of heresie, the meroure of ypocrisie, the norischer of scisme". Finally, judging from the inclusion of so many strange legends, we are forced to the opinion that Capgrave was astonishingly credulous. Compare, e.g., the following "In this zere, in the XX day of August, in the fest of Seynt Oswyn, the Kyng being at Newcastle upon Tyne, a wright hew on a tre, whech schuld long to a schip; and at every strook he smet ran oute blood, as it had be of a beste. He bethought him of the festful day, and left his werk. His felaw stood beside, having no reverens to this myracle, took the ax and smet, and anon blod ran owte. He fel for fere, and cryed mercy. And al the town merveylid, and gaf worchip to God. The tre was bore to Tynmouth, in token of this myracle."

Bibliography.
C.B.E.L., 1.260.

Discussion.
D.N.B. (*sub nom.*).

Language.
For a full account (of Hingeston's text) see W. Dibelius in *Angl.*, 23.153–94, 323–75, 427–72, 24.211–63, 269–308 (1900–1).

9. Wyntoun's *Oryginall Cronycle*

See p. 277 above.

10. Boece's *Chronicle*

See p. 278 above.

B. LATIN

These (like the English chronicles) are published in the official Chronicles and Memorials, commonly referred to as the "Rolls Series", with (as a rule) valuable introductions, and translations. They vary, naturally, in quality, but the method is usually the same; compilation so far as it will serve and original composition covering the author's own time. Only a few of the most important are listed here, to show how historical interest persisted, how the period is covered, and how every part of England shared in the work.

Florence of Worcester: to 1117, continued by John of Worcester to 1141. Translation in Bohn's Antiquarian Library.

Eadmer, monk of Canterbury, *Historia Novorum in Anglia*, gives contemporary history to 1122.

Ordericus Vitalis, an Anglo-Norman, ecclesiastical history to 1141. Translation in Bohn.

Simeon of Durham includes a version of some lost Northumbrian annals, and is original for 1121–9. Transl. by J. Stevenson, *Church Historians of England*, III, ii.

William of Newburgh in Yorkshire covers from the Conquest to 1198, mainly dealing with the reigns of Stephen and Henry II. He was a real historian with some idea of evidence. See Bruce Dickins, *A Yorkshire Chronicler*, Trans. Yorks. Dialect Soc., V, Part XXXV. Transl. J. Stevenson, *Church Historians of England*, IV, ii.

William of Malmesbury, half Norman and half English, wrote *De Gesta Regum Anglorum*, finally revised 1135–40. He searched widely in English legend and song as well as in written records, and produced an interesting and lively, as well as useful, book. Selected translations in Bohn's series.

Henry of Huntingdon, 1084?–1155, Archdeacon of Huntingdon in the diocese of Lincoln. Translation in Bohn's series.

Matthew Paris (d. 1259) followed Roger of Wendover (d. 1236) as chronicler in the great monastery of St. Alban's, and was followed by men he had trained. The whole Chronicle covers from the creation to 1440. The third great name is that of Thomas Walsingham (d. 1422?). See the prefaces in the Rolls Series, and V. H. Galbraith's edition of *La Estoire de seint Ædward*. The *Chronica Majora* reaches to 1253; the *Historia Minor* is an abridgement. Matthew gathered information where he could, with some independence of mind. The *Vitae duorum Offarum* is attributed to

Matthew, and twenty-three lives of abbots of St. Albans were compiled by him or under his direction. See H. R. Luard's prefaces to the Rolls Series edition of the *Chronica Majora*.

Higden, Ranulf [d. 1364]. A Benedictine monk of Chester, wrote *Polychronicon*. A translation into good colloquial English made in 1387 by John de Trevisa, was published by Caxton in 1482, Wynkyn de Worde in 1495 and Peter Treveris in 1527, and a portion, *The description of Britain*, by Caxton in 1480 and de Worde in 1498.

C. FRENCH

Wace, *c.* 1100?–*c.* 1174?, was not Anglo-Norman, but pure Norman, born in Jersey and living in Caen and Bayeux; but his *Brut* made tradition in England through Layamon (p. 320). Below is a selection of Anglo-Norman histories; for full lists and bibliography see J. Vising, *Anglo-Norman Language and Literature*, Oxford, 1923.

Geffrei Gaimar, c. 1150, in Lincolnshire: *Lestorie des Engles*; four MSS.; ed. T. Duffus Hardy and C. T. Martin, 2 vols., Rolls Ser., 1888: Vol. I, preface on text and language, and text; Vol. II, life of G. and translation. A first Book is missing in all MSS. which add *Lestorie* after Wace's *Brut*. The French *Haveloc le Danois* (used by G.) is added (see *Havelok*, p. 354), with other illustrative matter. G.'s sources (A.-S. Chronicle, etc.) are interesting and significant.

Jordan Fantosme, c. 1175, schoolmaster at Westminster: Chronicle of war with William the Lion, 1173–4; ed. R. Howlett, Rolls Ser., 1886, in *Chronicles of Stephen, Henry II and Richard I*, Vol. III, and transl. in J. Stevenson's *Church Historians of England*, IV, 242–288. He was possibly an eyewitness of some events. His verse already departs from French rules.

Anon., c. 1225, *The Song of Dermot and the Earl*, ed. G. H. Orpen, Oxford, 1892; on the conquest of Ireland—cf. Giraldus Cambrensis.

Peter of Ickham, c. 1275, has been credited with *Le Livere de Reis*, a Chronicle from Brutus to 1274; ed. J. Glover, Rolls Ser., 1865.

Peter of Langtoft, early fourteenth century; a *Chronicle* from the fall of Troy to 1307; ed. T. Wright, Rolls Ser., 1866. See Robert of Brunne, p. 324.

Anon., mid-fourteenth century: *Chroniques de Londres*, 1260–1344, in prose; ed. G. J. Aungier, Camden Soc. 28, 1844.

Sir Thomas Gray of Heaton, d. 1369?; the prose *Scalacronica*, begun to beguile his imprisonment in Scotland, 1355–7—in which case Geoffrey of Monmouth, Bede and Higden were in circulation there. He is good evidence for the three Edwards, from his father's experience and his own, for this is a knight, not a monk. Ed., in part, J. Stevenson, Maitland Club, 1836; tr. Sir Herbert Maxwell, 1907.

DEBATES

1. *The Owl and the Nightingale*

Critics usually speak of this poem of 897 four-stress couplets in superlatives. It is extant in two MSS., viz., B.M. Cott. Calig. A IX (before 1250) and Jesus Coll. Oxf. 29 (Bodl. Lib.; c. 1275). Both are copied from the same exemplum, itself a copy. Discussion still centres round the identity of the author and the date of composition. Various persons called Nicholas have been suggested including the Nicholas of Guildford selected in the poem as the umpire and there stated to be an inhabitant of Portisham, Dorset. For the date of composition various years round about 1200 have been proposed.

Very briefly the poem, the first of its kind in English, consists of a debating contest between the Owl and the Nightingale about their personal worth in general and their value to mankind in particular. In the end, and accompanied by a flock of birds which, after the manner of human beings, has gathered round, they fly off to the afore-mentioned Nicholas to request arbitration from him. At this point the poem concludes.

It is a notable debate, always highly interesting, well constructed, vivacious and genuine. The verse is believed by Wells to be unequalled by any poetry before Chaucer. The poem is thought to be essentially didactic and to have some inner meaning, though precisely what, is still in dispute. Maybe it is an allegory of the discord between Duty and Pleasure, between Gravity and Joy, or again of the challenge of the new secular poetry of love to the traditional poetry of religion.

Bibliography.
C.B.E.L., 1.181–2.

Editions.
Atkins, J. W. H. *The Owl and the Nightingale*. Cambridge, 1922. [An ed. of both texts, with full critical apparatus, and trans-

lation. Excellent. A. assigns poem to Nicholas of Guilford, and the date of composition to the reign of John, 1199–1217.]

Gadow, W. *Das mittelenglische Streitgedichte Eule und Nachtigall.* Berlin, 1907.

Grattan, J. H. G., and Sykes, G. F. H. E.E.T.S., 119.

Wells, J. E. *The Owl and the Nightingale.* Rev. ed. London, 1909. [Gives both texts, with full critical apparatus. Excellent. Assigns to about 1216–25.]

Translation.

Atkins (above); Weston, *Ch. M.E. P.*, 310–24—parts only.

Discussion.

Atkins (above).

Hall. *Sels.*, 563–7. [Dialect, metre, date, source, author.]

Hinckley, H. B. (1) "The Date of the O. and N." in *M.Ph.*, 17.247 ff., 1919. [Suggests 1177 or 1178 as date.] (2) "The Date, Author and Sources of the O. and N." in *P.M.L.A.*, 44.329–59. 1929. [Suggests 1178–9 as date.] (3) "Notes on the O. and N." in *P.M.L.A.*, 46.93–101. 1931. [Textual notes.] (4) "The Date of the O. and N." in *Phil. Quart.*, 12.339–49. 1933. (5) "Science and Folk-lore in O. and N." in *P.M.L.A.*, 47.303–14. 1932. [Believes the poet a close observer of nature.] (6) "Date of Vivian's Legation in Med. England" in *Phil. Quart.* 12.339ff.

Huganir, K. *The Owl and the Nightingale, Sources, Date and Author.* Philadelphia, 1931. [Much criticised. Attributes, but improbably, to Nicholas of Guilford, an itinerant justice in S.W. England. Date: c. 1182–3. Considers author's description of birds is not based on direct knowledge.]

Owst. *Lit. Pul.*, 22 ff. [General interpretation.]

Tupper, F. "The Date and Historical Background of the O. and N." in *P.M.L.A.*, 49.406–27. 1934. [Assigns to c. 1195, and accepts Nicholas of Guilford as the author.]

Wells, J. E. Review in *J.E.G.Ph.*, 32.408–412. 1933. [Evidence for date and authorship.]

Wells. IX [8].

Wrenn, C. L. "Curiosities in a Medieval Manuscript" in *Essays and Studies*, 25.101 ff. [On the Jesus MS. and the dialect thereof.]

Other M.E. debates are extant as under (see Wells, IX [9–12]).

2. *The Thrush and the Nightingale*

Two MSS., Auchinleck (1330–40), 74 ll. (beginning of poem): and Digby 86 (1272–83), 192 ll. Stanza: aabccbddbeeb, the *b*-lines having three stresses, the other four. Date: probably Edw. I. Dialect: Southern. Theme: the worth of women. Eds.: F. Holthausen, "Der me. Streit zwischen Drossel und Nachtigall" in *Angl.*, 43.52–60. 1919; C. Brown, *English Lyrics of the 13th Century*, Oxford, 1932, pp. 101–7. *C.B.E.L.*, 1.183.

3. *A Disputation bitwene a God Man and the Devel*

987 ll. in verse dating from c. 1350 and preserved in two MSS., Vernon 288 (1370–80) and B.M. Add. 22,283 (1380–1400). Theme: Seven Deadly Sins. Ed. C. Horstman, E.E.T.S. 98, p. 329 ff., and F. J. Furnivall, E.E.T.S. 117, p. 750.

4. *The Book of Cupid* or *The Cuckoo and the Nightingale*

A poem of fifty-eight pentametres, aabba, composed c. 1389–1400, and extant in several fifteenth-century MSS. Ed. Skeat, *Oxford Chaucer*, 7.347 ff. Discussion: A. Brusendorff, *The Chaucer Tradition*, London, 1925, pp. 441 ff. [Assigns to Sir Thos. Clanvowe (see p. 288 above) and dates poem 1392]. C. E. Ward, "The authorship of the C. and N." in *M.L.N.*, 44.217–26, 1929 [Accepts Brusendorff's theories]. *C.B.E.L.*, 1.187.

DIALOGUES

1. Dialogues between the Soul and the Body

Dialogues between the body and the soul—a widespread literary genre—fall into two types: A, those in which the Soul alone speaks, chiding the Body for its sinful life, and B, those in which the Body reciprocates the Soul's accusations. Type B, apparently derived from a twelfth-century Latin poem of unknown authorship, is much the more numerous. Note the O.E. examples, both of Type A (pp. 192, 220).

The M.E. examples are all of Type B. The following is a representative specimen. *Debate between the Soul and the Body.* Extant in six MSS. (the earliest being Laud 108, c. 1290), all from a single original and varying in length between 490 and 590 4-beat ll., rhyming ababab. Ed.: Emerson, *Reader*, 47–64, T. Wright, *Latin Poems commonly attributed to Walter Mapes*, Camden Soc., 1841. Trans.: Weston, *Ch. M.E. P.*, 304–10. Discussion: J. D.,

Bruce, "A Contribution to the Study of 'The Body and the Soul' Poems in English" in *M.L.N.*, 5.385–401; Wells, IX [1]. *C.B.E.L.* 1.171 (under Version IV).

2. *The Vices and Virtues*

A lengthy prose dialogue, earliest of all M.E. dialogues, preserved in MS. B.M. Stowe (c. 1200) in the dialect of the S.E. The text is imperfect at the beginning. The Soul opens with a confession of its sins to Reason and then asks for guidance upon how to become reconciled with Christ. A discussion on the Virtues follows. The piece is stated by the writer to have been compiled from many sources. Wells (pp. 1125, 1311) notes the existence of a fourteenth (or fifteenth)-century MS.

Bibliography.
C.B.E.L., 1.181.

Editions.
Francis, W. N. *The Book of Vices and Virtues*. E.E.T.S., 217. 1942. [Of special interest to the student of medieval popular religion.]
Holthausen, F. *Vices and Virtues*. E.E.T.S., 89 and 159.

Discussion.
Hall. *Sels.*, 444 (on sources and author): Wells, IX [2].

Other M.E. dialogues are: *The Dialogue between the Virgin and Christ on the Cross* (stanzaic), *A Disputison Bitwene Childe Jesu and Maistres of the Lawe of Jewus* (stanzaic), *The Lamentation of Mary to St. Bernard* (two versions, in stanzas), *The Dispute between Mary and the Cross* (stanzaic), *A Disputison Bytwene a Christenemon and a Jew* (stanzaic). See further Wells, IX [3–7].

DRAMA

This study suffers a little from the praiseworthy efforts of scholars to make a connected history out of disconnected documents. The histories make much of liturgical drama, for it has the advantage of being documentary, but it does not follow that it explains the whole story. Thirty years ago it was fashionable to seek literary origins in "folk festivals", the spring-goddess, the corn-lord, and so on, and though that hypothesis was overworked, it exists. The "folk play" may be older than the liturgy for all we know. Certainly cross-talk and dressing-up are perennial and ubiquitous, and the clerics may well have been exploiting tastes and aptitudes rather than inventing them. Liturgy, again, is not uniform, and the reasons for variation are to be sought neither in Rome nor in Jerusalem, but locally, so that the religious and secular customs of one province may not too readily be assumed for another without direct evidence, and it follows that the development may differ even if it can be assumed that the general intention is identical.

One question is crucial, and it has not been answered: why the "miracles" in England, and in England alone, became the business of the craft guilds. The sequence "dramatic liturgy—religious guild—secular company" may hold for France, but it cannot be paralleled with the English sequence "dramatic liturgy—craft custom—his lordship's servants". So also the sequence from the customs of a Benedictine monastery like Durham to the habits of a town like Chester is a chronological sequence. The affiliation is merely a deduction, even allowing for the (just possible) intermediary of the Franciscans. And there is no trace in the cycles of any monastic participation in the town plays—for that matter, the great age of English miracle is that in which the people were on the side of the secular clergy against the regulars. We are free to guess, and our guess may be right, but we must recognise the two solutions of continuity in the history of English acting—in the evidence for the formation of the craft custom and for the formation of the sixteenth-century companies of players. These were fresh starts, at some time and somewhere. It follows that an admirable book like Gustave Cohen's *Histoire de la Mise-en-Scène dans le Théatre Religieux Français du Moyen Age* (1926) is valuable in itself and for purposes of comparison, but should not be read as if it described the sources of English staging. It follows also that Dr. Creizenach's thesis (e.g., in his useful chapter in *C.H.E.L.* Vol. V)—that whereas England possesses the greatest body of mediaeval drama, it must be derived from other countries for which no such body of evidence exists—is based largely upon the usual assumption that the English could never have any ideas of their own. The student, then, being careful to distinguish evidence from deduction and deduction from conjecture, will find all three, in varying proportions, in the following books. The full bibliography is given by Wells, *Manual*, Chap. XIV.

The indispensable book is still E. K. Chambers, *The Mediaeval Stage*, 2 vols., 1903, for its historical chapters, its wide range of evidence, and the valuable collection of documents in Vol. II. There is food for thought when we continue with the same author's *The English Folk Play*, 1933. His final summing up is contained in Chap. I of his *English Literature at the Close of the Middle Ages*. A. W. Ward, *English Dramatic Literature*, Vol. I, Chap. I, gives the bones of the matter, and the relevant chapters of Allardyce Nichol, *British Drama: An historical survey*, 1928, and *The Development of the Theatre*, 1927. A. Mantzius, *A History of Theatrical Art*, trans. L. von Corsell, 1903, is European in scope, but may provide points. Karl Young, *The Drama of the Medieval Church*, 2 vols., 1933, is admirably documented. K. L. Bates, *The English Religious Drama*, New York, 1893, and S. W. Clarke, *The Miracle Play in England* (n.d.) are useful elementary introductions, but the student will probably find C. M. Gayley, *Plays of our Forefathers*, 1907, most useful, especially as it treats of the plays critically and has a good succinct appendix on the sources of the miracles. For the best text of the centrally important Chester "banns" and other documents that reveal both the organisation and the breakdown of guild production, see below, Salter and Greg, *The Trial and Flagellation*. W. W. Greg, *Bibliographical and Textual Problems of the English Miracle Cycles*, in *The Library*, 3rd series, V (1914), and in book form, deals with real evidence and with relevant and practical questions. For mummings and suchlike, see R. Brotanek, *Die Englischen Maskenspiel*, 1902, R. J. E. Tiddy, *The Mummers' Play*, Oxford, 1923; Enid Welsford, *The Court Masque*, 1927, Chaps. I, II, and *The Fool, his Social and Literary History*, 1938.

Selections are in A. W. Pollard, *English Miracle Plays, Moralities, and Interludes: Specimens of the Pre-Elizabethan Drama* (many editions), and J. M. Manly, *Specimens of the Pre-Shakespearian Drama*, 1897 etc. *Everyman: with other Interludes*, ed. E. Rhys (Everyman's Library), contains *inter alia*, eight miracles; the texts are modernised.

A. MIRACLE PLAYS

1. *York Plays*.

B.M. MS. Addl. 35290 (often called the Ashburnham MS. from an earlier owner), written c. 1430–40, contains forty-eight plays, being the usual Old Testament "types" (eleven plays), the New Testament story from the Annunciation to Pentecost, three plays of Our Lady, and Doomsday. There is an excellent edition by Lucy Toulmin Smith, 1885, with useful introduction. She prints the music of the songs in an appendix, though she did not think much of it. The Scriveners' Play, *The Incredulity of Thomas*, No. 42 in the series, exists also in the "Sykes MS." owned by the York Philosophical Society. It was edited by J. P. Collier, *Camden Soc. Miscellany*, IV.

See W. A. Craigie, *The Gospel of Nicodemus and the York Mystery Plays*, in An English Miscellany presented to Dr. Furnivall, 1901.

2. *Ludus Coventriae* or *The Plaie called Corpus Christi.*

The MS. in the B.M., Cotton Vespasian D.VIII, is mid-fifteenth-century, but bears these titles in later hands. There is no internal evidence to connect it with Coventry or with the Grey Friars there as earlier scholars believed, but the name is convenient and may be correct. The series has been worked over, and the technique varies from simple procession (e.g., *The Prophets*) and monologue (*Moses*) to quite elaborate contemporaneous staging in the two parts of *The Passion*. It comprises forty-two sections, beginning with the Creation and ending with the Assumption of the Virgin and Dooms-day, with an explanatory prologue at the opening and three other prologues interpolated. These are not craft plays, but may have been acted by a guild formed for the purpose.

The first complete edition is by J. O. Halliwell, Shakespeare Soc., 1841: a good text and introduction, but that of K.S. Block, E.E.T.S., ex. ser. CXX (1922 for 1917), closer to the form of the MS., has a good introd., index and glossary. Part of one play is in Pollard, two in Manly, and five in Hemingway. A "diplomatic" text of one was edited by W. W. Greg, 1915. The make-up of the series is discussed by Esther L. Swenson, *An Inquiry into the Composition of the Ludus Coventriae*, Univ. of Minnesota Studies, 1914.

Two *Coventry Corpus Christi Plays* were edited by H Craig, E.E.T.S. ex. ser. LXXXVII, 1902. These are not part of the same series, but are craft plays. (*a*) The Shearman and Tailors' Pageant, containing the Annunciation, Nativity, Shepherds, Prophets, Kings, and Slaughter of the Innocents, was printed by T. Sharp, 1817 and 1825, from a MS. since burnt, and his print is the only text-source. It is included by Manly, and a modernised text of the Nativity by Pollard, in *Fifteenth Century Prose and Verse*, 1903. (*b*) The Weavers' Pageant, which exists in MS. in the archives of its native city, contained the Prophets, Simeon and Anna, the Presentation in the Temple, and Visit to Jerusalem. The Presentation was printed by Sharp for the Abbotsford Club in 1836. Craig's introduction and appendices contain valuable excerpts from Coventry documents: note especially App. II, extracts from account-books.

3. *Digby Plays.*

The *Digby Plays*, edited by F. J. Furnivall, New Shakespeare Society, 1882, E.E.T.S., ex. ser. LXX, 1896, contains The Killing of the Children, The Conversion of St. Paul, and Mary Magdalene from MS. Digby 113 (c. 1480–90) in the Bodleian Library, and The Burial and Resurrection from MS. *e Museo* 160 in the same, with Wisdom from the Macro Plays (below) intercalated. As an edition it is not very helpful. The Magdalene play is interesting especially for its comic and satiric scenes.

4. *Chester Plays.*

The *Chester Plays* exist in five MSS., all late copies: viz., in the B.M., Addl. 10305, and Harl. 2013, both written by George Bellin, 1592 and 1600; Harl. 2124, part written by James Miller, 1607; in the Bodleian, MS. 175, written by Wm. Bedford, 1607; and one belonging to the Duke of Devonshire, written by Edward Gregory, 1591. The first was edited by T. Wright, Shakespeare Soc., 1843–7, and Harl. 2124, by H. Deimling, E.E.T.S. ex. ser. LXII, 1892, and Matthews, ib., LXV, 1914, with introduction concerning MSS. and text. The series contains "banns" (i.e., prologue or proclamation) and 24 "pageants": the Fall of Lucifer, four O.T. subjects, sixteen N.T. subjects from Salutation to Pentecost, and The Prophets of Antichrist, the Coming of Antichrist and Doomsday. The "prophets" play is of the usual non-dramatic expository type, the remainder are straightforward plays, the comic elements less developed than in the Towneley cycle.

To these add: F. M. Salter and W. W. Greg—*The Trial and Flagellation, with other Studies in the Chester Cycle.* Malone Society, 1935. I. The "Trial and Flagellation"; a new MS. II, The Manchester Fragment of the "Resurrection". III, "Christ and the Doctors", and the York Play. IV, The Lists and Banns of the Plays. I contains the texts, some highly specialised discussion of the relations of the MS., and valuable notes on gilds and their plays in the sixteenth century. IV contains accurate copies of the important descriptions, not easily accessible elsewhere. This is a capital document.

5. *Towneley Plays.*

The *Towneley Plays*, so called from the family which long owned the MS. now in America, are sometimes called the Wakefield plays because the name is found on the first page. They were published first by the Surtees Soc., 1836, and again by G. England and A. W. Pollard, E.E.T.S., ex. ser. LXXI, 1897. The MS. is mid-fifteenth-century, the plays somewhat older. The set consists of thirty-two pieces: the Fall of the Angels and Creation, seven Old Testament and twenty-two New Testament episodes (including the legendary Harrowing of Hell), and Doomsday, with a monologue, the Hanging of Judas, added in a later hand. Six plays and the Judas episode are imperfect, and twelve leaves missing after the Creation presumably contained the Fall and Expulsion from Eden. The MS. is not a straightforward play-book like the Chester and York MSS., since the Shepherds' Play is duplicated, the order is incorrect, and only four plays are assigned to crafts. Five plays—Pharaoh, the Doctors, the Harrowing of Hell, the Incredulity of Thomas, and Doomsday—are versions of the same episodes in the York cycle: for this and allied questions see Pollard's introduction and Greg, *Bibliographical and Textual Problems*. The technique varies from simple presentation to the most highly-developed realistic drama, of which the second Shepherds' Play is the best-known example. Pollard, *English Miracle Plays*, prints the second Shepherds' Play; Manly, *Specimens*, prints Noah's Flood, Isaac, Jacob, and the second Shepherds' Play, which is also in Rhys's Everyman selection.

6. *Non-Cycle Mystery Plays*.

The Non-Cycle Mystery Plays, edited by O. Waterhouse, E.E.T.S., ex. ser. CIV (1909) contains: (1) dramatic fragments from a MS. in Shrewsbury School, specially important as transitional between pure liturgy and drama. (2) *The Creation of Eve and Temptation*, from an eighteenth-century transcript of certain pages in the Norwich Grocers' Book, now lost. It differs from the dramatisations in the existing cycles. (3) *Noah's Ark*, from the printed texts in Henry Bourne, *History of Newcastle upon Tyne*, 1736; a late and bad version, modernised by Bourne, of the Newcastle Ship-wrights' Play.(4) *Abraham and Isaac*, an excellent play in two versions, one from MS. D. IV. 18 in Trinity Coll., Dublin, printed by R. Brotanek, *Anglia*, XXI, 1899, and one from a MS. among the manorial papers of Bourne in Suffolk, a late fifteenth-century version of an older play, first printed by Lucy Toulmin Smith, *A Commonplace Book of the Fifteenth Century*, 1886, where it appears among various religious poems. (5) *The Play of the Sacrament*, called the Croxton Play because the name is mentioned in the prologue, from MS. F. IV. 20 in Trinity Coll., Dublin. It is not a biblical play, but anti-Semitic legendary, rather crudely but realistically done for village audiences. (6) *The Pride of Life*, from a MS. at Christ Church, Dublin, is the earliest extant morality, dating from the early fifteenth century. Unfortunately it is imperfect.

All but the last are included by Manly. Waterhouse gives the bibliography.

B. MORALITIES

The *Macro Plays* are so called after a former owner of the vol. which contains the MSS., bound together, of three plays: *Mankind*; *Mind, Will and Understanding* (called by Furnivall, *Wisdom*); and *The Castle of Perseverance*. They were edited by F. J. Furnivall and A. W. Pollard, E.E.T.S., ex. ser. XCI, 1904, rep. 1924. In his valuable introd. Pollard dates them about 1475, 1460, and 1425 respectively. The last is earliest, longest, and best, and is accompanied by stage-diagrams, reproduced by Pollard. See also under *Non-Cycle Mystery Plays* above, No. 6; also under Skelton, *Magnificence*, p. 312; Scottish Drama, below, and in Vol. II of this series, Chap. VIII.

LEGENDS

I. LEGENDS OF SAINTS

For a good general account, see G. H. Gerould's *Saints' Legends*, Boston, 1916. For a detailed bibliography, see Wells, V. 3.

A. LEGEND COLLECTIONS

1. *The Smaller Vernon Collection*

Nine items in short couplets, totalling 6,643 ll., extant in MS. Vernon (1370–80; Southern dialect). The first eight are closely rendered from *Legenda Aurea* (a Latin collection written 1260–70 by Jacobus a Voragine for use in church services, cf. Wells, 306), and the 9th from *Vitae Patrum*, Ed.: C. Horstmann, *A.E. Leg.*, 1878, 174. See Wells, V [21]; *C.B.E.L.*, 1.175.

2. *The Scottish Collection of Legends*

Fifty items in Scots dialect, composed, apparently for private reading, at the end of 14th c., and extant in a somewhat defective text in MS. Cbg. Univ. Lib. Gg. 2, 6 (15th-c. hand). Metre: 4-stress ll. in couplets. In all, and including prologue, 33,533 ll. Two of the legends are of Scottish saints, but none of English.

The author was an aged priest of the church, and used the *Legenda Aurea* as his chief source. Ed.: Metcalfe, W. M. *Legends of the Saints*, 3 vols., *S.T.S.*, 1896. See Wells, V [22]; *C.B.E.L.*, 1.175.

3. *Osbern Bokenham's Lives of Saints*

Comprises 13 legends, all of women. Composed (1443–6) in the Suffolk dialect and extant in MS. Arundel 327. Source: *Legenda Aurea*. Metre: short couplets in 8-line stanzas rhyming ababbcbc. Ed.: C. Horstmann, Heilbronn, 1883; M.S. Serjeantson, E.E.T.S., 206.

B. LEGENDS IN INDEPENDENT TEXTS

The following lives of individual saints deserve special notice. They are found at least once outside the collections. See Wells, 308.

1. *Cuthbert*

Found independently in a version (c. 1450) in MS. Castle Howard, as well as in two collections. 8,362 short (usually 4-beat) lines rhyming in couplets. Ed.: J. T. Fowler, *The Life of St. Cuthbert in English Verse*, Surtees Soc., 87. See Wells, V [37]; and, for background, B. Colgrave's *Two Lives of Saint Cuthbert*, C.U.P., 1940.

2. *Erkenwald*

This highly interesting and attractive poem of 352 long alliterative lines, preserved in a single paper MS. (Harley, 2250) dating from the late 15th century, deals with the life of St. Erkenwald, Saxon bishop of London, 675–93. It is written in the N.W. Midl. dialect, was probably composed c. 1386, and is attributed to the Pearl-poet (see p. 300). Bibliography: *C.B.E.L.*, 1.203. Editions: Gollancz, I. *St. Erkenwald, an Alliterative Poem, written about 1386, narrating a Miracle wrought by the Bishop in St. Paul's Cathedral (Select Early English Poems*, Vol. IV), O.U.P., 1922; Savage, H. L. *St. Erkenwald*, O.U.P., 1926. Translation: See Gollancz (above). Discussion: R. W. Chambers, pp. 65–6 of Article on "Long Will" in *Essays and Studies*, 9, 1923; G. H. Gerould, *Saints' Legends*, pp. 238– , 272– , 372– ; J. R. Hulbert, "The Sources of St. E. and the Trental of St. Gregory" in *M.Ph.*, 16.485–9; H. Koziol, pp. 170–1 of article on "Zur Frage der Verfasserschaft einiger mittelenglischer Stabreimdichtungen" in *E. St.*, 67. 1922–3; Oakden, *Allit. Poetry*; Wells, V [41].

3. *Juliana*

One of the "Katherine Group" (on authorship, see R. M. Wilson, Leeds Stud., I. 24 ff.). Found independently in an alliterative prose version in MSS. Royal 17, A, 27 (c. 1230), and Bodl. 34 (c. 1230). Source: probably a Latin version. Found in other two collections. Ed.: Cockayne and Brock, E.E.T.S., 51 (both texts); d'Ardenne, S.T.R.O., *An Edition of þe Liflade ant te Passiun of Seinte Iulene*, Liège, 1936; Hall, *Sels.*, 1.138–49 (both texts), 2.543–53 (apparatus); Morris, *Specimens*, 1.96–109 (both texts). See Wells, V [49]; *C.B.E.L.*, 1.169.

4. *Katherine*

Extant in alliterative prose in 3 MSS. all of 1200–50, viz., Royal 17, A, 27, Bodl. NE. A, 3, 11, and Cott. Titus D, 18. This version gives the name to the so-called "Katherine Group". Also found in other versions, including the three following: (*a*) 8-line stanzas, (*b*) short couplets, and (*c*) ll. of 6 or 7 stresses in couplets. Ed.: E. Einenkel, *The Early English Life of St. Katherine and its Latin Original*, E.E.T.S., 80 (R. with varr. of B. and T.). Sel.: Hall, *Sels*, 1.128–31 (text R), 2.524–31. See Wells, V [50]; *C.B.E.L.*, 1.169.

5. *Margaret*

Extant in alliterative prose (forming one of the "Katherine Group") in 2 MSS. (both c. 1230): Royal 17, A, 27 and Bodl. 34. Other versions occur in (*a*) stanzas of ll. with 7 or 6 stresses, (*b*) ll. of 7 or 6 stresses in couplets, and (*c*) short couplets. Ed.: F. M. Mack, *Seinte Marherete*, E.E.T.S., 193 (B. and R. texts: full critical apparatus). Discussion: E. E. Francis, "A Hitherto Unprinted Version of the *Passio S. Margaritae*" in *P.M.L.A.*, 42.87–105, 1927: Gerould, G. H. "A New Text of the *Passio S. Margaritae* with Some Account of its Latin and English Relations" in *P.M.L.A.*, 39.525, 1924. See Wells, V [52]; *C.B.E.L.*, 1.169–70.

II. BIBLICAL LEGENDS

1. *The Gospel of Nicodemus*

For an O.E. version, see p. 257, above. Several M.E. versions are extant, one being metrical and strophic, the others prose. Notable as a source book for the York Plays.

A.   Metrical version, 12-ll. stanzas of 4-stress ll., totalling about 1,800, rhyming ababababcdcd. Composed c. 1300–25, probably in the North, and extant in several 15th-c. MSS. Source: Latin. Ed.: W. H. Hulme, *The Harrowing of Hell, and the Gospel of Nicodemus*, E.E.T.S. E.S., 100.

B.   Prose versions. The extant MSS., mostly 15th c., fall into six groups. Note early printed versions by Notary (1507), de Worde (1509), Skot (1529).

See Wells, V [73]; *C.B.E.L.*, 1.188.

2. *The Harrowing of Hell*

Extant in 3 MSS., Digby 86 (late 13th-c., 256 ll.), Harley 2253 (c. 1300; 249 ll.), and Auchinleck (c. 1330–40; 201 ll., defective). Composed before 1250. Metre: 4-beat ll. in couplets. The piece is conversational and dramatic. Ed.: W. H. Hulme, *The Harrowing of Hell*, E.E.T.S.E.S., 100 (all versions). Discussion: J. A. MacCulloch, *The Harrowing of Hell. A Comparative Study of an Early Christian Doctrine*, Edinburgh, 1931. See Wells, V [74]; *C.B.E.L.*, 1.188.

III.   LEGENDS OF VISITS TO THE UNDERWORLD

Three pieces are extant in English before 1400, evidently all popular. On the subject generally, see E. J. Becker, *Medieval Visions of Heaven and Hell*, Baltimore, 1899; H. R. Patch, "Some Elements in Medieval Descriptions of the Other-world" in *P.M.L.A.*, 33.601–43, 1918; Willson, *The M.E. Legends of Visits to the Other-World*, Chicago, 1917. See also A. B. Van Os, *Religious Visions: The Development of the Eschatological Elements in Medieval English Literature*, Amsterdam, 1932; St. J. D. Seymour, *Irish Visions of the Other World*, London, 1930; Wells, V, 3, II (B.d.).

1. *Vision of St. Paul* or *The Eleven Pains of Hell*

Six versions are found, the most comprehensive being in MSS. Vernon (1370–80; 346 ll.) and Jesus Coll. Oxford 29 (c. 1275; 290 ll.). Both of these are in short couplets. The ultimate source is Greek, and two versions of this existed already in the fourth century, but one has since been lost. There are 6 Latin versions, represented by 22 MSS. (See M. R. James, *Texts and Studies*, Vol. 2, Cambridge, 1893.) In the Vernon text, St. Paul, in company with St. Michael, makes a tour of Hell and sees the souls in torment. The Jesus version differs considerably in detail: there, for example, the tour is described to Satan by a returned sinner. Texts from different MSS. are available in E.E.T.S., 49.147 ff., 98.251 ff., 117.750 ff., 49.223 ff., 49.210 ff. Discussion: Hall, *Sels.*, 2.413–15. See Wells, V [79]; *C.B.E.L.*, 1.176–7.

2. *St. Patrick's Purgatory*

This popular legend, perhaps suggested by the cave "Purgatory" near Lough Derg in Donegal (on which, see Harvey, *Patrick's Purgatory*), and probably first committed to writing, in Latin prose, by Henry, a monk of Saltrey, Hunt., is preserved in 3 M.E. versions: (1) Laud MS. 108 (c. 1280–90; 773 7-stress ll. in couplets) and various others; (2) MS. Auchinleck (1330–40; 198 tail-rhyme stanzas aabccb. This version is known as *Owayn Miles*, Sir Owayn being the hero); MSS. Cotton Calig.A II (341 short couplets) and Brome (342 short couplets), both fifteenth-century. In this legend, Sir Owayn, a deep-dyed sinner, pays a visit to the underworld via the great pit, Sir Patrick's Purgatory, and is there subjected to various torments, but on praying, escapes to Paradise, ultimately returning to earth where he becomes a holy man. Ed.: C. Horstmann, *A.E. Leg.*, 1875; E.E.T.S., 87.199 ff.; G. P. Krapp, *Legends of St. Patrick's Purgatory*, Baltimore, 1900. Trans: Shackford, *Leg. Sats.*, 33; Weston, *Ch. M.E. P*, 83–9. Discussion: S. Leslie (Comp.), *St. Patrick's Purgatory: A Record from History and Literature*, London, 1932. Wells, V [80]; *C.B.E.L.*, 1.177.

3. *The Vision of Tundale*

This "epic of torment" is preserved in one English version in short couplets in several fifteenth-century MSS. It enjoyed European popularity, being found in numerous versions in Latin, French, German and Icelandic. The prologue mentions 1149 as the date of composition. The English recension, however, only dates from c. 1400. In the story, a rich, but very wicked, Irishman called Tundale, is stricken unconscious at a meal, thence removed to Hell, where he is cruelly tortured. Purged of his sins, he then recovers consciousness and repents. Ed.: W. D. B. Turnbull, *Visions of Tundale*, Edinburgh, 1843; A. Wagner, Halle, 1893. See Wells, V [81]; *C.B.E.L.*, 1.177.

LYRICAL POETRY

This section is closely allied to those on *Music* (p. 438) and *Latin writers* (p. 400). It is arranged so as to lead from Latin lyric, through French, to English. This may be a true historical sequence, and some would have it so; but the student is warned that so little is known of vernacular arts and customs that he must not take it for granted. Many tribes and tongues are fused in the tradition of Europe. In the time of Walter Map, who is credited with some Latin songs, the Welsh (according to Giraldus Cambrensis) had already a custom of singing in three-part harmony, and there is early evidence of developed song in parts of England. The strict distinction between "folk" and "art" song is dangerous at best. We have only what was written down by people who had the habit of writing, which has less to do with the habit of making songs than with any other literary habit; and it was only in the nineteenth century that anyone thought of ignoring the evidence and describing England as "the land without music". It is quite conceivable that the sequence should be exactly the reverse: but if we remember that we are following the sequence of *writing-down* and keep an open mind as to the process of *making*, no harm is done, and it is convenient to have a sequence of some kind, if only as a mnemonic. For full bibliography, see Wells, *Manual*, Chap. XIII.

For Latin lyric, see the section on *Latin Writers* (p. 400). F. Brittain, *The Mediæval Latin and Romance Lyric* (1937), and S. Gaselee, *Transition from the Late Latin Lyric to the Mediæval Love Poem* (1911) assume that the sequence of form and feeling goes with the linguistic development, and (since it may be true and the student has been warned) may be read with much profit. H. J. Chaytor, *The Troubadours* (Cambridge Manuals, No. 39, 1912) is a short and satisfactory introduction to a subject which may be exemplified in Barbara Smythe, *Trobador Poets* (selections translated with notes and introduction, the *Mediæval Library*, No. 11, 1929) and C. Colleer Abbott, *Early Mediaeval French Lyrics*, 1932, and followed up in J. Anglade, *Les Troubadours, leurs vies, leurs ouvres, leur influence* (1919), a reliable work with a good bibliography, and A. Jeanroy, *La Poésie Lyrique des Troubadours* (1934), a complete and authoritative survey of literary forms and a good biographical dictionary. Pierre Aubry, *Trouvères et Troubadours* (1909) should be noted here as well as under *Music*.

A. Jeanroy, *Les Origines de la Poésie Lyrique en France au Moyen Age* (1925) is standard. See also E. Faral, *Les Jongleurs en France au moyen age* (1910). The link between France and England is attempted by H. J. Chaytor, The *Troubadours and England*, and by J. Audiau, *Les Troubadours et l'Angleterre* (1927), an interesting little book vitiated by abject acceptance of Taine's fancy picture of the sombre English crouching in the mud as they watch the eternal rain with lacklustre eyes.

For lyric in England, see the article by E. J. Dent in the *Oxford History of Music*, noted under *Music* (p. 438); also F. M. Padelford, in C.H.E.L., II, Chap. XVI. The best anthology is E. K. Chambers and F. Sidgwick, *Early English Lyrics* (1907), which contains also an admirable essay by Sir E. K. Chambers (reprinted in *Sir Thomas Wyatt*, 1933) and an excellent bibliography. Dr. Carleton Brown has specialised in religious lyric, and for this his collections are indispensable: *English Lyrics of the XIII Century* (1932), and *Religious Lyrics of the XIV Century* (1924). See also his bibliography, *A Register of Middle English Religious and Didactic Verse*, two vols., published by the Bibliographical Society, 1916 and 1920. The chief MS. collections are described by Chambers and Sidgwick; we may note here Harleian 2253 in the British Museum as containing some of the best fourteenth-century songs. Sets of lyrics from MSS. have been published by F. M. Padelford, *Anglia* XXXI, 1908; see also notes by N. Bolle, ib., XXXIV, 1911, and XXXVI, 1913; Zupitza in Herrig's *Archiv*. 89; Fehr, ib., 106; and F. M. Padelford and A. R. Benham, *The Songs of Rawlinson MS. C. 813*, Univ. of Washington Studies, I, Seattle, 1909. W. Heuser, *With an O and an I*, in *Anglia* XXVII, 1904, is a comparative study of a kind more of which is needed.

For carols see R. L. Greene, *The Early English Carol* (1935). The Oxford Carol Book is good—see under *Music* (p. 438). One collection in modern spelling is in A. W. Pollard, *Fifteenth Century Prose and Verse* (1903), but better in R. Dyboski, *Songs, Carols, etc. from Richard Hill's Balliol MS.* E.E.T.S., E.S., Cl. 1907. (See also E. Flügel in *Anglia*, XXVI 1903). Others are F. J. Furnivall, *Political, Religious, and Love Poems*, E.E.T.S. 15, 1866, and *Hymns*, E.E.T.S., 24, 1867; G. G. Perry, *Religious Pieces from the Thornton MS.*, E.E.T.S. 26, 1867, revised 1913; J. Kail, *Twenty-six Poems . . . from the Digby MS.*, E.E.T.S. 124, 1904; Mabel Day, *The Wheatley MS.*, E.E.T.S. 155, 1917; J. Ritson, *Ancient Songs and Ballads* (3rd ed., W. C. Hazlitt), 1877; Chappell, under *Music* (p. 438).

PROVERBS

1. *The Proverbs of Alfred*

This collection of proverbs, the chief in M.E., is a hotch-potch of traditional wisdom and superstition, and religious and moral precepts. The connexion with Alfred the Great claimed for it in the introductory paragraph and repeatedly reaffirmed in the text, is probably only nominal and is due either to the king's reputation for sagacity or to the author's endeavour to secure reflected prestige for his compilation. Connoisseurs of proverbial wisdom and trite sayings will appreciate this interesting collection.

Three MSS. are extant, Jesus Coll. Oxf. 29 (c. 1275; 456 ll.); Trin. Coll. Cbg. B, 14, 39 (beginning of thirteenth century; 709 ll.), and (best of all) Maidstone MS. A 13 (266 ll.; before 1250), while there are three surviving leaves (ed. N. R. Ker, *Med. Ævum*, 5.115) of a fourth, the archetypal text from MS. Cott. Galba A 19 now destroyed. The compilation probably dates from c. 1150–80, and is in the Southern dialect. The verse is transitional: alliteration and rhyme occur: the lines are of unequal length and have two stresses. The lines are paragraphed according to sense.

Bibliography.
C.B.E.L., 1.180.
Taylor, A. "Introductory Bibliography for the Study of Proverbs" in *M.Ph.* 30.195. 1932–3. [Useful catalogue of books in various languages.]

Editions.
Borgström, E. *The Proverbs of Alfred*. Lund, 1908. [Ed. of J. and T., with apparatus.]
Brown, C. "The Maidstone Text of the 'P. of A.'" in *M.L.R.*, 21.249–60. 1926.
Hall. *Sels.*, 18–28 (J. text), 285–308 (full apparatus).
Morris, R. *An Old English Miscellany*. E.E.T.S., 49. Pp. 102–38.
Skeat, W. W. *The Proverbs of Alfred*. Oxford, 1907. [J. and T. Texts.]
South, H. P. *The Proverbs of Alfred, Studied in the Light of the Recently Discovered Maidstone Manuscript*. London, 1931. [Full apparatus. Dates original 1150–75.]

Translation.
Weston. *Ch. M.E. P.*, 289–94.

Discussion.

Anderson, O. S. .*The Proverbs of Alfred* (*I. A Study of the Texts*). Lund., 1942

Brown, C. "A Thirteenth-Century MS. at Maidstone" in *M.L.R.*, 21.1–12. 1926.

Oakden. *Allit. Poetry*, 140–2.

Skeat, W. W. *Early English Proverbs*. Oxford, 1910.

Taylor, A. *The Proverb*. London, 1931. [A general descriptive and historical survey of the proverbs in European languages.]

Wells. VII [5].

Whiting, B. J. *The Origin of the Proverbs*. O.U.P., 1931. [General survey.]

2. *The Proverbs of Hendyng*

This collection is similar in content to the *Proverbs of Alfred*, but for the tone, which is worldly and cynical. Nothing is known of Hendyng, except that he is here stated to be the son of Marcolf. The latter, be it noted, is one of the contestants in German versions of the *Dialogue of Salomon and Saturn*.

The text is preserved in three MSS., Digby 86 (1272–83; 47 stanzas), Harley 2253 (c. 1310; 39 stanzas), and Cbg. Univ. Lib. Gg. I. I (1300–30; 46 stanzas). Altogether, there are 51 separate stanzas, each of which has 7 ll., the first six rhyming aabccb, of which the *b*-ll. have three stresses, the others 4, while the seventh line contains a proverb and ends with *Quop Hendyng*.

Bibliography.
C.B.E.L., 1.183.

Editions.

Morris. *Specimens*, 2.35–42.

Schleich, G. "Die Sprichwörter Hendyngs" in *Angl.*, 51.220–77, and 52.350–61, 1927–8. [Excellent.]

Translation.

Weston. *Ch. M.E. P.*, 294–8.

Discussion.

Kneuer, K. *Die Sprichwörter Hendyngs*. Leipzig, 1901. [Compares H.'s proverbs with English and continental collections.]

Wells. VII [6].

Other proverbial collections include the (popular) *Distichs of Cato* (earliest M.E. version is Northern of fourteenth century; also in O.E.), *How the Wyse (Gode) Man Taught Hys Sone* (several fifteenth-century MSS.) and *How the Good Wife Taught her Daughter* (3 or 4 versions in 8 MSS.). See further Wells, VII [8–10].

ROMANCES

Bibliography.

Billings (below), *passim.*

C.B.E.L., 1.128–130.

Herbert, J. A. *Catalogue of Romances in the Department of MSS. of the British Museum.* London, 1910. [Vol. III of Ward's *Catalogue*, q.v. Describes those items of MS. that deal with the "popular collections of Exempla, or short stories used for illustrations by medieval preachers, and of similar tales, moralised or otherwise, both in prose and verse".]

Hibbard (below), *passim.* [See also pp. 321–6 for select list of special studies on romances.]

Ward, H. L. D., and Herbert, J. A. *Catalogue of Romances in the Department of MSS. of the British Museum.* 3 vols. London, 1883–1910.

Wells. *Manual*, 761 ff., 1003 ff., 1100 ff., 1203 ff., 1295 ff., 1382 ff., 1483 ff., 1562 ff.

Texts.

E.E.T.S. Includes standard editions of most of the romances.

French, W. H., and Hale, C.B. *Middle English Metrical Romances.* New York, 1930. [Book of texts (19 being complete) intended for classroom study. With apparatus.]

Hartshorne, C. H. *Ancient Metrical Tales, Chiefly Printed from Original Sources.* London, 1829.

Halliwell-Phillipps, J. O. *The Thornton Romances.* Camden Soc. London, 1844. [Contains text of *Perceval, Isumbras, Eglamour* and *Degravant*, with introd. and notes.]

Ritson, J. *Ancient English Metrical Romances.* 3 vols. London, 1802. Rev., Goldsmid, Edinburgh, 1884.

Robson, J. *Three Early English Metrical Romances.* Camden Soc. London, 1842. [Contains *Aunters of Arthur, Sir Amadace*, and *Avowynge of King Arthur.*]

Thoms, W. J. *A Collection of Early Prose Romances.* Rev. Ed. London, 1907.

Weber, H. *Metrical Romances of the XIII, XIV and XV Centuries, published from Ancient Manuscripts, with an Introduction, Notes and a Glossary.* 3 vols. Edinburgh, 1810.

Discussion.

Barrow, S. F. *The Medieval Society Romances.* O.U.P., 1924.

Billings, A. H. *A Guide to the Middle English Metrical Romances, dealing with English and Germanic Legends, and with the Cycles of Charlemagne and of Arthur.* New York, 1901. [Gives short specimen[s], abstract, synopses, notes on source, metre, dialect and author, and a bibl. of thirty-two of the more important romances, and of five poems on Gawayn. The introd. contains a general survey of the history and character of the English verse-romances, which relies on Ten Brink and Brandl. Though partly superseded by Wells's *Manual* and Hibbard (below), still a useful compilation.]

Dunlap, A. R. "The Vocabulary of the M.E. Romances in Tail-rhyme Stanza" in *Delaware Notes*, 1941 (May). [Discredits the theory of a "school" of tail-rhyme poets.]

Ellis, G. *Specimens of Early English Metrical Romances.* Rev. J. O. Halliwell-Phillipps, London, 1848. [Designed to "exhibit a general view of our romances of chivalry." Tells the story of each in prose.]

Everett, D. "A Characterisation of the English Medieval Romances" in *Essays and Studies by Members of the English Association.* Vol. XV. Oxford, 1930. [Concerned with the fundamentals of the Mediaeval Romance and shows how to differentiate it from other literary types. Important.]

Gautier, L. *Les Epopées Françaises.* 5 vols. 2nd ed. Paris, 1878–97. [Exhaustive study of the French romance. Should be consulted.]

Geissler, O. *Religion und Aberglaube in den mittelenglischen Versromanzen.* Halle, 1908.

Gist, M. A. *Love and War in the Middle English Romances.* Philadelphia, 1947. [But the account of medieval morality has been adversely criticised.]

Hibbard, L. A. *Medieval Romance in England, a Study of the Sources and Analogues of the non-Cyclic Metrical Romances.* Oxford, 1924. [An excellent book, superseding earlier works in this field. Also contains good selective bibl. to each romance. Indispensable.]

Ker. *Epic and Romance.*

Lawrence, W. W. *Medieval Story, and the Beginnings of the Social Ideals of English-Speaking People.* New York, 1911.

Leach, H. G.   *Angevin Britain and Scandinavia*. Cambridge, 1921. [A study of mediaeval relations between the literatures of Britain and Scandinavia. See especially Chaps. VI–IX on the romances.]

Lewis, C. S.   *The Allegory of Love. A Study in Medieval Tradition.* Oxford, 1936. [See particularly Chap. I on "Courtly Love".]

Mason, E.   *French Medieval Romances from the Lays of Marie de France.* Ev. Lib., 557. 1924. [A book of translations useful for comparison.]

Mott, L.   *The System of Courtly Love*. London, 1904.

Nutt, A.   *The Influence of Celtic upon Mediæval Romance.* London, 1904.

Spence, L.   *A Dictionary of Medieval Romance and Romance Writers.* London, 1913. [Summaries, brief mentions of writers, works and personages. Useful.]

Taylor, A. B.   *An Introduction to Medieval Romance.* London, 1930. [A general survey of the chief themes and features of mediaeval romance.]

Thompson, S.   *Motif-Index of Folk-Literature.* Bloomington, 1932.

Trounce, A. McI.   "The English Tail-rhyme Romances" in *Medium Ævum*, I–III. Oxford, 1932–4. [Characterises and analyses the form of the tail-rhyme romances and endeavours to show that the twenty-three extant examples were either all written in E. Anglia or are closely related to the E. Anglian group. But see Dunlap above.]

Wägner, W.   *Epics and Romances of the Middle Ages, adapted from the work of Dr. W. Wägner,* by M. W. Macdowell, and edited by W. S. Anson. 1st ed. 1882. London, 1917. [See especially pp. 419–74 for "Legends of Arthur and the Holy Grail". Contents:—Part I: Retelling of the Amelung and kindred legends. Part II: Retelling of the Nibelung and kindred legends. Part III: Retelling of the Carolingian, Arthurian legends and Tannhauser.]

1. ENGLISH AND GERMANIC LEGENDS

1. *Horn*

The mediaeval popularity of the *Horn* legend is attested by the existence of versions in A.N. (*Horn et Rymenhild*, ascribed to the twelfth century), in English (*King Horn* [below], composed c. 1225 and *Horn Childe* [below], early 14th c.), and of the late fourteenth century French prose *Pontus et la belle Sidoyne* (translated into both English [middle of fifteenth century] and into German [c. 1465], whence it passed [16th c.] into Icelandic). Versions also exist in some ten Scottish ballads. Briefly it tells of how Horn, a boy prince, is deprived of his kingdom by invaders, is exiled in a foreign court, where, after pressure, he falls in love with Rymenhild, the daughter of the king, who shortly after banishes him, of how after seven years he rescues his lady from two distasteful suitors, and finally returns with her as his queen to reign happily over his motherland. The origin of the story, which evidently combines the exile-and-return- with the love-motive, is still in dispute, but is to be sought amongst Anglo-Saxons, Danes, Norse Vikings, or Anglo-Normans. See Billings, 3–4; Hibbard, *Med. Rom.*, 83–4; Wells, pp. 7–8; *C.B.E.L.*, 1.147.

A. *Geste of King Horn*

Three MSS. preserve this lively but unadorned tale, which seems to have been intended for reciting to a popular audience:—
(1) MS. Cbg. Univ. Lib. Gg. 4, 27, 2 (c. 1250–60), 1,530 ll.;
(2) MS. Laud Misc. 108 Part II (c. 1300–20), 1,569 ll.; (3) MS. Harley 2253 (c. 1,310), 1,546 ll. The relationship of the MSS. is uncertain, but the first is probably nearest to the original, which was very likely composed in the (South) Midlands, c. 1225.

Structurally the poem is transitional, and accordingly provocative of controversy. The lines are short, with three or four stresses, are developed out of the long alliterative line, and rhyme in couplets. The influence of the French short couplet on the traditional metre is thus clearly revealed. Alliteration both within the line and between successive lines may also be noted.

Bibliography.
C.B.E.L., 1.147.

Editions.
Hall, J. *King Horn*, Oxford, 1901. [Excellent ed. of all three texts in parallel, with full critical apparatus and glossary.]
Lumby, J. R. *King Horn*. Re-edited by G. H. McKnight. E.E.T.S., O.S., 1901.
Morris. *Specimens I*, 237–86.
Wissmann, T. *Das Lied von King Horn*. Strassburg, 1881. [With full apparatus.]
French and Hale. 25–70.

Translations.
Weston. *Ch. M.E. P.*, 93–109.

Discussion.
Billings. 1–12.
French, W. H. *Essays on King Horn.* O.U.P., 1939. [Discusses type, metre, text, and personal names. The text is contained in an appendix. A challenging study.]
Hartenstein, O. *Studien zur Horn Sage.* Heidelberg, 1902.
Hibbard. *Med. Rom.*, 83–96.
Leidig, P. *Studien zu King Horn.* Borna-Leipzig, 1927.
Oliver, W. "King Horn and Suddene" in *P.L.M.A.*, 46.102–14. 1931. [Localises legend in Roxburghshire.]
Schofield, W. H. "The Story of King Horn and Rimenhild" in *P.M.L.A.*, 18.1–84. 1903. [Important survey of sources and localisation of legend.]
Wells. I [1]
West, H. S. *The Versification of King Horn.* Baltimore, 1907.

B. *Horn Childe and Maiden Rimnild*

This unique, rather pedestrian version of the *Horn* legend, preserved in MS. Auchinleck, f. 317 v. (1330–40), consists of 1,136 ll. in twelve-line tail-rhyme stanzas usually rhyming aabaabccbddb. Probably composed about 1300–25 in the N. Midlands, and carefully localised in the N. Riding of Yorkshire, it shows "in contrast to the abundance of matter, the native power, and the unconscious spontaneity of *King Horn* . . . poverty, inefficiency and anxious effort", Wells, *Manual,* p. 12.

Bibliography.
C.B.E.L., 1.148.

Editions.
Hall, J. *King Horn.* Oxford, 1901. [Text only, pp. 179–92]
Ritson. *A.E.M.R.*, 3.282–329.

Discussion.
Hibbard. *Med. Rom.*, 97–102.
Trounce. *Engl. Tail Rhymes.*
Wells. I [2].
See also under *King Horn* above.

C. *King Ponthus and the Fair Sidone*

This is a fifteenth-century prose rendering, extant in MS. Digby 185 and MS. Douce 384 (fragment) of the French prose romance *Ponthus et Sidoine* (composed before 1445).

Edition.
Mather, F. J., Jr. *King Ponthus and the Fair Sidone.* *P.M.L.A.*, 12.1–150. 1897. [With full apparatus.]

Discussion.
Wells. I [4].

2. *Havelok*

The *Havelok* legend, which exemplifies the exile-and-return motive, tells how the heir to the Danish throne, Havelok, having been treacherously deprived of his heritage and exiled to England, is brought up by humble fisherfolk and becomes a simple scullion in the service of the wicked Regent. The latter, learning of his diligence and remarkable athleticism, accordingly insists on marrying him to Goldborough, the English heiress, with the intention of thereby degrading her. But Havelok's royal birth is soon revealed and on returning to Denmark, he regains the kingdom. He subsequently wins England too, and prospers.

There are four main versions of the story:—(1) The earliest, an episode in Gaimar's *L'Estorie des Engleis,* composed 1145–51, (2) the French metrical romance, *Lai d'Havelok* (12th century), (3) the M.E. *Havelok the Dane* (below), and (4) a summary mention (82 ll.), in the Lambeth MS. of Robert Manning of Brunne's *Chronicle* (q.v., p. 324). The history of the legend is still controversial. See further Billings, 17–22; Hibbard, *Med. Rom.,* 103–13; Wells, I [5].

The English version, *Havelok the Dane,* comprises 3,001 four-stress ll., mostly in short couplets and is preserved in MS. Laud Misc. 108 (1300–20; the MS. also contains *King Horn,* p. 352), as well as in four short fragments in MS. Cbg. Univ. Lib. 4407 (14th c.). The story is localised at Grimsby and was probably originally composed in the North Midland dialect of Lincolnshire. With its vigorous, realistic portrayal of humble life, it was clearly intended for the ears of a popular audience.

Bibliography.
C.B.E.L., 1.148–9.

Editions.
French and Hale. 73–176.
Holthausen, F. *Havelok.* 3rd ed. Heidelberg, 1928. [Full apparatus. Prints also the Lambeth MS. interpolation and the Cambridge fragments. Excellent.]

Skeat, W. W. *The Lay of Havelok the Dane*. 2nd ed. rev. K. Sisam, Oxford, 1915. [With full apparatus. Includes Cambridge fragments. Standard ed.]

N.B.—Selections are given in most *Readers*.

Translations.
Darton, F. J. H. *A Wonder Book of Old Romance*. New York, 1907.
Weston. *Ch. M.E. P.*, 110–18. [ll. 465–1,274 only.]

Discussion.
Bell, A. *Le Lai d'Haveloc and Gaimar's Haveloc Episode*. London, 1925.
Billings. 15–24.
Bugge, A. "Havelok and Olaf Tryggvason" in *Saga Book of the Viking Club*, 6.257–95. 1910.
Creek, H. le Sourd. "The Author of Havelok the Dane" in *E.St.*, 48.193–222. 1915. [Relationship of different versions of the lay.]
Fahnestock, E. A. *A Study of the Sources and Composition of the Old French Lai d'Havelok*. New York, 1915.
Heyman, H. *Studies on the Havelok-Tale*. Upsala, 1903.
Hibbard. *Med. Rom.*, 103–14.
Schmidt, F. *Zur Heimatbestimmung des Havelok*. Göttingen, 1900.
Wells. I [5].

3. *Guy of Warwick*

The story of *Guy* was popular in England from the thirteenth to the nineteenth century, no doubt because of the great diversity of its interests. It should certainly be read. The narrative falls into two parts, the first, dealing with the knightly deeds of Guy up to the time of his marriage with Felice, being entirely romantic; whereas the second, or continuation, is pietetic, being concerned with Guy's (adventurous) activities as a pilgrim. The story was provided with a sequel in the romance of *Reinbrun, Gy sone of Warwicke* (1,524 ll. in twelve-line tail-rhyme stanzas, extant only in the Auchinleck MS., below).

Four English versions, all translations from the French and, except for (a) under 2 below, all in short couplets, exist as under:

1. (A) Auchinleck MS. (c. 1330–40). About 7,100 ll., another 200 or slightly more being missing.
   (C) MS. Caius Coll. Cbg. 107 (beginning of 15th c.). Also includes the continuation. In all, 11,095 ll.
   (S) MS. Sloane 1044 (14th c.). A fragment of 216 ll.

2. (a) Auchinleck MS. Contains the continuation (as well as the sequel *Reinbrun*). This part has 299 twelve-line tail-rhyme stanzas, aabaabccbddb or aabccbddbeeb.

3. (P) B.M. MS. Addit. 14408 (fragment; 14th c.).

4. (c) MS. Cbg. Univ. Lib. Ff. II 38 (15th c.), 11976 ll. MS. Caius Coll. Cbg. 107.

Bibliography.

C.B.E.L., 1.149.

Editions.

Zupitza, J. *The Romance of Guy of Warwick.* E.E.T.S., 25, 26. 1875–6. [Ed. of c, MS. Cbg. Univ. Lib. With copious textual notes.]

Zupitza, J. *The Romance of Guy of Warwick.* E.E.T.S., 42, 49, 59. 1883–91. [Ed., without apparatus, of both A and a, Auchinleck MS., and of C, Caius Coll. Cbg. 107.]

Discussion.

Billings. 25–32.

Crane, R. "Vogue of Guy of Warwick from the Close of the Middle Ages to the Romantic Revival" in *P.L.M.A.*, 30.125–94. 1915. [Surveys the history of the story in England up to c. 1900.)

Hibbard. *Med. Rom.*, 127–39.

Wells. I [6].

4. *William of Palerne*

William of Palerne, noteworthy because it is the earliest, or next earliest, of the poems marking the revival of the traditional composition, combines the love-motive with the werwolf theme. It was translated by a certain William (l. 5521) at the order of Sir Humphrey de Bohun (c. 1350) from the 9,663 ll. of *Guillaume de Palerne* (S.A.T.F., 1876), a French romance written 1150–1200, and is preserved in a unique W. Midland version of 5,540 long alliterative lines in MS. King's Coll. Cbg. 13 (c. 1350). Its beginning is fragmentary.

Bibliography.

C.B.E.L., 1.156.

Edition.

Skeat, W. W. *The Romance of William of Palerne.* E.E.T.S., 1867, reprinted 1890. [With critical apparatus.]

Translation.
Darton, F. J. H. *A Wonder Book of Old Romance.* New York, 1907.

Discussion.
Billings. 41–6.
Hibbard. *Med. Rom.,* 214–23.
McKeehan, I. P. "Guillaume de Palerne: A Medieval 'Best Seller' " in *P.L.M.A.,* 41.785–809. 1926. [An analysis of the contents of the story.]
Oakden, J. P. *Alliterative Poetry in Middle English.* Manchester, 1930. [Dialect, author and versification.]
Smith, K. "Historical Study of the Werwolf in Literature" in *P.M.L.A.,* 9.1–41. 1894.
Tibbals, K. "Elements of Magic in the Romance of *William o Palerne*" in *M.Ph.,* 1.355–71. 1903.
Wells. I [12].

5. *Sir Beues of Hamtoun*

During the mediaeval period, the *Bevis* legend achieved European currency: versions exist in Romance, Germanic, Celtic and Slav languages. Recounting the extraordinary adventures of a hero, Bevis, in particular the "loss and recovery of his inheritance, his fights with Saracens and dragons, his marriage with a converted princess, his gain of innumerable possessions, [it] is distinctive chiefly for its amazing absorption of familiar *motifs* and for its blending of elements drawn from romance, fairy tale, saint legend, and heroic epic" (Hibbard, below, 115). The legend is a hotch-potch of adventures garnered from the most diverse sources. The original version nowadays tends to be attributed to a Frenchman who put it together, probably not before 1200, out of his own knowledge of contemporary romance.

The M.E. version, perhaps first translated at Southampton, is extant in six MSS., the earliest being MS. Auchinleck (1330–40). The latter preserves it in 4,620 ll. The first 474 are in six-line tail-rhyme stanzas, aabaab or aabccb; the remainder are in short couplets.

Bibliography.
C.B.E.L., 1.150.

Edition.
Kölbing, E. *Sir Bevis of Hamton.* E.E.T.S. E.S., 46, 48, 65. 1885–94. [With full critical apparatus.]

Discussion.
Billings, 36–41.
Boje, C.   *Ueber den altfrz. roman* v. *Bueve de Hamtone.* Halle, 1909.
Hibbard.   *Med. Rom.,* 115–26.
Hoyt, P. C.   "The Home of the Beves Saga" in *P.M.L.A.,* 17.237–46. 1902. [Argues that it is developed out of the Horn legend in England.]
Matzke, J. E.   "The Oldest Form of the Beves Legend" in *M.Ph.,* 10.19–54. 1912–13.
Wells.   I [13].
Zenker, R.   *Boeve-Amlethus, Das altfrz. Epos Boeve de Hantone und der Ursprung der Hamletsage.* Berlin, 1905.

6.   *Athelston*

In 811 ll., mostly in twelve-line tail-rhyme stanzas, preserved in a unique copy in MS. Caius Coll. Cbg. 175 (15th c.), *Athelston* (composed c. 1350) tells the story of four blood-brothers, one of whom, viz., Athelston, became king of England, another Archbishop of Canterbury, and the other two, earls. The plot is simple: one of the earls falsely accuses his peer to the king, and the remainder of the poem is taken up with a graphic description of the various incidents that followed. These include a brutal assault (with earlier literary parallels), an excommunication, a threatened rebellion, trials by ordeal, a penance and finally an execution. The narrative holds the attention from beginning to end. Trounce (ed., below, p. 52) derives the poem from an A.N. metrical original written at Bury St. Edmunds, but Taylor (below) assigns it to the N.E. Midland dialect.

Bibliography.
C.B.E.L., 1.150–1.

Editions.
French and Hale, 177–205.
Trounce, A. McI.   *Athelston, a Middle English Romance.* O.U.P., 1933. [With full apparatus.]
Zupitza, J.   "Die Romanze von Athelston" in *E.St.,* 13.331–414. 1889. [Valuable notes.]

Translation.
Rickert.   *Early Eng. Rom.*

Discussion.
Billings, 32–6.

Hibbard. *Med. Rom.*, 143–6.
Taylor. Leeds Studies in English, 4.47.
Trounce (above).
Wells. I [14].
Zupitza, J. "Die Romanze von Athelston" in *E.St.*, 14.321–44.
1890.

7. *The Tale of Gamelyn*

Theme: the adventures that befell a youth in the course of regaining his heritage. MSS.: sixteen, none earlier than the fifteenth century, and all preserved after the fragmentary Cook's *Tale*, in MSS. of the Canterbury Tales. Source: an E.Midl. fourteenth-century version, compounded from tradition, fact and folk-tale. Metre: some 900 ll. of irregular length rhyming in couplets and each with a cæsura, the first half-line normally having four stresses, the second, three. Alliteration is found in stock phrases. Important as a predecessor of the Robin Hood Ballads, and as an indirect source of *As You Like It*.

Bibliography.
C.B.E.L., 1.150.
Hammond, E. P. *Chaucer: A Bibliographical Manual*. New York, 1908. Pp. 425–6.

Editions.
French and Hale, 209–35.
Skeat, W. W. *The Complete Works of Geoffrey Chaucer*. 7 vols. Oxford, 1894–7. 4.645–67, 5.477–89.

Translation.
Rickert. *Rom. Friendship*, 1.85 ff.

Discussion.
Hibbard. *Med. Rom.*, 156–63.
Lindner, F. "The Tale of Gamelyn" in *E.St.*, 2.94–114, 321–43.
1878–9.
Wells. I [15].

II. ARTHURIAN LEGENDS

For a general account of Arthur see some modern work of reference like *Encycl. Brit.* Here it must suffice to say that while there may have been a fifth or sixth century British chief who fought with distinction against the Saxons, the story of the romantic figure of King Arthur probably early achieved popularity amongst the Celts in this country and in Brittany. "Arthur gradually became a king, a conqueror of nations, one of the greatest heroes of the world, the foremost of the three Christian representatives among the Nine Worthies, and greatest of the nine. About him gathered a vast body of literature in all civilised tongues. Gradually there came to be associated with his story and that of his court, cycles of romance that developed in connexion with a number of originally independent heroes—Gawain, Perceval, Eric, Launcelot, Tristram—and also with the Holy Grail. Most of these cycles, as wholes and as individual tales, were loosely connected with the story of Arthur himself." (Wells, I. 2).

Following Wells's excellent arrangement, the romances will be treated below under the following heads: A, the Whole Life of Arthur; B, Merlin and the Youth of Arthur; C, Launcelot and the Last Years of Arthur; D, Gawain; E, Perceval; F, The Holy Grail; G, Tristram.

Bibliography.
Billings, 85.
C.B.E.L., 1.130–140.
Parry, J. J. *Bibliography of Arthurian Critical Literature for the Years 1922–9.* New York, 1931.
Parry, J. J., and Schlauch, M. *Bibliography of Arthurian Critical Literature for the Years 1930–5.* New York, 1936.

Discussion.
Baker, I. *The King's Household in the Arthurian Court from Geoffrey of Monmouth to Malory.* Washington, D.C., 1937. [On character and personnel.]
Bruce, J. D. *The Evolution of Arthurian Romance from the Beginnings down to the Year 1300.* 2 vols. 2nd ed., with supplement. Hilka, Göttingen, 1928. [An invaluable guide.]
Chambers, E. K. *Arthur of Britain.* London, 1927. [On origins and early history. Contains a valuable bibliographical note, pp. 283–94.]
Cross, T. P., and Nitze, W. A. *Lancelot and Guenevere. A Study in the Origins of Courtly Love.* C.U.P., 1930.
Dickinson, W. H. *King Arthur in Cornwall.* New York, 1900, etc.
Faral, E. *La Légende Arthurienne: Etudes et Documents.* 3 vols

Paris, 1930. [Deals with the earliest Latin writings concerned with Arthur, not with English Arthurian literature.]

Fletcher, R. H. *The Arthurian Material in the Chronicles*. Boston, 1906. [Contains an account of the various chronicles. A useful reference book.]

Jaffray, R. *King Arthur and the Holy Grail. An Examination of the Early Literature pertaining to the Legends of King Arthur and of the Holy Grail*. London, 1928.

Jones, W. L. *King Arthur in History and Legend*. C.U.P., 1911. [A brief but useful introd.]

Ker, W. P. *Epic and Romance*. 2nd ed. London, 1908. [See Chap. V: "Romance and the Old French Romantic School."]

Lewis, C. B. *Classical Mythology and Arthurian Romance*. O.U.P., 1932.

Loomis, R. S. *Celtic Myth and Arthurian Romance*. New York, 1927.

Loomis, R. S. "By what Route did the Romantic Tradition of Arthur reach the Continent" in *M.Ph.*, 33.225–38. 1936.

MacCallum, M. W. *Tennyson's Idylls and Arthurian Story from the Sixteenth Century*. Glasgow, 1894. [The introd., pp. 1–108, discusses the origin of the legend and its treatment in the romances.]

Malone, K. "The Historicity of Arthur" in *J.E.G.Ph.*, 23.463–91. 1924.

Maynadier, H. *The Arthur of the English Poets*. Boston, 1907.

Newell, W. W. *King Arthur and the Round Table*. Boston, 1897.

Nutt, A. *Celtic and Medieval Romance*. London, 1904.

Rhys, J. *Studies in the Arthurian Legend*. Oxford, 1891. [Standard.]

Saintsbury, G. *The Flourishing of Romance*. Edinburgh, 1897. [See Chap. III on "Matter of Britain".]

Van der Ven-ten Bensel, E. F. W. M. *The Character of King Arthur in English Literature*. Amsterdam, 1925. [Useful and well-documented analysis.]

Vinaver, E., and Williams, F. M. *Arthuriana: A Review of Medieval Studies*. 1–2. Oxford, 1929–31.

Weston, J. L. *King Arthur and His Knights. A Survey*. London, 1905.

Wells, I. 2.

A. THE WHOLE LIFE OF ARTHUR

Early English versions: Lawman's *Brut*; *Arthur* in the Latin chronicle of the British Kings; alliterative *Morte Arthure;* chronicles of Rbt. of Gloucester (p. 322), Robert Mannyng (p. 324), and Thomas Bek of Castleford; Malory's famous *Morte d'Arthur;* and the ballad, *The Legend of King Arthur.*

Arthur is first mentioned by Nennius (fl. 796) in his Latin prose *Historia Britonum,* where he is called "dux bellorum". He next appears in the Latin prose *Historia Regum Britanniae* (1135–1477) of Geoffrey of Monmouth (?1100–54, bishop of St. Asaph, 1152–4; see further, p. 403), who considerably enlarged Nennius's material out of his own imagination. Arthur is here idealised as an all-conquering potentate. Of the later accounts, all ultimately derive from Geoffrey's work. In particular, notice that the *Historia* was translated (c. 1150) into A.N. verse by Geoffrey Gaimar, and additionally, that it forms the basis of the A.N. versified *Roman de Brut* or *Geste des Bretons* that the cleric Wace wrote about 1155. The latter is notable as the source of Lawman's *Brut* and because it contains the first mention both of the Round Table and of the legend of the anticipated return of King Arthur. See Wells, I, 2, I; *C.B.E.L.,* 1.131.

1. Lawman's Brut

For a brief account and bibliography of Lawman's versified chronicle of English history in over 32,000 ll., see pp. 320–1.

The story of Arthur, who is here treated as an all-conquering king of England, though in a traditional heroic setting, is narrated in ll. 18,533–28,651. Novelties for which Lawman is responsible comprise the mention of the presence of elves at Arthur's birth— they enchant him—and the anglicisation of the figure of the king. For bibliography, see pp. 321–2, above; and Wells, I [19].

2. Arthur

An unadorned, matter-of-fact, somewhat pedagogic poem of 642 four-stress irregular ll. in couplets contained in an incomplete, Latin chronicle of the British Kings and preserved in the Marquess of Bath's MS. (1430–40). Dialect: Southern, of 1350–1400. Source: Geoffrey of Monmouth's *Historia,* or a similar version. Ed., Furnivall, E.E.T.S., 2. Discussion: Billings, 190–2; Wells, I [20].

3. Morte Arthure

A fine poem of 4,346 long alliterative ll. preserved in the Thornton MS. (1430–40) and composed in the North of England,

c. 1350–1400. Identified, probably incorrectly, with the *Gret Geste of Arthure* ascribed by Wyntoun (p. 277) to Huchown (p. 409). Based on Geoffrey's *Historia*, with features from Lawman. Also noteworthy as the source of Malory's fifth book. Ed.: G. G. Perry, E.E.T.S., 8, 1865, rev. Brock, 1871; M. M. Banks, London, 1900; E. Björkman, Heidelberg, 1915. Discussion: Billings, 181–9; Wells, I [21]; Gordon, E. V., and E. Viagner, "New Light on the Text of the Alliterative 'Morte Arthure'" in *Medium Ævum*. 6.81–99. Trans. Ev. Lib., 634. Bibliography: *C.B.E.L.*, 1.136–7. See also p. 410.

B. MERLIN AND THE YOUTH OF ARTHUR

The accounts are of two types: (1) historical or chronicle, and (2) literary or romance.

(1) Merlin, famous among the Welsh as a seer and sorcerer (see *Encycl. Brit.*), is first associated with Arthur in the *Historia* (1135–47) of Geoffrey of Monmouth, who, however, before 1135 had written a *Book of Merlin*, now lost. The germ of the Merlin legend probably lies in Nennius's account (*Historia Britonum*) of the boy Ambrosius who gave King Vortiger valuable prophetic assistance during the erection of his citadel. In his narrative of Merlin in his *Historia*, Geoffrey elaborates Nennius's account, and identifies Ambrosius with Merlin.

(2) The romance treatments of the figure of Merlin all ultimately derive from Robert De Borron's French, fragmentary poem, *Merlin* (504 ll.), dating from the end of the twelfth century.

For a bibliography of *Merlin*, see Wells, I.2.II; *C.B.E.L.*, 1.131–3; and in particular W. E. Mead's *Outlines of the Legend of Merlin*, E.E.T.S., 112.

Of the three English romances on Merlin, viz., *Arthour and Merlin*, the prose *Merlin* (c. 1450–60) and Lovelich's tedious metrical *Merlin*, (c. 1450; ed. E. A. Kock, E.E.T.S. E.S., 93, 112) in some 28,000 ll. in couplets, only the first is noteworthy.

Arthour and Merlin

Two metrical recensions, A and Y, both in four-stress couplets, are extant: (A) MS. Auchinleck (1330–40), 9,938 ll., composed in the S.E. about 1250–1300, and (Y) MS. Lincoln's Inn Lib. 150 (c. 1400), 2,490 ll., Percy Folio MS., 2,378 ll., and two later MSS. containing shorter texts. Ed.: Kölbing, A. E. B., Leipzig, 1890. Discussion: Billings, 111–23; Wells, I [24]. Bibliography: *C.B.E.L.*, 1.133.

C. LANCELOT AND THE LAST YEARS OF ARTHUR

Whereas Lancelot (see *Encycl. Brit.*) was the hero of the huge, popular, influential, thirteenth-century French prose *Lancelot*, versions of which were made in all cultivated European languages, he appears only latish in English romances and, moreover, as a relatively unimportant figure, never attaining to equal fame with Gawayn. Only three romances prior to 1500 are concerned with him, viz., *Le Morte Arthur* (see below), *Lancelot of the Laik* and Malory's *Morte D'Arthur* (see p. 297).

Bibliography.
C.B.E.L., 1.131.

Discussion.
App, A. J. *Lancelot in English Literature, his Rôle and Character.*
Washington, D.C., 1929.
Bruce. *Evolution Arth. Rom.*, 1.192–216.
Cross and Nitze (above).
Wells. I. 2. III.
Weston, J. *Legend of Sir Lancelot du Lac.* London, 1901.

1. Lancelot of the Laik

This inferior and loose paraphrase of the French *Lancelot* is preserved in MS. Cbg. Univ. Lib. Kk. I. 5 (15th c.), and comprises 3,486 pentameters in couplets in Lowland Scots. It tells of how Lancelot in the service of Love achieves renown in the wars of Arthur and Guliot. Ed.: W. W. Skeat, E.E.T.S., 6; M. M. Gray, S.T.S., 12. Discussion: Billings, 192–200; Wells, I [27]. Bibliography: *C.B.E.L.*, 1.138–9.

2. Le Morte Arthur

This is one of the gems among M.E. romances and will be read with delight. Its themes are the loves of the Maid of Ascolot and Lancelot (undoubtedly the hero of the whole narrative), of the guilty passion of the Queen and Lancelot and its revelation by Gawayne, Modred's treason and seizure of Arthur's realm, the fateful battle in Cornwall, the bearing away of Arthur to Avalon, and the subsequent deaths of Lancelot and the Queen. Accordingly in subject-matter, the romance resembles Books XX and XXI of Malory's *Morte d'Arthur*. Probably both versions depend upon the same source, viz., a lost version of the French *Mort Artu*, the last part of the French *Vulgate Lancelot*.

The poem, preserved in a unique text written by two scribes

in MS. Harley 2252 (late 15th c.), was probably composed in the N.W.M. dialect about the end of the fourteenth century. It has 3,834 four-stress lines—136 are assumed to be missing after l. 1181—arranged in eight-line stanzas normally rhyming abababab. Alliteration is frequent. Ed.: Bruce, E.E.T.S. E.S., 88 [1903]; Hemingway, Boston, 1912. Discussion: Billings, 200–8; Wells, I [29]. Bibliography: *C.B.E.L.*, 1.138.

D. GAWAIN

The legend of Gawain probably originated amongst the Celts as a myth, but owes its development to the poets of Northern France.

Gawain is the first of the heroes to appear in Arthurian romances, in which he is the king's sister's son, and always his close associate. He figures in them all and is often more conspicuous than the supposed hero of the piece. He alone of Arthur's knights became the hero of a cycle of romances. In all the earlier prose narratives, he is the perfect knight. He is similarly portrayed in all the English romances except *Le Morte Arthur* and Malory's *Morte d'Arthur*. In later French stories, Gawain's character greatly deteriorates, but the only English tales to reveal him in his less virtuous rôle are the two just mentioned.

The Gawain cycle of English romances comprises:—*Sir Gawayne and the Grene Knight, The Grene Knight, The Turke and Gowin, Syre Gawene and the Carle of Carelyle, The Awntyrs of Arthur, Golagrus and Gawain, The Avowynge of Arthur, Ywain and Gawain, The Weddynge of Sir Gawen and Dame Ragnell, The Jeaste of Syr Gawayne,* and *Libeaus Desconus*. Three of these, viz., *Sir Gawayne and the Grene Knight, Golagrus and Gawain,* and *Ywain and Gawain,* are specially attractive, the first being generally acknowledged as supreme amongst romances in English.

Bibliography.
C.B.E.L., 1.131.

Discussion.
Bruce. *Evolution Arth. Rom.*, 2.91–103. [On "Miss Weston's Gawain-Complex".]
Encycl. Brit., s.n.
Kittredge, G. L. *A Study of Gawain and the Green Knight*. Cambridge (Mass.), 1916.

Weston, J. L.   *The Legend of Sir Gawain. Studies upon its Original Scope and Significance.* London, 1897.
Wells.   I.2.IV.

1.   Sir Gawayne and the Grene Knight

The unique text of this admirable poem in the W. Midl. dialect, is extant in MS. Cott. Nero A X (now X+4; 14th or early 15th c. hand). Its 2,530 ll. are arranged in unequal stanzas, the stanza comprising a number of long alliterative lines followed by a sequence of five short ones rhyming ababa, the first of which has one stress, the remainder three each. The poem, divided into four fyttes, was written c. 1370 by an unknown author, who may also have composed *Pearl*, *Purity* and *Patience* (see "The Pearl Poet," pp. 300 ff.). The source may be French. There are two main themes: a beheading, and a chastity test. See Wells I [31].

Bibliography.
C.B.E.L., 1.135–6.

Editions.
Gollancz, I.   *Facsimile of MS. Cotton Nero A. X* (*Pearl, Cleanness Patience* and *Sir Gawain*). E.E.T.S., 162. 1922, 1931.
Gollancz, I., Day, M., and Serjeantson, M. S.   *Sir Gawain and the Green Knight.* E.E.T.S., 210, 1940.
Tolkien, J. R. R., and Gordon, E. V.   *Sir Gawain and the Green Knight.* 2nd ed. Oxford, 1936. [Standard ed.]

Translations.
Hare, H.   *Sir Gawayne and the Green Knight.* With an Introduction, Notes, and Bibliography by R. M. Wilson. London, 1948. [In verse.]
Kirtlan, E. J. B.   *Sir Gawain and the Green Knight, with an Introduction on the Arthur and Gawain Sagas in Early English Literature.* London, 1912.
Neilson and Webster. *Chief British Poets.* Boston, 1916.
Weston, J. L.   *Romance, Vision and Satire.* Boston, 1912.

2.   Golagrus and Gawain

Theme: the glorification of Gawayn's courtesy and chivalry. Source: the French *Roman de Perceval*, but there is much divergence. The text, for which there is no MS., survives in a printed Scottish version, dated 1508, now in the Advocates' Library at

Edinburgh. Date of composition: 1450–1500. This anonymous romance, which really comprises two vigorous, independent tales (ll. 1–234, and 235–end), has 1,362 ll. in thirteen-line stanzas rhyming ababababcdddc. The first nine of each stanza are long-alliterative with a medial pause, while 10–12 have three stresses, and l. 13, two. The poet reveals a notable power of description.

Bibliography.
C.B.E.L., 1.139.

Editions.
Amours, F. J. *Scottish Alliterative Poems in Riming Stanzas.* S.T.S. Edinburgh, 1892–7.
Trautmann, M. "Golagrus und Gawain" in *Angl.*, 2.395–440. 1879. [With critical introd.]

Discussion.
Billings. 168–73.
Ketrick, P. J. *The Relation of "G. and G." to the O.Fr. "Perceval".* Washington, D.C., 1931. [Suggests author composed his poems after 1440 and used a French prose version of the *Perceval* Continuation.]
Wells. I [37].

3. *Ywain and Gawain*

This excellent metrical narrative recounts the adventures of a knight called Ywain who marries the widow of one of his vanquished foes, is separated from her, but after performing many heroic deeds is re-united with her. The figure of Arthur furnishes a convenient background, while Gawain's function is merely to enhance Ywain's distinction. The poem, which has two natural divisions, the second beginning at l. 1,449, is a condensed version of the court-epic, *Yvain, ou Le Chevalier au Lion*, the masterpiece of Chrétien de Troyes, most famous of the Old French romance writers.

Consisting of 4,032 octosyllabic ll. in couplets with some alliteration, especially in stock phrases, the text is preserved in MS. Galba E IX (early 15th c.). Very likely the poem was composed in the Northern dialect (c. 1300–50).

Bibliography.
C.B.E.L., 1.134.

Editions.

Schleich, G.   *Ywain and Gawain.* Oppeln and Leipzig, 1887.
Ritson.   *A.E.M.R.,* 1.1–169.

Selection.
French and Hale.   485–527. [1,448 ll.]

Discussion.
Billings.   153–60.
Brown, A. C. L.   *Ywain, A Study in the Origins of Arthurian Romance.* Boston, 1903.
Loomis.   *Celtic Myths,* Bks. I and II.
Wells.   I [39].
Zenker, R.   *Forschungen zur Artusepik: I. Ivainstudien.* Halle, 1921. [Contains complete bibliography, survey of theories about the source of the O.Fr. poem, and a discussion of the relationship of *Yvain* to the Welsh *Owain.*]

E. PERCIVAL

There is only one M.E. representative of the Perceval legend, a widely dispersed folk-tale of great antiquity, which became associated with Arthurian legend in the twelfth century. Note however its appearance in Malory. The first occurrence of the tale in metrical form was in Chrétien de Troyes' unfinished *Perceval* or *Conte del Graal.*

Bibliography.
C.B.E.L., 1.131–2.

Discussion.
Billings.   127–32.
Bruce.   *Evolution Arth. Rom.,* 1.313–41; 2.1–19.
Encycl. Brit., s.n.
Harper, G. M.   "Legend of the Holy Grail" in *P.M.L.A.,* 8.77–140. 1893.
Nutt, A.   *Studies on the Legend of the Holy Grail.* London, 1888.
Wells.   I.2.V.
Weston, J. L.   *The Legend of Sir Perceval.* 2 vols. London, 1906–9.

Sir Percyvelle of Galles

This metrical romance of 2,286 ll., arranged in sixteen-line tail-rhyme stanzas usually *aaabcccbdddbeeeb,* tells how (Arthur's sister's son) Percyvelle is, after his father's death, brought up by his mother in a forest away from mankind, how he returns to the world, accomplishes heroic deeds, for which Arthur knights him, wins a royal bride, and, finally, how he returns to rescue his mother from her misfortunes. It has no outstanding merits. Nor does it mention the quest of the Grail.

The text is preserved in the Thornton MS. (1430–40). Date of composition: 1350–1400; dialect: Northern.

Bibliography.
C.B.E.L., 1.137–8.

Editions.
Campion, J., and Holthausen, F. *Sir Percyvelle of Galles.* Heidelberg, 1913.
French and Hale. 531–603.

Translation.
Weston. *Ch. M.E. P.* 236–62.

Discussion.
Billings. 123–34.
Brown, A. C. L. "The Grail and the English Sir Perceval" in *M.Ph.*, 16.553 ff.; 17.361 ff.; 18.201 ff. and 661 ff.; 22.79 ff. and 113 ff.
Griffith, R. H. *Sir Perceval of Galles. A Study of the Sources.* Chicago, 1911.
Wells. I [44].

F. THE HOLY GRAIL

The only M.E. romances before Malory to deal with the quest of the Grail are *Joseph of Arimathie* and the *History of the Holy Grail* (see below). The legend first appears in an incomplete poem of 10,601 ll., entitled *Perceval* or *Le Conte du Graal* or *Le Conte del Graal* of Chrétien de Troyes, who began it before 1188. The subject may be studied in the following items.

Bibliography.
Bruce. *Evolution Arth. Rom.,* 2.398–402.
C.B.E.L., 1.132.

Discussion.
Billings. 99–108.
Brown, A. C. L. *The Origin of the Grail Legend.* London, 1943. [Scholarly.]
Bruce. *Evolution Arth. Rom.*

2A

THE BEGINNINGS OF ENGLISH LITERATURE

Encycl. Brit., see *Grail.*

Harper, G. M. "The Legend of the Holy Grail" in *P.M.L.A.*, 8.77–140. 1893. [Historical survey.]

Jaffray, R. *King Arthur and the Holy Grail.* London, 1928.

Newell, W. W. *The Legend of the Holy Grail and the Perceval of Crestien of Troyes.* Cambridge (Mass.), 1902.

Nutt, A. *Studies on the Legend of the Holy Grail.* London, 1888.

Nutt, A. *The Legends of the Holy Grail.* London, 1902.

Waite, A. E. *The Holy Grail, Its Legends and Symbolism.* London, 1933.

Wells. I.2.VI.

Weston, J. L. *The Quest of the Holy Grail.* London, 1913.

Weston, J. L. *From Ritual to Romance.* Cambridge, 1920.

1. *Joseph of Arimathie*

709 long alliterative ll. preserved in Vernon MS. (1370–80) and composed c. 1350. About 100 ll. at beginning lost. Source: the French *Grand Saint Graal* (c. 1240), attributed to Robert de Borron. Notable as one of the earliest alliterative poems in M.E. as distinct from O.E. Ed.: W. W. Skeat, *The Alliterative Romances of Arimathie*, E.E.T.S., 44. Discussion: Billings, 96–109; Wells, V [45]. Bibliography: *C.B.E.L.*, 1.134.

2. *History of the Holy Grail*

Author: Henry Lovelich, a skinner, who also wrote the metrical *Merlin* (p. 363). Extant in 23,794 4-beat ll. rhyming in couplets, in MS. C.C.C.C. 80 (late 15th c.). Beginning lost. Composed c. 1450. Source: the French *Grand Saint Graal.* Of little merit. Ed.: F. J. Furnivall, *Lovelich's History of the Holy Grail*, Parts I–IV, E.E.T.S., E.S. 95 (with discussion). Discussion: Billings, 109–11; Wells, I [46]. Bibliography: *C.B.E.L.*, 1.138.

G. TRISTRAM

There is only one romance in English prior to Malory concerned with the legend of Tristram, which may have originated in this country. See further Billings, 87–91; *Encycl. Brit.*, s.n., MacNeill (below) and Wells, I. 2. VII. Bibliography: *C.B.E.L.*, 1.132.

Sir Tristram

Preserved in MS. Auchinleck (1330–40) in 3,344 ll. arranged

in 11-line stanzas. The ll. have 3 stresses, except for l. 9, with 1 stress. Composed in the North (-Midlands) just before 1300 and doubtfully attributed to Thomas of Erceldoun. Is unmoral, distinctly popular in tone, apparently having been intended for recitation to the masses. Ed.: Kölbing, *Die Nordische und die Englische Version der Tristan-Sage*, I, II, Heilbronn, 1872–82; MacNeill, G. P., *Sir Tristrem*, S.T.S., 1886 [valuable historical introd.]. Trans.: Weston, *Ch. M.E.P.*, 141–73. Discussion: Billings, 85–95; Wells, I [48]. Bibliography: *C.B.E.L.*, 1.133–4.

III. CHARLEMAGNE LEGENDS

The best account of the legends of Charlemagne, the most notable historical medieval personage in medieval romance and minstrelsy, is J. L. Weston's *The Romance Cycle of Charlemagne*, London, 1901. See also W. P. Ker's *Epic and Romance*, Chaps. I and IV, also the *Encycl. Brit.*, s.n., A. B. Taylor's *Introduction to Medieval Romance*, Chap. II, and Wells, I. 3. *Bibliography: C.B.E.L.*, 1.140.

The cycle's extant English representatives, all of which are mainly based upon French sources, fall into three groups: (A) the *Firumbras*-group, viz., *The Sowdone of Babylone, Sir Firumbras*, and Caxton's *Charles the Grete* (1485); (B) the *Otuel*-group, viz., *Roland and Vernagu, The Siege of Melayne, Otuel, Duke Rowlande and Sir Ottuell*, and the so-called Fillingham *Otuel;* (C) detached romances, viz., *The Song of Roland, The Taill of Rauf Coilzear, The Four Sons of Aymon* and *Huon of Burdeux*.

A. THE FIRUMBRAS-GROUP

The source of the group is apparently a (lost) French poem *Balan*, now represented by Mousket's rhyming Chronicle of c. 1243.

1. *The Sowdone of Babylone*

The theme is the destruction of Rome by the Saracens. Extant in the Fenwick MS. (formerly Phillips). Composed c. 1400 in the E. Midlands, and comprises 3,274 4-stress ll. rhyming abab, but there is much irregularity. Ed.: E. Hausknecht, E.E.T.S., E.S., 38. Sel.: French and Hale, 239–84 (ll. 1,491–3,326). See Billings, 47–52; Wells, I [49]. Bibliography: *C.B.E.L.*, 1.142.

2. *Sir Firumbras*

This version of the favourite Charlemagne legend, consisting of 5,825 ll. (the beginning and end being missing), was composed in the South (c. 1375–1400), and is preserved in MS. Ashmole 33 (end of 14th c.; the author's autograph). Lines 1–3,410 are septenary couplets with internal rhyme; 3,411–end, in tail-rhyme 6-line stanzas aabaab. The theme is the historic combat between Roland, Charlemagne's nephew, and the Saracen, Firumbras, king of Alexandria. Ed.: S. J. H. Herrtage, E.E.T.S. E.S., 34. See also Billings, 52–8; Wells, I [50]; and, for a bibliography, *C.B.E.L.*, 1.141.

Another version in 1,842 ll. rhyming in couplets and derived from the same source as the above, is preserved in the fifteenth century (2nd half) Fillingham MS. (now B.M. Addit. MS. 37492). Each line consists of two parts separated by a cæsura, each half having 2 or (more usually) 3 stresses. Ed. (with valuable introd.): M. I. O'Sullivan, E.E.T.S., 198.

3. *Charles the Grete*

A prose translation made by Caxton and printed by him in 1485, from Jean de Bagnyon's *Fierebras*. Ed.: S. J. H. Herrtage, E.E.T.S. E.S., 36, 37. Wells, I [51].

B. THE OTUEL-GROUP

The Otuel-matter is thought to derive from a supposed cyclic poem *Charlemagne and Roland* about the warfare with the Saracens.

1. *Roland and Vernagu*

This disjointed and unpoetical account of Charlemagne's relief of Constantinople and his subsequent conquest of Spain, and of Roland's slaying of the pagan giant Vernagu, comprises 880 3-stress ll. in 12-ll. tail-rhyme stanzas, aabccbddbeeb, composed in the N. Midlands, and preserved in MS. Auchinleck (1330–40). Ed.: S. J. H. Herrtage, E.E.T.S. E.S., 39. See Billings, 58–63; Wells, I [52]. Bibliography: *C.B.E.L.*, 1.140.

2. *Sege of Melayne*

An incomplete poem about Roland's capture at Milan and subsequent rescue by Archbishop Turpin's crusading clergy is preserved in M.S. Additional 31,042 (15th c.), and was probably composed in the North 1350-1400. Contains 1,602 ll. in tail-rhyme stanzas aabccbddbeeb. Ed.: S. J. H. Herrtage, E.E.T.S

E.S., 35. See Billings, 63–6; Wells, I [53]. Bibliography: *C.B.E.L.*, 1.141.

3. *Otuel*

Acclaimed as the oldest Charlemagne romance in English, *Otuel*, an uninspired, incomplete poem (precise source undetermined) of 1,738 4-stress ll. rhyming in couplets and arranged in short irregular stanzas, survives in MS. Auchinleck (1330–40), probably being composed before 1330 in the S. Midlands. It tells of the Saracen Otuel and his (drawn) duel with Roland, the slayer of Otuel's uncle, Vernagu, of his sudden conversion and his subsequent heroic deeds in Lombardy while fighting against the heathen. Ed.: S. J. H. Herrtage, E.E.T.S., 39. Discussion: Billings, 67–71; O'Sullivan (below); Wells, I [54]. Bibliography: *C.B.E.L.*, 1.140.

A second version in 12-ll. tail-rhyme stanzas, aabaabccbddb, and apparently derived from the same source as the above, is preserved in the first 1,691 ll. of the romance called *Otuel and Roland* (Fillingham MS. [2nd half of 15th c.], now known as B.M. Addit. MS. 37492), Ed.: M. I. O'Sullivan, E.E.T.S., 198. On the relationship of this version to *Roland and Vernagu* (above), see R. N. Walpole, *Charlemagne and Rowland*, C.U.P., 1944.

4. *Duke Rowlande and Sir Ottuell of Spayne*

Contains 1,596 ll. in 12-ll. tail-rhyme stanzas aabaabccbccb and extant in B.M. Addit. MS. 31042 (15th c.). Probably composed c. 1400 in the North of England, the story is similar in general content to *Otuel*, above. Ed.: S. J. H. Herrtage, E.E.T.S. E.S., 35. Discussion: Billings, 71–3; O'Sullivan (above, pp. xlii–lx; relationships); Wells, I [55]. Bibliography: *C.B.E.L.*, 1.141.

C. DETACHED ROMANCES

1. *The Song of Roland*

This is an inferior poetic version of the *Chanson de Roland*, the French national epic. Composed, possibly by a cleric, c. 1400 in the S.W. Midlands, the story is concerned with the annihilation of Charlemagne's rearguard by Saracens in the mountain passes of Spain. The text is preserved in a fragment of 1,049 irregular ll. in couplets in B.M. MS. Lansdowne 388 (?c. 1450), the beginning and end being lost. Ed.: S. J. H.

Herrtage, E.E.T.S., 35. See Billings, 73–9; Wells, I [57].
Bibliography: *C.B.E.L.*, 1.141–2.

2. *The Taill of Rauf Coilzear*

Composed in Scotland 1475–1500 and preserved in the
Advocates' Library, Edinburgh, in a unique copy printed by
R. Lekpreuik, St. Andrews, 1572, this excellent poem recounts
Charlemagne's amusing experiences in the simple home of
Rauf the Collier, of the latter's rise to knightly rank at Charle-
magne's court and his subsequent adventures. The precise
source is unknown, but the background is Scottish. The romance
contains 975 ll. grouped in the popular 13-ll. stanza of the
Gawain-school, the first 9 being long, the rest short. Rhyme
scheme: abababababcddddc. Ed.: F. J. Amours, S.T.S., 27;
W. H. Browne, *The Taill of R. Coilyear*, Baltimore, 1903 (with full
apparatus); S. J. H. Herrtage, E.E.T.S. E.S., 39. Discussion:
Billings, 79–84; H. M. Smyser, "The Taill of Rauf Coilyear and
its Sources" in *Harvard Notes and Studies*, 14.135; Wells, I [58].
Bibliography: *C.B.E.L.*, 1.142. See also p. 411.

IV. LEGENDS OF GODFREY OF BOUILLON

The sole surviving examples of the popular cycle of romances
celebrating the famous crusader Godfrey of Bouillon (c. 1060–
1100), reputed descendant of a swan-maiden, and one of the three
Christian heroes among the Nine Worthies of the Middle Ages,
are the late fifteenth-century, short, but highly dramatic, poem
Chevalere Assigne, and a long prose version written by R. Copland
(fl. 1508–47) and printed by W. Copland (fl. 1556–69), and
again by Wynkyn de Worde under the title of *The History of the
noble Helyas, Knight of the Swanne*. For a bibliography and an
account of the legends, see Hibbard, *Med. Rom.*, 239–52. See
also R. Jaffray, *The Two Knights of the Swan, Lohengrin and Helyas,
A Study of the Legend of the Swan Knight*, London, 1910. See Wells,
I, 4; and, for a bibliography, *C.B.E.L.*, 1.146.

Chevalere Assigne

Consisting of 370 long alliterative ll. and preserved in an
E. Midland version in B.M. MS. Cott. Calig. A II (15th c.),
this poem tells how seven infants became transformed into
swans and were later humanised. Ed.: Lord Aldenham, E.E.T.S.
E.S., 6; French and Hale *M.E. Metr. Rom.*, 859–73. Discussion:
Billings, 228–9; Hibbard, 239; Wells, I [62]. Bibliography:
C.B.E.L., 1.146.

V. LEGENDS OF ALEXANDER THE GREAT

Testimony to the great popularity of the legends of Alexander in early English is furnished by Chaucer who in *The Monk's Tale* wrote:

> The storie of Alisaundre is so commune
> That every wight that hath discrecioun
> Hath herd somewhat or al of his fortune.

The ultimate source of all the Western versions of the legend is the anonymous Greek *Pseudo-Callisthenes* (c. A.D. 200). Thence it was redacted in Latin (c. 340) and later enlarged. By the twelfth century, it had appeared in French, subsequently being considerably expanded. In O.E., the story is represented by *Alexander's Letter to Aristotle* and the *Wonders of the East* (see respectively p. 237 and p. 259, above). Several post-Conquest versions have survived, all somewhat bookish in tone, the most important being mentioned below.

For a general account of the legend, the following may be consulted.

Bibliography.
C.B.E.L., 1.143-4.

Discussion.
Encycl. Brit., Alexander III (The Romance of Alexander). .
Budge, E. A. W. *History of Alexander the Great.* Cambridge, 1889.
Budge, E. A. W. *Life and Exploits of Alexander the Great.* London, 1896.
Lascelles, M. "Alexander and the Earthly Paradise in Medieval English Writings" in *Essays and Studies,* 5.31, 79, 173.
Magoun, F. P. (ed.). *The Gests of King Alexander of Macedon. Two M.E. Alexander Fragments, Alexander A and Alexander B.* London, 1929. [Introd. has a valuable account of works derived from *Pseudo-Callisthenes.*]
Meyer, P. *Alexandre le Grand dans la Littérature Française du Moyen Âge.* 2 vols. Paris, 1896.
Robson, E. I. *Alexander the Great: A Biographical Study.* London, 1929. [Chap. XI discusses the Greek romance.]
Wells. I.5.

1. *The Life of Alisaunder* or *King Alisaunder*

Probably the earliest of this group of legends, and extant in MSS. Laud I 74 (now Misc. 622; c. 1400; ll. 4,772-5,989),

375

Lincoln's Inn L 150 (c. 1400; ll. 1–4,772, 5,989–end), and
Auchinleck (1330–40; fragment), has 8,033 4-stress ll. in couplets.
Very likely composed in Kentish 1250–1300, being based upon
Eustache's *Roman de Toute Chevalerie*. Ed.: H. Weber, *Metr. Rom.*,
Vol. I. Sel.: French and Hale, 789–805 (ll. 3,857–4,281, 6,684–
6,743). See Wells, I[65].

2. *The Alliterative Alexander Fragments*

There are 3 such fragments, A, B, and C. A and B were
translated from the same poem into W. Midl., c. 1340, by one
person, who was not, however, the author of C. This rendering
may have been made in either Northumbrian or N.W. Midl.,
1400–(c.) 1450. All three are connected in theme and are
ultimately derived from a Latin version of Leo's *Historia de Proeliis*.

A. Sometimes called *Alisaunder*, survives in 1,249 long ll.
in MS. Bodley Greaves 60 (16th c.). Ed.: W. W. Skeat, E.E.T.S.
E.S., I (pp. 177 ff.), and (with Latin sources) F. P. Magoun,
Gests of King Alexander of Macedon, London, 1929.

B. Sometimes entitled *Alexander and Dindimus*, has 1,139 long
ll. extant in MS. Bodley 264 (c. 1450). Ed.: W. W. Skeat,
E.E.T.S. E.S., 31, and F. P. Magoun, ib.

C. Known as *The Wars of Alexander*. Preserved in the fifteenth-
century MSS. Ashmole 44 and Dublin Trin. Coll. D, 4, 12.
Ed.: W. W. Skeat, E.E.T.S. E.S., 47.

See Oakden, *Allit. Poetry*, *passim* (on metre, dialect and authorship); Wells, I [66].

3. *The Prose Alexander*

Translated from Latin into the Northern dialect and preserved
in the Thornton MS. (1430–40). Ed.: J. S. Westlake, E.E.T.S.,
143 (text and side-notes only). Wells, I[68].

4. *The Scottish Alexander Buik*

See p. 409.

VI. LEGENDS OF TROY

For their knowledge of the legends of Troy, mediaeval writers
in general depended, not upon Homer, who was both comparatively unknown and regarded with distrust and contempt,
but upon, though probably indirectly, Virgil, Dares Phrygius
(fl. between 400 and 600), and Dictys Cretensis (4th c.).
English authors, however, chiefly relied upon Dictys, Dares,

the Northern-French Benoît de Sainte-More, and the Sicilian Guido delle Colonne. Benoît about 1184 composed his *Roman de Troie*, the great masterpiece of mediaeval classical romances, an Anglo-Norman poem of some 30,000 ll. based upon Dares and Dictys. Guido in 1287, without acknowledgement, from Benoît's poem made a Latin prose translation, *Historia Destructionis Troiae*, which became both popular and authoritative. The following works may be consulted.

Bibliography.
C.B.E.L., 1.145–6.

Discussion.
Gordon, G. S. "The Trojans in Britain" in *Essays and Studies*, 9.
Encycl. Brit. See *Troy, Dares Phrygius, Dictys Cretensis.*
Griffin, N. E. *Dares and Dictys, Introduction to the Study of the Medieval Versions of the Story of Troy.* Baltimore, 1907.
Joly, A. *Benoît de Saint-More et le Roman de Troie.* Paris, 1870–1.
Parsons, A. E. "Trojan Legends in England" in *M.L.R.*, 24.253–264, 394–408. [1929.]
Taylor, H. O. *The Medieval Mind.* London, 1914. [See Chap. XXXII, Sect. 4.]
Wells, I.6.
See also the introductions to the editions of the several items below.

1. *The Gest Historiale of the Destruction of Troy*

A stirring poem preserved in a W. Midl. version of 14,044 long alliterative ll. in a MS. (c. 1450) in the Hunterian Museum, Glasgow University. Probably composed 1350–1400 in N.-W. Midl. Ed.: D. Donaldson and G. A. Panton, E.E.T.S., 39 and 56. Discussion: Oakden, *Allit. Poetry* (dialect, metre, authorship). See Wells, I [72]. Bibliography: *C.B.E.L.*, 1.144–5.

2. *The Seege of Troye*

This poem of some 1,900 ll. in short couplets is preserved in 4 MSS., Harley 525 (shortly after 1400; 1,922 ll.), Lincoln's Inn 150 (c. 1400; 1,988 ll.); Egerton 2862 (end of 14th c.; 1,828 ll.) and Arundel XXII (14th c.; 2,066 ll.). It seems to depend upon a version of Benoît's *Roman*, and was probably composed 1300–25 in the N.W. Midlands. Ed.: (all MSS.) M. E. Barnicle, E.E.T.S., 172; (3 MSS.) L. Hibler-Lebmannsport, *The Seege of Troye*, Graz., 1928. See Wells, I [73]. Bibliography: *C.B.E.L.*, 1.145.

3. *The Laud Troy Book*

The *Troy Book* is extant in MS. Laud 595 (early 15th c.). Consisting of 18,664 ll. in short couplets, with frequent alliteration, it was probably composed c. 1400 in the N.W. Midlands, being mainly founded upon Guido, perhaps supplemented from Benoît. Ed.: J. E. Wülfing, E.E.T.S., 121–2.

Note also the versions of the Troy-Legend made by Lydgate (the metrical *Troy-Book;* see p. 295) and Caxton (the prose *Recuyell of the Historyes of Troye*). See Wells, I [75], I [78]. Bibliography: *C.B.E.L.*, 1.145.

VII. LEGENDS OF THEBES

The fullest M.E. account of Thebes is Lydgate's versified *Siege of Thebes* (see p. 296, above). See Chaucer's treatment of a single phase of the story in his *Knight's Tale*. For a general bibliography, see Wells, I.7, and *C.B.E.L.*, 1.146.

VIII. EUSTACE—CONSTANCE—FLORENCE—GRISELDA LEGENDS

Following Wells (I.8), we may conveniently group under this heading a number of romances which are linked by form, theme, purpose, and region of origin. Each appears in 12-ll. tail-rhyme stanzas, extols the virtues of patience and endurance, and originates from the North of England or the East Midlands. On the figures of St. Eustace or Placidus, Constance, Florence and Griselda, see Hibbard, below. The undermentioned may also be consulted.

Gerould, G. H.   "Forerunners, Congeners, and Derivatives of the Eustace Legend" in *P.M.L.A.*, 19.335–448. 1904.

Gough, A. B.   *The Constance Saga*. Berlin, 1902. [Palaestra 23.]

Griffith, D. D.   *Origin of the Griselda Story*. Seattle, 1931.

Hibbard.   *Med. Rom.*, 1–48, 267–89.

Schlauch, M.   *Chaucer's Constance and Accused Queens*. New York, 1927.

Trounce, A. Mc. I.   "The English Tail-Rhyme Romances" in *Medium Aevum*, 1.87 ff., 168 ff; 2.34 ff, 189 ff; 3.30 ff.

Wells, I.8.

1. *Sir Isumbras*

Extant in one late fourteenth-century MS., and in five fifteenth-century MSS., including Thornton (1430-40), as well as fragmentarily in MS. Gray's Inn 20 (?c. 1350), this romance, composed 1350-1400 by a humble minstrel in the N.E. Midlands, has 804 ll. in 12-ll. tail-rhyme stanzas rhyming aabccbddbeeb. Despite its abundant didacticism and its far-fetched episodes, the piece achieved much popularity, and was printed early. The theme is the afflictions of a knight due to his neglect of God, and his final attainment, by deeds of prowess, of the rewards of Heaven. Ed.: Halliwell, *Thornton Romances*, London, 1844 [Camden Soc.]; G. Schleich, *Ysumbras*, Berlin, 1901 [Palaestra 15]. See also Hibbard, *Med. Rom.*, 3–11; Wells, I [81]. Bibliography: *C.B.E.L.*, 1.156–7.

2. *Sir Eglamour of Artois*

Composed in the North 1350–1400, probably by some unknown Englishman, this popular romance, a mosaic of stock incidents, contains, in the best MS., viz., Thornton (1,430–40), 1,335 ll., in 113 12-ll. tail-rhyme stanzas rhyming aabccbddbeeb. There are three fifteenth-century MSS., five sixteenth-century ed., and the transcript of a sixth in the Percy Folio. A single leaf written late in the fourteenth century is extant in MS. Egerton 2862. Ed.: Halliwell, *Thornton Romances*, London, 1844; G. Schleich, *Sir Eglamour*, Berlin, 1906 [Palaestra 53]. See Hibbard, *Med. Rom.*, 274–8; Wells, I [82]. Bibliography: *C.B.E.L.*, 1.157.

3. *Sir Torrent of Portyngale*

Extant in a single MS., Chetham 8009, and in a few fragments of a sixteenth-century printed ed., this prolix poem contains 2,669 ll., in 12-ll. tail-rhyme stanzas. It was probably composed by a cleric in the E. Midlands late in the fifteenth century, and its incidents are very similar to those of *Sir Eglamour* (above). Ed.: E. Adam, E.E.T.S. E.S., 51 See Hibbard, *Med. Rom.*, 279–82; Wells, I [83]. Bibliography. *C.B.E.L.*, 1.159.

4. *Octavian*

Two versions of this romance, wholly independent, exist. A South-Eastern version, composed c. 1350, is preserved in the fifteenth-century MS. Cott. Calig. A ii and comprises 1,962 ll. rhyming aabab, the *b*-ll. having two stresses, the *a*-ll. four.

Edited by Weber, *Metr. Rom.* 3.157–239. The second version was probably composed in the North c. 1350 and survives in 12-ll. tail-rhyme stanzas in two MSS., viz., Cbg. Univ. Lib. ff. ii, 38 (15th c.; 1,731 ll.), and Thornton (1430–40; 1,628 ll.). Ed.: Halliwell, *The Romance of the Emperor Octavian*, London, 1848. See Hibbard, *Med. Rom.*, 267–73; Wells, I [84]. Bibliography: *C.B.E.L.*, 1.156.

5. *Sir Triamour*

This readable and realistic poem, which besides stock themes includes a tale of a hound faithful unto death, has survived in the fifteenth-century MS. Cbg. Univ. Lib. Ff. II, 38, in the Percy Folio (c. 1650) and in B.M. Addit. 27879 (17th c.). It has 1,719 ll., in 12-ll. tail-rhyme stanzas and was probably composed in the N. Midlands 1400–50. Ed.: Halliwell, Percy Soc., 16, 1846; Schmidt, A. J. E., *Syr Tryamoure*, Utrecht, 1937. See Hibbard, *Med. Rom.*, 283–9; Wells, I [85]. Bibliography: *C.B.E.L.*, 1.159.

6. *The King of Tars*

Composed probably in the (?N.E.) Midlands before 1325, this didactic, theological romance in 12-ll. tail-rhyme stanzas is found in MSS. Auchinleck (1330–40; 1,228 ll.), Vernon (1370–80; 1,122 ll.) and B.M. Addit. 22283 (1380–1400; 1,122 ll.). Its theme is the love of a heathen Saracen Sultan for a Christian princess. Ed.: (all MSS.) Krause, *E.St.* 11.33ff. [1887]; (Vernon MS.) Ritson, *A.E.M.R.*, 2.156–203 [1882]. See Hibbard, *Med. Rom.*, 45–8; Wells, I [86]. Bibliography: *C.B.E.L.*, 1.154.

7. *Le Bone Florence of Rome*

Designed to illustrate Christian fortitude, this romance of 2,187 ll. in 12-ll. tail-rhyme stanzas rhyming aabccbddbeeb has for its theme the trials and sufferings of an innocent woman, who, becoming famous as a healer, brings about the conversion of her former persecutors. Despite the didacticism, it is a good story. Probably composed in the N. Midlands before 1325, and based upon a lost version of the French *Florence de Rome*, it is contained in MS. Cbg. Univ. Lib. Ff. II, 38 (15th c.). Ed.: Ritson, *A.E.M.R.*, 3. 1–92; W. Viëtor, Marburg, 1893. Discussion: Hibbard, *Med. Rom.*, 12–22; Wells, I [87]. Bibliography: *C.B.E.L.*, 1.158.

IX. BRETON LAIS

In English there are six to eight (*Sir Degare* and the *Earl Toulous* being the doubtful cases) romances that depend upon Breton *lais*. The latter are represented by the *lais* of Marie de France (ed.: K. Warnke, 3rd ed., Halle, 1925, and trans. Ev. Lib. 557). All these romances are comparatively short, direct, simple and compact, and all deal with the theme of true love. See Wells, I. 9; E. Rickert, *Seven Lais of Marie de France*. London, 1901; A. McI. Trounce, "The English Tail-Rhyme Romances" in *Medium Ævum*, 1.87, 168, 2.34, 189, 3.30. Bibliography: *C.B.E.L.*, 1.151.

1. *Lai le Freine*

Probably composed early in the fourteenth century, in the South or the S.E. Midlands, and preserved in MS. Auchinleck 1330–40, this highly meritorious story has 340 ll. (in which there is a gap of 13) in octosyllabic couplets. The ending is missing. The source is Marie de France's *Lai de Fresne*, and the writer may have been the person who wrote *Sir Orfeo* (below). Note that the Romance has a Prologue, which, besides being a virtual characterisation of the *lai*-genre, is repeated at the beginning of *Sir Orfeo*. Ed.: Weber, *Metr. Rom.*, 1.357–71; H. Varnhagen, *Angl.*, 3.415–23 (1880); M. Wattie, *The M.E. Lai le Freine*, Northampton (Mass.), 1929. Trans.: E. Rickert, *Rom. Love*, pp. 47 ff. Discussion: Hibbard, *Med. Rom.*, 294–300; Wells, I [88]. Bibliography: *C.B.E.L.*, 1.151.

2. *Sir Orfeo*

This charming tale of minstrelsy and true love, a mediae-valisation of the classical tale of Orpheus and Eurydice, was composed in the S. Midlands or the South shortly after 1300, probably being founded on some unknown French source. Its 602 irregular 4-beat ll. rhyming in couplets are preserved in MS. Auchinleck (1330–40), and in the fifteenth century Ashmole 61 and Harley 3810. The first 22 ll. (prologue) of these latter MSS. are repeated from *Lai le Freine* (above). Ed.: Cook, *Lit. M.E. Reader*, 88 ff.; French and Hale, 323–41; Sisam, *Fourteenth-Century Verse and Prose*, 13–31. Trans.: Rickert, *Rom. Love*, 32 ff.; Weston, *Ch. M.E. P.*, 133–41. Discussion: Hibbard, *Med. Rom.*, 195–9; Wells, I [89]. Bibliography: *C.B.E.L.*, 1.151–2.

3. *Emare*

Acclaimed as the "best M.E. representative of the Constance saga", this romance, composed in the N.E. Midlands towards the end of the fourteenth century and preserved in MS Cotton Calig. A II (1446–60), consists of 1,033 ll., in 12-ll. tail-rhyme stanzas with a variable rhyming scheme. Ed.: French and Hale, 423–55; A. B. Gough, *Old and Middle English Texts*. London, 1901; E. Rickert, E.E.T.S. E.S., 99. See Hibbard, *Med. Rom.*, 23–34; Wells I[90].

4. *Sir Launfal or Launfalus Miles*

From Marie de France's *Lai de Lanval* descend, through an English translation, two independent *M.E.* versions, one being *Sir Launfal*, and the other being represented by three pieces (see next item). An Arthurian romance, *Sir Launfal* was composed in the S.E. by Thomas Chestre (see D.N.B.) during the fourteenth century, and consists of 1,044 ll. in 12-ll. tail-rhyme stanzas, preserved in MS. Cotton Calig. A II (1446–60). Ed.: French and Hale, 345–80. Trans.: Rickert, *Rom. Love*, 57 ff.; Weston, *Ch. M.E. P.*, 204–16 (verse) and *Four Lais of Marie de France*, London 1900 (prose). Discussion: Billings, 144–53; Stokoe, W. C., "The Sources of Sir Launfal: Lanval and Graelent" in *P.M.L.A.*, 63.392–404, 1948; Wells, I [91]. Bibliography: *C.B.E.L.*, 1.152.

5. *Sir Landeval*

The longest of three items representing a second version of the *Launfal* story, this romance has 535 octosyllabic ll. in short couplets, extant in MS. Rawlinson C 86 (16th. c.) It was composed in the South in the fifteenth century. Edited by Kittredge, in *Amer. Journ. of Phil.*, 10.1 ff. Trans.: J. L. Weston in Blair and Chandler, *Approaches to Poetry*. London, 1935. See Billings, 144–53; Wells, I [92]. Bibliography: *C.B.E.L.*, 1.152.

On *Sir Lambewell* (632 octosyllabic couplets in the Percy Folio MS.) and *Sir Lamwell* (fragmentary text, in three MSS.), see Wells, I [93–4]. Bibliography: *C.B.E.L.*, 1.153.

6. *Sir Degare*

Extant in five MSS., the earliest being Auchinleck (1330–40, also the most perfect), and three sixteenth-century editions; was probably composed in the S. (?W.) Midlands 1300–25. Auchinleck preserves the romance in 993 ll. in short couplets.

The tale exhibits an unusually large number of folklore and romance motifs. Ed.: French and Hale, 287–320; G. Schleich, Heidelberg, 1929. Discussion: C. P. Faust, *Sir Degare: a Study of the Texts and Narrative Structure*, O.U.P., 1936; Hibbard, *Med. Rom.*, 301–5; C. H. Slover, "*Sire Degarre*": *a Study in a Medieval Hack Writer's Methods*, in *Univ. of Texas Studies in English*, 11.6–23 [1931]; Wells, I [95]. Bibliography: *C.B.E.L.*, 1.153.

7. *Sir Gowther*

This poem, a version of the *Legend of Robert the Devil*, which enjoyed a European popularity, tells the life-story of a man who commits every sin, is later converted and atones appropriately. Composed about 1400 in the N.E. Midlands or else the North and extant in the 15th-c. MSS. Advocates' Lib. Edbg. 19, 3, I and Royal 17, B, 43, the romance has 757 ll. in 12-ll. tail-rhyme stanzas aabccbddbeeb. Ed.: K. Breul, Oppeln, 1886, 1895 [both texts]; W. J. Thoms, *Early English Prose Romances*, London, 1906. Discussion: Billings, 227–8; Hibbard, *Med. Rom.*, 49–57; Wells, I [96]. Bibliography: *C.B.E.L.*, 1.153.

8. *The Earl of Toulous*

The theme of this rather ordinary poem, a blend of folklore, legend and history, is the Innocent Persecuted Wife. Its supposed Breton origin is nowadays suspect. Composed probably c. 1400 in the N.E. Midlands and preserved in MSS. Cbg. Univ. Lib. Ff. II 38 (15th c.; oldest and best text), Ashmole 45 and 61 (both 16th c.), and Thornton (1430–1440), it consists of 1,224 ll. in 12-ll. tail-rhyme stanzas rhyming aabccbddbeeb. Ed.: French and Hale, 383–419 [Cbg. text]; G. Lüdtke, Berlin, 1881 [critical ed. of all texts]. Trans.: Rickert, *Rom. Love*, 80 ff. Discussion: E. A. Greenlaw, "The Vows of Baldwin" in *P.M.L.A.*, 21.575–636 [1906; see especially 607–635]; Hibbard, *Med. Rom.*, 35–43; Wells, I [97]. Bibliography: *C.B.E.L.*, 1.153.

X. MISCELLANEOUS ROMANCES

A. ROMANCES OF GREEK OR BYZANTINE ORIGIN

1. *Apollonius of Tyre*

Versions of the *Legend of Apollonius* are found in O.E. (p. 244, above), and in Gower's *Confessio Amantis*, Bk. VIII 271 ff. (ed. G. C. Macaulay, Oxford, 1901), as well as fragmentarily in several MSS. of an English version of the *Gesta Romanorum* (edited by Madden, Roxb. Club, 1838). Shakespeare used Gower's story for *Pericles of Tyre*. See further Hibbard 164–73; Wells I [98].

2. *Floris and Blancheflur*

By general consent one of the most charming of the M.E. romances, this tale of true love was composed c. 1250 in the E. Midlands, being founded upon a lost French "aristocratic" version of a legend that was popular throughout Western Europe. The text is preserved in MSS. Egerton 2862 (end of 14th c.; 1083 ll.), Cott. Vitell. D III (1250–1300; 451 ll., 180 being imperfect), Auchinleck (1330–40; 861 ll.), Cbg. Univ. Lib. Gg. 4, 27, 2 (1250–1300; 824 ll.). The beginning is missing. Hausknecht's critical ed. (below) comprises 1,296 ll. with three or four stresses and rhyming in couplets. Ed.: French and Hale, 823–55 (MS. Egerton); E. Hausknecht, Berlin, 1885 (all MSS.); G. H. McKnight, E.E.T.S., 14 (Cbg. Cott. and Egerton); A. B. Taylor, Oxford, 1927 (Egerton and Auchinleck). Trans.: F. J. H. Darton, *Wonder Book of Old Romance*, New York, 1907; Rickert, *Rom. Love*. Discussion: Hibbard, *Med. Rom.*, 184–94; Wells, I [99].

B. COMPOSITES OF COURTLY ROMANCE

Under this heading it is convenient to group five romances, all late and all apparently artificial composites of stock incidents.

1. *Sir Degrevant*

This piece, consisting of 1,904 ll., in 16-ll. stanzas rhyming aaabccccbddddbeeeb, composed in the North 1350–1400, and preserved in MSS. Thornton (1430–40) and Cbg. Univ. Lib. Ff. I 6 (15th c.), is notable for its many excellent descriptions of beautiful and luxurious things. Ed.: (Thornton MS.) Halliwell, *Thornton Romances*, London, 1844, [Camden Soc. 30]; K. Luick, *Wiener Beiträge* 47, Vienna, 1917 [both MSS.]. Trans.: Rickert, *Rom. Love;* 107 ff. Discussion: Hibbard, *Med. Rom.*, 306–11; Wells, I [100]. Bibliography: *C.B.E.L.*, 1.158.

2. *Generydes*

Two versions of this romance extant, but both were probably composed c. 1430 or later, and, despite the difference in length, are closely similar in essentials. One version has 10,086 ll. in short couplets preserved in the Helmingham MS. (1400–1500), whereas the other has 6,995 ll. in rhyme-royal extant in MS. Trin.

Coll. Cbg., Gale O, 5, 2 (? c. 1440). Ed.: (Helmingham) F. J. Furnivall, Roxb. Club, 1866; (Cbg.) W. A. Wright, E.E.T.S., 55, 70. Discussion: Hibbard, *Med. Rom.*, 231–8; Wells, I [101]. Bibliography: *C.B.E.L.*, 1.159.

3. *Parthenope of Blois*

The very popular French story of Partenepeus of Blois and his fairy love Meloir, often accounted one of the loveliest of mediaeval romances, is represented by two M.E. versions, one a mere fragment of 308 4-beat ll., in quatrains abab found in Lord Delamere's MS. (15th c.). The fuller version is preserved in five fifteenth-century texts, the oldest being MS. Univ. Coll. Oxon C 188 (c. 1450; 7,257 ll., with gaps), and the longest, in couplets, in MS. B.M. Addit. 35288 (late 15th c.); 12,195 ll. Despite its inordinate length, prolixity and excessive detail, the rendering has its merits. Ed.: A. T. Bödtker, E.E.T.S. E.S., 109 (all texts). See Hibbard, *Med. Rom.*, 200–13; Wells, I [102]. Bibliography: *C.B.E.L.*, 1.159.

4. *Ipomadon*

The Anglo-Norman romance *Ipomédon* (over 10,000 ll.) written by Hue de Rotelande (Flintshire) is the source of three M.E. versions: (A) *Ipomadon*, composed in N. Lancs., c. 1350 or earlier; 8,890 ll., in 12-ll. tail-rhyme stanzas, aabccbddbeeb, in MS. Chetham 8009 (15th c.); (B) *The Lyfe of Ipomydon* composed shortly after 1400 in the E. Midlands, in 2,343 4-beat ll. in couplets extant in MS. Harley 2252 (late 15th c.); and (C) the prose *Ipomedon*, preserved in MS. Bath 25 (c. 1400; some 1,700 ll. of print).

Ipomadon, the longest and most important version, faithfully reproduces the matter of the French narrative, though not literally. Its subtle analysis of emotions, detailed introspection, wealth of characters, incidents and motives, make it one of the most impressive of M.E. romances. The *Lyfe* is a condensed redaction of the original reproduced from memory. Ed.: (all texts) Kölbing, Breslau, 1899. See Hibbard, *Med. Rom.*, 224–30; Wells, I [103]. Bibliography: *C.B.E.L.*, 1.155.

5. *The Sqyr of Lowe Degre*

The chief textual authority of this romance, composed c. 1450 in the E. Midlands, is W. Copland's ed. (1555–60) in 1,132 ll. Ed.: French and Hale, 721–55; W. E. Mead, *The Squyr of Lowe Degre*, Boston, 1904. Trans.: Rickert, *Rom. Love*, 153 ff. See

Hibbard, *Med. Rom.*, 263–6; Wells, I [104]. Bibliography: *C.B.E.L.*, 1.159–60.

C. HISTORICAL ROMANCES

1. *Richard Coer de Lyon*

Seven MSS. preserve this romance, of which there are apparently two versions very different in content. A lost A.N. romance written about 1230–50 is the source. The first English recension, represented by the fragment of 696 ll. in MS. Auchinleck (1330–40), the earliest MS., was probably composed in Kent before 1300. The author evidently gloried in stories of violence and held Frenchmen in utter contempt. Ed.: K. Brunner, *Der me. Versroman über Richard Löwenherz*, Vienna, 1913 (critical ed. of all the MSS. with introd. notes and German trans.). Trans.: Weston, *Ch. M.E. P.*, 123–32 (parts only). See Hibbard, *Med. Rom.*, 147–55; Wells, I [105]. Bibliography: *C.B.E.L.*, 1.150.

2. *Titus and Vespasian* or *The Destruction of Jerusalem*

Two versions, allegedly independent, of this versified tale are found in M.E., one in short couplets, the other in alliterative ll. The former, founded upon French and Latin sources, is contained in nine fifteenth-century MSS., and in a critical text would amount to some 5,770 ll. The latter is similarly preserved in seven MSS., at least six dating from the fifteenth century. It seems to have been based upon a French version, the latter probably being derived from a Latin account.

Ed.: (Complete version) J. A. Herbert, Roxb. Club, 1905; (Alliterative version) E. Kölbing and M. Day, E.E.T.S., 188. Discussion: Oakden, *Allit. Poet*; Wells, I [106]. Bibliography: *C.B.E.L.*, 1.157–8.

D. ROMANCES FROM FAMILY TRADITION

1. *Melusine*

This prose romance (371 pages of print), preserved in MS. Royal 18 B II (c. 1500) is a close rendering, made about 1500, of a French tale, with the same title, written in 1387 in honour of the Duchess de Bar, first in Latin and then translated into French, probably by the author himself, viz., Jean d'Arras.

Ed.: A. K. Donald, E.E.T.S. E.S., 68. See Wells, I [107].
Bibliography: *C.B.E.L.*, 1.160.

2. *The Romauns of Parthenay* or *Lusignen*

This consists of 6,615 ll., in rhyme-royal preserved in MS. Trin.
Coll. Cbg. R, 3, 17 (late 15th c.), and composed in the N. Midland dialect at the end of the fifteenth century. It was founded
upon a French version, in octosyllabic couplets, of the popular
story of *Melusine* (above) that had been written at the request of
the Dukes of Parthenay to exalt the house of Lusignan. Ed.:
W. W. Skeat, E.E.T.S., 22. See Wells, I [108]. Bibliography:
C.B.E.L., 1.160.

3. *The Knight of Courtesy and the Fair Lady of Faguell*

A poem of 504 4-stress ll., rhyming abab, perhaps composed
from memory, 1450–1500, in the London dialect, and printed by
Copland in 1568. Incorporates the gruesome motif of the Eaten
Heart. Source: French. Ed.: McCausland, Northampton (Mass.)
1922; Ritson, *A.E.M.R.*, 3.172 ff. Trans.: Rickert, *Rom. Love*,
141 ff. Discussion: Hibbard, *Med. Rom.*, 253–62; Wells, I [109].
Bibliography: *C.B.E.L.*, 1.160.

E. DIDACTIC ROMANCES

1. *Amis and Amiloun*

Preserved in four MSS., viz., Auchinleck (1330–40), Douce
326 (15th c.), Harley 2386 (16th c.), and Egerton 2862 (shortly
before 1400), this somewhat melodramatic recension of a
well-known mediaeval tale appears to have been composed
in the N.E. Midlands towards the end of the thirteenth century.
Closely related to the A.N. *Amis e Amilun*, it contains 2,508 ll.,
in 12-ll. tail-rhyme stanzas aabccbddbeeb. The theme is the
life-long devotion of two knights. Ed.: (All texts) Kölbing,
A.E.B., Heilbronn, 1884; Leach, M., *Amis and Amiloun*, E.E.T.S.,
203. Trans.: F. J. H. Darton, *Wonder Book of Old Romance*, New
York, 1924; Rickert, *Rom. Friendship*, 1 ff.; Weston, *Ch. M.E. P.*,
174–204. Discussion: Hibbard, *Med. Rom.*, 65–72; Wells, I
[110]. Bibliography: *C.B.E.L.*, 1.154.

2. *Sir Amadace*

This romance, or more correctly moral tale, extant in two
independent versions in MS. Ireland (Hale, Lancs.; 1450–60)

and MS. Auchinleck (1330–40), was composed, from an unde-termined source, before 1325, in N.W. England, perhaps Lancs. It extends to 864 ll. in 12-ll. tail-rhyme stanzas aabccbdddbeeb. The central theme is the "service which Amadus renders to a dead man [viz. payment of his debts] and the Grateful Dead's subsequent actions". Ed.: (Auch.) H. Weber, *Metr. Rom.*, 3.241 ff.; (Ireland) Robson, Camden Soc., 1842. Trans.: Rickert, *Rom. Friendship*, 40–67; Weston, *Ch. M.E. P.*, 216–28. Discussion: G. H. Gerould, *The Grateful Dead, The History of a Folk Story*. London, 1907; Hibbard, *Med. Rom.*, 73–8; Wells, I [111]. Bibliography: *C.B.E.L.*, 1.154–5.

3. *Sir Cleges*

Apparently a minstrel's tale, this "combination of humo[u]r, piety and romance" in tail-rhyme usually aabccbdddbeeb, has been preserved in two fifteenth-century texts that seem to have been written down from memory or recitation. Perhaps composed in the N. Midlands shortly after 1400, it is extant in MSS. Advocates' Lib. Edin. Jac. 19, 1, 11 (531 ll.) and Ashmole 61 (570 ll., 6 being missing). The poem emphasises the virtue of generosity and the wickedness of greed. Ed: (both MSS.) A. Treichel, *E.St.*, 22.374ff.; (Auch.) G. H. McKnight, *M.E. Humorous Tales*, London, 1913. Trans.: J. L. Weston, *Libeaus Desconus and Sir Cleges*, London, 1902. Discussion: Hibbard, *Med. Rom.* 79–80; Wells, I [112]. Bibliography: *C.B.E.L.*, 1.158.

4. *Roberd of Cicyle*

This popular tale, immediate source unknown, found in eight MSS., three from 1370–1400, and the rest from the fifteenth cen-tury, consists of 444 ll., in short couplets, being composed before 1370 in the S.E. Midlands. It recounts how an Angel usurped the position of the arrogant King Robert of Sicily and so humili-ated him as to bring about a complete change of heart. Excel-lently handled in every way, it may well be considered a pious legend rather than a romance. Ed.: (MS. Vernon [1370–80], the oldest text), French and Hale, 933–46. Trans.: F. J. H. Darton, *Wonder Book of Old Romance*, New York, 1907. Discus-sion: Hibbard, *Med. Rom.*, 58–64; Wells, I [113]. Bibliography: *C.B.E.L.*, 1.157.

SERMONS AND HOMILIES

The following general works should be consulted.

Caplan, H. *Mediaeval Artes Praedicandi, a Hand-List*. New York, 1934.
Crane, T. F. *Medieval Sermon Books*. Proc. Amer. Phil. Soc. 56, No. 5. No, 114, p. 49. 1883.
Deanesly, M. *The Lollard Bible*. Cambridge, 1920.
Little, A. G. *Studies in English Franciscan History*. Manchester, 1917.
Mosher, J. A. *The Exemplum in the Early Religious and Didactic Literature of England*. New York, 1911.
Owst, G. R. *Preaching in Medieval England c. 1350–1450*. C.U.P., 1926.
Owst, G. R. *Literature and Pulpit in Medieval England*. C.U.P., 1933.
Smith, L. T. "English Popular preaching in the Fourteenth Century" in *E.H.R.*, 7.25–36, 1892.
Wells, V.

A. SINGLE SERMONS OR HOMILIES

1. *Hali Meidenheid*

Composed beginning of thirteenth century in the South and preserved in MS. Cott. Titus D 18 (1200–50), and MS. Bodl. 34 (c. 1210), is an alliterative prose homily exalting virginity. Three others, *Juliana* (p. 342), *Margaret* (p. 342), and *Katherine* (p. 342) are concerned with the same theme. Edited by O. Cockayne, *Hali Meidenheid, c. 1200*, E.E.T.S., 18, but rev. ed., with a variant MS., Bodl. 34, by F. J. Furnivall; Colborn, A. F., *Hali Meiðhad*, O.U.P., 1940. See Wells, V [1]. Bibliography: *C.B.E.L.*, 1.168.

2. *Sawles Warde*

A notable prose homily, actually an allegory, with excellent personification and dramatic conversation, based on St. Matt. xxiv, 43. Composed c. 1200 in the W. Midl. dialect and preserved in three MSS.: Cott. Titus 18 (1200–50), Royal 17, A 27 (c. 1230) and Bodl. 34 (c. 1210). It is a free expansion of Chaps. XIII–XV of Bk. IV. of Hugo de St. Victor's treatise *De Anima*. Edited by R. Morris. *Old English Homilies (before 1300)*. *Series 1*., E.E.T.S., 34, pp. 244–67 (with trans.); Hall *Sels.*, 1.117–28, 2.492–524 (apparatus); R. M. Wilson, *Sawles Warde*, Leeds School of English Language, 3, 1939. See Wells, V [2]; *C.B.E.L.*, 1.168–9.

B. GROUPS OF SERMONS OR HOMILIES

1. *The Bodley Homilies*

Preserved in MS. Bodley 343 in a twelfth-century hand. Consist of fourteen prose homilies mostly on themes from the New Testament and pastoral theology. Ed.: A. O. Belfour, *Twelfth-Century Homilies in MS. Bodley 343*. E.E.T.S., 137 [Text with translation] Wells, V [11].

2. *The Lambeth Homilies*

Preserved in MS. Lambeth 487 in a late eleventh-century hand. Originally composed in a S.W. dialect. Comprise sixteen in prose, and one in verse on the *Pater Noster*, which is the first poem in English written in the short couplet. The first five homilies, characterised by homely illustration and the modes of address "good men" and "dear men" may come from the one author. The collection discourses upon a variety of themes, including biblical stories, Shrift, Sunday in general and particular Sundays, the Creed, the *Pater Noster*, the Nativity, Christian duty, etc. Ed.: R. Morris, *Old English Homilies* (c. 1220–30), E.E.T.S., 29. Sel.: Hall, *Sels.*, 1.76–82, 2.407–27 (critical notes, etc.). Discussion: H. E. Allen, "The Author of the 'Ancren Riwle' ", in *P.M.L.A.*, 44.635–80 (see pp. 671 ff.). R. M. Wilson, *Leeds Studies* 4 (collation and provenance). See Wells, V [12]. Bibliography: *C.B.E.L.*, 1.170.

3. *The Trinity College Homilies*

Extant in MS. Trin. Col., Cbg. B, 14, 52 (early fourteenth century; ?London dialect). A collection of thirty-four rambling, prose homilies, probably composed, as the need arose, in the twelfth century. The themes show great variety, and include stories from the Old and New Testaments, Feast Days and particular Sundays, as well as pastoral topics. The author, a folk-etymologist, uses many interesting illustrations, but no *exempla*. Ed.: R. Morris, *Old English Homilies, Series II*, E.E.T.S., 53. Sel.: Hall, *Sels.*, 1.82–8, 2.427–38 (notes). See Wells, V [13]. Bibliography: *C.B.E.L.*, 1.170.

4. *The Ormulum*

Written in the E. Midl. dialect by Orm, a canon-regular possibly of Elsham Priory in N. Lincs. Extant in MS. Bodl.

390

Jun. I (1200–10, though possibly even earlier, cf. Hinkley, *Phil. Quart.* 14.193 ff.), and written by Orm himself, or under his supervision, this is a collection of thirty-two homilies, designed to instruct ordinary people in Church doctrine. Preceding the homilies we have 342 ll. of dedication, a table of contents giving the names of 242 homilies in Latin (the series is therefore incomplete) and a preface of 102 ll. Altogether there are 19,992 ll., and 67 fragmentary ones at the end. Each homily comprises a translation of the Gospel for the day, an exposition thereof and its application. The metre is the septenary, rhymeless, monotonously regular with 15 syllables, and soporofic.

Perhaps the chief interest of the *Ormulum* is its orthographical system, which, invented by Orm himself, has long exercised the minds of philologists (cf. the bibl. in Wells, V [14]), most of whom appear to have assumed that he was a phonetician. But the latest suggestion is that it was in reality a practical system of pointing, to help the reader in putting it over to the hearers (cf. Sisam, below). Ed.: R. Holt, Oxford, 1878 (a new ed. is needed). Sel.: Hall, *Sels.*, 1.112–7, 2.479–92 (apparatus). Discussion: H. C. Matthes, *Die Einheitlichkeit des Orrmulum.* Heidelberg, 1933 (Textual criticism, sources, language); and "Quellenauswertung and Quellenberufung im Orrmulum" in *Angl.*, 59.303–18 (1935); K. Sisam, "MSS. Bodley 334 and 342" in *R.E.S.*, 9.1–12, 1933 (purpose of Orm's orthographical system). See Wells, V [14]. Bibliography: *C.B.E.L.*, 1.170.

5. *Five Kentish Sermons*

Prose: Pre-1250; MS. Laud 471. Ed.: R. Morris, *An English Miscellany*, E.E.T.S., 49; Hall, *Sels.*, 1.214–22, 2.657–75 (apparatus). See Wells, V [15]. Bibliography: *C.B.E.L.*, 1.171–2.

6. *Cotton Vespasian Homilies*

Three prose, plus a scrap of a fourth; MS. Cott. Vesp. A 22; composed 1200–50. Ed.: R. Morris, *Old English Homilies* E.E.T.S., 34. Sel.: Hall, *Sels.*, 1.12–17, 2.269–85 (apparatus) Wells, V [16]. Bibliography: *C.B.E.L.*, 1.172.

C. CYCLES

1. *The Northern Homily Cycle*

The numerous MSS. fall into three distinct groups as follows:—
(i) Earliest form. 59 homilies for Sundays. Usually the homily comprises a paraphrase of the gospel for the day, an exposition, and an illustrative *narratio* or tale (legendary or popular) as

exemplum. Best represented by MS. Royal Coll. of Phys., Edinburgh (Northern: early 14th c.). Ed.: J. Small, *Engl. Metrical Homilies*, Edinburgh, 1862.

(ii) Second great form. 79 homilies, in two divisions, a *Temporale*, and a *Proprium Sanctorum*, with no legends. For Sundays, Vigils and Weekdays. Best represented by MS. Vernon (1370–80: Southern) and B.M. Add. 22283 (1380–1400).

(iii) Third great cycle. In two divisions, a *Temporale* (121 items) and a *Legendary* (31 items). Best represented by MS. Harley 4196 (early 15th c.). Note that this MS. introduces a group of legends as readings for Christmas week, and that only about 20 *narrationes* are retained. Ed.: C. Horstmann, *A.E. Leg.*, 1881.
On the collection as a whole, see G. H. Gerould, *The North. English Hom. Collection*, Oxford, 1902, and Wells, V [18]. Bibliography: *C.B.E.L.*, 1 173–4.

2. *The Southern Legend Collection*

This extremely popular collection probably originated among the monks at Gloucester, c. 1275–1300, but was later considerably modified. Its numerous MSS., covering the period 13th–16th centuries, fall into 8 groups, some with sub-divisions. The metre is usually septenaries in couplets. For a detailed account, see Wells, V [19]. Ed.: C. Horstmann, *The Early South-English Legendary*, E.E.T.S., 87. Bibliography: *C.B.E.L.*, 1.174–5.

TALES

1. PIOUS TALES

For a summary account and bibliography, see Wells II.1.

A. MIRACLES OF THE VIRGIN

The Vernon Miracles

The most representative group of Virgin miracles in English, these *Miracles* are extant in the Vernon MS., fol. 123 ff. (1370–1380), the index to which gives the titles of forty-two Virgin miracles that were, or were to be, included in the collection (also in Horstmann, below, pp. 138–9). But nine only are included one being incomplete. All are in verse. The shortest has 74, the longest 186 lines. The group, totalling altogether 1,064 lines, comprises the following pieces :—(1) The Deliverance of the City of Crotey; (2) The Child Slain by the Jews; (3) The Harlot's Prayer; (4) A Jew Boy in an Oven; (5) How a Man got a New Leg; (6) The Virgin a Surety for a Merchant; (7) The Fornicating Priest; (8) The Monk with the Quinsy; (9) [Incomplete] The Incontinent Monk, (Wells, II[1]). At the end of each piece is an exhortation to the service of the Virgin. Ed.: C. Horstmann, E.E.T.S., 98. Discussion: R. W. Tryon, "Miracles of Our Lady in M.E. Verse" in *P.M.L.A.*, 38, 1923 [see esp. pp. 332–340, on sources of tales]; Wells, II [1]. Bibliography: *C.B.E.L.*, 1.162–3

B. OTHER TALES

1 The Gast of Gy [or The Ghost of Guy]

This is extant in both poetic and prose versions. The poetic version, of 2,064 four-stress lines in couplets, is contained in MSS. Cotton Tiberius E. VII (c. 1400) and Rawlinson F. 175 (c. 1350). It is in Northern English of c. 1325–50, and is apparently derived from the prose rendering, also originally Northern. The latter, which is included in MS. Vernon (1370–80) and (fragmentarily only) in MS. Caius Coll. Cbg. 175 (1340–1400), is drawn from a Latin source, *De Spiritu Guidonis*, preserved in MS. Cotton Vespasian A VI. For an edition of the prose version, see Bowers, R. H., *The Gast of Gy: a M.E. Religious Prose Tract preserved in Queen's College, Oxford.* Leipzig, 1938.

The story concerns the miracle of the ghost of a French burgess of Alexty, who died in 1323. The ghost appeared to the prior, a master of Geometry, and a master of Philosophy, and converses with them about purgatory, morality and the efficacy of masses for the dead. The tale is interesting, not because of any special literary merit, but for the insight it gives into current problems in theology. Ed., G. Schleich, *The Gast of Gy*, Berlin, 1898; C. Horstmann, *Yorkshire Writers*, 2. 292 ff. See Wells, II [9]; *C.B.E.L.*, 1.162.

The following are worth consideration:—

2. Narratio Sancti Augustini

84 lines in tail-rhyme, aabccb, Southern dialect, MS. Harley 3954 f. 75 r. (c. 1420). The devil is a stenographer recording the gossip of three women. Amusing. Ed. T. Wright and J. O. Halliwell, *Reliquiae Antiquae*, 2 vols., London, 1845 [See 1.39 ff.]. See Wells, II[12].

3. The Eremyte and the Outelawe

387 lines, Midland dialect, MS. B.M. Add. 22577 (c. 1806).

Emphasises Doctrine of Lost Sheep and Workers in Vineyard. Ed. M. Kaluza, *E.St.*, 14.165 ff. See Wells, II [14]; *C.B.E.L.*, 1.163.

4. *Child of Bristowe*

558 lines, North dialect (1350–1400), MS. Harley 2382 (15th c.). No literary merit. Shows virtue of good deeds, of supporting Church, efficacy of masses for dead and a son's piety. Ed. Horstmann, *A.E. Legenden*, 1881, 315 ff.; C. Hopper, Camden Soc. 73 (O.S.), 1859. See Wells, II [15].

There are also, in all the languages, collections of *exempla*, anecdotes for the enlivening of sermons (see Owst, p. 396), and these are worth looking at, as specimens of the floating ideas common in men's minds and for the glimpses they give of mediaeval life and ways of feeling. See T. Wright, *Latin Stories*, Percy Soc., 1842, and his introd. The most famous and influential is *Gesta Romanorum*, originating in England in the late thirteenth century, and current all over western Europe in various selections and versions, but deriving originally from more ancient and even, perhaps, oriental sources. The Latin was translated into English in the early fifteenth century and three MSS. of different selections remain. Wynkyn de Worde printed forty-three stories c. 1510 and reprinted; rev. version by R. Robinson, 1595, and 16 editions before 1700: *G.R.* is edited by S. J. H. Herrtage, E.E.T.S. E.S. xxxiii, 1879, with introd. and commentary. See (with caution) Warton's *Dissertation* in his *History*; the ed. of the Latin version by H. Oesterley, Berlin, 1872, has a standard introd.

An Alphabet of Tales is a fifteenth-century translation from the Latin of Arnold of Liège: the tales are mere anecdotes, but carry an authentic feeling of life. They are edited by Mary M. Banks, E.E.T.S. 126–7, 1904–5; no apparatus has appeared.

2. HUMOROUS TALES

Although probably current in England from an early period, actual examples of humorous tales (equivalent to French fabliaux) are scarce before 1400. Besides *Dame Sirith* (alternatively, but unwarrantably *Siriz*), which is one of the most typical (see below), we may note Chaucer's tales told by the Merchant, the Miller, the Reeve, the Shipman and the Summoner. The earliest example is perhaps the *Land of Cokaygne* (95 couplets, probably composed 1250–1300, in MS. Harley 913, written in 1308–25), though some classify it as a satire (Wells, IV [29]). Its theme is the Land of Fair-Ease, to which admission was possible only after "waiting for seven years in swine's ordure".

Dame Sirith of 450 lines, "copied by a scribe of the South-West from an East Midland MS., the original probably being Southern" (Wells, 178), is extant in MS. Digby 86 (1272–83).

The story concerns a merchant's wife who is ultimately persuaded by Dame Sirith, under threat of metempsychosis, into yielding herself to a rich aristocratic clerk. It is typical of the fabliaux-middle-class milieu, illicit love facilitated by trickery, broad humour, realism and directness. The piece, which is indirectly from a Latin source, though ultimately of Indian origin, is chiefly conversational, the links being either very brief or non-existent; in fact it is, in form, more dramatic than narrative.

Bibliography.
C.B.E.L., 1.160.

Editions.
McKnight, G. H. *M.E. Humorous Tales*. Boston, 1913.
Cook. *Lit. M.E. Reader*, 141–58.
Sampson. 416–28.

Discussion.
Schröder, E. *Dame Sirith*. Göttingen, 1936. [A useful introduction to the poem.]
Wells. II[20].

3. FABLES, BESTIARIES, ANIMAL TALES
A. FABLES

Despite that England was the home of the mediaeval fable and that books of fables in French and Latin still survive from this period, no such English collection is extant. The twelfth century collection translated from Latin into English by Alfred of England, and later attributed to Alfred the Great by Marie de France (fl. 12th c.), who used an English version as the basis of her own French book *Ysopet* comprising over 100, has unfortunately been lost. In fact, up to Chaucer scarcely a dozen English fables exist. Moreover each occurs singly as part of a larger work. Two of them, the fables of the *Owl and the Falcon*, and of the *Fox and the Cat*, are readily accessible in *The Owl and the Nightingale*, the former being provided with a moralistic interpretation (ll. 99–138, and 809–37 respectively). A third, the *Belling of the Cat*, is allegorised in *Piers Ploughman*, B-text (Prol., ll. 146–209). For the other examples, see Wells, II[23].

The earliest English collection probably dates from the early fifteenth century and is the work of Lydgate (?1370–?1451), who wrote seven fables, possibly while still at Oxford. Note also the (13) *Moral Tales of Aesop the Phrygian* (c. 1475) of the Scotsman Henryson (?1430–?1504) and Caxton's publication, *Aesop*, [1484].

Discussion.

Bastin, J.   *Recueil Général des Isopets.* 2 vols. S.A.T.F. 1929–30.

Canby, H. S.   *Short Story in English.* New York, 1909.

Harry, P.   *Comparative Study of Aesopic Fable in Bozon.* Cincinnati, 1903.

Hervieux, L.   *Les Fabulistes latins depuis le siècle d'Auguste jusqu'à la fin du moyen âge.* 2nd ed. 5 vols. Paris, 1893–8. [Contains the fable literature of Anglo-Latin *Romulus*, Odo of Cheriton, John of Sheppey.]

Jacobs, J.   *Fables of Aesop.* 2 vols. London, 1889.

Keidel, G. C.   *Manual of Aesopic Fable Literature.* Baltimore, 1896.

McKenzie, K., and Oldfather, W. A.   *Ysopet-Avionnet: The Latin and French Texts.* Urbana, 1919.

McKnight, G. H.   "The M.E. Vox and Wolf" in *P.M.L.A.*, 23. 497–509. 1908.

Mosher, J. A.   *The Exemplum in the Early Religious and Didactic Literature of England.* New York, 1911.

Owst, G. R.   *Preaching in Medieval England.* C.U.P., 1926.

Owst, G. R.   *Literature and Pulpit in Mediæval England,* Cambridge, 1923.

Plessow, M.   *Geschichte der Fabeldichtung in England.* Berlin, 1906.

Smith, L. T., and Meyer, P.   *Les Contes Moralisés de Nicole Bozon.* Paris, 1889.

Warnke, K.   *Die Fabeln der Marie de France.* Halle, 1898.

Wells. II.3.I.

B. BESTIARIES

Bestiaries were known in England from very early times. Their purpose was to convey moral and religious instructions through expositions of the actual and supposed natural history of both living and fabulous creatures of the animal world, beasts, birds, fish and insects. In form they are stereotyped: first the description, then the allegorical interpretation or application. Very probably all of them ultimately derive from the so-called *Physiologus* (or *Bestiary*), which, since lost, arose among the Christians of Alexandria in Egypt during the second century. Originally in Greek, it was translated into Latin, whence it passed into the vernacular literatures of the West. In England, versions in both English and Anglo-French appeared. The oldest of these, indeed the oldest in any Teutonic language, are the O.E. poems, *The Panther* and *The Whale* (see p. 191) Yet only one M.E. collection of bestiary material has survived, viz., *The Bestiary* (see below), although sporadic specimens are extant in various MSS. Bestiaries have had an important influence on the literature of England, as well as on its symbolic art (viz., the fantastic creatures of mediaeval illuminations and sculptures) and its science.

Discussion.
Encycl. Brit. s.v. *Physiologus* in the 11th ed., and s.v. *Bestiary* in the 14th ed.
Wells. II.3.II.

1. *The Bestiary*

The *Bestiary*, a poem of 802 lines, contained in only one MS., viz., Arundel 292, was written in the late thirteenth century in the E. Midland dialect (perhaps originally in Lincs., but later copied in Essex, Hall, *Sels.*, 591). Written in a variety of verse forms, including the alliterative measure, it is mainly a translation of the Latin *Physiologus* of Thetbaldus. The latter treats of thirteen creatures:—the lion, serpent, eagle, ant, fox, hart, spider, whale, mermaid, centaur, elephant, turtle-dove and panther. The English version deals with only twelve of these, the centaur being excluded; but it adds a passage on the culver or dcve, from the Latin of Neckham's *De Naturis Rerum* (c. 1180–94). After stating the supposed nature and habits of each creature, the author, following ancient practice, points out the spiritual truths they symbolise.

A difficult piece of M.E., but of peculiar interest for the light it throws upon the mediaeval methods of presenting religious doctrine.

Bibliography.
C.B.E.L., 1.182–3.

Edition.
Morris, R.   *An Old English Miscellany*. E.E.T.S., 49. 1872.

Selections.
Morris. *Specimens*, 1.132–40.
Hall. *Sels.*, 76–96.

Cook. *Lit. M.E. Reader*, 316.
Emerson. *Reader*, 14–20.

Translations.
Shackford. *Leg. Sats.*, 101. [Parts.]
Weston. *Ch. M.E. P.*, 325–34.

Discussion.
Wells. II[24].

C. ANIMAL TALES

For a bibliography of Animal Tales, see Wells, II.3.III. For a discussion of the subject, see C. F. Fiske, "Animals in Ecclesiastical Literature 650–1500" in *P.M.L.A.*, 28.368–87, 1913 [concludes that their function is to vivify spiritual truth and religious story].

The Fox and the Wolf

The Fox and the Wolf, contained in MS. Digby 86 (1272–83) and consisting of 295 ll. emanating from the South (c. 1250–75) is a vigorous, humorous and realistic account of how a fox, whilst raiding the friar's poultry, had the misfortune to fall down a well, and of how he escaped therefrom by a clever stratagem at the wolf's expense. The source, not yet ascertained, may be a version of the French *Roman de Renard*.

Bibliography.
C.B.E.L., 1.161.
McKnight, G. H. *M.E. Humorous Tales*, 85–9. [Full.]

Editions.
Cook. *Lit. M.E. Reader*, 188.
McKnight. ib., 25–37.

Translation.
Weston. *Ch. M.E. P.*, 275–9.

Discussion.
Canby. *Short Story*, 51.
McKnight, G. H. "The M.E. Vox and Wolf" in *P.M.L.A.*, 23.497–509. 1908.
Wells. II [25].

4. UNIFIED COLLECTIONS

Under this heading, it is convenient to mention the interesting tales of the *Seven Sages of Rome*. In the Middle Ages and before the introduction of printing into England, the compilation of manuscript collections of material of the same general type was a useful and frequent form of literary activity. In this way were put together the single collections of e.g., popular songs, recipes, homilies, fables, exempla, anecdotes, moralistic tales, descriptions of fabulous animals, miracles and saints' legends that have come down to us (Wells, 185). Of the narratives, two main classes may be distinguished: those that are simply collections of essentially disconnected pieces (e.g., Chaucer's *Legend of Good Women* [1385] and the English version of *Gesta Romanorum* [MS. Harley 7333, c. 1450], ed., E.E.T.S. E.S. 33), and those that form an artistic unity, in which "the single stories are narratives within a narrative" [Wells, l. c.]. To the latter class belong Chaucer's *Canterbury Tales*, Gower's *Confessio Amantis* and *The Seven Sages of Rome*. The first two are dealt with on p. 283 and p. 289 respectively.

The Seven Sages of Rome

The Seven Sages of Rome, of Oriental origin, is extant in eight M.E. versions (besides several Early Modern ones). These eight occur in nine different MSS., two being copies of the same *exemplar*. Seven are derived from the same thirteenth-century original, now lost. The longest version has over 4,300 lines, the shortest only some 2,500 lines. The earliest MS. dates from 1330–40. Altogether the renderings form three, if not four, different groups.

Briefly, the framework of the poem is as follows. Inspired by jealousy and the interests of her own children, the young queen of Diocletian, Emperor of Rome, tries to poison her husband's mind against her stepson, who, while away from the capital, has acquired exceptional wisdom under the guidance of seven sages of Rome. On returning home, the son, fearing the Emperor, agrees to remain silent for seven days. Denounced by the queen for alleged attacks upon her honour, he is condemned to death by the Emperor. But the punishment is deferred. Each night for a week the queen tells a tale of the machinations of underlings and the consequent dangers to their master. Each dawn the Emperor gives orders for the boy's execution, but countermands them under the influence of a narrative of female cunning and of hasty action told by one of the sages. At the end of the period, the boy, breaking his silence, tells an appropriate tale, denouncing the queen. The lady, admitting her guilt, is suitably punished at the stake.

Bibliography.
C.B.E.L., 1.155.
Hibbard. *Med. Rom.*, 181–2.

Edition.
Brunner, K. *The Seven Sages of Rome.* E.E.T.S., 191, 1933.
Campbell, K. *Seven Sages of Rome.* Boston, 1907. [With critical apparatus.]

Translation.
Weston. *Ch. M.E. P.*, 281–6. [Parts.]

Discussion.
Campbell, K. "A Study of the Seven Sages, with Special Reference to the M.E. Versions" in *P.M.L.A.*, 14.1–107. 1899.
Hibbard. *Med. Rom.*, 174–81.
Wells. II [27].

SOME MEDIAEVAL LATIN WRITERS

For the mediaeval varieties of Latin, use Du Cange, *Glossarium ad Scriptores Mediæ et infimae Latinitatis.* The best edition is that of 1883–7, but a new revision is in preparation. There is an abridged version in one vol., 1868, not easy to find. J. H. Baxter and C. Johnson, *A Medieval Latin Word-Book*, Oxford, 1934, is a good brief Lexicon. Glossaries are attached to many of the published texts. The first English-Latin dictionary was *Promptorium Parvulorum sive Clericorum* (i.e., The Boys' or Clerks' Store-house), compiled about 1440 by Geoffrey the Grammarian (Galfridus Grammaticus), also called G. Starkey; first ed. by Pynson, 1499; edited by A. Way, Camden Society, 25, etc., 1843– , and (better) by A. L. Mayhew, E.E.T.S., X ser. cii, 1908. It is more useful to English than to Latin philologists, but it is a source for obscure fifteenth-century Latin words. Bale ascribes to Geoffrey also *Ortus Vocabulorum*, the first Latin-English dictionary printed in England; Wynkyn de Worde, 1500. F. J. E. Rabey, *Christian-Latin Poetry*, 1928, and *A History of Secular Latin Poetry*, 1934, cover the whole ground, but the English sections are easily picked out, and in any case English writers cannot be studied in isolation.

The extensive bibliographies give reliable guidance to the whole subject.

Helen Waddell's *The Wandering Scholars*, 1927, is a learned and sympathetic study, somewhat excited and romantic, but delightful as an introduction and valuable as a contribution to scholarship. It contains some neat translations (with originals in an appendix which is in effect a small anthology), and a very good bibliography. Her *Medieval Latin Lyrics* is pleasant reading.

F. Brittain, *The Medieval Latin and Romance Lyric to A.D. 1300* (1937), is not concerned with English, but is full of good material for the subject in general.

See also W. P. Ker, *The Dark Ages* (2nd imp., 1911), G. Saintsbury, *The Flourishing of Romance and the Rise of Allegory* (1897), and G. Gregory Smith, *The Transition Period* (1900), all in the "Periods of European Literature" series; *The Cambridge History of English Literature*, Vol. I, Chaps. V (M. R. James) and X (Sir J. E. Sandys); Claude Jenkins, *Some Aspects of Medieval Latin Literature*, in *The Legacy of the Middle Ages*, edited by Crump and Jacobs, 1926. The "Rhythmorum Exempla", Appendix X in W. P. Ker, *Form and Style in Poetry*, edited by R. W. Chambers, 1928, exemplify synoptically the parallels between Latin and vernacular verse-forms. There is an interesting historical note on the English pronunciation of Latin by Henry Bradley, Soc. for Pure English Tracts, IV, 1920, reprinted in Collected Papers, 1928. See also G. H. Fowler, *Notes on the Pronunciation of Medieval Latin in England*, in *History*, Sept. 1937.

The student of English literature will probably find all he needs in Stephen Gaselee, *The Oxford Book of Latin Verse* (reprinted 1937) and *An Anthology of Medieval Latin*, 1925. The latter, a delightful selection of brief prose and verse extracts, is perhaps the best introduction of all, and the sources are given, so that an attractive line may be followed up. The following are useful collections for our purpose:

Thomas Wright, ed. *Latin Poems attributed to Walter Mapes*, Camden Society, No. 16, 1841, a collection of Goliardic poems, anonymous pastimes of the international *corpus studentium*. Some are certainly not by Map; none can be proved his; but he was quite capable of writing them, so the tradition of his authorship may be respected if not believed. For him, see below. The great collection of such things is *Carmina Burana*, ed. Schmeller, 1848, or, better, by Hilks and Schumann, 1930– . Versions by J. A. Symonds, *Wine, Women and Song*, 1884, and by Helen Waddell *ut sup.*

Satirical Poets of the Twelfth Century, Rolls Series, 1871. Vol. I includes the *Speculum Stultorum* of Nigel Wireker (fl. 1190), a comprehensive satire on society in general and the clerical orders in particular. This is the tale of Dan Burnell the Ass, cited by Chaucer. Vol. II includes the great *De Contemptu Mundi* (the authorship of which is disputed but which may be English), the two influential works of Alain de l'Isle (1114–1203), *Anticlaudianus* and *De Planctu Naturae* (*vide* Chaucer, *Hous of Fame*, etc.), and various *Ænigmata*, among them those of Tatwin (Archbishop of Canterbury, d. 734) and Aldhelm (Bishop of Sherborne, 640?–709), which may be compared with vernacular Riddles.

The Political Songs of England, Camden Society, No. 6, 1839, with translations, is less important than *Political Poems and Songs*, Rolls Series, 1859, of which some are Latin. The great international collections are those of E. du Méril *Poésies Populaires Latines au Moyen Age*, 1847; *Carmina Burana* (see above); Drèves, *Analecta Hymnica Medii Aevi*.

See also Stevenson, *Latin Hymns of the Anglo-Saxon Church*.

There is, of course, an enormous mass of philosophical, ecclesiastical, and theological writing, which may be sought in J. P. Migne, *Patrologia Latina*, 1844–55. There are printed the letters and minor works (as well as major) of such as Bede, Alcuin, Aldhelm, and so on. The index is adequate. More secular works such as chronicles may be sought for in *Monumenta Germaniae Historica, Auctores Antiquissimi*, edited by T. Mommsen, 1871–, and *Monumenta Germaniae Historica, Scriptores*, edited by G. H. Pertz and others, 1826–96. Of direct and notable interest, is the wonderful group of courtiers of Henry II, for whom see Kate Norgate, *England under the Angevin Kings*, 1887, and of whom we must remark, besides the poets noted above:—

Walter Map or Mapes (fl. 1200), Archdeacon of Oxford, wit, scholar, and busybody. *De Nugis Curialium* is one of the first and best of bedside books, full of humours and curiosities. Edited by T. Wright, Camden Society, and admirably by M. R. James, 1914. There is a good translation with brief but useful introduction and notes, by F. Tupper and M. B. Ogle, 1924. For the poems traditionally ascribed to Map, see the ed. by T. Wright, above.

Giraldus Cambrensis (1146?–1220?). Gerald de Barri, son of a Norman knight and grandson of Nesta, a Welsh princess famous for her beauty, and Archdeacon of Brecknock. *Works*, edited by Brewer and Dimock, Rolls Series, 1861–77.

Topographica Hibernica and *Expugnatio Hibernica* are the record of the Norman conquest of Ireland.

Itinerarium Cambriae describes a journey with Archbishop Baldwin to preach the Crusade. A translation, with the *Description of Wales* by Sir R. C. Hoare (1806), in Bohn's Antiquarian Library and in Everyman's Library (No. 272).

Gemma Ecclesiastica, and Lives of St. Hugh of Lincoln, St. David, etc., are more professional, but

De Rebus a se Gestis is a lively book of memoirs.

Gerald's personal reminiscences, collected from various works, were translated by H. E. Butler, as *The Autobiography of Giraldus Cambrensis*, 1937: this is a book to read, for the events, the descriptions, and above all for the man.

John of Salisbury (d. 1180), pupil of Abelard and friend of Thomas à Becket, professor and Bishop of Chartres, and "the most learned classical writer of the Middle Ages".

Life by C. C. J. Webb, 1932.

Works, edited by J. A. Giles, 1848.

Policraticus, first printed 1476, an important treatise on political theory, contains many personal reminiscences. Best ed. by C. C. J. Webb, 1909.

Metalogicon, a treatise on logic, in Migne, *Patrologia Latina* and edited by C. C. J. Webb, 1929.

Historia Pontificalis, edited by R. Lane Poole, 1927.

Life of St. Anselm; *Entheticus* is a Latin elegy on Becket. See also *The Early Correspondence of John of Salisbury* by R. Lane Poole, in Proceedings of the British Academy for 1924, and Helen Waddell, in Essays and Studies, XIII, 1928.

Geoffrey of Monmouth, 1100?–1154, Bishop of St. Asaph.

Historia Britonum was compiled from the British history ascribed to Nennius and from a History of Britain which, he says, was brought from Brittany by Walter Calenius. This "fabulous history" (Giraldus's *Description of Wales*, Chap. VII) was vulgarised in the Norman versions of Wace and Gaimar and the English versions of Layamon and Robert of Gloucester, and has supplied stories to many generations of English poets since, as well as providing the backbone of the Arthurian legend.

The first edition was printed in Paris, 1507. The best modern edition by J. A. Giles. Translation "with a large Preface" by Aaron Thompson, 1718, revised by J. A.

Giles for Bohn. A translation by Sebastian Evans (1903) is No. 577 in Everyman's Library.

The book is discussed by all writers on Arthurian legend, but see especially E. Faral, *La Legende Arthurienne des Origines à Geoffrey de Monmouth* (Paris, Champion, 1929)

See also under Chronicles (p. 329), Education (p. 425), Science (p. 266).

A NOTE ON ANGLO-NORMAN

The line between insular and continental French is hard to draw precisely. At first the Norman of the duchy and the Norman of the kingdom were one and the same, and there would always be coming and going: but the purely Norman phase is brief. Nor were William's adventurers all Norman. In a generation or two, personal, feudal, ecclesiastical and educational relations connected England with all northern and western France. Thus, though certain Anglo-Norman traits may be isolated, the dialect of writers is very variable, and the provenance of certain texts is much debated. We have to think along feudal rather than racial or geographical lines—and those lead us out of England. The student of the twelfth to fourteenth centuries had best go direct to the French literary historians first, for French literature was in circulation and in men's minds. The study of technique is not much more helpful. Anglo-Norman verse broke down in the twelfth century—that is, almost as soon as it can be said to exist. Also macaronic lyrics appear as early as any in Anglo-French. The line between "local" and "bad", in verse as in language, is very precarious. It is to be hoped that the Anglo-Norman Society founded in Manchester by Miss Muriel Pope will make the texts available—which few are at present—and help to bring the whole subject out of its present confusion.

Schofield attempts, in his *English Lit. from the Conquest to Chaucer*, to bring French (and Latin) literature into relations with English. For the material, see especially J. Vising, *Anglo-Norman Language and Literature*, Oxford, 1923, a good reference book listing the 404 texts, with bibliography, lists of MSS., and a lucid and succinct note on the English dialectical forms of French.

See under Grosseteste, p. 290, Bozon, p. 279, Chronicles, p. 330, Walter of Henley, p. 441. The following exemplify the appearance of insular matter (other than chronicles) in the French language. *La Vie Seint Edmund le Roi*, by Denis Piramus, c. 1170–80; Thomas of Canterbury, by Benet, c. 1185; *Tristan*, by Thomas, c. 1170, edited by J. Bédier, Soc. Anc. Textes Francais, 1902–5, the first of the Tristan romances; *Horn* by Mestre Thomas (not the author of *Tristan*), see *King Horn*, p. 352; *Waldef*, late twelfth century; *Haveloc*, c. 1130–40, see *Havelok*, p. 354, and Gaimar, p. 330; *Le Lai du Cor*, mid twelfth century; *L'Estoire du Saint Graal*, by R. de Borron, late twelfth century, is claimed for France; *The Vision of Tundal*; *Guy of Warwick*, early thirteenth century, see p. 355; *Boeve de Haumtone*, early thirteenth century, see p. 357; ed. L. Brandin, *Fouke Fitz Warin* (Classiques Français du Moyen Âge), Paris, 1930; *Foulques Fitz Warin*, in prose, c. 1258, edited by T. Wright, 1855; *St. Hugh of Lincoln*, see Chaucer, the Prioress's Tale, and Skeat's notes thereon. See also T. Wright, *Political Poems*, Rolls Series (p. 317). The Anglo-Norman Text Soc. has published one vol. yearly since 1939 (Oxford, Blackwell)

In the fourteenth century works on French language appear—see Walter de Bibbesworth, c. 1300, in Wright and Halliwell, *Reliquiae Antiquae*, Vol. II. Henceforth it is French that matters; a man like Gower was not working on an insular tradition, but, whatever his accent, on lessons imported from France. Ed. A Owen. Paris, 1929.

ADDENDA

P. 317 POLITICAL POEMS

Mum and the Sothsegger

This interesting poem on the evils of Richard II's rule is dated 1403-6. The anonymous author was apparently connected with Bristol; the dialect is S.W. Midland, and the verse alliterative. Two incomplete MSS. of the mid 15th century exist, giving independent texts separated by a gap of some 250 ll., *viz.*—(i) 857 ll. in Cambridge Univ. Lib. MS. Ll. iv. 14, divided (unnecessarily) into a Prologue and 4 Passus in imitation of *Piers Plowman* and long known as *Richard the Redeless;* and (ii) 1751 ll. in the recently discovered B.M. Addl. 41666. Ed. Mabel Day and R. Steele, E.E.T.S. 199, with full apparatus. Discussion: Oakden, *Alliterative Poetry* (dialect, verse, etc.); Wells, IV[54].

P. 404 LATIN WRITERS.

Roger Bacon, 1214?–1294?–, an Oxford Franciscan and the greatest mediaeval scientist, left many treatises, of which many MSS. exist, but few were printed until modern times. His *Opus Majus* was ed. J. H. Bridges, 1897, but his interesting fusion of Aristotle, the Arabs, tradition, and vigorous original thought, and his interesting method of exposition, may be most easily observed in any of the shorter works—*e.g, de Vitiis Contractis in Studio Theologiae, Questiones de Plantis,* or *de Coloribus*—ed. R. Steele and others. Oxford, 1909-. See also SCIENCE, pp. 266-7.

CHAPTER XI

SCOTTISH LITERATURE

The documents of this period are usually divided into *Early* and *Middle* Scots, the line of demarcation being, roughly, 1450, or the acceptance of the mastership of Chaucer, for which see W. P. Ker, *Form and Style in Poetry*, 1928. "Early Scottish" literature is differentiated from other Northern English literature by its local or national sentiment and not by cultural or linguistic variation of any deep significance. For this reason some of the works usually included in "Early Scots" will be found among their congeners elsewhere in this volume.

The literary language called "Middle Scots", which prevailed until the Union of the Crowns or thereby, differs from Northern English in the more conscious cultivation that follows from its being a *sermo regius* and not an outlying dialect; in variations of vocabulary due to the accidents of separation; ·and in true variation of culture and of vocabulary which by that time had come about largely by the different political and social relations with French and (continental) Latin. But, throughout, the only difference that need trouble anyone who knows more than Addisonian English is the system of spelling, a habit of artifice for which see Gregory Smith's introduction to *Specimens* of Middle Scots, noted below.

Bibliography: Dickson and Edmond, *Annals of Scottish Printing*, 1890, and H. G. Aldis. *A List of Books printed in Scotland before 1700*, 1890, deal with texts, and Scottish books are included in *S.T.C.* William Geddie, *A Bibliography of Middle Scots Poets* (Scottish Text Society, New Series 61, 1912) lists texts and critical works; it is useful if not a model, and the introduction summarises the history of criticism and scholarship up to its date. Hugh Walker, *Three Centuries of Scottish Literature*, Vol. I (1893), T. F. Henderson, *Scottish Vernacular Literature* (1898 . . . 1910) and J. H. Millar, *A Literary History of Scotland* (1903) are uninspired, but useful for reference. Agnes Mure Mackenzie, *An Historical Survey of Scottish Literature to 1714* (1933) is a lively partisan essay, which should be read. The best work on the subject is that of G. Gregory Smith, in *Scottish Literature* (1919) only in part concerned with the earlier periods, but a shrewd analysis of the character of Scottish literature by one who really understood it; in *The Transition Period* (1900), Ch. II; in his chapters in *C.H.E.L.* (Vol. II, Chap. IV, X, XI) and his articles on Scottish men of letters in the *Encyclopaedia Britannica;* and in *Specimens of Middle Scots* (see below). Janet M. Smith, *The French Background of Middle Scots Literature* (1934) is primarily a thesis on Scottish relations with France, but is generally valuable and contains the best bibliography of the subject; J. Veitch, *The Feeling for Nature in Scottish Poetry*, 1874, is in an old-fashioned mode of criticism, but is still worth attention, as is John Nichol's *Sketch of Scottish Poetry* in the E.E.T.S. ed. of Lindsay, Vol. V. F. Brie's *Die nationale Literatur Schottlands von den Anfängen bis zur Renaissance* (1937) is admirably clear and thorough. John Speirs, *The Scots Literary Tradition* (1940), if less scholarly, gives some real criticism.

The most scholarly book of selections is Gregory Smith, *Specimens of Middle Scots* (1902), containing a useful linguistic introduction and a descriptive bibliography of text-sources. M.M. Gray, *Scottish Poetry from Barbour to James IV* (1935) is a very pleasant and useful anthology of extracts and short pieces, drawn from all available sources; spellings are slightly and judiciously normalised: the best anthology for the general reader. G. Eyre Todd, *Early Scottish Poetry* (1891) and *Mediaeval Scottish Poetry* (1892) are useful enough as brief introductions, and some early fragments are included in W. Macneile Dixon, *The Edinburgh Book of Scottish Verse* (1910), and Sir George Douglas, *A Book of Scottish Poetry* (1911), and John Buchan, *The Northern Muse*, wherein also are some good general observations among the notes.

The Scottish Text Society began publication in 1884, and has now published almost all extant texts up to 1600 or thereby, with the notable exception of the works of Gavin Douglas. By including complete transcripts of the great MS. collections it has made the materials available as well as collated and edited texts. These great collections, to which we are indebted for practically the whole of Dunbar as well as of minor writers, are well described in Gregory Smith, *Specimens*.

The most important are:—The Asloan MS. written by John Asloan (or Sloane) "towards the beginning of the sixteenth century". Twenty-six pieces remain out of sixty listed in the table of contents. Printed complete by the Scottish Text Society, edited by W. A. Craigie. 2 vols. 1923–5.

The Bannatyne MS., Scot. Nat. Lib. MS. 1.1.6, written in 1568 by George Bannatyne (1545–1608?), to pass the time when detained at Leith by plague. It contains 334 separate poems (and forty-two duplicates and additions in other hands). Printed complete by S. T. S., edited by W. Tod Ritchie. 4 vols. 1928, 1930, 1934.

The Maitland Folio MS., Magdalene Coll., Cambridge, Pepysian Library, written by Sir Richard of Lethington, between 1570 and 1590, and bought by Pepys at the Lauderdale sale in 1692. It contains 182 separate poems. Printed complete by S.T.S., edited by W. A. Craigie. 2 vols. 1919, 1927.

The Maitland Quarto MS., also in the Pepysian Library, written by Maitland's daughter Marie in 1586. It contains ninety-five separate poems. Printed complete by S.T.S., edited by W. A. Craigie, 1920.

The scientific study of the language as a whole has been somewhat neglected, but some specialist studies of texts are listed below and a sound foundation is being laid by Sir W. A. Craigie in his Dictionary of the Older Scottish Tongue, now in progress.

A. EARLY SCOTS

JOHN BARBOUR, 1316?–1395

Here is the first identifiable Scottish poet; student and teacher at Oxford and Paris, archdeacon of Aberdeen, and royal auditor. For his life, see Skeat's editions below (Vol. IV of E.E.T.S. ed.,). The two MSS. of his great historical poem, *The Actes and Life of the most Victorious Conquerour, Robert Bruce King of Scotland* are in St. John's College, Cambridge (G. 23) and the Scottish National Library (19.2.2), both written by John Ramsay, in 1487 and 1489 respectively. David Laing had a unique copy of an edition printed by Lekprevik for H. Charteris, Edinburgh, 1571, but it is lost, and the earliest surviving editions are those of Hart, Edinburgh, 1616 and 1620. The most useful modern edition is that of W. W. Skeat, E.E.T.S., extra ser. XI, XXI, XXIX, LV, 1870–89; reprinted 1896. The same edition was revised for the S.T.S., 2 vols. Nos. 31–2, 1894. The edition by W. M. Mackenzie, 1909, will be found convenient. Selections appear in Morris and Skeat's *Specimens of Early English*, Vol II; G. Gregory Smith, *Specimens of Middle Scots* (appendix); O.F. Emerson, *Specimens*, and in all the anthologies.

Criticism is found in Warton, Jusserand, and the usual histories. See also F. Brie's valuable *Die nationale Literatur Schottlands* (1937).

J .T. T. Brown, *Wallace and Bruce Restudied*, Bonn, 1900, is here mentioned to warn off the student from the controversy which followed it—pretty fighting, much erudition, and little judgment. The attribution of other works has led to similar differences of opinion. So few early Scottish documents have escaped the long series of depredations and devastations from Edward I to Cromwell that the evidence does not exist for adequate checks upon arguments and theories, especially when based on linguistic points of dialect, etc. The works attributed may in any case be noted conveniently here.

The Buik of Alexander is a version in eight-syllable couplets of two French romances, *Li Fuerres de Gadres* and *Les Vœux du Paon*. The text depends on a unique copy of a print by Alexander Arbuthnet, Edinburgh, c. 1580. This was reprinted (edited by David Laing) for the Bannatyne Club, 1831. An elaborate edition by R. L. G. Ritchie, S.T.S., new ser., 12, 17, 21, 25, 1920, 1924, 1926, 1928, contains, in Vol. I, bibliography, discussion of originals, authorship, language and metre. The controversies on authorship are summarised in Chap. IV, and Ritchie concludes in favour of Barbour. The text begins in Vol. I; the French originals are printed facing the Scottish version. This must be studied by any critic of the *Bruce*, and is worth study for its own sake.

The Lives of the Saints exist in one MS., Cambridge University Library, Gg. II. 6. Part was edited by C. Horstmann in *Altenglischen Legenden*, Heilbronn, 1881, and all by W. M. Metcalfe, in 6 vols., with introduction and notes, S.T.S. 18, 23, 25, 35, 37, 1888, 1890-1, 1894-5, Vol. I containing introduction, V and VI, notes. Henry Bradshaw, who found the MS. (*Collected Papers*, 1888), and Horstmann, believed it Barbour's, but P. Buss decided against it, *Anglia*, IX (1886). The poems are, however, of Barbour's time and region. There are fifty legends, including the Seven Sleepers and the Aberdonian St. Machar.

The Troy Book found in MS. Kk.v. 30 in Cambridge University Library by Henry Bradshaw was also claimed by him for Barbour (see above), but Buss (above) and E. Koeppel, in *Englishe Studien* X (1887) disprove it on linguistic grounds.

HUCHOWN OF THE AWLE RYALE AND OTHERS

The mysterious Huchown, who *floruit* (if at all) in the fourteenth century, is mentioned by Andrew of Wyntoun (edited by Amours, V, 4332):

409

He maid the gret Gest of Arthure
And the Anteris of Gawane,
The Epistill als of Suete Susane.

The third of these is certain; the others are believed to be *Morte Arthure* and *The Awntyrs of Arthur* (see below). In *Huchown of the Awle Ryale*, Glasgow, 1902, G. Neilson identified Huchown with Sir Hew of Eglinton, mentioned by Dunbar in *The Lament for the Makaris*, and made extravagant claims for him. Amours (see below) thinks him a priest rather than so important a political figure. Henry Bradley (*Collected Papers*, p. 222) argues for a Cumbrian origin, the (equally mysterious) *Awle Ryale* or *Aula Regalis* being Oriel College. There is now an official Huchown-Problem, the nature of which may be illustrated by citing two papers: that of MacCracken, *P.M.L.A.*, 1910, who proves that the three poems cannot be by the same author but gives *Susane* to Huchown; and that of S. O. Andrew, *R.E.S.*, 1929, who proves that the poems are by the same author, an inhabitant of the N.W. Midlands. Wyntoun's mention by no means proves Huchown a Scot, but the evidence for Sir Hew of Eglinton does not consist merely of a few dialectal forms to which little external check can be applied. The poems at least exist.

The Epistill (or *Pistill*) *of Susane* tells the story of Susanna and the Elders in twenty-eight 13-line stanzas of romance type with "bob and wheel", viz., eight 5-beat lines rhymed ababbab, one 2-syllable line (the "bob"), three 6-syllable (the "wheel"), one 4-syllable, rhymed cdddc; the whole alliterated. Five MSS. exist: the Vernon (c. 1370–80) in the Bodleian; Cotton Caligula A II (c. 1430) and Addl. 22283 (c. 1380–1400) in B.M., and two privately owned. The poem was edited by D. Laing (*Select Remains*, 1822, re-edited by Small, 1885, and by W. C. Hazlitt, 1895); by C. Horstmann in *Anglia*, I, 1877, from Vernon MS., and in Herrig's *Archiv*, 62 and 74 from Cotton and Phillips MSS. In F. J. Amours, *Scottish Alliterative Poems*, S.T.S., 27, 38, 1892, 1897, the Vernon text (as oldest) is printed by itself, the other four, parallel, in an appendix. Huchown here lacks control over detail, but shows considerable sensitiveness and emotional imagination.

Morte Arthure is contained in the Thornton MS. in Lincoln Cathedral Library, and has been edited by G. G. Perry, E.E.T.S., 8, 1865, re-edited by E. Brock, 1871. It consists of 4,346 alliterative lines without rhyme, and is based ultimately on Geoffrey of Monmouth, covering Arthur's war with Rome, Modred's treachery, and Arthur's last battle and death. There are some good touches of nature and religion. See also p. 362.

The Awntyrs of Arthure at the Terne Wathelyne is a congener of *Gawaine and the Green Knight*, not so good, but a very fair vigorous romance, with moral interludes, telling first of the meeting of Guinevere and Gawaine with a ghost (whose pedigree would be worth working out) near Wadling Tarn in Cumberland, then of one of the usual challenges which Gawaine accepts and wins. The verse is fifty-five 13-line romance-stanzas, rhymed and alliterated with "wheel" but without "bob", the verses being linked by rhetorical repetition as in *Pearl*. There are three MSS.: Thornton, Ireland, and Douce (Bodleian). Laing edited the poem in *Select Remains* (see above, *Susane*). Amours, *Scottish Alliterative Poems*, prints the Thornton MS., as most northerly, and Douce, as most complete, with references to the other.

Gologras and Gawane, in 105 similar stanzas, has been assigned to Clerk of Tranent on the strength of Dunbar's reference in the *Lament*:

> Clerk of Tranent eik he (*sc.* Death) has tane
> That maid the aenteris of Gawane.

But as this is all we know of Clerk, we are not much helped. The poem is of the late fifteenth century, a good version of part of *Perceval le Gallois* by Chrétien de Troyes; it is a straightforward tale of fighting and courtesy, without the religious note of the others. The name appears in the index of the Asloan MS., but the pages are missing, and the one text-source is the print by Chepman and Myllar, 1508, reprinted by Laing, 1827, and by Sir F. Madden in *Syr Gawayne*, Bannatyne Club, 1839 (an important collection); edited by M. Trautmann in *Anglia*, II, 1879, and Amours, *Scottish Alliterative Poems*.

The Taill of Rauf Coilzear is the freshest of this group, though the latest. No source is known, but the theme is common in tale and ballad—the adventure of the wandering king with his free-spoken and independent subject, here attached to the Charlemagne cycle. It is in seventy-five stanzas of the same form. The name stands next to *Gologras* in the Asloan index, but the poem is missing likewise, and the text depends on a unique copy of Lekprevik's print, St. Andrews, 1572. This was printed by Laing (*Select Remains, ut sup.*); by S. J. H Herrtage, *Charlemagne Romances*, Part VI, E.E.T.S., 4 ser. XXXIX, 1882; by M. Tonndorf, Berlin, 1894; by W. H. Browne, Baltimore, 1903; and by

411

Amours, *Scottish Alliterative Poems*. This poem has been allowed to remain Scottish so far. See also p. 374.

BLIND HARRY, *alias* HENRY THE MINSTREL, c. 1460

Dr. W. H. Schofield proves (below), that he was not blind, nor Harry, nor a minstrel, but John Major, a contemporary and a historian, says he was. In any case, he wrote *The Actis and Deidis of the Illuster and Vailzeand Campioun, Schir William Wallace, Knicht of Ellerslie*, of which the MS. written in 1488 by John Ramsay, another contemporary (the scribe of Barbour's *Bruce*) is in the Scottish National Library. Only a fragment remains of an edition printed by Chepman and Myllar about 1508, a unique copy (in B.M.) of one printed by Lekprevik for H. Charteris, 1570, reprinted 1594, 1600, 1611, 1618, 1620, and so on. The most useful modern edition is by J. Moir, S.T.S. 6, 7, 16, 1885–6, 1889.

A facsimile of the 1570 ed. is publ. by "Scholars Facsimiles and Reprints", New York, 1938, and S.T.S., with introd. by Sir W. A. Craigie.

Selections are in Eyre Todd, *Early Scottish Poetry*, Skeat, *Specimens*, and in Douglas's and Gray's anthologies. A modernised edition by W. Hamilton of Gilbertfield, Glasgow, 1722, was often reprinted, and was influential though bad: see Burns's letter to Dr. Moor, 2nd Aug., 1787. See also F. Brie's *Die nationale Literatur Schottlands* (1937).

Harry claimed as his authority a Latin book by John Blair, Wallace's chaplain. It is not extant, but may well have existed, since, though Harry knew the romances and used the conventional gambits, the incidents are not all conventional. This knowledge of romances, and even of scraps of classical mythology, is best explained by the supposition that Harry, a professional minstrel, knew his job. See the histories, W. H. Schofield, *Mythical Bards and the Life of William Wallace*, Cambridge, 1910, and George Neilson in *Essays and Studies*, Vol. I, 1910. The language is studied by H. Heyne, *Die Sprache in Henry the Minstrel's "Wallace"*, Kiel, 1910.

B. MIDDLE SCOTS POETRY

JAMES I, 1394–1437

The Kingis Quair is a garden-allegory, and the best imitation of Chaucer in his French and courtly style, written c. 1423 on James's courtship of his wife, Lady Anne Beaufort. The 197 stanzas are in the common Chaucerian 7-line form, rhyming ababcc, called *rime royal* from his use of it in this poem. The one MS. is in the

Bodleian Library, Arch. Selden, B.24. It was first printed by W. Tytler in *Poetical Remains of James the First, King of Scotland*, 1783, and (in recent times) edited by W. W. Skeat, S.T.S., 1, 1884; revised S.T.S. new ser. 1, 1911; R. Steele, 1903; A. Lawson, 1910 (with *The Quair of Jelusy*); W. M. Mackenzie, 1939. Skeat's revised edition is the most useful, but another is in preparation by Sir W. A. Craigie. For James's life (besides the histories of Scotland and introductions in the above editions), see J. J. Jusserand, *Le Roman d'un Roi d'Ecosse*, 1895, translated as *The Romance of a King's Life*, 1896, and E. M. W. Balfour-Melville, *James I, King of Scots*, 1936. He was noted as a poet in his own century, and Bale (1548) lists a *De regina sua futura* which is probably the *Quair*, but there has been long controversy as to his authorship, though James was probably as able to write English as Charles d'Orleans. In *The Language of the King's Quair* (Essays and Studies, XXV, 1939) Sir W. A. Craigie not only studies the text, but concludes for the royal authorship.

A Ballad of Good Counsel is added by Skeat, from MS. Cambridge Univ. K.K.1.5. and *The Gude and Godlie Ballatis* (1578 and 1621); printed also in *Ratis Raving*, edited by J. R. Lumley, E.E.T.S., 43, 1870.

Two very popular poems have been attributed to James I, with (so to speak) remainder to James V: *Christ's Kirk on the Green* and *Peblis to the Play*. Either or neither may be royal, but it is convenient to put them here, and the tradition itself is noteworthy evidence of the Scottish view of royalty, since these are rough, lively descriptions of popular festivals, ancestors of many later Scottish poems and important vehicles of the tailed romance-stanza to later ages. *Christ's Kirk* is in the Bannatyne and Maitland MSS., and appears first in print as a broadsheet of 1643. It may be most easily found in Dixon's, Eyre-Todd's, Douglas's and Miss Gray's anthologies. Allan Ramsay added two cantos.

SIR RICHARD HOLLAND, fl. c. 1450

Holland was a clerk in orders and secretary to two (Douglas) Earls of Moray.

The Buke of the Howlat is akin to *The Parlement of Foules* as one of the many mediaeval bird-poems. Like them, it contains more than bird-watching, but all that can be gleaned from it is praise of the Douglases. Like Hawes, Holland has left a couplet that is remembered:

> O Douglass, O Douglass,
> Tendir and trewe.

The poem is taken seriously by some, but Gregory Smith is indubitably right in emphasising its daftness (*Transition Period*, 1900, p. 74). Holland may have had an allegorical purpose, but he enjoyed the possibilities of the *genre* as Chaucer did, and, unlike Chaucer, allowed them to run away with him. There is also good farce in it. Fragments of an edition of about 1520 exist (D. Laing, *Adversaria*, 1867), but the text-sources are the Bannatyne and Asloan MSS. Recent editions are by F. J. Amours, *Scottish Alliterative Poems*, S.T.S., 27, 38, 1891, 1896, from the Asloan MS., and A. Diebler, Leipzig and Chemnitz, 1893, from the Bannatyne. Laing's introduction in his Bannatyne Club edition 1823 has matter in it. Gaelic phrases are given different interpretations by Diebler and by Campbell, *Popular Tales of the West Highlands*, 1862, Vol. IV, p. 53: Holland's Gaelic is only a shade more serious than that of Henryson in *Sum Practeis of Medycine*, and may well be left obscure.

ROBERT HENRYSON, ?1430–?1506

Master of the Grammar school attached to the Benedictine Abbey of Dunfermline, but not certainly the Robert Henryson incorporated in the University of Glasgow in 1462 or the notary public who witnessed certain Dunfermline deeds, since the name was common. Dunbar mentions him as dead in the *Lament for the Makaris*, which was printed in or about 1508; and that is all we know. He lacks Dunbar's metrical ingenuity, and in place of his exuberance exhibits a gentle middle-aged quietude; but technically he is more than adequate and keeps his poems moving. Of all the Scottish Chaucerians he is the least rhetorical and the likest to his master in his more sober moods. The burlesque *Sum Practysis of Medecyne*, however, proves that he had his share of the mediaeval notion of farce and of the native pleasure in satirical nonsense.

Henryson's works were edited by David Laing, 1865. The best edition is that of G. Gregory Smith, Sc.T.C., 3 vols.; Vol. I, 1914, introduction (valuable) and notes; Vol. II, 1906, parallel texts of the Fables; Vol. III, parallel texts of the other poems. That by H. H. Wood, 1933, is convenient and useful. Selections appear in many collections from Allan Ramsay's *Evergreen*, 1724, down.

The Testament of Cresseid appears in the index of the Asloan MS., but is lost from the volume. Published in Thynne's edition of Chaucer (1532) as a fifth book of *Troilus and Criseyde*, and thence in other editions. Published separately in a better text by Charteris, 1593; well edited by Bruce Dickins, Porpoise Press, Edinburgh, 1925. A Latin translation by Sir Francis Kinaston (1587–1642) was partly printed in Urry's edition of Chaucer (1721–) and by F. Waldron (1796); MS. in Bodleian Library. The poem is a sequel to Chaucer's, and better than most sequels. The body of the poem is in rime royal (553 lines) with sixty-three lines, *The Complaint of Cresseid*, in 9-line stanzas rhyming aabaabbab.

Orpheus and Eurydice is less important. It appears in the Bannatyne and Asloan MSS., and was printed by Chepman and Myllar, 1508. The 414 lines in rime royal are followed by 164 (209 in MS. texts) of *Moralitas* in 10-syllable couplets.

Robene and Makyne is in the Bannatyne MS., was included by Percy in his *Reliques* (1765) and appears often in anthologies, for it was long and deservedly popular in Scotland. It is a humorous *pastourelle* after the mediaeval French manner—not a Virgilian Bucolic. The dialogue is in sixteen 8-line stanzas of eight and six syllables alternately, rhyming ababab.

Ten *Fables* appear in the Bannatyne MS. (1568), and one in the Asloan (c. 1515), an extract in the Makculloch (see G. G. Smith, *Specimens*), and all fourteen in Harleian MS. 3865 in the British Museum, dated 1571. They were printed by Lekprevik for Charteris, 1570; in English versions by R. Smith, 1577; and by Andro Hart, 1621 (reprinted by the Maitland Club, 1832). They are all in rime royal, of varying length but of almost equal merit. The beginner may select, say, *The Cok and the Iasp* for its neatness, observation and humour; *The Uponlandis Mous and the Burges Mous* which Wyatt may have known; and *How the Fox maid his confessiun to Frier Wolf*, which Sir Thomas More may have known.

The Abbay Walk comes next, for its resigned philosophy. It appears in both Bannatyne and Maitland MSS., and was first printed (modernised) by John Forbes, Aberdeen, 1686. It is a recension of earlier English work (see G. G. Smith's ed., Vol. I), but has Henryson's mark plain upon it. The seven stanzas are of a neat form: eight lines of eight syllables, rhyming ababbxbx, the borrowed refrain (x) being "Obey and thank thy god of all".

The other poems are mainly moral and religious. *The Bludy Serk*, twelve stanzas and three of *moralitas* in the *Robene* verse, is an allegory from the *Gesta Romanorum*. The average fifteenth-century poet would have expanded the material indefinitely; the discreet Henryson keeps it short, and improves the technique by omitting names. *The Garmont of Gud Ladeis*, forty lines in quatrains which are half the *Robene* stanza, is also of a comely simplicity, suggesting an origin in a secular song, as the grim *Thre Deid Pollis* suggests a wall-decoration. The nonsensical *Sum Practysis of Medecyne* may be a satire on a practitioner or practitioners, predecessors of Burns's Dr. Hornbook. No poet has written better *In Prais of Aige*.

WILLIAM DUNBAR, 1465?–1530?

An East Lothian man of good family, perhaps M.A. of St. Andrews, and destined from childhood for the Church, was for a time a Franciscan: but see *How Dunbar was desierit to be a Frere*. He was employed about the court of James IV, and was silenced, along with so much of promise and fulfilment, by the disaster of Flodden. Dunbar is the greatest of Scottish poets, and the student or lover of poetry should not allow the artificial diction and strange spelling of this Scottish school to stand in his way, especially as the grammar is simple and regular.

Dunbar's allegories, in the old manner of the *Rose* learned from Chaucer and Lydgate (see *The Goldyn Targe*, 253 ff.), preserve more of the charm of their original than any others except Chaucer's. Their brevity and lucidity show how he kept control of himself and his matter as few poets could. His conciseness and economy in general would, indeed, be remarkable at any time; at that period they would be extraordinary, were it not that the Scottish poets usually have some notion of keeping to the point. His formal allegories are: *The Thrissil and the Rois*, 189 lines in rime royal, on the marriage of James IV and Margaret Tudor in 1503; and two love-allegories, *The Goldyn Targe*, 2,791 lines in 9-line stanzas rhyming aabaabbab, and *Bewty and the Prisoner*, 112 8-syllable lines in 8-line stanzas rhyming ababbxbx—x being a constant refrain-rhyme. The allegorical formulas are carried over into smaller poems as usual.

The Satires are not easy to disentangle from the comic poems. The *Flyting of Dunbar and Kennedy*, for instance, might be termed a series of satires and replies, but the thing was a game, a set sparring match between two poets who were probably excellent friends. Skelton's *Invectives against Garneysche* are of the same nature, except that we may surmise it was a less equal contest, and the replies were not preserved. *The Testament of Mr. Andro Kennedy* is also a comic poem; when Dunbar wished to damage anyone he did it in more deadly fashion. The principal satires, however, are general—*The Twa Merrit Wemen and the Wedo*, traditional but realistic: Dunbar does not require, like Hawes, the *exempla* of Socrates and Virgil—he has the figures in his eye.

416

The Devil's Inquest and the poems on burgess folk like the *Tailzeouris and Soutaris* show that this court poet was not blind to common life, and *The Dance in the Queen's Chalmir* that he carried his grotesque vision into the most exalted circles and that it included his own figure. The familiarity of his addresses to the king seem to justify this lack of dignity. *The Dance of the Seven Deidly Synnis* is of another order, but comes from the same imagination.

Finally, there are the moral and religious poems. *The Merle and the Nychtingaill* treats in the old debate-form of earthly and heavenly love, a theme treated directly elsewhere. He addresses the king on *The Worldis Instabilitie*, using his favourite device of a refrain, as again in *All Erdly Joy Returnis in Pane*, and, magnificently, in the *Lament for the Makaris*. The Latin refrain in that poem tolls like a bell, but he could use Latin as he pleased: compare the poem on the Nativity, and the *Ballat of Our Lady*. His hymns indeed are beautiful, and they are both accomplished and singable, an unusual combination of virtues in hymnary.

Most of his poems are preserved in MSS., especially in the Bannatyne MS. A useful table of MS. appearances is in C. Steinberger (see below). Unique copies exist in the Scottish National Library of these texts: *The Ballade of Lord Barnard Stewart; The Flyting of Dunbar and Kennedy; The Goldyn Targe*; printed by Chapman and Myllar, probably in 1508; facs. ed., W. Beattie, Edinburgh Bibliographical Soc., 1950; and *The Two Marret Wemen and the Wedo*, perhaps printed in France.

The MS. poems were printed piecemeal in the eighteenth century; modern editions are: David Laing, 1834, 2 vols. and supplement; W. Gregor, Scottish Text Society, 1893, J. Schipper, Vienna, 1891–5, and W. M. Mackenzie. The last is the most useful and convenient edition.

Selections in W. M. Dixon, *The Edinburgh Book*, in Sir George Douglas, and John Buchan, *The Northern Muse*, in G. Eyre Todd, *Mediæval Scottish Poetry*, and a good selection in M. M. Gray, *Scottish Poetry*.

The most elaborate study of Dunbar is that of J. Schipper, *Wilhelm Dunbar, sein Leben und seine Gedichte*, Berlin, 1884; excellently studied, though it is doubtful whether the daft Scottish character could be appreciated at a German professorial desk. Rachel Annand Taylor's *Dunbar, The Poet and his Period*, 1931, is interesting and over-emphatic, to be read with pleasure and caution. Cécile Steinberger, *Etude sur William Dunbar*, 1908, is a pleasant descriptive essay. O. Smeaton published a *Life*, 1898—any "life" of Dunbar resolves itself into a sketch of his times and a study of his poems. See the usual histories, *passim*, and notably Gregory Smith in *C.H.E.L.*, II, Chap. X, and in *Scottish Literature*. H. B. Baildon, *The Rimes in the Authentic Poems of William Dunbar*, 1899, will interest the philological student.

GAVIN DOUGLAS, 1474?-1522

The son of the great Earl of Angus was born to great place and to trouble and intrigue. As a younger son, his place was in the church; trouble came to him in both church and state. The scenes of his life may be well observed in the relevant portion of *Tales of a Grandfather*, or in Scott's favourite source Pitscottie; for if Scott lightens the dark shades a little, his lack of "scientific" method is a virtue in describing that tangle of personal and family hates and ambitions, and he really understood the mixed and often irrelevant motives. But the life of the politician Bishop of Dunkeld seems equally irrelevant to his poetry. Poetry was a pastime, but he had gleams of inspiration; and he studied his pastime, though the amateur betrays himself in the difficulty of his synthetic language as well as in the obsolescence of his mediaeval models. The enduring interest of his work—as distinct from its considerable historical and still greater philological interest—lies in some fine passages of subtle description and in the phrasing that was his amateurish pleasure. It is difficult to believe that (except for one short moral epigram) he wrote only three long and elaborate poems, but if he produced any *juvenilia* or *minora* he—and others—treated them as of no account and nothing was heard of them: in which he seems to resemble David Lindsay.

The Palice of Honour, 2,142 lines in 9-line stanzas rhyming aabaabbab, is a learned allegory, by *The House of Fame* out of *The Court of Love*, but ending with a moral disquisition that Henryson would have done better. As a picture of the literary content of the contemporary mind it is invaluable, curious, and not unattractive in the native roughness of style that gives it an archaic rather than a decadent feeling as compared with Hawes. No MS. is preserved. It was printed first in London, Copland, ?1553; Edinburgh, Ros for Charteris, 1579, which was used in the Bannatyne Club edition, 1827.

King Hart, 960 lines in 8-line stanzas rhyming ababbcbc; a moral-religious allegory descended from Grosseteste's *Château d'Amour*; is less interesting for its conventional matter, but keeps moving. This appears in the Maitland folio MS., and was first printed by Pinkerton, *Ancient Scotish Poems*, 1786—a bad edition.

Conscience, 28 lines in 7-line stanzas rhyming ababbcc: an

416

epigram. This also is in the Maitland folio MS., and was first
printed by Pinkerton.

Eneados, a translation of Virgil (including the thirteenth book
by Mapheus Vegius) in 10-syllable couplets, was the first great
effort of translation into English, and is by no means despicable,
as a fair test-passage (V.134–43) may show:

> The remanent of the roweris, every wycht,
> In pople tre branschis dycht at poynt,
> With spaldis nakit, schene with oil anoynt,
> Apon thair settis and thortis all attanis
> Thair placis hint, arrayit for the nanis,
> With armis reddy outour thair airis fald,
> Abidis lisnand the takin to behald,
> Thair hartis on flocht, smythin with schame sum deill,
> Bot glaid and ioly, in hope for to do weill,
> Rasis in their breistis desyre of hie renoun.
> Syne, but delay, at the first trumpettis soun,
> From thair marchis attanis furth they sprent.
> Vpsprang the clamour, and the rerd furth went,
> Heych in the skyis, of mony maryner.
> The fary stour of seis rais thair and heir,
> Throw fers bak drauchtis of feil gardeis squair.
> Thai seuch the fludis that souchand quhair thai fair,
> In sondir slydis; ourweltit eik with ayris,
> Fra thair foirstammys the buller brauis and raris.

The most remarkable passages, however, are in the original prologues to the Books, various in matter and in verse-form. The
descriptions of the winter night in the seventh prologue and of
the summer morning in the twelfth are deservedly famous.

The *Eneados* is preserved in five MSS.: Trinity College, Cambridge (Gale MSS. O 3.12), the first copy from the original,
written by Mathew Geddes, Douglas's chaplain; University of
Edinburgh, written by James Elphinstone before 1527; in the
same library, the "Ruthven" MS., a little later; Lambeth Palace,
dated 1545–6; the Marquis of Bath's library, Longleat, dated
1547. The one early printed edition is London, Copland, 1553,
edited with protestant alteration of religious phrases. The Cambridge MS. was printed for the Bannatyne Club, 1839. The one
modern edition of Douglas's works is by John Small, 1874, in
4 vols.: Vol. I, life and bibliography, and minor poems; Vols.
II–IV, *Eneados* (from Elphinstone MS.), and glossary. There is a

dissertation on the *Eneados* by Aloys Schumacher, Strasbourg, 1910; and one on the interesting language by J. L. Larue, Strasbourg, 1908. Lauchlan Maclean Watt, *Douglas's Æneid*, 1920, though amateurish and occasionally naïve, contains some facts and the beginnings of a criticism.

SIR DAVID LINDSAY, ?1490–?1555

A scion of the large and powerful Lindsay family of Fife, Sir David of the Mount spent his life in court employments. His most conspicuous post was that of Lyon King of Arms—head of the Scottish college of heralds—which entailed attendance at parliaments and councils and also diplomatic journeys; his duties as guardian to the young King James V doubtless helped to breed the habit of advice and admonition. Lindsay was no youthful warbler: he must have been about forty when he wrote the earliest extant poem, *The Dreme*. So we have no love-poems, but only the comments and opinions, pungent and full-flavoured, of a shrewd, humorous, experienced but sympathetic man of the world; and instead of hymns, the anticlerical satires of a reformer, no theologian nor mystic, but a moralist who conducted a frontal attack on abuses in State and Church—especially such as bore hard on poor folk—and who hit hard and feared none. The manner is coloured by study of mediaeval romance and of Chaucer and Lydgate and his Scottish predecessors; the outlook is contemporary and even advanced.

For bibliographical details, see Douglas Hamer, *The Library*, 4th ser. X, and in his edition of the Works (below), Vol. IV. He argues for lost earlier editions of several poems.

Collective eds. Partial collections appeared at Paris, 1558; Edinburgh, 1559; London, 1566, 1575, 1581 (anglicised versions): see Hamer (above). Complete collections, except for *Squire Meldrum* and *Ane Satyre of the Thre Estaitis*, were printed by John Scot for H. Charteris, Edinburgh, 1568,?1569, 1571; by T. Bassandyne, 1574; by Ross, ?1580, 1582; by R. Charteris, 1592, 1597, 1604, etc. A Danish translation appeared at Copenhagen in 1591. The long list and inclusion in MSS. prove Lindsay's popularity, which continued up to the nineteenth-century revolution.

Of modern editions, those of Chalmers, 1806, Laing, 1879, and Murray, E.E.T.S., 1865–71, are superseded by the elaborate and admirable edition by Hamer, S.T.S., 3rd ser., 1, 2, 6, 8, 1930–4. Vol. I contains the poems; Vol. II, *Ane Satyre of the Thre Estaitis*; III and IV, notes, life, bibliography, appendices and glossary.

Personal details appear especially in *The Dreme* and *The Complaint*. *Squire Meldrum*, a romantic biography of a friend, is one of the brightest poems, less aureate in diction, moving quicker. *The Complaint of Bagsche*, the king's old hound, is neither fable nor allegory, but really about a dog: Lindsay, like Henryson, has sympathy with beasts, but unlike any earlier poet, makes that sympathy a sufficient motive for a poem. *The Testament of the Papingo*—the king's parrot—on the other hand, is a human poem, of the sort displayed at length in the *Monarche*. For the rest, one or two are satires; the *Tragedie of the late Cardinal Beaton* is after the Boccaccio-Lydgate manner, but decidedly unsympathetic to Beaton. Lindsay uses the rime royal for serious poems, 10-syllable and 8-syllable couplets for comic and satiric verse. *Squire Meldrum* is also in 8-syllable couplets, *The Complaint of Bagsche* in a comic 8-line stanza of 8-syllable lines rhyming ababbcbc, and the Exhortation to the king before *The Dreme* in 9-line stanzas rhyming aabaabbab. Much the longest poem is *Ane Dialogue betwix Experience and ane Courteour, Off the Miserabyll Estait of the World*, also called *The Monarche*, 6,338 lines in all, part in rime royal, part in 8-syllable couplets. The subject is universal history, mainly from the Bible; the motive, admonition to the king. It is the dullest of the poems, but is saved from the impersonal dullness of its type by Lindsay's evident earnestness.

For *Ane Satyre of the Thre Estaitis*, see under Drama, p. 423. Lindsay is noticed in all the histories of literature, but see especially Warton, John Nichol in Ward's *English Poets*, Vol. I, and Jusserand, Vol. I. W. Murison, *Sir David Lindsay*, 1938, gathers the relevant facts and adds some remarks on the Scottish Reformation.

C. SIXTEENTH-CENTURY SCOTTISH POETRY

The strong mediaeval strain in the Scottish poets makes it proper to include them in this vol. Throughout the century the new strains learned from France, Italy, and England mingle in increasing proportions, from Gavin Douglas, whose contempt for Caxton's mediaeval version of *Eneados* is of the Renaissance but who has otherwise nothing of the "new poetry", down to Drummond, who properly belongs to the next vol. (p. 213) as a follower of Spenser, but is credited with a macaronic *Polemo-Middinia* possible only to a compatriot of Dunbar and Urquhart of Cromarty. The group which centres in James VI is not very exciting, but these men had their moments, and to understand

their peculiar mixture, and also their failure to found an enduring
school of poetry, would be to understand a very important and
interesting turn in the intellectual and artistic history of Scotland.
But some strenuous work must be done before that can be accomplished. Some dull source-hunting is required to trace the lines
of descent, and much comparative study before we shall understand, for instance, why the "Spenserian" sonnet-form was popular in Scotland before Spenser published his, or even wrote more
than one.

Nothing is known of the life of ALEXANDER SCOTT (*florit* 1545–
68). His amorous and occasionally graceless poems, lyrical in
style and cheerful even in satirical moments, are contained in the
Bannatyne MS. along with those others—Harry Stewart, Merser,
and so on—of whom we know and have even less. The first complete edition was that of David Laing, 1821, the latest those of
J. Cranstoun, S.T.S., 36, 1896, and A. K. Donald, E.E.T.S.,
ex. ser. LXXXV, 1902. The texts of Laing and Cranstoun should
be checked by the S.T.S. edition of the MS., but they print some
of the music from the Aberdeen *Cantus* (see under Music, p. 439)
in appendices. ALEXANDER MONTGOMERIE (1545?–1611?) had a
considerable reputation, though little was published in his lifetime—James VI quotes in his *Reulis and Cautelis* (see below) from
poems printed from thirteen to thirty-four years later. His works
were edited by J. Cranstoun, S.T.S., 1887, with biography, bibliography and notes, but the supplementary vol. by G. Stevenson,
S.T.S., 59, 1910, is necessary for corrections and additions in both
text and apparatus. *The Cherry and the Slae*, a mediaeval allegory in
114 14-line stanzas, was twice published by Waldegrave in 1597,
and remained popular. *The Flyting between Montgomerie and Pol-
wart* (i.e., Patrick Hume), published by Hart, 1621, in an edition
now lost but often reprinted, is another survival of the days of
Dunbar. His other poems are lyrical on themes of love and religion, and his use of the sonnet and of varied stanzas is to be
noted. ALEXANDER HUME (1560?–1609) younger brother of Pol-
warth and minister of Logie, published *Hymnes or Sacred Songs*,
1599: edited by A. Lawson, S.T.S., 48, 1901. These are dull, but
The Day Estivall has merited frequent reprinting, especially when
judiciously cut as by Dixon. STEWART OF BALDYNNIS (1550?–
1605?) is a lesser man but of the same breed. JAMES VI (1566–
1625) is Scot only in language, and poet only by dint of perseverance; but he did persevere, and his verses and his critical *Schort
Treatise containing some Reulis and Cautelis to be observit and eschewit
in Scottis Poesie* (1884) are the more valuable as documents of the

school that their author was a mere school-product. For the verse, see the editions by R. S. Rait; for the *Treatise*, G. Gregory Smith, *Elizabethan Critical Essays* (1904), Vol. I. The many anonymous scraps include some poetry as good as any of these: a useful selection is conveniently gathered in Miss Gray's *Scottish Poetry*. David Laing, *Early Popular Poetry of Scotland*, 1895, is important.

D. SCOTTISH DRAMA

For this see A. J. Mill, *Mediæval Plays in Scotland*, 1927, where the documents are printed. Records are fairly numerous; Dunbar's *Droichis Part of the Play*, and Montgomerie's *The Navigation* and *The Cartel of the Thre Ventrous Knichts* seem to be parts of entertainments of the early masque type; but only two plays are extant, Sir David Lindsay's *Satyre of the Thre Estaitis* (see p. 420) and the anonymous *Philotus*. A contemporary description of the first version of Lindsay's elaborate morality, performed at Linlithgow, 1540, exists in the Public Record Office: a complete transcript is printed by Hamer (below). The version produced at Cupar-Fife in 1552 is preserved in the Bannatyne MS. as a series of interludes, and the version (similar but omitting a prefatory interlude) acted at Edinburgh in 1554, was printed by Robert Charteris, Edinburgh, 1602, and frequently thereafter. The two are printed on opposite pages by Douglas Hamer, in Vol. II of his edition of Lindsay's Works, S.T.S., 3rd ser., 2, 1931. The play, in two parts and some 3,500 lines in length, is a coarse, outspoken indictment of immorality and injustice in king, law, trade and church, two-thirds plain denunciation of contemporary evils and one-third anti-clerical propaganda. It bears witness both consciously and unconsciously to the state of Scotland at the time, and also suggests that the Scottish reformation might have had a different character if James had lived to control it. For its affiliations, see Anna J. Mill, *Influence of Continental Drama on L.'s Satyre*, in M.L.R., 1930.

Philotus, by an unknown author, but written probably about 1600, was published by Charteris, Edinburgh, 1603, and by his successor Hart in 1612. The best modern edition is by Miss A. J. Mill, S.T.S., Miscellany Vol., 3rd ser. 4, 1932. The plot is close to the eighth tale in Barnabe Riche's *Farewell to Militarie Profession*, 1581, but parallels with *Gli Ingannati*, 1538, suggest a possible common Italian source. *Philotus* is a romantic comedy of the School of Plautus, a Renaissance work in a different world from Lindsay's, parallel to English comedy before Lyly and Greene.

E. SCOTTISH PROSE

There is little here to attract the literary student outside the historians who are listed elsewhere; they, by a kind of compensation, are readable indeed. In the earlier period, the translations of GILBERT OF THE HAYE (*The Buke of the Law of Armys*, etc., 1456; edited by J. H. Stevenson, S.T.S., 44, 62, 1899, 1908) provide useful specimens of late-chivalric doctrine. The first original prose is in the theological tracts of JOHN OF IRELAND (c. 1480). His *Meroure of Wysdome*, composed for the young James IV, is edited by C. Macpherson, S.T.S., 2nd ser., 19, 1925; the prose is painstaking but not accomplished. JOHN BELLENDEN's workmanlike translation of five books of Livy, about 1530-40, is edited from the Scottish National Library MSS. by W. A. Craigie, S.T.S., 47, 51, 1900-2. But such things as Gau's *Richt Vay to the Kingdom of Heaven*, and the religious controversialists like Ninian Wingate, Nicol Burne, Mure, and the rest, are merely dull even in invective. There is a touch of preacher's rhetoric here and there in Knox, but even the humanists failed to adapt their skill to vernacular prose, though George Buchanan wrote excellent Latin prose and was deservedly famous among neo-Latin poets.

Some of the best prose is in official papers (e.g., Records of the Privy Council, and Pitcairn's *Trials*), and passages in James Melvill's Diary (1556-1614; printed 1829, reprinted Woodrow Soc.) prove that he had an eye for a dramatic scene and a gift for description. But the storms were too high for lighter craft. There is but one piece of prose with artistic intention, *The Complaynt of Scotlande*, a controversial tract adapted in the main from Alain Chartier's *Quadrilogue Invectif*, with the rhetorical vices of the original elaborated in a strained and deliberately *recherché* dialect. It was published in Paris about 1550, edited by John Leyden, 1801, and by J. A. H. Murray, E.E.T.S., E.S. XVII–XVIII, 1872-3, with other tracts of the time. See W. A. Neilson, J.G.P., 4.

CHAPTER XII

THE ARTS

I. A. EDUCATION AND SCHOLARSHIP

Most manuals of the history of education glance at mediaeval schools, but (partly owing to a certain self-complacency in the writers) seldom to any great purpose. The difficult question of "literacy" has not been studied for the period as a whole, but very interesting points emerge in the discussions by C. L. Kingsford, in *English Historical Literature in the 15th Century*, Chap. VIII, and *Prejudice and Promise in XVth Century England*, Chap. II; by J. W. Adamson, in *The Extent of Literacy in England in the 15th and 16th Centuries*, a paper in *The Library*, 4th ser. X (1930); and by C. J. Sisson in *Marks as Signatures*, ib., Vol. IX (1929). F. Leach's *The Schools of Medieval England* is the best for reference, and his *English Schools at the Reformation* adds to it. See also his *Educational Charters and Documents*.

The magisterial work on the mediaeval Universities is H. Rashdall, *The Universities of Europe in the Middle Ages* (revised edition, 1935), but (again) the restricted subject allows of more personal understanding in histories of single universities like Willis and Clark's and Mullinger's histories of Cambridge, Brodrick's of Oxford, the published muniments of the Scottish universities, and the series of Oxford and Cambridge College Histories. See also Sir R. S. Rait's *Life in the Medieval University* (Cambridge Manuals, No. 38) and (for a small example of daily life) H. E. Salter's *An Oxford Hall in 1424* in *Essays . . . presented to R. L. Poole*. Sir J. E. Sandys, *A History of Classical Scholarship*, Vol. I, is the standard work on the classical attainments of mediaeval scholars. For Helen Waddell, *The Wandering Scholars*, etc., see p. 401.

B. PHILOSOPHY

Not many students may have time or energy to enter this labyrinth, especially as it is European in extent and the English contribution cannot be treated separately. But some notion of its general aspect may be required. C. R. S. Harris's chapter, No. 4 in the Oxford *Legacy of the Middle Ages*, may serve (with the usual encyclopedias) as an introduction. Thereafter, consult H. O. Taylor, *The Mediaeval Mind*, 1911 (2nd ed. 1914). Almost better, although—or because—more succinct and restricted in scope, is the same author's *Classical Influence on the Middle Ages*, 1925. Along with this goes A. de Wulf, *Philosophy and Civilisation in the Middle Ages*, 1922. The same author's *Mediaeval Philosophy*, translated by E. C. Messenger, Harvard, 1922, is very valuable, as is Etienne Gilson, *The Spirit of Medieval Philosophy*, 1936, especially (for our purposes) the last three chapters. F. Picavet, *Historie Générale et Comparée des Philosophies Mediévales* and M. de Wulf, *History of Medieval Philosophy*, translated by E. C. Messenger, 1926 and 1935, may be consulted. (The French originals of de Wulf and Gilson are usually more lucid than the translations.) R. L. Poole, *Illustrations of the History of Medieval Thought*, 1884, is full of material. G. M. Trevelyan, *England in the Age of Wiclif*, 1899, will help in this study also. R. McKeon, *Selections from Mediaeval Philosophers*, New York, 1930, gives translated extracts which illustrate most usefully both the principal doctrines and the method of argument. A brief extract from St. Thomas Aquinas in S. Gaselee's *An Anthology of Medieval Latin* will show the formula of presentation.

A. II. BOOKS AND LIBRARIES

RICHARD DE BURY, 1281–1345.

The name of Richard Aungerville, called Richard de Bury, tutor to Edward III, bishop of Durham, lord chancellor, and a prince of book-collectors, must appear at the head of this section. His *Philobiblon*, half rhapsody on books and half advice on keeping a library, is a bookman's book, the first of many and father of them all. There are many MSS., and an edition was printed at Cologne in 1473, and another at Spire in the same year. An English translation by J. B. Inglis appeared in 1832, of which there are many reprints, the best being those edited by E. C. Thomas, 1888, and by E. F. West, New York, Grolier Club, 1889. See F. S. Merryweather, *Bibliomania in the Middle Ages*, 1849, and subsequently; also J. de Ghellinck in *Revue d'Histoire Ecclésiastique*, Vols. XVIII (1922) and XIX (1923).

B. MANUSCRIPTS

The student must first decide for himself whether he requires information on books or on works of art; he must not imagine that the text-books of his forebears were like the noble service-books and princely histories usually exhibited in library show-cases. For either purpose he may well begin with Falconer Madan, *Books in Manuscript*, 2nd ed., 1920.

For the reading of MSS., see Sir E. Maunde Thompson, *History of English Handwriting*, and Falconer Madan's useful article in *Medieval England*, Oxford, 1924. The beginner will find the following helpful: *Twelve Facsimiles of English MSS.*, edited by W. W. Skeat, 1892; and *Facsimiles of Twelve Early English MSS.*, edited by W. W. Greg, 1913. *Durham Cathedral MSS to the End of the Twelfth Century*, introd. R. A. B. Mynors, O.U.P. 1939, contains good reprod. of important MSS. The literary student may be concerned only with formal "book-" or "text-hands", but may have to study other documents, for which consult H. Jenkinson, *Palaeography and the Practical Study of Court Hand*, or C. Johnson and H. Jenkinson, *Court Hand Illustrated*, and Jenkinson, *The Later Court Hands of England*, or T. Wright, *Court Hand Restored*, edited by Martin. He will require help with tiresome abbreviations, and will find it in the above vols., and in A. Chassant, *Dictionnaire des Abbréviations*, A. Cappelli, *Lexicon Abbreviaturarum: Dizionario di Abbreviature* (a handy pocket book), or C. T. Martin, *The Record Interpreter*.

For the art of illumination, continue with O. Elfrida Saunders, *English Illumination*; J. H. Middleton, *Illuminated Manuscripts*; J. A. Herbert, *Illuminated Manuscripts*; and *Schools of Illumination*, magnificent reproductions from MSS. in the British Museum, with introductions and descriptions by J. A. Herbert, viz.: Part I, Hiberno-Saxon and Early English Schools, II, twelfth-thirteenth centuries, III, 1300-50, IV, 1350-1500. F. Harrison, *Treasures of Illumination*, published by *The Studio*, with fair reproductions, may be more accessible. J. O. Westwood, *Palaeographia Sacra Pictoria*, may also be found useful. Reproductions of more or less complete books are: *The Book of Kells* (eighth-century Irish), published by *The Studio*; *The Lindisfarne Gospels* (eighth-century Northumbrian), *Queen Mary's Psalter* (early fourteenth century), and the *Luttrell Psalter* (mid-fourteenth century, East Anglian), published by the British Museum trustees. Various facsimiles are noted above, e.g., under Beowulf, p. 162. The British Museum sells large reproductions of single pages, and cheap and handy sets of postcards in colour, and its *Guide to the Exhibited MSS.* contains much useful information succinctly conveyed, the notes in Part III on the schools of illumination providing an admirable guide. There are many articles in periodicals, e.g., Roger Fry, *The Burlington Magazine*, Vol. XIII, pp. 128–9, 261–73, but more is to be learned from personal examination of even a poor MS. than from many reproductions of splendid pages. Walter Oakeshott carries the study to a higher plane in *The Artists of the Winchester Bible*, C.U.P., 1945. G. A. Plimpton, *The Education of Chaucer*, Oxford, 1935, is an odd, attractive little book on books.

For technical points on colours and methods, D. V. Thompson's translation of *De Arte Illuminandi*, with the editor's invaluable notes, will serve for English practice, though it is of Italian origin. Thompson has also a lucid article on *Medieval Parchment-Making* in *The Library*, 4th ser. XVI (1936). But the student will learn most from a practical modern handbook such as Edward Johnston, *Writing, Illumination, and Lettering*, which contains historical as well as technical matter: both repay study.

The methods and regulation of book-supply for universities can be studied in J. Destrez, *La "Pecia" dans les Manuscrits Universitaires du XIIc et XIIIc Siècle*. See also an article on *The Pecia* (the copyist's unit of calculation) by R. Steele, *The Library*, 4th ser. XI (1931), and a scribe's bill of 1469 among the Paston Letters, No. 596 in Gairdner's edition. In *The Price of Books in Medieval England*, in *The Library*, 4th ser. XVII, 1937, H. E. Bell discusses admirably what is after all a crucial point. J. W. Clark, *The Care of Books*, contains valuable material on copyists, libraries, etc. Monastic scriptoria are described in J. Taylor, *The Monastic Scriptorium*, *The Library*, 1st ser. II, 1890, in books on monastic life and incidentally in catalogues as noted below. For the St. Albans scriptorium and its ways, see Luard's prefaces to his edition of Matthew Paris (above, p. 330), and Claude Jenkins, *The Monastic Chronicler*.

For libraries, see Clark (above) and B. H. Streeter, *The Chained Library*. The contents and organisation of a college library are best documented in F. M. Powicke, *The Medieval Books of Merton College*; P. S. Allen, *Early Documents connected with the Library of Merton College*—a very valuable paper—in *The Library*, 4th ser. IV; and H. W. Garrod, *The Library Regulations of a Medieval College*, ib., VIII, 1928. See also the history of Cambridge libraries in Willis and Clark, *History of the University of Cambridge*, III, vii, and the catalogues of Cambridge College libraries by M. R. James. Several monastic catalogues have been published: e.g.,

Durham, by B. Botfield, Surtees Soc., Vol. 7; Dover Priory, by M. R. James; Westminster Abbey, by J. A. Robinson, and M. R. James; Worcester, by J. K. Floyer and S. G. Hamilton, Worcs. Historical Soc. These are the best evidence for monastic study and book-production alike. Note also Joseph Hunter, *English Monastic Libraries; The Localisation of Manuscripts*, by Falconer Madan, in *Essays in History presented to Reginald Lane Poole*—an interesting and practical study in technique, as is M. R. James, *The Wanderings and Homes of Manuscripts*, S.P.C.K., *Helps for Students of History*, No. 17. Private libraries are more difficult to estimate, but see the book-list of a fifteenth-century gentleman among the Paston Letters, edited by Gairdner, No. 869, and an excellent article (not without significance for Chaucer), *King Richard II's Books*, by Edith Rickert, *The Library*, 4th ser. XIII, 1933; also E. A. Savage, *The Old English Library*, one of *The Antiquary's Books* series.

Gottlieb, *Mittelalterliche Bibliotheken* is particularly valuable as a means of reference to all available catalogues of mediaeval libraries.

C. PRINTED BOOKS

For the subject in general, read E. Gordon Duff, *Early Printed Books* (1893) and the first two chapters of H. R. Plomer, *A Short History of English Printing* (1900), and consult Joseph Ames. *Typographical Antiquities*, edited by W. Herbert, 1785; E. Gordon Duff, *A Century of the English Book Trade, 1457–1557*, (1905) and *Fifteenth Century English Books* (Bibliographical Society, 1917) His *Early English Printing* is a technical work consisting of type-facsimiles, and may be prefaced by H. G. Aldis, *The Printed Book* (Cambridge Manuals, No. 89, 1916). The British Museum *Guide to the Exhibition in the King's Library* has the virtues of its kind. For early editions of specified authors, look up the indispensable *Short-Title Catalogue of English Books, 1475–1640*, edited by Pollard and Redgrave (Bibliographical Society, 1926). The growth of publication and the run of taste are both easily observed in the equally indispensable *Annals of English Literature* published by the Oxford University Press, 1935.

WILLIAM CAXTON (1422?–1491).

The standard work is W. Blades, *The Life and Typography of William Caxton*, 1861–3, 2nd ed., 1882. E. Gordon Duff, *William*

Caxton, Chicago, 1905, is to be recommended, and H. R. Plomer, *Caxton* (The Roadmaker Series, 1925) is good and concise, and contains recently-discovered details not available to Blades and Duff. Biographical facts and documents are well collected and arranged in J. W. B. Crotch's *Caxton's Prologues* and *Epilogues*, E.E.T.S. 176, 1927. See also S. de Ricci, *A Census of Caxtons*, Bibliographical Society, 1909. There are many articles on technical points, but we are concerned more with the literary aspect, with which Miss N. S. Aurner deals intelligently in *Caxton. Mirrour of Fifteenth Century Letters*, 1926. There is also a valuable paper by A. T. P. Byles, *W. Caxton as a Man of Letters* in *The Library*, 4th ser., XV, 1935. H. B. Lathrop, *The First English Printers and their Patrons*, ib., III, 1923, is very relevant here.

Lists of Caxton's publications are given in all the Lives. We have ninety-two works from his press, of which six are single leaves (five indulgences and one advertisement). The other eighty-six represent seventy-four different books, being second or third editions. He published 6 vols. of Chaucer (see p. 284); five works of Lydgate, viz., *The Hors the Shepe and Ghoos* (2 editions), *The Chorle and the Birde* (2 editions), *Stans Puer ad Mensam*, and *The Temple of Glas* in 1477, and *The Lyf of Our Lady* (2 editions) in 1484; Gower's *Confessio Amantis*, 1483: and Malory's *Morte d'Arthur* in 1485. His prose books might be divided thus; though the divisions are not always clear-cut and calculations might differ slightly: ten books of morality, sixteen religious, six service-books, eight of social teaching, including fables, two of history, one of statutes, two political works (his only publications in Latin), three scientific, nine romances, and four school-books including a French-English vocabulary which he himself may have compiled.

Of his own works, *The Life of Robert Earl of Oxford* is lost. *The Lives of the Fathers*, which he finished on his death-bed, was printed by W. de Worde, 1495. The translation of *Ovyde his Methamorphose*, left unprinted, was edited by S. Gaselee and H. T. B. Brett-Smith in 1924 from the unique MS. in the Pepysian collection in Magdalene Coll., Cambridge. His other translations, all in prose and all from French except *Reynard the Fox*, which is from Dutch or Flemish, are:

The Recuyell of the Historyes of Troye. Printed at Bruges, 1472, from Raoul de Fevre. Edited by H. O. Sommer, 1894.

The Game and Playe of the Chesse. Bruges, 1475: Westminster, 1483. Moral Tales, from Jean de Vignay and Jean de Faron's versions of J. de Cessolis, *Liber de Ludo Scaccorum*. Facsimile,

V. Figgins, 1855, 1860. Edited by W. E. A. Axon, 1883.

The History of Jason. 1477. From Raoul de Fevre. Edited by J. Munro, (text only) E.E.T.S., extra ser. LXI, 1913. There is a MS. in the University Library, Cambridge, and another (with considerable variants and independent of the printed text) in the Hunterian Library, University of Glasgow.

The Mirrour of the World. 1481, 1490. Popular science, through French mainly from the *Speculum* of Vincent of Beauvais. The first English book illustrated with woodcuts. Edited by O. H. Prior, E.E.T.S., ex. ser., CX, 1913.

Reynard the Fox. 1481, 1489. Beast-fable, apparently from a Dutch or Flemish version. Edited by E. Arber, 1875.

Godefroy of Bologne. 1481. From French version of William, Archbishop of Tyre's history of the First Crusade. Edited by Mary N. Colvin, E.E.T.S., ex. ser., XLIV, 1893.

The Golden Legend. 1483, 1488. His greatest work, a compendium of Saints' lives, based on but enlarged from the *Legenda Aurea* of J. de Voragine: "for as moche as I had by me a legende in frensche, another in Latyn, & the thyrd in englysshe which varyed in many and dyvers places ... therefore I have wryton one oute of the sayd thre bookes." Edited by F. S. Ellis, Temple Classics, 1900. Selection edited by G. V. O'Neill, 1914.

The Boke callid Cathon. 1483. From a French commentary on the Latin school-books *Magnus* and *Parvus Cato*, of which he had printed a verse translation by Benedict Burgh.

The Knight of the Toure. 1484. Instructions in religion, manners and morals for young women, from Geoffrey de la Tour Landry. Edited in part by G. Rawlings, 1902, and (as supplementary to an earlier translation) by T. Wright, E.E.T.S. 33, 1868: corrections in 41, 1870.

Æsop. 1484. From Jules Machault's version of the well-known fables. See in M. J. Jacobs, *History of the Æsopic Fables*, 1889.

The Ordre of Chivalrye. 1484. The moral teachings of an old knight to a young squire. Edited by F. S. Ellis, 1892.

The Curiall. 1484?. From Alain Chartier's prose complaint of the miseries of court life. Edited by F. J. Furnivall and P. Meyer, E.E.T.S., ex. ser. LIV, 1888.

The Lyf of St. Wenefrede. 1485?. An addition to *The Golden Legend.*

Charles the Grete. 1485. Compiled from the *Speculum Historiale* of Vincent of Beauvais and the Charlemagne romances. Edited by S. J. Herrtage, E.E.T.S. ex. ser. XXXVI–XXXVII, 1880.

Paris and Vienne. 1485. French romance. Edited by W. C. Hazlitt, 1868.

The Book of Good Manners. 1487. Moral and religious teaching from Jacques Legrand's *Livre de Bonnes Mœurs.*

The Fayttes of Armes and of Chyvalrye. 1489. A book of military science, compiled out of Vegetius *De Re Militari, L'Arbre de Batailles,* etc., by Christine de Pisan. Ed.: A. T. P. Byles, E.E.T.S., 189, 1932, revised with corrections, 1937.

Blanchardyn and Eglantyne. 1489. French romance. Ed.: L. Kellner, E.E.T.S., ex. ser. LVIII, 1890.

The Four Sons of Aymon. 1489. French romance. Ed.: O. Richardson, E.E.T.S., ex. ser. XLIV–XLV, 1884.

The Gouvernayle of Helthe. 1489. Popular medicine. Facsimile, W. Blades, 1858.

Eneydos. 1490. A chivalric re-telling of the story, like *The Recuyell* and *Jason,* soon to be condemned by the men of the new school. Ed.: M. T. Culley and F. J. Furnivall, E.E.T.S., ex. ser. LVII, 1890.

The Art and Craft to Know Well to Die. 1490–1. Abridged from *Ars Moriendi,* a popular work of religion, of which a French version had been printed by Caxton's partner Colard Mansion at Bruges. The second ed. has the Latin title.

Caxton's native style in original composition is to be sought in his Prologues and Epilogues, conveniently collected by J. W. B. Crotch, E.E.T.S., 176, 1927 and by Miss Aurner. Nine of the most important are printed in modernised spelling in A. W. Pollard, *Fifteenth Century Prose and Verse,* 1903, one of Arber's "English Garner" series. Besides the information they convey, these short pieces present a clear picture of Caxton's sober character and his praiseworthy motives. The most important are those in *The Recuyell* (for biographical details), *Eneydos* (on the difficulties of writing English), *Morte D'Arthur* (on morals and on King Arthur), *The Ordre of Chyvalry* (on contemporary degeneracy), but all contain some honest and pious phrases, none the worse for occasional naïveté. Here is a specimen of his conscientious view of his work, from the prologue to the second edition of *The Canterbury Tales:*

> "I fynde many of the sayd bookes/whyche wryters haue abrydged it and many thynges left out/And in somme place haue sette certayn versys/that he neuer made ne sette in hys booke/of whyche bookes so incorrecte was one brought to me vj yere passyd/whyche I supposed had ben veray true &

correcte/And accordyng to the same I dyde do enprynte
a certayn nombre of them/whyche anon were sold to many
and dyuerse gentyl men/of whome one gentylman cam
to me/and said that this book was not accordyng in many
places vnto the book that Gefferey chaucer had made/ To
whom I answered that I had made it accordyng to my
copye/and by me was nothing added ne mynusshyd/Thenne
he sayd he knewe a book whyche hys fader had and moche
louyd/that was very trewe/and accordyng vnto hys owen
first book by hym made/and sayd more yf I wold enprynte
it agayn he wold gete me the same book for a copye/how be it
he wyst wel/that hys fader wold not gladly departe fro it/
To whom I said/it caas that he coude gete me suche a book
trewe and correcte/yet I wold ones endeuoyre me to enprynte
it agayn/for to satysfye thauctour/where as to for by
ygnouraunce I erryd in hurtyng and dyffamyng his book
in dyuerce places in settyng in somme thyngs that he neuer
sayd ne made/and leuying out many thynges that he made
whyche ben requysite to be sette in it/And thus we fyll
at accord/And he full gentylly gate of hys fader the said
book/and delyuerd it to me/by whiche I have corrected my
book/as here after alle alonge by thyde of almyghty god
shal folowe/whom I humbly beseche to gyue me grace and
ayde to achyue/and accomplysshe/to hys laude honour and
glorye/and that all ye that shal in thys book rede or heere/
wyll of your charyte emong your dedes of mercy/remembre
the sowle of the sayd Gefferey chaucer first auctour/and
maker of thys book. And also that alle we that shal see and
rede therein/may so take and vnderstonde the good and
vertuous tales/that it may so prouffyte/vnto the helthe
of our sowles/that after thys short and transitorye lyf we may
come to euerlastyng lyf in heuen/Amen"

For Caxton's immediate followers see H. R. Plomer, *Wynkyn
de Worde and his Contemporaries*, and the general histories cited
above. Gavin Bone's *Extant Manuscripts printed from by W. de Worde*,
in *The Library*, 4th ser. XII, 1932, is interesting. Except (perhaps)
for the unknown printer who—probably in some relations with
Caxton—continued in the new medium, in 1479–80, the traditions of St. Albans, Caxton's successors were foreigners. Wynkyn
de Worde, an Alsatian, was Caxton's apprentice, succeeded to his
business which he largely increased, and continued till his death
about 1534. John Lettou (which may mean "the Lithuanian")

began in 1480 and was joined by William de Machlinia, who
worked from 1482 to 1490, specialising in law-books. Richard
Pynson, a Norman, succeeded him about 1490 and continued
in London till his death in 1530, and Julian Notary, a Frenchman,
was at work in London from 1498 to 1520. The growth and
organisation of the book trade is a matter for the next volume,
rather than for this.

In Edinburgh, Walter Chepman (1473?–1538?), a merchant,
financed the setting up of a press by Androw Myllar, a book-
seller who learned printing in Rouen. They printed the Aberdeen
Breviary, but most of their output seems to have been of Scottish
poetry. Not much survives—the most important volume is a
mutilated bundle of poems in the Scottish National Library—
but what exists is priceless. See R. Dickson, *Introduction of the
Art of Printing into Scotland*, 1885; R. Dickson and J. P. Edmond,
Annals of Scottish Printing, 1890; and H. G. Aldis, *A List of Books
printed in Scotland before 1700*, 1904.

III. OTHER ARTS

[NOTE. This is a strictly limited selection of books which the
literary student may need, or may care, to consult.]

A. ARCHITECTURE

For "Anglo-Saxon" and "Norman" Architecture, the two
volumes by A. W. Clapham, *English Romanesque Architecture*
(1930 and 1934) are all the more valuable that they deal with
decoration as well as structure. There are innumerable guides
to mediaeval architecture in general, but Cyril E. Power's
English Mediaeval Architecture, in three small volumes, cheap,
concise, and fully illustrated, is the most useful compendium for the pocket and for quick reference. Francis Bond's
Gothic Architecture in England (1906) is authoritative and comprehensive, or the relevant sections of "the architects' bible"
may be consulted—Sir Banister Fletcher's *History of Architecture
on the Comparative Method* (various editions). Less technical works
are W. H. Godfrey's *Story of Architecture in England*, Vol. I and
the admirably illustrated *Cathedrals of England* by H. Batsford
and C. Fry, *England's Greater Churches* by C. B. Nicholson, and
The Mediaeval Styles of the English Parish Church by F. E.
Howard. More specialised, A. Hamilton Thompson's *The
Ground Plan of the English Parish Church* and *The Historical*

Growth of the English Parish Church (Cambridge Manuals, Nos. 15 and 16) are concise, learned, and lucid; so also his *English Monasteries* (No. 67), to which we may add R. Liddesdale Palmer's *English Monasteries in the Middle Ages* for studies in buildings and their arrangements, uses, and layout. For secular buildings there is less evidence and less help, but see Ralph Dutton, *The English Country House* (1935), Chaps. I and II; Sidney H. Heelt, *The Houses and Buildings of Other Days* (1929); Clapham and Godfrey, *Some Famous Buildings and their Story;* *The English Castle* by Hugh Braun; Ian C. Hannah, *The Story of Scotland in Stone* (1934); and Sir John Stirling Maxwell, *Shrines and Homes of Scotland*, 1937. Something may be gleaned from *The Villages of England* by A. K. Wickham, and *Homes and Gardens of England* by Batsford and Fry. But local studies, and visits to the sites themselves, will be found of more benefit than many books. John H. Harvey's *Henry Yevele* is an interesting life of a great 14th-century architect. (See also under Economic History, p. 264.)

B. SCULPTURE

W. G. Collingwood, *Northumbrian Crosses* (1927), deals with one art-form only, the free-standing stone cross, and only in one part of the country, but is valuable as a fairly complete record so far, and well illustrated. A photographic index of early crosses has been compiled in the British Museum and may be consulted on application. A. S. Napier describes one famous small example in an article on the Franks Casket, in *An English Miscellany presented to F. J. Furnivall* (1901). More generally, see J. Brøndsted, *Early English Ornament*, translated from the Danish by A. F. Major, 1924; Arthur Gardner, *A Handbook of English Mediaeval Sculpture;* notes in books on architecture, *passim;* Baldwin Brown, *The Arts in Early England*, the greatest and most comprehensive survey of the Anglo-Saxon period, and T. D. Kendrick, *Anglo-Saxon Art* (1937). Notice also such special studies as F. H. Crossley, *English Church Woodwork and Furniture*, and *English Church Monuments*.

C. PAINTING

Bibliographies for 1934 and for 1935 are published by the Courtauld Institute, University of London, and will, it is to be hoped, be continued annually. The importance of mediaeval painting in England has been recognised only recently, so the student should beware of the casual remarks which appear in histories of art published before, say, 1920. In 1927 Tancred Borenius and E. W. Tristram published *English Mediaeval Painting*, which set the subject on its feet, and is indispensable. Frank Kendon's *Mural Paintings in English Churches during the Middle Ages* (1923) is useful, and, for other forms of picture, the illustrated catalogue of the Burlington Arts Club exhibition of "British Primitives", 1923. *A History of English Art in the Middle Ages* (1932) by O. Elfrida Saunders is the most valuable general study of this and other arts, but (here as elsewhere) much is gained by restriction of subject, as in the very valuable *Franciscan History and Legend in English Mediaeval Art* edited by Dr. A. G. Little for the Society for Franciscan Studies (1937) and containing articles on wallpaintings, screenpaintings, glass and embroidery, illuminated MSS., and seals. Professor Tristram has published the first volume of what we hope will be a complete conspectus of English wallpaintings, O.U.P., 1945. For methods in general, see D. V. Thompson, *The Materials of Medieval Painting*, 1936. For wood engraving (late, scanty and poor), see Edward Hodnett, *English Woodcuts*, 1480–1535, Bibliographical Society, 1935.

For the lesser arts, the British Museum *Guides* and the catalogues of the Victoria and Albert Museum and the London Museum provide useful introductions and are invaluable for reference. The proceedings of archaeological societies, and particularly those of the (London) Society of Antiquaries, published in *Archaeologia*, contain many articles on pottery, jewellery, weapons, etc. Since English embroidery had a European reputation, such a study as A. F. Kendrick's *English Embroidery* (revised 1913) may be mentioned. Of more general interest is Withington's *English Pageantry*, which includes various arts. For brasses, consult H. W. Macklin, *The Brasses of England* (1907), for stained glass, Herbert Read, *English Stained Glass*, 1926.

D. COSTUME

A good collection of mediaeval examples is in Hartley and Elliot, *Life and Work of the English People*, 1931. J. R. Planché, *A History of British Costume*, is not yet superseded. The relevant portions of Dion Clayton Calthorp's *English Costume* gain from the author's keen interest, but it is rather "popular". In preference consult Dorothy Hartley, *Mediaeval Costume and Life*, which contains photographs of actual people in mediaeval clothes as well as reproductions from MSS., or F. M. Kelly and Randolph

Schwabe, *A Short History of Costume and Armour*. These two give instructions for making costumes. For this purpose C. Kohler, *A History of Costume*, translated by A. K. Dallas, 1928, is excellent: the costumes are German, but the details can be adapted. In G. G. Coulton, *The Chronicler of the Middle Ages* (*i.e.*, Froissart), published by *The Studio* (1930), pictures from MSS. of Froissart are reproduced: they appear in full in a volume supplementary to Johnes's editions, often well hand-coloured, and are valuable though, being French, not reliable for England. Brasses and other funeral monuments are a great source of information and any well-illustrated book on these subjects may be consulted.

E. HERALDRY

The theory of heraldry has suffered from exaggerations and consequent depreciations, but it was a normal part of mediaeval education. One of the treatises in *The Boke of St. Albans*, (see p. 440) is "of blasyng of armys". For amusement read John Guillim's famous *Display of Heraldry* (1610, and often reprinted); for business, J. R. Planché, *The Pursuivant of Arms*, Fox-Davies, *A Complete Guide to Heraldry*, or Boutell, *Heraldry Historical and Popular*, 1864. Elvin's *Dictionary of Heraldry* is useful for explanation of terms. Sir J. Balfour Paul, *Heraldry in Relation to Scottish History and Art* (1900) is interesting. For heraldic design, G. Eve, *Decorative Heraldry* (1897), or St. John Hope, *Heraldry for the Craftsman and Designer* may be consulted, but most of all the best mediaeval examples. Various rolls of arms are published in *The Genealogist* and separately; note Wright's or Nicholas's facsimiles of the important Caerlaverock Roll, a roll of arms of persons present at the siege of Caerlaverock in 1300. For Scotland, Sir David Lindsay's Heraldic MS. is available in facsimile. St. John Hope, *Stall Plates of the Knights of the Order of the Garter* (in St. George's Chapel, Windsor) is also important. County Histories are useful, and there are many pictures and articles in the proceedings of societies on armorial seals (one of the main sources of evidence) and the like, which will probably be the best resource for the student looking for obscure persons: *Archaeologia* for England generally, *Archaeologia Aeliana* for the north, and so on.

To find the arms when the name is known, consult Burke, *General Armoury* (1884 ed.); for the name when the arms are known, Papworth and Morant, *Ordinary of British Armorials*, 1874. Burke's *Peerage* and *Landed Gentry*, Doyle's *Official Baronage of England* (for the higher nobility) and Balfour Paul's *Scots Peerage* and

An Ordinary of Arms (2nd ed., 1903), may be searched, and (for ecclesiastics) J. Woodward, *Ecclesiastical Heraldry*, and Bedford, *The Blazon of Episcopacy*. Joseph Foster, *Some Feudal Coats of Arms* (1902) is useful though not to be trusted without checking. The edition of Froissart published by the Shakespeare Head Press provides, in an armorial index in the last volume, a useful quick-reference selection for the fourteenth and early fifteenth centuries.

F. MUSIC

The transcription, publication, and elucidation of existing MS. music are professional tasks which the literary amateur awaits. As it is, we can sympathise with the weary chorister whose complaint is printed in Wright and Halliwell's *Reliquiae Antiquae*, Vol. I, p. 291:

"The song of the cesolfa dos me syken sare".

Wright describes this rhyme from MS. Arundel 292 as "written in a hand of the time of Edward II"—i.e., 1307-27. Nothing is known of O.E. music except that it existed; but see F. M. Padelford, *O. E. Musical Terms*, Bonner Beiträge zur Anglistik IV, Bonn, 1899. Early treatises on the theory of music, from Bede down, are usually mathematical, and derive, directly or eventually, from the *De Musica* of Boethius.

In *Music in the Middle Ages* (1940-41), Gustave Reese provides useful information (see esp. Ch. 8 and 14) and also lists of gramophone records and a full bibliography. For ecclesiastical music, see the Oxford History of Music (2nd edition), Vols. I and II. The student may be helped by the gramophone records, series I, of the Columbia Gramophone Company's *History of Music*, Nos. 1 to 5, with accompanying notes by Percy E. Scholes. These are not of English music, but church music, like the Church itself, is international. The history of English secular music has been neglected, but see the important chapter by E. J. Dent on *Special Aspects of Music in the Middle Ages*, in the Introductory Vol. to the Oxford History. In his *Plaine and Easie Introduction to Practicall Musicke*, 1597 (facsimile published by the Shakespeare Association), Thomas Morley refers often to earlier and superseded methods and devices. For examples, examine *Early Bodleian Music*, edited by Sir J. Stainer, and *Early English Harmony* (Quaritch), and search W. Chappell's *Collection of National English Airs* and *Popular Music of the Olden Time*. Chappell's "olden time" is anywhere before 1750 or thereby: but there is no knowing how old some well-known tunes

like *Chevy Chase* or the Helston Furry Dance are. Chappell's
introductions are very valuable: for the tunes, the later editions
revised by Wooldridge are more reliable. The Columbia History
contains a record (No. 12) of *Somer is i-comen in*. The fine contemporary song on Agincourt is in the *Oxford Song Book* in singable
form, and the *Oxford Carol Book*, in addition to an admirable
(though too brief) introduction, contains many carols of the
fifteenth century and earlier, including the sequence *Angelus ad
Virginem* which the clerk Nicholas sang (The Miller's Tale, 30),
and the exquisite *Lully, lulla, thou little tiny child* from the Coventry
Nativity Play, with Elizabethan harmony to the old tune.
English Carols of the Fifteenth Century, by Fuller-Maitland and
Rockstro, is another great repertory. Some relics survive in most
church hymnals: they have to be carefully inspected in view
of the ways of editors and (still more) of their clerical employers:
but these are improving. The carol collections and Chappell's
are the best resource for the literary amateur who wishes to learn
something of the "feel" of mediaeval music in those phases which
concern him most.

Since French influence may be important and some parallel
development is certain, help may be sought from T. Gérold, *La
Musique au Moyen Âge* (Les Classiques Français du Moyen Âge),
Paris, 1932; Pierre Aubry, *Trouvères et Troubadours*, Paris: Alcan,
n.d., and *La Rhythmique Musicale des Troubadours*, Paris: Champion, 1907: from Bédier and Aubry, *Les Chansons de Croisade*,
Paris: Champion, 1909, in which No. VI is Anglo-Norman, and
I and XXII are copies from Anglo-Norman MSS.: and from
such collections as the *Chansonnier de S. Germain*, edited by Aubry,
published by Alcan, and also by the *Société des Anciens Textes
Français*, and sensible editions like that of Colin Muset in *Les
Classiques du Moyen Âge* (Champion), where tunes are printed as
well as words.

The Aberdeen *Cantus, Songs and Fancies*, is as late as 1662,
but it includes music of earlier times. A facsimile of the third
edition, 1682, was printed for the New Club, Paisley, 1879. See
also H. G. Farmer, *Music in Mediaeval Scotland*, 1930.

For musical instruments—remembering that their mechanics
may influence the structure of tunes and therefore the verse of
songs—the best resources (failing access to a collection) are
F. W. Galpin, *Old English Instruments of Music* (revised 1932)
and G. Kinsky, *The History of Music in Pictures*. For musical
notations, see H. M. Bannister, *Monumenti Vaticani di Palaeografia
Musicale Latina*, 1913.

THE BEGINNINGS OF ENGLISH LITERATURE

G. SPORT

Some 19 MSS. exist of *The Master of Game*, translated from the
Livre de Chasse of Gaston (Phébus) Comte de Foix (for whom see
Froissart) with some slight interpolations and five original
chapters (XXII, on hunting-horns, and XXXIV–XXXVI),
and dedicated to Prince Henry (Henry V) by Edward, 2nd Duke
of York (*d.* 1373–1415: the "Aumarle" of Shakespeare's *Richard
II*, killed at Agincourt). It was edited in 1904 by W. A. and F.
Baillie-Grohman in an unfortunately expensive and limited
edition, with excellent illustrations, notes, and bibliography, from
MS. Cotton Vespasian B XII in the British Museum. A modern-
ised version is appended, and this was reprinted in 1909, with
abbreviated but still useful notes and bibliography. From the
same MS. comes *The Art of Hunting according to John Gifford and
William Twety* in Wright and Halliwell's *Reliquiae Antiquae*, Vol. I
(*Twety* should be *Twici* or *Twich*—an Anglo-Norman of c. 1300).
In the same volume is *The Booke of Hawkyng after Prince Edwarde
Kyng of Englande* from MS. Harleian 2340 of Henry VI's time.

The Boke of St. Albans contains four treatises: of hawking,
of hunting, of heraldry, and of angling, the last being added in
the second edition, 1469. The name of Dame Juliana Berners
or Barnes, an early fifteenth century prioress of Sopwell in Herts,
has been attached to it, but the parts are not all from the same
hand. It is an unpretentious manual for country gentlemen,
less elaborate than the royal *Master of Game*, and has the simple
charm that such books often possess. The author of the section
on angling is the father not only of Isaak Walton, but of all
English angling writers since, and his best-known passage is
worth quoting from again: "Thus me semyth that huntynge and
hawkynge and also fowlynge ben so labourous and grevous
that none of theym may perfourme nor bi very meane that
enduce a man to a mery spyryte: which is cause of his longe lyfe
acordynge unto the sayd parable of Salamon. Dowtless there
folowyth it that it must nedes be the dysporte of fysshynge wyth
an angle . . . And yet atte the leest he hath his holsom walke
and mery at his ease: a swete ayre of the swete sauoure of the
meede flowers: that makyth hym hungry. He hereth the melo-
dyous armony of fowles. He seeth the yonge swannes: heerons:
duckes: cotes and many other fowles, wyth thyr brodes, whyche
me semyth better than alle the noyse of houndys: the blasts of
hornys and the scrye of foulis that hunters: fawkeners and foulers

440

can make. And yf the angler take fysshe: surely thenne is there noo man merier than he is in his spyryte". Dame Juliana was surely not the author of that—or any other woman.

This popular work was printed at St. Albans in 1485; the second edition printed by Wynkyn de Worde in 1496 with the "treatyse of fysshynge wyth an angle" added: reprinted 1540, 1563?, 1561, 1586, and revised by Gervase Markham in 1596 with the title of *The Gentleman's Academie*. Modern editions are by W. Blades, J. Haslewood (1810), and others. A facsimile of the treatise on angling was published in 1880, with introduction by M. G. Watkins.

In *A Chapter of Mediaeval History: The Fathers of the Literature of Field Sport and Horses*, the Rt. Hon. D. H. Madden wrote pleasantly on Gaston de Foix and others. There is something to be got from Lady Apsley's *Bridleways through History*, 2nd edition, 1936, about horses, riding and hunting.

For other sports the classical work is J. Strutt's *Sports and Pastimes of the People of England*, itself an excellent pastime. The edition by J. C. Cox, 1903, should be used. The British Museum publishes a set of postcards of Sports and Pastimes from early fourteenth century drawings.

H. AGRICULTURE

The working of the manor is discussed in most economic and social studies (see p. 264). A lucid explanation is given by John Orr, *A Short History of British Agriculture*, Oxford Manuals, 1922. N. S. B. Gras, *A History of Agriculture*, Part I, Chap. IV–V, is abominably "educational" but selects well in the bibliography. For an admirable detailed study see H. S. Bennett, *Life on the English Manor, 1150–1400*. Cambridge, 1937. The recognised father of English agricultural writers is Walter of Henley, fl. 1250, whose *Boke of Hosebondrie*, printed by Wynkyn de Worde about 1510, is edited by E. Lamond, Roy. Hist. Soc., 1890, with other allied works. It exists in Anglo-French and English. Vising treats the English as a translation from French; J. Murray, in her edition of Grosseteste's *Chasteau d'Amour*, says G. translated Walter's English into French; D.N.B. denies G.'s connexion altogether: such is the state of knowledge. Miss Lamond prints *Les Reules Seint Roberd*, being notes on estate administration by Grosseteste. There are many MSS., often adapted to different practice. See also D. Macdonald, *Agricultural Writers*, 1908, for extracts and bibliography, and F. H. Cripps-Day, *The Manor*

Farm, 1931, for a facsimile. A fifteenth-century translation of Palladius (fourth century) on Husbandry is edited by B. Lodge and S. J. H. Herrtage, E.E.T.S., 52, 72 (1872, 1879) from MS. Bodl. Addl. A. 369, and by M. H. Liddell from another MS. Miss Hammond prints the prologue (not in the E.E.T.S. ed.) and another passage. The main interest is in the language and metre, which await special study.

Mediaeval gardening is discussed in most histories, usually badly and at second-hand: the Hon. Alicia Amherst, *A History of Gardening in England*, 1896, and reprints, is as good as any. The largest work is Sir Frank Crisp, *Mediæval Gardens*, 2 vols. 1924; the scholarship is uncritical and the period extends into the seventeenth century, but some information is there, and the illustration is lavish. See T. Wright, *History of Domestic Manners*, 1862; the Quennell's *History of Everyday Things:* for more direct contact, Bartholomaeus Anglicus, Bk. XVII. A poem by "Jon Gardener" called *The Feate of Gardening* is still in MS.; the MS. is ascribed to c. 1440, the poem may be older: see Crisp (above), Vol. I, p. 42, and W. L. Carter, in *My Garden*, No. 36 (Dec. 1936).

INDEX

References in roman numerals are to the Introduction, in *italic* to the Student's Guide. Main entries are in black numerals.

PA2111
M3